The MILITARY And The STATE In LATIN AMERICA

The
MILITARY
And The
STATE
In LATIN
AMERICA

Alain Rouquié

Translated by
PAUL E. SIGMUND

UNIVERSITY OF CALIFORNIA PRESS

Berkeley • *Los Angeles* • *London*

University of California Press
Berkeley and Los Angeles, California

University of California Press, Ltd.
London, England

First published in France under the title
L'Etat Militaire en Amerique Latine
©1982 Editions du Seuil.

Library of Congress Cataloging-in-Publication Data
Rouquié, Alain.
    The military and the state in Latin America.
    Bibliography: p.
    Includes index.
    1. Civil-military relations—Latin America.
2. Military government—Latin America. 3. Latin
America—Politics and government—1948–
I. Title.
JL956.C58R6813 1987   322'.5'098   86-14666
ISBN 0-520-05559-4 (alk. paper)
Printed in the United States of America

1 2 3 4 5 6 7 8 9

CONTENTS

ACKNOWLEDGMENTS

This work is the result of a long period of research and reflection carried out in the stimulating setting of the Center of International Studies and Research of the Fondation Nationale des Sciences Politiques (Paris). The book owes much as well to my teaching at the Institut d'Etudes Politiques and the *Institut des Hautes Etudes d'Amérique Latine*. I thank the colleagues, researchers, and students at these institutions for their comments, criticisms, and suggestions.

Some of the analyses put forward here have already been published in scholarly journals in another form. Others have been subjected to criticism in colloquia or roundtables. The discussions that they have provoked have enabled me to complete, deepen, or correct my approach. I wish to express my thanks to the organizers of, and participants in, these meetings. I owe special thanks to the Institut d'Etudes Politiques at Aix-en-Provence, the Latin American Council of Social Sciences (CLACSO) in Buenos Aires, the Instituto de Investigaciones Sociales of the Autonomous National University of Mexico (UNAM), the Getulio Vargas Foundation in Rio de Janeiro, and the Latin American Program of the Woodrow Wilson International Center for Scholars in Washington.

Finally, I should thank the many civilian and military observers and actors who shared in my field research, provided documents, and assisted me in understanding the complex series of events that comprise the raw material for my analysis. Although they are not cited in the text, it is in a way to them that this book belongs, even if they do not agree with all of its hypotheses and conclusions.

INTRODUCTION

In September 1973 a horrified French public discovered Latin American militarism—in the unexpected form of terrorism in Chile. Even people on the left had been largely indifferent to the massacres in Djakarta, but so much had been said, pro and con, about the *via Chilena* in France that attempts were hastily made to exorcise this coup d'état that was not unusual but yet was different from what had happened in other countries. The dark continent-wide tide of a praetorianism that was novel only in its date and manner of execution ended by confirming our earlier views. We came to terms with the intolerable through a few simple ideas. The involvement of the International Telephone and Telegraph Company (ITT) obscured the vast number of underlying, more fundamental causes. An abundance of rhetoric did the rest, and indifference followed. Latin America was no longer a model. At least since 1959 we had loved it only for its revolutionary and epic qualities. Once it was under the jackboot, martyrology replaced any desire to understand. Superficial approaches soon reappeared. It is always easy to demonstrate one's knowledge of the 120th Bolivian coup or the grotesque and banal outbursts of the monstrous Pinochet or the pallid interchangeable Uruguayan jailors. But who seeks to understand why armed men obey unarmed civilian power, or to fathom the strange and almost miraculous magic involved in the workings of those fragile liberal democracies where we live—whatever the convictions and societal purposes that we favor?

The militarization of the Latin American political systems is not a recent phenomenon, but neither is it a permanent and fundamental element in the political order of the independent states of the subcontinent. In 1954, out of twenty Latin American states, thirteen were governed by military men. In 1980 two-thirds of the total population of Latin American lived in states under military rule or dominated by the military. In South America around the same time—before the return of civilian rule in Ecuador and Peru—eight nations representing nearly four-fifths of the territory of South America were governed by officers who held power on the basis of a recent or earlier coup. The hegemony of the military in these "derivative" nations that belong culturally to the West, in their language, religion, and juridical norms and institutions, cannot fail to trouble the consciences of those in the "industrial democracies." With the help of angry participant-observers, ingenious and unverifiable theories appeared. These universally applicable explanations or keys to the universe are merely more or less coherent extrapolations based on fragile or spectacular evidence. They serve to set out some guidelines in an area in which great confusion reigns, precisely because of the lack of serious empirical study; however, they also reassure those who accept them. Successive interpretations emerge at each stage, adjusting themselves to the contemporary situation. Models bloom and fade. A new orthodoxy eliminates an earlier one, which in turn reemerges a little later in a more sophisticated and equally convincing form that is both coherent and applicable, but often neither true nor false.

Some Simple But Erroneous Ideas

Obviously both troubling and disturbing, this endemic hegemony of military power is not easy to explain. There is no doubt that it is not the same over space and time. These variations suggest the need for great caution. The interpretation of the tendencies that seem to emerge is very difficult. It would be cruel to recall the number of carefully documented theories and definitive judgments that history has suddenly refuted and destroyed. Thus, an able observer of Latin America could write in

1929 at a time when Argentina was about to enter an era of militarism from which it has not yet emerged: "Today Argentina is one of the most stable and civilized states not only in Latin America but in the world. A revolution there is as improbable as one in England."[1] At the beginning of the 1960s, one of the American experts on the political role of the military in Latin America asserted that, along with Uruguay and Chile, Bolivia was one of the nations in which militarism had been definitively eliminated.[2] In Chile, it is true, the politicians and leaders of Allende's Popular Unity were not only attempting to convince themselves and to flatter the officers when they kept repeating that their military—unlike others—were legalistic and obedient but in that pathetic rhetoric there were elements of both credulousness and manipulation. On this subject nothing is more unreliable than the contemporary, the transient insight, the perception based on current events.

Nevertheless, the persistence of a phenomenon that seemed in its beginnings to be restricted to an area that was culturally homogeneous led to the development of global and nonhistorical explanations. Was there perhaps a type of relationship between the military institutions, power, and civil society that was peculiar to the Iberian world? Was not the very vocabulary of militarism predominantly Spanish? From the time of General Riego to Generalissimo Franco and including the well-named *"Espadones"* (sword-rattlers) in the nineteenth century, the Iberian Peninsula indeed appeared to be a classic locale for *pronunciamentos* and *juntas* of officers. The persistence of the phenomenon might therefore be explained as a transplantation from Spain.

The cultural and "essentialist" explanation has sometimes given way to more elaborate versions that, despite their descriptive richness, come dangerously close to tautological popular psychology. In particular, they insist on the normality of authoritarianism in the Latin American political systems with the army most often as its instrument. This lack of capacity for democracy is said to be the result of the juridical tradition, of the heritage of Spanish jurists and theologians since the sixteenth century, and especially of the *Siete Partidas* of Alfonso X, the contemporary of St. Louis in France.[3] This recourse to the "Ibero-Latin tradition" conceptualized as the "Corporatist Model," "Neo-Falangism," or "Mediterranean Syndicalism" is useful in emphasizing the specificity of sociopolitical forms and mechanisms. But why would the norms of the medieval Iberian city have been more influential on the other side of the Atlantic than those contained in the codes and constitutions of nineteenth-century European and Anglo-Saxon liberalism? Does this not ignore the fact that the same social causes produce similar effects? It is symptomatic of the ignorance or ethnocentrism of "the chosen people"—all the authors involved are Americans—that the non-Iberian component of this world, suddenly baptized as Latin, are in effect conjured away. Why choose Alfonso the Wise rather than Atahualpa or Montezuma? What should we say more specifically about the actors? How much do generals Stroessner, Geisel, Medici, Leigh, and Pinochet owe to Castile? And in the British capital called Buenos Aires, has the population, made up largely of Italians who speak Spanish with a Genoan accent, been any less supportive of military rule for the last fifty years? Is it necessary to raise further doubt by citing the 1980 coup in neighboring Surinam, which speaks Dutch?

In a more historical fashion some authors have tried to explain the frequency of military intervention in the political life of contemporary Latin America by referring to "cultural residues of the nineteenth century civil wars" in that area. Militarism goes back to the collapse of the Spanish colonial state, which produced the centrifugal and anarchic forces of the *caudillos*. The "decentralized violence" of the wars of independence is said to extend to the coups d'état of today and tomorrow. Today's general staff officers and antiguerrilla special forces are supposed to be the descendants of the local strongmen who were followed by their men at arms. Equating the military caudillos who were amateurs using inflated military titles with career officers leads to confusion. Those improvised warriors were the product of the disorganization of society and the collapse of the state, while the career officer is an organization man who only exists by and for the state.

Furthermore, this view is historically incorrect in a number of countries. There was stability and continuity, at least in Argentina, Chile, Peru, and even in Bolivia, between the period of turbulence associated with independence and the beginning of the military era in the twentieth century. Civilian rule was sovereign in those countries for several decades after the annihilation of *caudillismo*. It hardly existed at all in Chile—to say nothing of Brazil, where national independence took place, if not smoothly, at least without societal breakdown and extended conflict. On the contrary, the countries where the phenomenon of caudillismo was most evident earlier have had several decades without military regimes and interventions—Mexico since the 1930s and Venezuela since 1958. All of this suggests that we should look elsewhere for the roots of militarism than to a complex and diverse human "climate."

In the second half of the twentieth century, this interpretation was matched by theories that linked militarism and underdevelopment. The role of the military in the former colonial states of black Africa gave rise to increasing doubts about the cultural explanation. Emphasis was placed on the economic, social, and international implications of American militarism. America was rediscovered in the phenomenon of decolonization and the resulting neocolonial disappointments. We might be ignorant of the mechanisms of military power, but we generally know the principal indicators of underdevelopment. The temptation to make use of quantitative comparisons was great. Studies were devoted to the correlations between indicators of development and the "degree" of military intervention in political life. The devotees of "exact" science viewed political instability as a set of equations. These methods of "contextual" and statistical explanation, often based on statistics that were not comparable, and lacking any historical perspective or theoretical framework, increased our appetite, but did not satisfy our hunger.

It does not seem unreasonable to think that, in less developed countries where social structures are weak and qualified technicians are rare, the professional army will constitute a leadership force; this reservoir of abilities results in an image and a consciousness of competence that opens the door to power. Besides, do not the tensions associated with growth operate against the possibilities of political pluralism? Are not civilian regimes and party struggles almost incompatible with orderly modernization? Is not, therefore, the democracy expressed in all the constitutions of the continent a luxury belonging to wealthy nations? Without authoritarian government, the capital accumulation necessary for the famous "takeoff" will not take place. The positivists of the end of the last century thought that the turbulent South American republics were naturally incapable of representative government and they called for a "democratic Caesarism," a "necessary strongman" who would be appropriate to the idiosyncrasies of their varied peoples. With their more scientific trappings the theorists of modernization and development are saying the same thing. In this very old and unresolved debate, explanation often becomes justification for existing regimes. Nevertheless, recent history does not support these coherent, but fallacious, arguments. The economic performance of military regimes in Argentina, Ecuador, and Peru in the 1970s hardly supports the military version of modernization, to say nothing of the long reigns of military dictators like Leonidas Trujillo or Alfredo Stroessner who contributed to the underdevelopment of their fiefdoms.

According to the enthusiasts of development, the more complex the social system and the more modern the economy, the fewer the opportunities for the armed forces to engage in political intervention. Reality contradicts this view; the three most advanced societies on the continent have suffered the most violent and tenacious military regimes. Uruguay, Chile, and Argentina are precisely the nations that are most eminently pluralistic and modernized. It is even difficult to classify Argentina—which is European, urbanized, and dominated by the middle class—as an underdeveloped nation. Yet, since 1930 the hegemony of the military has become the norm in that country. The current "executioner-states" (*bourreaucraties*) of the Southern Cone do not seem, therefore, to demonstrate any economic backwardness, much less an archaic social structure.

At the end of the 1960s and especially beginning in 1973, new interpretations emerged that linked militarization with the actions of external agents upon Latin American societies. This marked some progress in the analysis, finally taking into account the external orientation of the Latin American economies and their domination by the industrialized countries, especially the United States. The theory also took cognizance of the increasing dependence of the Latin American countries, especially in the formation and functioning of their military institutions. In correctly emphasizing the importance of the training of the Latin American military under North American auspices, and the coordination of military planning by the Pentagon, the specific functioning of the military institutions was finally given its rightful place.

The outrage of civilian analysts at the prospect of these soldiers, with the more or less open blessing of a foreign country, turning upon their own people the arms that were supposed to be used for their defense led to some deceptive simplifications. While the psychological approach had lost its appeal, a conspiracy theory of history, backed by an undifferentiated economism, only provided the illusion of understanding. National elites sometimes adopted this tactic of blaming the tutelary power, thus killing two birds with one stone. With their radical rhetoric they were able to cover over class conflict and even make the military themselves appear innocent, while raising at little cost the banner of anti-imperialism. The "radical chic" of the intellectual elite constituted a third world conformism that refused to be concerned with nuances. The naive or partisan instant expert proceeded to make vast affirmations and happily adopted a deductive approach. Thus the Latin American armies, "programmed" by Washington, the "simple appendages" of the Pentagon, only acted because they were manipulated at the behest of Yankee interests. Finally, these armies became little more than the "political parties of large international capitalism" or, as a Brazilian military man and Marxist historian likes to repeat, "It is not the generals in uniform that count—but General Motors and General Electric . . . they are the most powerful generals." The instrumental conception of military power goes farther. The establishment of military authoritarian regimes is said to respond to the present necessities of world capitalism and the resulting new international division of labor. The present stage of development is described as "requiring" a strong power that will repress social movements, guarantee investments, and accelerate accumulation.

These cosmic economistic interpretations that disregard national differences and internal mediating factors such as the nature of the military structure—indeed, any sociological analysis—call for several comments. The "business dictatorships" did not arise in Latin America as a result of the so-called internationalization of the domestic market, nor did they emerge from the suggestions of the Trilateral Commission. If the theory asserts once more that foreign investors prefer orderly regimes, this was also true of the dictatorships of the nineteenth century. And we are only stating the obvious. Yet the two countries that are among the most economically dependent, Mexico and Venezuela, have civilian governments and an inactive military, and despite the activities of ITT in Chile, since 1973 the large American industrial firms have avoided the Chile of "the Chicago boys," as well as Uruguay, which welcomes foreign investment, and they have even "disinvested" from Argentina since 1976. It is a strange capitalism that is able to establish regimes at its convenience but cannot make a profit from them.

Although the military influence of the United States is clear and undeniable, its effects are not automatic. It did not prevent the radicalism of the Peruvian colonels around General Juan Velasco Alvarado after 1968 or the revolutionary regime of General Torres in Bolivia. In fact, U.S. influence cuts both ways. Did not U.S. training produce the "best and most able guerrilla leaders in Guatemala, Luis Turcios Lima and Yon Sosa"?[4] As for the quasi-theological explanation that regards the doctrine of "national security" as a decisive influence on the establishment of today's military dictatorships, it seriously overestimates the effect of ideology and of counterrevolutionary rhetoric; this was demonstrated by Franco Spain for forty years, as well as by the war plans that have been drawn up by all the Western countries, including France. That is not to say that the ideological dimension of the regimes in question is unimportant—nor are external military dependence, the actions of the omnipresent Central Intelligence Agency (CIA), and the desire of the United States for long-term control over the armed forces of the continent. However, to argue that the desire to achieve control and penetration have brought about the ability to manipulate events always and everywhere is to ignore crucial differences among the actors, their values, and their positions in their respective nations.

The weakness of instrumental conceptions is demonstrated by the shifting positions of their authors, who do not hesitate to attribute the most astonishing versatility to American imperialism. When these theorists observed the military in certain countries giving up power to civilians, and martial regimes gradually or suddenly liberalizing in 1977, where a year earlier they had stigmatized the necessary complementary relationship between large-scale capitalism and military repression, they discovered that "democratic transformations are desired and encouraged by the multinationals and through the direct or indirect domination of the capitalism of the central nations and of their enormous power" or that "the American government and the multinationals are making policy for the year 2000 when domination can no longer be exercised through strong dictatorial regimes that employ unhuman methods." One would have thought that such cold monsters would be immune to such sudden reversals.

This critical review does not exhaust the subject, but it permits us to make our own view clear. We do not believe in historical determinism or in any sort of historical, economic, or geographic fatalism. We are not looking for a single thesis that explains every situation. If we are determined to disprove the grand conceptions of Latin American militarism, it is not to add our own theoretical grain of salt to what is already an ample discussion. We propose, instead, to carry out in this book a realistic empirical examination of military power in all its diversity, taking into account the fact that we are talking about *military* power and that from the moment it usurps constitutional authority, it cannot be considered a "passive" or a negligible actor.

A Reexamination of Military Power

If we reject metaphorical interpretations of contemporary Latin American militarism—whether instrumental or simply tautological—it is because their oversimplified a priori character leaves out the essential element in any political analysis: power. The impasse among the intervening variables is no minor methodological defect. Whether it is the result of conviction or of facile generalizations, the explanation of one reality by another—whether it is historical, geographic, or social—cannot be considered as sound. In fact, however, the great majority of the most careful studies of the political role of the military focus on factors other than the military institutions as political forces and their insertion in the state and society. Two approaches are favored by analysts of this phenomenon. The defenders of the theory of modernization emphasize the performance and the specific accomplishments of noncivilian regimes. In contrast, the majority of adherents to the sociology of social conflict seek to identify the class nature of the interventions. In both cases the analysis remains on a different level from that of the power of the military.

This study, by contrast, concentrates on the physiology of that power—on its mechanisms, functioning, and functions. The "global" or essentialist theories neglect to tell us the how, while we are going to give it a special place. The roundabout approaches regard military institutions as a mysterious black box. We are going to try to open that box and look inside. This does not mean that we will explain everything in corporate terms—far from it. The basic roots of militarism are obviously not found within the military structure, no more than armies are responsible—whatever the ambition or cupidity of their leaders—for the chronic instability that certain nations have experienced. Moralism is not compatible with sociological knowledge.

We believe, therefore, that only a knowledge of the formation, evolution, and political functioning of Latin American armies can permit us to move beyond accepted ideas and theories—however correct and seductive they may appear. Likewise, the analysis of the transformations of the state and the political system that military usurpation produces seems to us indispensable if we are to understand this disconcerting and unexplored phenomenon. That is why this book relates at the same time to Latin American military institutions (the military *estate*) and to the militarization of its political systems (the military *state*). The resemblance is more than one of words. The two realities cannot be separated if we are to understand Latin American history. The army and the state in Latin America—and elsewhere—are indeed closely associated realities; the creation of a permanent army is the foundation of state sovereignty.

This book is not a reflection on the state in Latin America. Since I am not attracted to the metaphysics of politics or to abstract theorization, I have not been tempted to erect large conceptual structures to explain social institutions. Since, in addition, confusion reigns supreme in this area, overall analytic schemes are premature. Instead, by clarifying a limited but identifiable and central component of its institutional structure, I will throw some light on the mystery of the state—especially the state in Latin America.

This work is also not an analysis of the causes and types of military coups d'état in Latin America, since this would have little meaning in countries in which the army is such a permanent actor in public life that its participation is generally accepted. Besides, it would be a kind of ethnocentrism to devote our attention exclusively to the overthrow of constitutional government in countries in which civilian or legal governments are either nonexistent or of very short duration. Neither a history of the army nor a sophisticated typology of military regimes, this book is also not presented as one of the traditional boring collections of national case studies that focus on a single theme. It is difficult for the Latin Americanist to give up such a comfortable approach, since it enables him to avoid speaking of Latin America as a single whole. Thus, it is with some apprehension that we will adopt here an approach that is cross-national but also takes into account the diversity of the subcontinent. While we are aware, as well, that there is another danger—that of triviality—in the all-purpose generalization that confuses Argentina with Salvador and Brazil with Honduras, we believe that the juxtaposition of national studies does not allow us to perceive larger transnational movements and mechanisms that are fundamental for our purpose.

This book therefore is written from a comparative perspective—the only one that is appropriate for the realities of Latin America. It is possible to define the principal characteristics of the subcontinent called Latin America as combining internal heterogeneity with external homogeneity. That is, the diverse Latin American societies share a common underlying reality: the constraints of international domination and location on the periphery. In addition, the general characteristics of the military model and the external material and moral orientation of Latin American armies make the comparative approach all the more imperative.

This work, based on many years of field work on military power and on a research strategy that we have described elsewhere[5] constitutes, therefore, a comparative synthesis that draws on existing research—often unpublished—and on primary sources. We do not argue a thesis or a single explanation. Could there be one explanation that applies to a half century of military rule and to more than twenty countries distributed over 80 degrees of latitude, other than an unlikely response to a startling question that our cultures hesitate to contemplate: Why are the military not in power everywhere? We will only pose a few questions by way of leading hypotheses:

1. Are the armies of Latin America professionalized sectors of the state with their own values, interests, and particular ways of functioning—and therefore related more to the state than to society?

2. Are those armies by definition or formation essentially in the service of internal or external social or political forces? Do they constitute a pawn that will be used from time to time, through mediating mechanisms, to defend certain social interests?

3. Are the armies politically monolithic and culturally and ideologically homogeneous?

4. Are the military and the civilian sectors two separate and hostile camps in opposition to each other, with the civilians defending progress and liberty that the military perversely and single-mindedly wish to destroy?

These questions do not have explanatory value in themselves, but they can guide our investigation and facilitate our analysis and comprehension. They are useful only if the case-by-case answers are placed in an overall context and related to the distribution of social power and to the distorted or frustrated development of the individual countries under consideration. Part I of the book provides a historical overview of the development of the military estate in South America. Chapter 1 surveys the sociopolitical background of the Americas, emphasizing both the variety of their national experiences and the similarity of their problems. Chapter 2 is devoted to the close—and at times contradictory—relationship between the creation of the army and the construction of the state. Chapter 3 analyzes the military profession from a concrete sociological point of view, focusing on the time-lag between the modernization of the military and the modernization of the state. Chapter 4 attempts to identify the immediate causes of the emergence of new military institutions in the 1920s and 1930s. Chapter 5 evaluates the political impact of post–World War II imperialism on the armies of the subcontinent and assesses the effects and limits of military dependence on the United States.

Part II tries to distinguish, situate, and make comprehensible the many varieties of military power in Latin America today, from the more or less patrimonial dictatorships (chap. 6) to the institutionalized and progressive military governments (chap. 10). Chapter 7 covers the mechanisms of civilian supremacy in the nations that have had relatively stable constitutional governments over a long period. The recurrent militarism of the praetorian republics and their methods of institutionalization are discussed in chapter 9, and the brutal intervention by military forces in previously democratic Latin American countries are analyzed in chapter 8. A final summary (chap. 11) poses the question of the future of the military state, particularly the possibilities of demilitarization, thus providing a logical conclusion to a book devoted to the degrees, mechanisms, and limits of the militarization of the state. An epilogue, written in April 1986, focuses on the causes and future prospects of the return of civilian rule in most countries of Latin America.

Part I

1

IN SEARCH OF
THE AMERICAS

Societies and Powers

We cannot understand the power and role of the military in Latin American public life without a knowledge of the societies within which the military establishments are situated and the forces they control. This is a difficult and ambitious task. What are we suggesting? That we should avoid being content with vague and convenient generalities or stereotypes? Words themselves are deceptive. Does Latin America exist? To speak of a number of Latin Americas does not make things any easier. Culture, language, and geography are not helpful. Is not Mexico part of North America? Who has ever thought that Canada, even if part of it speaks French, belongs to what is called Latin America? And the recently created organization for economic cooperation called the Latin American Economic System (SELA) includes several English-speaking countries.

That group of countries conveniently referred to as Latin America is defined above all by a set of political and economic relationships. It is an America that is dominated and dependent, that speaks mainly Spanish and Portuguese, but also in some cases French, English, and even Dutch. In other words, it is an America that is "peripheral" in relation to the metropoles of the industrial world. Its nations possess a parallel—although not identical—history, to the extent that they have generally experienced the same stages in their development. Without ignoring the differences in size that separate them, we cannot fail to recognize that they share a common destiny. However, the unique characteristic of this subcontinent in relation to other dependent

17

areas is that culturally it belongs totally to the West. Conquest and colonization did not simply influence these societies; it created and molded them, imposing on them the language, religion, values, and attitudes of Europe. Thus, whatever the impact of the pre-Columbian past and of its resurgence, Latin America is the part of the Third World that is Western. In addition, the colonization of the major part of this "New World" by the Spaniards and the Portuguese took specific forms that we know in their overall historical characteristics but not in their present effects and undeniably lasting impact.

A CONQUERED CONTINENT

It may seem paradoxical to make a detour through the myths of *El Dorado* in order to understand the contemporary societies of Latin America. Nevertheless, the colonial heritage and the mechanisms of the conquest have affected the evolution of these societies in an irreversible way. One can even maintain that the conquest never ended and that it continues today. This is true in part because of the continued extermination of the aboriginal populations as a continuation of the demographic catastrophe inflicted by the sixteenth-century conquerors on the indigenous populations of the Caribbean and of Mexico and the Andean countries, but also because of the social regression and degradation that have been imposed on the descendants of the great American civilizations. In addition, however, local ruling classes have worsened the situation of economic dependence by their predatory behavior, which is not unlike (at least in its motivation) that of the original *conquistadores*.

Since the discovery of America, the riches of the continent conquered by the Spaniards and Portuguese have been exploited not on the basis of the needs of the local populations but rather to fulfill the needs of Europe. This is the definition of the dependency relationship—which some today call "the pillage of the third world." In the present phase of development the contradictions between the international and the domestic markets have adopted new forms; despite industrialization, they have not disappeared. When the lower classes demonstrate in

Rio de Janeiro because they cannot obtain *feijao preto* (black beans), the reply is that the balance of payments requires that everything be sacrificed to the need for exports: soy beans for export rather than black beans to eat.

As producers of raw materials for the world market in the colonial past[1] and to a large extent today, the states of Latin America are marked by the fact that they were established specifically for exploitation. The gold fever that characterized the beginnings of the Latin American adventure did not die out when the "flight of the birds of prey" was over. Quick riches, the desire for immediate profits without thinking of the future, and an immediate preference for products that are "instantly rewarding" continue to influence economic attitudes.[2] Brazil has had a cyclical history of dominant products. Booms and rushes likewise mark the evolution of the Spanish-speaking areas of America. The external domination of the economies institutionalized the conquest and introduced speculation into the productive order. The most dynamic sectors of the subcontinent's economic elites were more like conquistadores than the conquering bourgeoisie, sacrificing everything to the current speculative venture without thinking too much of the future. Then and now one can speak of a "rapist agriculture" in the countryside, characterized, as Claude Lévi-Strauss aptly observed, by a soil that is "violated and destroyed" and by a nature that is "more fierce than ours because less populated and less cultivated but still lacking in true originality—not savage, but uprooted."[3]

That "seduced and abandoned" nature and the dehumanization of the countryside of which it is made up are not the only current manifestations of the "bandeirante dream of a quick fortune," or the walking madness of a Lope de Aguirre—to employ two symbols of the continuation of the conquest. The European immigrants of the nineteenth century who landed by the millions in temperate zones of South America came in order to "make America." The ease with which the Latin American economies can be adapted to different purposes, their astonishing plasticity that translates into the easy movement of capital from agriculture to industry and back depending on the international market, the importance of the financial sector, the rapidity of an imitative industrialization that conveniently associates itself with the large international conglomerates, are all indicators of the unstable availability of men who are ready to engage in adventures that are proposed and developed from abroad. The continuing presence of the conquest is also to be taken in a more literal sense that directly affects social relationships.

FEUDAL CONQUEST AND SOCIAL OUTCASTS

One cannot speak of the social structures of the Latin American world without emphasizing the concentration of landed property. The dualism, *latifundio-minifundio,* if those two terms are not limited to a geographical significance, affects almost all Latin American countries, whatever their degree of urbanization; this would include those that have various forms of medium- and family-sized properties, such as Costa Rica, Colombia, Argentina, and the south of Brazil. We will spare our readers monotonous columns of figures or dramatic exaggerations. Reference is often made to the case of prerevolutionary Mexico in the period of Porfirio Diaz when the Terrazas family owned 2.5 million hectares (6 million acres) in Chihuahua, and one railroad line ran for 120 kilometers (72 miles) through a single property in the state of Hidalgo. It is less well known that Chile in 1964 had a very high concentration of property ownership, largely unproductive, with 6.9 percent of the properties comprising 81.3 percent of the land.[4] One should not assume that the large landholdings only involve uncultivated or low-quality land. A list of the proprietors who own more than 30,000 hectares (75,000 acres) in the very rich province of Buenos Aires shows that two families before World War II owned more than 400,000 hectares (1 million acres) each of the fertile land in the pampas.[5] Even today, more than 11 million hectares (27 million acres) are divided among 500 landowners.

Over and above these bare facts, it is the mechanism of monopolization and dispossession that interests us here. This activity has been carried out since the beginning of the European occupation; it does not belong exclusively to the colonial period. Even after independence the large landholdings were extended and consolidated thanks to the seizure of Indian lands and the sale of church properties. The elimination of the guarantees granted to the Indians by the Spanish crown and the formally egalitarian spirit of liberalism that dominated the new republics opened the way to the breakup of the Indian communities, the annexation of their territories, and even to the expulsion of their members. The secularization of the lands of a clergy that was often rich and monopolistic and the distribution of the common lands of the villages—always in the name of progress and liberty—which took place in the second half of the nineteenth century benefited a small number of buyers with good connections. In the same period the states themselves, in order to get revenue or to pay off debts, sold remote and inaccessible land that had become valuable with the "pacification" of the Indians in Chile and Argentina and with the progress of communications.

We should not believe that the extension and exaggerated size of the large landholdings was a direct response to the necessities of the world market. In contrast to the slow advance of the frontier carried out by the pioneers of North America, land was taken over south of the Rio Grande before it could be developed, or even before there was any desire to settle it. Were such acquisitions made out of a spirit of conquest, a desire for prestige, or a wish to live like the nobility? In numerous cases the hacienda was as valuable because of the population that it contained as for its lands and potential riches. Its economic significance was less important than its political role and its social function. In fact, it has been said that the relatively equitable distribution of property in areas such as Costa Rica was based precisely on the absence of an indigenous population that could be exploited and dominated.[6]

Feudal conquest still goes on today. But motives related to profitability and capitalist rationality have replaced and sometimes aggravated archaic precapitalist motivations. We see the creation and recreation of large landholdings, sometimes out of tracts that were previously divided in a transitory fashion by agrarian reforms, in every country where agriculture plays a decisive economic role. Even in Mexico where, as the Zapata movement demonstrates, expulsion from agricultural holdings was the cause of the great revolutionary outbreak of 1910 and where an agrarian reform has been carried out which is the pride of the regime, the present situation, despite the legal limits on the property right, is not very different from that before the Revolution. It is estimated that in 1910, 11,000 land-owners owned 60 percent of the national territory while, in 1970, 0.8 percent of the properties (around 10,000 units) com-prised approximately the same area.[7] Ninety-six hundred prop-erties amount to 95 million hectares in area, while only a little more than half that area has been redistributed in fifty years of agrarian reform. The number of landless peasants has also nearly doubled between 1950 and 1966.[8] In Pinochet's Chile an agrarian counterrevolution since 1976 has reestablished the large landholders in their properties and power.

In Colombia the *violencia*, the civil war that ravaged the countryside beginning in 1948, had among other consequences the effect of fostering agrarian capitalism at the price of the expulsion of the farmers and small landholders from the lands that they had been cultivating.[9]

In Brazil in the 1980s, which because of the economic crisis and the absence of petroleum has turned back to agriculture, virgin territories are offered to large European, Japanese, and American companies. The Amazon region is sold at auction, and the heart of the continent is savagely deforested with no concern for the ecological consequences. Everywhere the large companies use their henchmen—the *jagunços* and *grileiros*—to uproot settlers who lack legal titles in order to clear patches torn from the forest. The most spectacular case of this feudal expan-sion is the private empire that has recently been carved out by an American businessman on the Jari River, not far from Belem and French Guyana[10]—1, 5, or 6 million hectares, no one knows—at the same time that land invasions by dispossessed peasants are daily occurrences in nearly all Latin American countries.

Rapacious acquisition of land is not a marginal, residual, or insignificant phenomenon in semi-industrialized societies that are characterized by rapidly expanding cities. Paradoxically, in the most urbanized countries of the continent, Uruguay and Argentina, the agrarian export sector is still the driving force of the economy, and it is only in certain mineral-based economies such as that of Venezuela that agriculture has little importance in social relations. It is on this level that the phenomenon that we are describing is so significant. There is a theory that in Central Europe and the Mediterranean countries the weakness of the small peasantry and family farms was one of the causes of political instability and the rejection of liberal democracy. In contrast, the small French peasantry that owned half of the land in the kingdom prior to the Revolution of 1787 is said to have been the basis of the French Revolution. The pioneers on the frontier and the beneficiaries of the Homestead Act were supposed to have guaranteed the stability of American democracy. Whether or not this theory, which needs confirmation, is true, the profound and lasting social impact of the land tenure system has produced societies very different from our own, in which domination has never ceased to be more important than production, and capitalist rationality is often subordinated to social reproduction and the maximization of power.

The Order of the Manor and Capitalist Modernization

More important than the devastating but brief period of mineral development during the first period of colonization, the long-lasting landholding system in the countryside was, with only a few exceptions throughout the continent, the true foundation of social relations. The model of hierarchy in the *hacienda* had a deep impact on the social fabric, influencing conduct and creating a deep chasm of unbridgeable social distinctions. The usurpation of the lands belonging to indigenous communities, the widespread forms of tenure shareholding paid for by days of labor or personal and family service in the master's house,[11] were sources for and models of the rigidity of social structures. Between the boss and *los de abajo*, the master and those "without importance," there is a difference assumed to be intrinsic. The peasants are the responsibility of the masters, who are expected to treat them in a paternalistic fashion, like children to be punished when appropriate and kept in their places. These dispossessed classes do not act as social partners, participate in contractual relationships, or take collective action, since violence is always present as a potential sanction. It is even possible, as in the case of the Peruvian peasants described by novelist Manuel Scorza, that the peons might have a "collective heart attack" after a meal offered by the landowner, as a result of daring to wish for a peasant union.[12]

It is only a step from unlimited social authority rooted in traditional relations to the privatization of power. At the beginning of the century protesting workers in the Chilean mines were put in chains, and private prisons were still functioning in the large landholdings, whether traditional or modern. Plantations and public work camps, run by transnational companies and protected by private police, have existed in Brazil and Central America in recent years. When Juan Perón published an agricultural laborers statute in 1945 which provided for a modest legal improvement in the condition of the peon in Argentina, the *estancieros* denounced the government for attacking private property. In addition, one cannot overestimate the importance of local power, sometimes reinforced by the difficulty—or the monopoly—of communications. The distant and external state traditionally delegated its powers to the local notables—*caciques* or *coroneis*—who were the source of its support and whom it backed with the police force when necessary. The expansion of the state and enlargement of its responsibilities sometimes had the unintended modernizing effect of working against the social control exercised by the local notables.

This historical heritage has directly affected present-day mental outlooks, since its impact is not limited to the backward precapitalist sectors of the economy or to societies that are particularly retarded in their development. Thus, noneconomic coercive measures have been utilized frequently in labor relations during the twentieth century in contexts that are completely capitalistic. Through debts that are contracted in the obligatory company store and cannot be repaid, or through monopoly control of the agricultural food-producing land that permits owners to obtain a large and stable work force during the *zafras* on the plantation,[13] capitalist enterprises linked to the international or domestic market never turn to free labor. We have even seen the establishment or reestablishment of various forms of forced labor—for instance, in Chiapas in 1936[14]—in response to the increased demand for exports. Conversely, it was the creation of an efficient export agriculture that eliminated the stable agricultural workers from the *fazendas* and replaced them with itinerant day workers (*boias frias*) recruited by middlemen who provided them to the landowner who pays the highest price.[15]

There is no trace here of structural pluralism. On the contrary, we observe the emergence of two complementary aspects of a single system of domination. The continued existence of the archaic traditional pole can be explained precisely because of the ascendancy of the modern pole. I am not trying to provide a complete description of the whole complex of social relations. I only want to locate the mechanisms, the recurring schemes or extreme models, that without exception have structured Latin American societies. For my purpose, societal memory is no less decisive than the features of real stratification that it affects.

Postcolonial Societies

Brazil and the Spanish-speaking states of Latin America, with the exception of Cuba, have been independent for more than 150 years. The colonial period thus seems to be well behind them. However, when Ecuadorean Indians were asked what the notion of *patria*—fatherland—meant to them, they answered—after a century and a half of independence, national symbols, and patriotic affirmations—"A bus company." (There is a company with that name in Quito.) The enslavement and repression of the Indians along with the massive importation of black slaves from Africa (Brazil did not abolish slavery until 1888) contributed to the establishment of disparate and badly integrated societies. It is not surprising that ethnic and cultural differences, as well as skin color, reinforced social segmentation. Official legal discrimination no longer exists today.[16] Status and wealth create "whites" but there is still a bit of "enlightened racism" among the elites who embraced social Darwinism at the beginning of the century. Drawing on a "scientific" basis for their prejudices, they continued the tradition of the fastidious colonial "pigmentoc-racy" that used institutional methods for three centuries to pre-vent the ascendancy of "castes" with impure blood.

Even in that apparent extension of Europe that is twen-tieth-century Argentina, social distinctions retain a discreetly colonial and surreptitiously ethnic character. Everyone knows that "the Mexicans descended from the Aztecs, the Peruvians descended from the Incas, but the Argentines descended from the ships" that brought their forefathers from Europe to the pampas. In spite of that celebrated aphorism, mass immigra-tion also had its nobility and commoners, those with prestige and those who were despised. First there is a hierarchy in date of immigration—a Mayflower in miniature that only involves a few decades in the nineteenth century. Then there is a hierar-chy of national origin. The Italian handyman and the crude Galician Spaniard are at the bottom of the scale, while the En-glishman and the Basque are at the top. When a hostile aristoc-racy wanted to calumniate Perón, they whispered in the salons of Buenos Aires, "His real name is Perone . . . ." And in a "white" country where it is bad taste to assume that there are any traces of Indian blood in the population, the way to dismiss the *descamisados*, often of rural background, who followed Perón's wife Evita was to refer to their mixed-blood features and jet-black hair by alluding to the *cabecitas negras*, and even *los negros*.

The objection could be made that similar or worse hierarchi-cal structures based on ethnicity are operative in North Amer-ica. There is a difference of scale, however. The colonial dimen-sion of Latin America societies is not to be found solely in the ethnic basis of social distinctions. The characteristics that we have described must be considered in the context of Latin America's "peripheral" situation. They are reinforced by their incorporation in a social whole in which the dominant actor is the foreigner. The external orientation of the process of accumu-lation and of the Latin American economies since their initial incorporation into the Atlantic market has produced social dis-tortions that are unknown in North America.

In fact, the development of the Latin American economies was always induced from the outside—in the initial export phase, in the brief period of autonomous national industrialization aimed at replacing imported manufactured products, and obviously today in the stage of national subsidiaries and "internationalized industrialization." At each stage modernization began with patterns of consumption, not with the creation of a productive apparatus. That "indirect access to civilization," as Celso Furtado calls it, even affected "import substitution"—the process by which local industry tries to produce manufactured goods similar to those created by the central economies. In the first or export phase an advanced "modernization" of consumption patterns was associated with accumulation that had no effect on the productive apparatus. The expansion of the primary export sector that drives dependent economies does not imply the transformation of the methods of production and any change in social relations. On the contrary, the control of the surplus, the support derived from profitable external alliances, and the cultural participation in the industrial world of the metropole reinforce the pattern of social domination. That "indirect assimilation" of industrial civilization and its values and conduct was accompanied by a remarkable immobility of the structures of society. Today the model of industrialization "associated" with multinational capitalism produces an increasing concentration of income and an expanding social heterogeneity due to the integration of new privileged social groups into the world of "developed" consumers. The growth of industry, rather than providing the driving force of national integration and social progress, only aggravates inequality and increases and "massifies" social distinctions.

In these penetrated and externally oriented societies we do not see the interplay of basic social classes characteristic in Europe, the contradictions that Marxism systematically analyzed. The confrontations and permutations of ruling classes that marked the evolution of the old continent are not the central dynamic of Latin American society. It is only by a dogmatic projection of the European experience—another form of dependence—that one can see the industrial bourgeoisie of the continent mounting an assault on the power of the agrarian aristocracy. In fact things happened in a totally different way. The exclusionary logic produced by the economic system forced the dominant groups to compromise among themselves; the leading role of primary product export produced an industrial development that was subordinated to agricultural development rather than antagonistic to it. The industrialist, once the ties to the artisan were broken, was hardly distinguishable from the small group of large landholders and financiers from which he had sometimes originated. In addition, the conscious search for a quick profit resulted in the diversification of investments and their transfer from a stagnant sector to more profitable areas including industry. This does not mean that the bourgeoisie does not exist, but it is not always easy to identify and it is not very aware of the historical role that is sometimes attributed to it. The "relevant effects" of its actions are not comparable to those of the European bourgeoisie, since the movement from one sector to another, further complicated by its association with foreign capital, makes it in most cases only intermittently bourgeois in character.

Rather than speaking of a dualism involving an opposition between the traditional and the modern as two coherent paradigms, it is necessary to think of two contradictory and complementary aspects of a single structure of domination. More concretely, the ruling groups among the upper classes, with all the continuity and immobilism of their social structure, manage to be at one and the same time both modern and archaic; thus, this group combines the most elaborate technical progress with the most retrograde social conduct, and reflects the most up-to-date and refined European culture while exercising social power through the latest brutal methods. The "fusion effect" of this dichotomous set of behaviors and values is precisely a result of the place that these social groups have in the functioning of the overall system. Guaranteeing external domination, they use exogenous legitimation to exercise internal hegemony. In other words, enlightened oligarchies can be both modern in their ideas and tastes and committed to the most traditional system of social control.

This is why, as Alain Touraine has correctly pointed out in his analysis of the "disarticulation" of dependent societies, for those elites social reproduction is often more important than production; the maintenance of privilege can sometimes be more important than the maintenance of the profit rate. The principal characteristics of these societies, apart from their profound differences and irreducible particularities, are the result of an effort to preserve a traditional social structure through the process of industrialization. Induced and imitative industrialization without an industrial revolution has sometimes been compared to "conservative modernization," and the adverse effects of this phenomenon in Germany and Japan have been described by Barrington Moore. The assumed contradiction involved in the desire to "resolve the unresolvable" has produced bastard regimes, militarism, and adventures. Without going further with the comparison, we simply note that this kind of social configuration is certainly more prone to the triumph of despotism than to the establishment of liberal representative systems.

SOCIAL CONTROL AND STYLE OF AUTHORITY

The concentration of economic and social power, the rigidity of the cleavages, the permanence of structures of domination even in the most secularized urban societies—all have contributed in different degrees throughout the continent to the structure of authority and specific types of relationships. One is struck both by the vertical character of social relations and by the general applicability of a model of authoritarian domination. In fact, not only do free and equal social links seem to be rare and at least difficult but the style of the relation of elite and masses is at once repressive, paternalistic, and monopolistic. We mean by this that the mechanisms for the exclusion of those who are dominated are ambivalent and involve both together and separately the methods of obligatory cooptation and marginalization.

Clientelism and the different patronage systems express both the vertical nature of social relations and the modalities of domination. The cacique, whether a large landholder, a merchant, or a local notable, is the pivotal intermediary with the rest of society. He controls a network of those obliged to him, and often dispenses to them as a favor what would otherwise result from the laws of the market or free contractual obligations. Geographical isolation, insecurity of status, scarcity of goods (land, water, jobs) ensure relations of reciprocity based on inequality. A network of favors, organized around the powerful man, appears to be established on an individual basis according to which each individual who receives largesse remains the external debtor and prisoner of his benefactor. This is especially true in the most archaic forms of agrarian production. Thus in Chile at the time of Popular Unity (1970–73), one could see miserable *inquilinos*—landless peasants who pay for their small plots by labor for the owner of the *fundo*—engaging in public demonstrations against agrarian reform. But the politics of scarcity affects not only the traditional rural sector. The city is likewise characterized by more or less institutionalized vertical solidarity. The illegal dwelling place and the informal job impel the individual to find protectors who will give him security and favors.

To assure the loyalty of those dependent on him (*clientes*) it is not unusual for the boss (*patron*) to become the godfather of their children, thus creating complex and ambiguous relationships through godparentage (*compadrazgo*). The compadrazgo gives a sacred significance through links of a putative and quasi-religious parentage to the clientelized relations of domination. It assures the undying loyalty of the weak to the strong, of the clients to the cacique. These mechanisms are not just attributes of old "patriarchs" or the caudillos of earlier times. We can cite the case of the manager of a sugar mill in Pernambuco in Brazil who is proud to be the godfather of one of the children of each of his workers. He addresses each of them by the informal *voce* and in return is addressed—with respect—by his first name.

Without always taking this quasi-religious form, systems of reciprocal obligation are the tissue of social life and affect the political culture. Even the trade union monopoly of hiring in certain countries and industries produces a clientelism that was not foreseen by the legislator. "You can do nothing without friends," says a Mexican, but those relations of friendship are rarely egalitarian. They are nearly always hierarchic and vertical, without completely reproducing the social distance involved in the classic patron-client relationship of the rural areas. Even in

Cuba under Castro, one finds that in the construction of socialism, Leninist-Soviet rationalism is confronted with Gordian
knots of the *sociolismo* of personal friendships (*socio*—partner,
friend) aimed at circumventing bureaucratic rigidities and the
demands of ideologically motivated programs.[17]

With few exceptions nearly all the established party systems and government political organizations, whether monopolistic or pluralistic, are structured in a pragmatic way around
local social authorities and "natural leaders." On the local level
the responsible leaders of the parties in power—whether it is
the dominant "revolutionary" party in Mexico, the conservative
two-party system of the National Democratic Union (UDN) and
Social Democratic Party (PSD) in Brazil before 1964, the Conservatives and Liberals in Colombia, or even the Radicals and
Peronists in Argentina—are most often those who because of
their position control the local population as a result of services
rendered or debts contracted. They are the ones who organize
the vote and can produce votes (even unanimous ones) for the
electoral market through procedures that involve a return for
favors that is not far from coercion.

To give some Brazilian examples: The *mandonismo* of the
violent strongman is the other side of his paternalistic concern
(or *filhotismo*). That is why during the democratic period, Brazilians would say "Electoral rallies do not win elections."[18] In other
words, free voting hardly exists. In addition, the parties and
governments contribute to this type of control through lucrative
favors, individual services, and the political exploitation of a
highly personalistic welfare state. Social security and health care
are not the result of the legislation of an anonymous administration but of the benevolent concern of the sovereign, whether it is
a man or a party. Thus the system functions harmoniously,
avoiding the pressures of the demands and requirements of
open democratic procedures. The individual resolution of social
questions utilizes the mechanisms of group cooptation to atom-
ize larger socioeconomic aggregates.

It is evident that these links of vertical solidarity adversely
affect attempts to organize horizontal groups based on class or
common interest. Those who are dominated have little opportunity to choose their patron or godfather. The social pyramid is

not static but is rather a dynamic reflection of the reality of social links. The style of command that emerges from these unequal or nonneutral relationships has as its counterpart a violence that theologians have recently baptized "structural" and that observers rarely see. Only the violence initiated by those who are excluded is reported in the papers. The daily violence that expels the peasant without a title to his land or the *colon* who has given offense, that of the troops that eject from the factory workers who are simply demanding the payment of their wages, is not a thing of the past. Violence from above emerges at any moment, in the most apparently modernized societies, and even in those industries with a modern wage-system and an organized and combative proletariat, as a chance result of a social conflict or economic disagreement.

This violence did not begin with its institutionalization in the numerous terrorist states that have flourished in recent years in the shadow of gold braid and the gallows. Torture was used in the police stations of Brazil, Argentina, and Chile against the maid accused of stealing from her mistress and the *roto* who stole farm animals long before the military launched their antisubversive wars with their sophisticated techniques. It was only when those same techniques were applied to the political sectors and the urban middle class that they were discovered in the depth of their horror.

Finally, let us emphasize the importance of this social verticality for the attitudes and practices of an institution that has magnified nonegalitarian and hierarchical values—the army.

POLITICAL CULTURE AND LEGITIMACY

If one had to identify in a few words the most striking aspect of Latin American politics it would certainly not be the prevalence of coups d'états or seizures of power, or the *continuismo* of its presidents for life, or sophisticated schemes of electoral fraud, but rather its indefeasible idealistic attachment to the representative institutions of the West. Even when liberal principles and constitutional provisions are violated or distorted, appeals are made to the permanent values of democracy. The salesmen of the New Order have not been successful south of the Rio Grande. Whether they are civilians or military men, they refer only to democracy and to no other source of legitimacy than the dominant liberalism. The dependence of the leading elites of Latin America upon "the mother of parliaments" and later on the country that is "the leader of the free world" is evidence of that surprising loyalty. In the "Third World" part of the West even the most rudimentary dictators mind their democratic manners. The Trujillos, Somozas, Stroessners, and many others before them have arranged to be reelected regularly by their people, and when the constitution forbade their reelection, they yielded to a faithful confederate, modestly reserving for themselves the command of the army.

It is true that an abyss separates the written constitution from actual practice. In his classic study, *Democracy in Mexico*, Gonzalez Casanova observes that "every citizen . . . becomes accustomed to comparing the model of orthodoxy with the reality of the paganism in which he lives and now or in the future he commits his sins," and he adds "While in Europe the theoretical and legislative models are the result of a direct creative relation between experience and political and legislative theory which produces particular instruments and techniques, in our country creative activity is the result of the application of a foreign way of thinking that we make our own through a process of imitation. In our legislation there is a process which is like that of some religions where the idols are hidden under the altars with the same sense of persecution and idolatry." The values that ought to underlie the practice resulting from the adopted institutions fulfill the function of a utopia, an inaccessible ideal that can only be reached through a miraculous process. Thus political life is played on two levels. The juridical inspiration and the manifest ideology are representative and formally egalitarian. The concentration of social power and the modes of domination that flow from them are largely incompatible, or more incompatible than in the older democracies, with the official sources of legitimacy. The appropriation of economic and political resources by a minority on the one hand, and the despoiling of the masses in a cumulative situation of inferiority on the other, demonstrate the essential dichotomy between words and actions. These asymmetrical relations may not otherwise be obvious in the most modernized societies. Nevertheless they constitute insurmountable obstacles to social participation. Behind the "public stage" of popular sovereignty there is a "private stage" based on relations of domination. Every attempt at participation that is not controlled, that is not the result of an agreement by the participants on "the private stage," is therefore seen as a threat to the "pact of domination."

That is why one finds in the Latin American states two types of legitimacy. On the one hand there is legitimacy based on the legal order and majority rule in conformity with constitutional provisions, while on the other there is a legitimacy that one can call oligarchic, whose justifying principle is usually historical or traditional. This duality can be found in systems as different as modern Argentina and the very backward black republic of Haiti. In the Caribbean "pigmentocracy" and in the most European countries of Latin America one finds a confrontation between the defenders of the power of the "most able" and of that of the "most numerous"[19]—the principles of liberalism against those of democracy. Thus we can understand why a policy that does not reflect the relations of domination results in the illegitimacy of the government that it has promoted.

The vertical character of social relations and the almost cosmic distance between institutional ideologies and social conduct produce a political culture of deception. The painted façades of a juridical universalism cover the particularism of personalistic relations and forces. The laws are not only made, as elsewhere, to be broken; they are often adopted, as they say in Brazil, *para inglês ver*, to make the English believe in perfectly advanced legislation that is never applied, those ethereal "blue sky" laws that are cited at the International Labor Office or international gatherings. Judicial institutions suffer the same fate as the law. In the popular language of the *refraneros* they say, "Justice is for friends and the law for enemies" and "The courts are for those who wear *ruanas*" (the Colombian poncho typically worn by peasants). These quasi-schizophrenic distortions are not, as is sometimes written north of the Rio Grande, the result of a psychological incapacity for democracy that is characteristic of Latin American societies, or of the Hispanic world, but rather of social and historical conditions, a knowledge of which is essential to understand the phenomena of politics.

On the State

At the center of those networks of specific determinants is the state—which is unknown or little known. One cannot analyze military power in Latin America without speaking of the state—indeed of a particular form of the state, that of dependent societies. Furthermore, discussions of the state that forget the central role of the military bureaucracies are only serving up abstractions. This state either is ignored or the term is applied selectively to disparate realities—the nation and its territory, the political system or the center of political life and the public bureaucracy, or the legal state, which is too often simply a pale instrument of social forces. This state, for which the evidence compels the calculation of a relative degree of autonomy in accordance with a poor and distorted version of Marxist writings, is certainly not easy to define or analyze. But here we cannot enjoy the luxury of imprecision or ambiguity. We will use the term "state" to mean a single political center that controls a territory and the population that occupies it,[20] and bases its legitimacy and power on a relationship to the forces of society.

Given this definition, we can trace certain characteristics of the development of the state in Latin America. In accordance with the historical and structural situation of the Latin American societies, the state is first of all, even during the colonial period, the place for transactions and bargaining between local propertied groups and the foreign bourgeoisie. In this sense we can make the paradoxical claim that the state in dependent societies is relatively independent of internal interests. We must qualify this assertion by excluding the patrimonial political systems governed by family dictatorships and making use of a now classic economic distinction.[21] The role and the capabilities of the bourgeoisie and the state organizations are not the same in the nations in which local economic groups control production, and in those countries with an enclave economy.

Nevertheless, in both of these cases the state functions to harmonize the divergent interests of the different propertied classes. It is rarely the instrument of one part of the ruling classes. Its margin of maneuver is relatively large, even in societies in which the export sector is in the hands of local property holders.

The dynamic equilibrium between the internal and external bourgeoisies within the state continues to be not only conflictive but very fragile. With a passing market crisis, the end of a speculative cycle, or the failure of a project, the balance collapses. The state apparatus alone both acts as arbiter and controls the direction of society, proceeding to dictate changes that no social force has the means to carry out successfully. It is easy for the state to take charge of the interests of the nation—as defined by its personnel—because the local ruling class has failed to do so or is involved in endless debates and, except during periods of euphoria and prosperity, can hardly ever persuade the subordinate classes that its interests of the moment are identical with the common good. This is so for two reasons: first, because of the foreign associations of the bourgeoisie and the difficulty of making foreign capital appear to be national in character, and second, because of the exclusionary nature of the political systems. A "clientelistic" type of redistribution that assures the consent of the dominated is only possible in periods of prosperity. Long before anyone spoke of the "welfare state," that government function was decisive in Latin America.

In fact, historically the center of national power played an original and decisive role in the creation of the social classes. At the extreme one can even say that it was not the dominant classes that created the state as an instrument of domination, but the state that helped to establish those social groups. The *latifundista* aristocracy and the rural bourgeoisie emerged in the nineteenth century through the distribution of land to friends and clients, to those under obligation, and to those who either possessed the financial means to aid the treasury or the "military" means to support provisional rulers. The grant of inexhaustible public lands facilitated the initial enrichment of a "progressive" or traditionalist leisure class that owed its start to the state. Later the selective distribution of credit or judicial decisions, as well as favorable business activities involving foreign capital and the state, reinforced a nucleus of property holders that dominated the economy and politics. Whether the issue was a plan for agricultural expansion, the encouragement of immigration to the Southern Cone, industrial development, or labor policy, very few groups of social prominence were independent of such state support. Some owed their establishment to state capital and manipulation, others their organization, still others their self-awareness. It is one of the paradoxes of Latin America (for once, this is true of all those countries) that the productive classes and capitalist elites never fail to manifest an aversion to state control and intervention, however slight, despite the fact that those sectors owe everything to the power of the state.

The paradox is perhaps only apparent, for the role of the state in the redistribution of national revenue is continuous. Even if the economists' famous cake gets larger, redistribution always involves a transfer from the productive sectors to those that are not directly involved in production. And those with economic power rarely view the results of this liberality in terms of social stability and political peace. Faced with populist governments that expand public employment to strengthen and satisfy the middle classes, the rich are defenders of the "minimalist" state and budget-cutting policies. The huge inefficient bureaucracies that are so frequent in Latin America are simply a reflection of the state role in the division of benefits and the cooptation of new social groups, and not just a kind of congenital administrative irrationality in which perverse *mañana* attitudes are combined with a shameful passion for paperwork. In fact a "public employee" in Latin America is neither the French fonctionnaire nor the British civil servant. If his function appears to be identical, the reasons for his being hired and the origins of his status are radically different. In no European country could one say, as Mario Benedetti did of Uruguay before 1973, that it was not only a country of bureaucrats, but "the only bureaucracy in the world to have become a nation."[22]

Furthermore, we must recognize that in Latin America economic policy is not a matter of chance. Radical shifts produce brutal reversals that are carried out by the state. Today it is the Chicago boys against the populists. An administration that is diametrically opposite to its predecessor ruins those who benefited from the largesse of past regimes. Those swings of the pendulum that long antedate 1973 explain the central role of the state, which derives less perhaps from the fragility of civil society than from its inertia and immobility.[23]

When we speak about the state in Latin America, it is necessary to consider the role of the army. The military coup d'etat can be understood as the director and arbiter among the societal sectors. The state, in the form of the coup, acts to preserve a status quo that can be reorganized and even overturned from top to bottom in order to guarantee the one essential requirement, the relations of domination and social and/or political exclusion—even at some sacrifice. Whatever the individual, historical, or national explanations that are given for the cycles of military interventions, they always result in a transfer of revenue and new social redistribution. These regulative coups—the innocence of the term is not meant to deny their crudeness, even their barbarity and ferocity—are therefore first of all actions by the state against social sectors whose power has grown to the point that they threaten government autonomy or endanger its functioning. The apparent desire of the military to free the state from civil society allows the armed forces to accomplish the goals of the state even against its will and acting in its defense. This in no way signifies that the military institution is above class, but that it defends the status quo in accordance with its own logic. For if an army by definition only defends what exists, its logic is that of war and not of social reproduction.

2

THE
ESTABLISHMENT
OF THE
MILITARY AND
THE BIRTH OF
THE STATE

When discussing countries that we think of as new, our ignorance of their past produces distorted interpretations of the present. The exaggerated importance given to the current situations gives rise to a fallacious model of a living and moving reality. Lacking a historical dimension, these "exotic" countries appear to be characterized by improvisation and chaotic caprice. We study monstrosities rather than societies. Belief in these images produces surrealistic visions of a political life that is not subject to laws, or social science, or rational understanding—of a fixed and immovable society, immature people incapable of self-government. Historical fatalism and popular psychology result only in an intellectual void. In Latin America, more than in other areas, a historical perspective is required if we are to overcome partisan mythologies and fantastic caricatures.

Armies also have a history. However, a short-range nominalism produces confusion. What are the armed forces and the military in twenty nations over more than a century? Are we speaking of the same subject over time and space when we refer to the army of this or that country? What is the point of describing a regime as military in these latitudes, or of asserting that there is strong military influence in a political system? A dictatorship does not necessarily have to be based upon the army, and a military regime is not necessarily established or maintained by means of a high level of repression. García Márquez's "patriarch," the five-star "general of the universe," was intensely interested in his military men, "not because they were the basis of his power, as everyone believed, but because they were his most dangerous natural enemies."[1]

There is a vast difference between the improvised warrior and a member of the military profession. The "Gaucho Chieftains of the Pampas" are in no way comparable to line officers. A strongman utilizing violence for political ends is fundamentally different from a high-level officer of the armed bureaucracy, even if they both wear gold braid and stars. The cards have been shuffled. Under an identical military visor, there are very different individuals. In societies with different levels of state modernization, social complexity, and functional differentiation, military personnel can come from unlikely different walks of life. For example, a former schoolteacher in twentieth-century Mexico can become a political chief and a leader of men during a revolutionary upheaval (this is a description of Plutarco Elías Calles, who was first a general and then president). A modest municipal clerk may be given the rank of captain at the time that he joins the revolutionary armies (we are referring to the popular General Cárdenas, Calles's successor in the presidency in 1934). Likewise, an army stenographer in Cuba with the rank of sergeant was able to promote himself rapidly in the course of a coup d'état (this was the case with Batista, Fidel Castro's adversary), and experts in court intrigue can rise in the military as a result of patronage: this happened with Lopez Contreras in Venezuela, and it has also occurred in Nicaragua and the Dominican Republic. But everywhere the military officer can also be someone trained in a national or foreign military school who is promoted on the basis of merit or seniority in the hierarchy, and who has never done anything else but command troops and carry out general staff exercises.

At the turn of the century and during the first quarter of the twentieth century in certain countries that were most divided by civil war among the oligarchical groups, it was not unusual for the leaders of the elite and the clan chieftains to use two titles—the civilian title of "doctor" and the military one of "general." Lawyers and warrior chieftains, they gave eloquent testimony to the nonexistence of the state and the preponderance of private interests. Even in societies that were more developed, if not more civilized, the prestige of the uniform was such that togas yielded to arms, and the top levels of the civil service were granted military titles. Miguel Cané, the ambassador of Argentina to Venezuela at the time of Guzmán Blanco (who ruled until 1886), was amazed to find that the minister of foreign affairs, a peaceful civil servant and former director of the chancery archives, bore the rank of general. "He held that rank," the Argentine diplomat tells us, "along with several hundred of his compatriots, but he had received it as a simple decoration, without ever feeling the least desire to exchange his peaceful existence for the agitated world of the military."[2]

Are they really military men? The boundaries are difficult to determine if one does not establish certain clear criteria. The peasants on horseback in the great plains (the *pampa* of the La Plata River, the *llanos* of Venezuela, the north of Mexico) are armed reserves who can easily become the elements of irregular armies. In the nineteenth century, at least, we can speak of a "civilian-agrarian-military" continuum involving the men on horseback.[3] Until the twentieth century, increasing numbers of private armies belonging to clans or parties in countries as different as the Dominican Republic and Uruguay attested to the fragility, weakness, and backwardness of the state. The national army—it was sometimes in this context only the forces of a caudillo who had seized power at the point of a gun—did not have a monopoly of control over the instruments of violence. The ease with which one could acquire arms of a relatively simple technological level, the absence in this respect of a qualitative difference between professionals and amateurs, between permanent public armed forces and private armed bands, increased the number of violent political mobilizations. The improvement in armament and in heavy arms of a technical nature—the end of the Iron Age—in the twenties (in 1930 in the case of Brazil) rendered this type of military opposition passé. The victories of the guerrilla army in Cuba in 1959 or of a popular party-led army in

1979 in Nicaragua can be explained essentially by the collapse of the ruling regimes and the demoralization of the military. In the case of Nicaragua, this led to both a mass civilian uprising and access of the Sandinista army to sophisticated arms, thanks to aid from foreigners who were opposed to Somoza.

In discussing the diversification and evolution of the military, particular emphasis will be placed on the armies that we call *statist*—that is, those that are responsible to the state alone and are its military branch. These are the modern standing armies that we know throughout the world. They are also the armies that carry out coups d'état. The degree to which the military apparatus is identified with the state varies. At the opposite extreme, irregular or private armies are totally *societal* in character, as are also some national armies that have been deeply penetrated by society. A second, more chronological, distinction refers to military professionalization. The appearance of professional cadres whose sole way of life and means of existence is the military institution totally changes the nature of the armed forces. Here too one can distinguish gradations and levels of professionalization. The three characteristics listed by Huntington—technical orientation, discipline, and esprit de corps—[4] apply to the state armies in which the military "profession" has developed a high degree of autonomy. There is no doubt that there is, if not a break, at least a difference, between a preprofessional and a fully professionalized military. The first has little permanence, and the officers, especially those in the higher grades, are members of a civilian elite who temporarily assume a social role; the modern armies, in contrast, are "total" institutions that aim at self-sufficiency and are characterized by a more or less evident absence of "lateral" relations with society.[5] We can ask if the same word applies to both realities. It is therefore no doubt a fallacy to speak without qualification of the "Brazilian army" in both 1830 and 1964 as an organization that indeed has evolved but is supposed to have remained essentially the same.

This does not mean that the collective institutional memory does not take into account the heroic past of the improvised or inchoate armed forces that existed at the dawn of national independence. The impact of that glorious past is not unimportant, especially in the area of politics. In Argentina, the native land of the liberator, General San Martín, the "saint of the spear," many people believe that one hundred generals created the nation. The streets of Santiago or São Paulo are as full of the names of famous or unknown generals as is Buenos Aires. Are they real generals, self-appointed young upstarts, or warrior chiefs recognized by the state and history? It does not matter. In all of South America, in the beginning was the army. However, we must recognize that in the armies of independence that expelled Spain from the continent there were very few military men, even if it is true that once these soldiers left civilian life they became permanent members of the military.

That is why the political history of the Latin American armies—or more precisely of the South American armed forces that today are almost entirely modern state organizations of the Western type—involved three stages closely linked to the emergence and modernization of the state. One phase of this transition was the "professionalization" of the military. Just after the achievement of independence by force of arms there was a period that one can call *militarism without the military*. We cannot speak of that period of military intervention in politics as we do today, for politics was only war carried out by military means involving fighting men as its protagonists. The liberating armies, when demobilized, often became large companies headed by the improvised and hardened leaders who had led the *montoneros* in the struggle against the Spaniards and now sought to take power and live on the country. This "predatory militarism" emerged in an institutional void. Those political armies sometimes looked like regular armies, but in fact they were an obstacle to the construction of the state that was to be established in opposition to them.

When the state coalesced without being stabilized, a national army was created; the members of the military during this period were identified with the political administrative personnel and drawn from the ruling classes. The functions of those ruling classes were diversified, and they included a military sector. Nearly all the Spanish-speaking republics, as well as the empire of Brazil, experienced a period of civilian preponderance—that is, one involving *a military without militarism*.

The third stage we know today. Depending on the country, it began at the turn of the century or in the 1920s. For different reasons analyzed later, the armies at the heart of the state were modernized, given technical training, and reorganized following the model of the most prestigious military institutions of the time. The military were militarized in order to make the army part of the state, but in the process they were given the organizational and moral resources—especially in the countries that established compulsory military service, "the school for a nation"—to intervene in political life. The officer corps, having developed a sense of its own competence that also was related to the weaknesses of the civil service and an acute sense of national identity, henceforth possessed the means to make its influence felt as a special public organization whose goal and legitimation were based on the ability to kill.

ARMIES BEFORE THE STATE

Morris Janowitz, the American expert on the military, divides the armies of the so-called developing countries into ex-colonial armies, national liberation armies, and armies created after independence. That division, while useful for other continents, is not applicable in Latin America since in varying degrees its national armies possess all three characteristics at the same time; in addition, there are "personal armies" that are difficult to relate to the three classifications. After independence in Bolivia elements of all three were present—that is, the army of liberation of Grand Colombia belonging to Marshal Sucre that had liberated Peru and Ecuador but had been organized for action in the captaincy-general of Venezuela, the remnants of the former Spanish army, and the Bolivian guerrilla troops who had revolted against the Spaniards. The first attempt to organize a genuine national army in Bolivia was carried out by General Santa Cruz in 1829, but the 5,000 well-disciplined and trained men that he organized formed the first of many "personal armies" that existed in that country throughout the nineteenth century.

It may be appropriate to say a few words about the status of the military in the colonial period in Spanish- and Portuguese-speaking America, especially since some writers do not hesitate to trace the origins of contemporary militarism to the pre-independence period. In fact, until the eighteenth century the Latin American colonies were only defended by a few detachments of the armies of the mother country and those born in the colonies were strictly excluded from membership. Only the local militias that assured the maintenance of internal order were open to them. However, the reforms carried out by Charles III and Charles IV between 1759 and 1808 in response to the danger from England changed that situation. The Spanish crown reinforced its garrisons on the basis of local recruitment so as to have less need for troops from the Iberian Peninsula. The militias were reorganized and their officers received the same rights as those of the regular army. Because of the insufficient numbers of peninsular Spaniards, the native-born *criollos* were admitted to the officers' ranks in the army. The privileges that were associated with the "military class" in a status-based and caste society such as that of the colonies had an undeniable attraction.

Thanks to the *fuero militar*, the group of rights enjoyed by officers and sergeants, the military acquired an enviable and prestigious social standing. Thus, military personnel were not subject to the regular courts but had their own judicial system, whether they were plaintiffs or defendants, and this was true for life if they had served a certain number of years.[6] Because of those legal privileges many Latin Americans from good families entered the army as cadets, obtained the rank of officer because of certain individual or family services rendered to the crown, or bought their commissions. Because of the fuero militar, the colonial army after the Bourbon reforms became an independent organism within the state that acted as a "self-governing" institution that was answerable only to itself.

This has led some to conclude that the arrogant and overbearing autonomy of the modern armies in a great many Latin American countries is directly related to the privileged status of the military in the colonial period. It is very unlikely, however, that this history had a bearing on the military after the permanent restructuring associated with independence and the repeated breakdowns in the various military organizations. This is all the more true since the reforms were applied especially to the garrisons responsible for the protection of the key ports needed for trade with the mother country and the defense of the adjacent coasts: essentially Cuba, New Grenada (present-day Colombia), and New Spain (today, Mexico). If we leave Cuba aside we find that these are precisely the countries in which the army is weak and its sovereignty limited, while in Mexico the fueros of the military were only abolished in 1856. However, this is not the essential point. Certainly, because of that reform the Spanish-speaking parts of America experienced a new institution—the army, but the motivations of its leaders were far from militaristic. Into the officer corps came an indolent and inglorious "army" in order to secure the privileges and exemptions that were granted to its members by the *cédula real*. The result: captains fit only for the salons and colonels with fine uniforms and gold braid. The military career became a way to join the nobility, but these young men had little authority over the enlisted troops who were recruited by force from the dregs of society, and would desert at the least opportunity in order to become highway robbers.

The situation was the same and even clearer in the case of colonial Brazil—epaulettes made an officer a noble. The line officers became members of the nobility as soon as their rank was recognized by the king.[7] Their descendants were also nobles and could thus become officers, since after 1757 in the Portuguese Empire it was necessary to belong to the nobility to become an officer. That rule continued in Brazil after independence, extending the requirement of membership in the nobility to all military functions. Being an enlisted man was no more attractive than in the Hispanic world. Manhunts and corporal punishment were the basis of recruitment and discipline.

The practically uninterrupted institutional continuity maintained in Brazil during the process of independence reinforces, of course, the historicist argument. Even if we take into account the difference in character between the Brazilian army around 1810 and at the end of the century, we can guess that the arrogance of the military and their messianic sense of superiority were not simply elements that derived from a corporate ethos but rather could be based just as well on an aristocratic nostalgia, the subtle effect of the collective memory of their status under the empire.

In any case the role and influence of the military in the

colonial period were considerable, and not simply a matter of protocol or precedence. Thus the officers in the technical branches and the physicians in the military shared a knowledge of mathematics, civil engineering, or physics that only they possessed. In a way they were the representatives in the colonies of the most enlightened elements of the Bourbon state at the time that the upheaval took place that produced the independent republics.

The Spanish American nations were established in wars of independence. The new republics had an army even when they did not have a state. Those independence armies forged nations out of the ruins of the colonial political institutions. The emancipation struggles against the Spanish crown were devastating and often bloody, even if they were led by and benefited the native-born bourgeoisie that desired freedom to pursue their economic interests—interests that were already dominant, although limited by colonial controls. Those socially conservative revolutions sometimes lasted for ten years—as in the case of Mexico—and divided vast sectors of the population into two camps. The struggles for independence were above all genuine civil wars among opposing ruling groups, and not simply, as the republican mythology claims, a battle waged by patriot heroes supported by a wave of popular sentiment against the regular armies of the mother country. In fact both royalists and patriots engaged in guerrilla warfare, recruited armies by force when necessary, and armed local militias. Since when warfare was prolonged and intensified, they extended the recruitment of troops into the popular classes and broadened their political audience to wider sectors of the population, the upper class, whether royalist or patriot, was quite often carried away by the mobilization that they had produced. In the areas where the victory of the Latin Americans was not rapid, the war became more intense, and racial struggles were superimposed on class hatreds to unleash a brutal anarchy. This was the case in Venezuela where the lower classes and the racially mixed social elements (the *Castas*) who had nothing to gain from the independence desired by the native-born elite massacred both the Spanish colonizers and the vanquished "insurgents."

The specter of a racial war hovered over the Spanish colonies in revolt. Long-repressed social and regional tensions emerged in full view. Both the Spaniards and the rebels tried to exploit them for their benefit but never succeeded in controlling them. In Venezuela again—where the social aspects of the war were particularly evident—the royalists recruited *mestizos, zambos,* and *mulattoes,* situated at the bottom of the social hierarchy, against the rebels who belonged to the native-born aristocracy. Boves, "the centaur of the llanos," organized his hordes of mixed-blood horsemen for the cause of the king of Spain. And the same men who followed "the Attila of Apure" could be found among the troops of "General" Paez, the hero of independence. The frightening picture of the civil war that is given to us by the positivist Venezuelan historians involves a comparison with "the Roman world at the time of the barbarian invasions." Is this a biased exaggeration that reflects the great fear of the property holders of popular insurrection and racial war? Of course, but the violent overturn of the colonial equilibrium that was partially maintained against the plebeian danger in the other viceroyalties by agreements among the adversaries to guarantee the right of property released centrifugal forces, broke down social structures, and shook up social hierarchies everywhere.[8]

The collapse of Spanish institutions left the area free for the warlords. The fragmentation of the territorial and administrative units of the colonial period resulted from the nature of the war carried on against the colonial power. It was also facilitated by the economic organization of Hispanic America at the beginning of the nineteenth century. The importance of the agricultural production of foodstuffs, the self-sufficient forms of social life, the difficulty of transportation despite the penetration of the market economy under the aegis of Great Britain, and the long history of the export of its products to Europe, resulted in societies in which precapitalist traits were politically prevalent. The archaic character of the relations of production—which one author has called "the reactionary method of capitalist development"[9]—accentuated these characteristics still more. In addition, like the precapitalist societies described by Georg Lukács, in the first quarter of the last century in Latin America "the autonomy of the parties is much greater because their economic interdependence is more limited and less developed than in capitalism," because "the weaker the role of the circulation of goods is in the life of a society, . . . the less the unity and organizational cohesion of the society and the state has a genuine foundation in the real life of the society."[10] Political disintegration has its roots in the economy, but expresses itself in warfare. A generalized state of war was the normal situation on a more or less permanent basis for the Hispanic republics at the dawn of their independence.

Armies against the State

That underlying anarchy of the postcolonial societies of the subcontinent produced the age of the caudillos. While certainly a man at arms, the caudillo is the opposite of the career military man. The career officer is the product of the workings of a bureaucracy. The caudillo is produced by the institutional decomposition of society. Once victory was achieved, in most countries around 1825, the leaders of the emancipating armies quickly transformed themselves into caudillos, sometimes carving out a fiefdom, but most often making efforts to gain control of "national" power. More often the victorious armies followed their leaders across the continents seeking their fortunes without any concern for national frontiers that were still fluid and existed only in theory. The generals sought the throne; their men, booty and an easy life. The civilian elites that had initiated the revolution in order to consolidate their power and serve their interests began to complain of the arrogance of those veterans who had gained their stripes on the field of battle, and the armies were a considerable expense for the states that were still being established. It was not rare for half the expense of the new republics to be devoted to the military budget.

In some countries the "voracious militarism" which was the result of a period of generalized violence took the place of a political system. Since other institutions no longer existed, the army was everything, since in almost every case there "was no power superior to that of arms" at the end of the wars of independence.[11] Thus from 1825 until 1879 Bolivia had a sinister series of "barbarian caudillos" whose intemperance and picturesque megalomania have become legendary. They emerged from the "liberating" troops to form personal armies in order to seize the government and plunder its riches. This was the case with the popular Isidoro Belzú (1848–1855) who destroyed the elite army of Santa Cruz and formed his own force made up of *cholos* and representatives of the lower classes in order to despoil an aristocracy that despised him as an opportunist of mixed blood. Again, there is the blustering Mariano Melgarejo, the antihero of Bolivian history. If one believes the thousands of anecdotes contained in popular tradition, he was an outrageous tyrant who seized the presidency by force in 1864.

The struggles among the civilians and the oppositions of interests and ideologies, when they were not arbitrated by the veterans of independence, likewise led to the force of arms. Whether the factions were liberal or conservative, supporters of unity or federalism, they established party-armies to mount an assault on power. Against the "official" party or the "situation," as they termed it, the opposition had no other means of expression than an uprising. The monopoly of collective violence did not exist. A weak state controlled nothing. Private, personal, or pseudopublic armies prevented the emergence and establishment of a state apparatus. One can even say that nearly everywhere in Hispanic America, sometimes down to the end of the nineteenth century, the armies that formed the nation prevented the construction of the state.

The crisis of independence and the period of anarchy that it initiated involving the fragmentation of the former Spanish empire, as well as the militarization of the new political units, plunged the subcontinent into what Halperin Donghi has called "a long waiting period."[12] From an economic point of view the instability that followed the ravages of war was not favorable to successful integration into the world market. When for economic reasons the new international division of labor that was dominated by England encouraged the involvement of countries that produced primary products, a political truce was imposed in the nations of the subcontinent. To enter "the age of economics" and to profit from the enormous European demand and the improvement in transatlantic transportation, it was necessary to construct the state. If the economic bases permitted the emergence of a dominant group that was capable of carrying out the great transformation required by the neocolonial order, it was compelled first to end decentralized militarism and the revolts of the legionnaires. The economic modernization of which the exporters of primary products were the guarantors and the beneficiaries could not take place without a state monopoly on violence and the establishment of a new type of army. "Peace and administration," "order and progress," were the slogans of the moment for the positivists. General Roca, the constitutional president of Argentina (1880–86 and 1898–1904), was not the only one to think that "revolutions—that is political uprisings—are not quoted on the Stock Exchange in London." For the dominant supporters of material—and at times cultural, but never social—progress who embraced dependence on the Western metropolitan countries, it was important to disarm civil society and to demilitarize political life so as to produce, export, and inspire the confidence of foreign capital.

The goal of state building was attained slowly in the countries of South America. Some countries of Central America and the Caribbean (such as Nicaragua and the Dominican Republic) were torn by permanent convulsions in the first third of the twentieth century without succeeding in establishing a recognized political structure that possessed a minimum of consistency and permanence. Elsewhere the process of demilitarization followed very different—at times unexpected—paths, as in Ecuador. It was also facilitated by the lack of capacity of even predatory military men to justify their existence, that is, to make war.

These turbulent military men, these noisy veterans, these saber-rattlers (among them "the heroes of July or December," "supreme protectors," "benefactors" or "restorers") who desired national recognition—that is, benefits from the public treasury—did not fail to bring discredit upon themselves when faced with a foreign enemy. General Santa Anna, one of the most extravagant of the caudillos and for thirty years the scourge of his country, Mexico, demonstrated a military incapacity that was at least equal to his political adroitness when he faced a war with the United States in 1847 resulting from the secession of Texas. This admirer of Napoleon and devotee of cockfights was four times dictator and four times overthrown; he also lost three undisciplined and poorly trained armies to the Yankee military forces, allowing the Americans to occupy Mexico City and dismember the territory of the nation. The seriousness of the disaster destroyed the prestige of the army and a few years later the exorbitant privileges of the officers inherited from the colonial period were suppressed.

The armies of Peru in power without interruption until 1872 and those of Bolivia that occupied the government—if not the country—when the War of the Pacific against Chile broke out in 1879, went down before the offensive of a country in which the military had been controlled by civilians for nearly fifty years. In spite of certain heroic episodes, Peru, because of its defeat, lost all its rights to the rich mining province of Tarapacá, and Bolivia was henceforth deprived of an outlet to the sea.

Chile represents the best example of the construction of the state against the army. The troubles at the time of independence, described by official historians as "anarchy," were shorter but no less intense than in the neighboring countries. But while five revolutions broke out in the three years before the battle of Lircay (1830), the last confrontation between the factions, the country experienced an era of political stability from the time of the adoption of the conservative and authoritarian constitution of 1833 that contrasted with the disorganization that characterized all of Spanish America at that time. The defeat of the *pipiolos*, who were liberals, rabid republicans, and federalists, by their adversaries, the *pelucones*, who were conservatives and centralists who sought an orderly government under the tutelage of the Spanish Basque aristocracy, was also a victory of civilians over the army. At Lircay civilian militias wiped out a part of the army that was linked at the outset with the liberals. Portales became a minister and organized the conservative republic that was characterized by a surprising equilibrium lasting until 1891. That "Portalian Republic," with its strong executive, was able to impose civilian control through thorough purges of the liberal elements in the officer corps, as well as of all those who had demonstrated a tendency to *pronunciamentos* and uprisings. To counterbalance the army which he had reduced to 3,000 men in 1837,[13] Portales reorganized a civilian militia that included as many as 25,000 men. The continuing "pacification" of the southern frontier with the Araucanian Indians and the wars against the alliance of Peru and Bolivia (1836–39 and 1879–83), as well as fear of Argentine power to the east at the end of the century, also contributed to keeping the Chilean military out of politics. In a strange irony of history, General Pinochet and his ideologues, who today call for the reestablishment of the authoritarian republic of Portales, seem to forget that the man who restored the "principle of authority" and who created the Chilean state had as his primary objective the demilitarization of public life.

In Peru the situation was very different. The most dynamic ruling groups struggled with only limited success to establish civilian supremacy. From 1821 until 1872 military leaders succeeded one another in power practically without interruption. Even the idea of a nonmilitary government seemed bizarre or utopian. It even reached the point that a "procivilian party" was established with a moderate program advocating the alternation of civilians and military men in power. With the support of this party Manuel Pardo became the first constitutional president of Peru in 1872, having been elected by the congress after a popular revolt had driven the military from power. Pardo reduced military spending and created a national guard that was larger than the army in order to neutralize it, but Peru's defeat in the War of the Pacific against Chile provided the opportunity for the praetorians to take their revenge. Following the customary pattern, the defeated army, stronger because of the blood that had been shed in vain and because of a few individual acts of heroism, blamed its reverses on a lack of equipment and on the incompetence of the civilian "politicians" who, according to the military, were ambitious, corrupt, and lacking in national feeling and a sense of the general interest. Three years after the catastrophe that included occupation of Lima by Chilean troops, General Andrés Caceres, the hero of La Breña, one of the battles with Chile, took over the presidency in a coup d'état in 1886.

Caceres ruled with an iron hand. The people quickly grew tired of his arbitrary government, while the financial oligarchy that was linked to English capital complained that the restored military did not recognize the laws of progress and it denounced their authoritarian statism in economics. The large guano and nitrate interests that favored laissez faire and general concessions to foreign companies opposed the government. Demilitarization was considered a necessity by the defenders of liberalism and of the participation of Peru in the world economy. The "civilianists" supported Nicolas de Piérola, a liberal and a former proponent of state direction of the economy, when he organized civilian troops and rose up against the government. The result of the war that lasted several months was that the regular army was defeated by poorly equipped civilians with no military training. Piérola took control of Lima in 1895 and occupied the presidency—a new humiliation for the Peruvian army. The civilians stayed in power for twenty years. However, the oligarchy and the dominant groups would not abandon their deep-seated antimilitarism until 1930.

The most surprising case of political consolidation against a dominant militarism is that of Ecuador in the middle of the last century. The Ecuadorian process was associated with the name of one man: Gabriel García Moreno, the creator of the "Republic of the Sacred Heart of Jesus," the amazing leader of a theocratic state, revered in France by the Christian Brothers religious order. In fact, he was a politician who used the church to build the state.

From 1830 until 1845 Ecuador was under the boot of a military regime that retained absolute control of the country. However, a regional and political division emerged involving opposition between the coast and the highlands. In 1852 General Urbina negotiated an alliance between the army and the liberal commercial bourgeoisie of the coast. When his government adopted some liberal measures to help the peasants in the highlands, the conservative landowners in the interior resisted and then revolted. Local uprisings threatened the country with dissolution. Autonomous governments were formed in Guayaquil, the coastal capital; in Quito, the national capital in the highlands; and in Cuenca and Loja on the high Andean plateaus. Peru took advantage of the situation to occupy part of the territory of its neighbor, and the principal port was blockaded.

At that moment García Moreno, an energetic and unusual

man with a background in chemistry and canon law, and a strange personality that is much discussed by historians of Ecuador, was able to seize power and took forceful action to resist the centrifugal tendencies. This man—who is considered by some to be "the avenger and martyr for Christian righteousness"[14]—appears in the eyes of his detractors as a false saint or simply as a religious fanatic and a sadist who loved repression. In fact, García Moreno was pitiless in his repression since he thought that he was carrying out a divine mission. He consecrated the country to the Sacred Heart in 1873, the same year that Paris was constructing the basilica of the same name. However, since he was aware of the danger in which the state had been in 1859, he soon made efforts to modernize the country and to centralize power in order to overcome the regional and sectoral divisions. He built highways (with forced labor), schools (for the Jesuits and Christian Brothers), introduced technical education (but closed the university), initiated large-scale public works, and reformed the fiscal and financial system. For some, he is the creator of modern Ecuador. In his effort to modernize he could not rely on the army, since it was a decentralizing force, or on parties, which were nonexistent. There remained the church, the only national institution—as García Moreno said, the "sole link among the Ecuadorians."

The paradoxical aspects of the situation were evident. While García Moreno's liberal enemies, led by writer Juan Montalvo, exalted cosmopolitanism in opposition to the obscurantist character of the government, García Moreno appealed to an ultramontane church to help him to transform the country. Furthermore, it was the church of the *Syllabus of Errors of the Modern World* to which their theologian chemist entrusted the responsibility of promoting science and progress and granted total monopoly control as a single party. García Moreno built up the state against "thirty years of militarism," the formula of the Peruvian García Calderon, the ardent admirer of all the "great Latin American leaders."[15] However, this did not prevent this "theocrat," imbued with his divine mission, from sending Ecuadorian officers to Prussia. Also, faced with the anarchy of 1860, Moreno sought without success to establish a French protectorate over Ecuador.

A MILITARISM WITHOUT THE MILITARY?

Once the postindependence anarchy was overcome, the Latin American states were pacified and the social structures and the place in the world market could be assured; these turbulent armies gave rise to the modern forces that were to be the central support and guarantee of the state. In the age of the caudillos, permanent state armies with a monopoly on the control of violence were a rarity in the continent, and officers were adventurers and warriors rather than military men. Nevertheless, there already were some professionals who tried to create an embryonic military organization. In this respect we can contrast two dissimilar figures who symbolized the career officers involved in the wars of independence: San Martín in Buenos Aires, the "liberator" of Argentina, Chile, and Peru, and Miranda in Caracas, whose policies are viewed by Venezuelan historians as the precursor of emancipation.

San Martín, who came to Spain at the age of eight and entered the college of nobles in Madrid, was incorporated in the Murcia regiment in 1789 and thus followed the normal route to become a Spanish officer. When he retired from the Spanish army in 1811, he was a lieutenant-colonel. Returning to his native land in 1812, he organized the Army of the Andes, the spearhead of the emancipation of the Southern Cone, following the best military models. This was very different from the pattern of the *montonera*. Unity of command, hierarchic structure, division into branches and services, uniform equipment—all of the specific characteristics of a regular army—were to be found there. This army included four infantry battalions, five squadrons of grenadier cavalry, and an artillery unit that were divided into three corps, each with its own general staff. In addition, General San Martín was not the only professional soldier in his army.

Miranda was the son of a tailor who went to Spain, bought a captain's commission in the Princess Regiment after some military study, and took part in 1774 in the Moroccan campaign in the ranks of the Spanish army. He served in Florida against England and reached the rank of lieutenant-colonel before he was stripped of his commission because of illegal trading activities involving contraband in slaves and merchandise in the North Atlantic. His role as adventurer in the service of the idea of independence dates from that inglorious turn of events. A general without a country or an army, he went to Pitt, Catherine the Great, and the leaders of the French Revolution to plead his cause and to look for support for the emancipation of his country from Spanish rule. Dictator for a brief period and defeated generalissimo, he was finally handed over to the Spaniards by his own officers.

More often, however, the leaders of the independence armies had never been in the regular army or received a military education. These men were leaders of bands or factions—the captain of a *montonera* of ragged peasants is happy to take on a high military rank. The caudillos of the troubled period of early Latin American independence were civilians who acquired some military experience in the course of the uprisings that they initiated. It was no different a century later during the Mexican Revolution. John Reed, in his penetrating and colorful description of the this uprising, has left us precise observations on this subject. Thus writing about Venustiano Carranza, who became president of the republic in 1915, Reed observes, "When Madero's revolution broke out, Carranza went to war in a totally medieval fashion. He armed the *peones* who worked his lands and took their lead as a feudal lord would have done. . . ."[16]

The officers in this kind of army, with their troops dressed in serapes and ponchos, were entirely ignorant of the art of war. Former soldiers, fighters by vocation, they were characterized by courage, ferocity, fearlessness, and endurance. If they did not die in battle, they were promoted rapidly. They secured their commissions in action when they distinguished themselves. Emerging in epic times, they forged a hierarchy that was very loose and easy to enter. Latorre, first a general, then dictator in Uruguay, was believed to be insensitive to pain. El Chacho Peñaloza, the caudillo of the plains of the Rioja district in northern Argentina, obtained the rank of captain for capturing the enemy cannons with his lasso. Other more politically oriented officers in less violent periods owed their epaulettes to their "revolutionary merits," that is, their friendship with a leader whom they had assisted in seizing power. Named in an arbitrary way, they had no technical formation. In this kind of army, discipline and hierarchy count less than loyalty and confidence. John Reed says, referring to the officer in the revolutionary armies, "Their role did not go beyond fighting at the head of their troops. All the soldiers considered the general who had recruited them as a feudal overlord. They were devoted to him entirely and no other officer from another group could exercise authority over them."[17] Thus, we can understand why the division between private and state armies was not very clear, all the more so since military schools existed only on paper and membership in the national army was demonstrated by wearing a uniform.

The officers were not a caste, since they did not even form a body with clearly defined rules for admission. The militarism of that period exhibited different social characteristics according to the country, but followed the same general pattern. Most often the hierarchy in the military was modeled on that of society. The caudillos, the generals, were the large landowners or their sons, the notables. But violence and the emphasis on courage and daring were democratizing factors that opened the way to prestige, status, and power.

Facundo Quiroga, the caudillo general in the province of La Rioja, was the son of a grand *hacendado* and inherited the position of captain of the provincial militia. Later and until the end of the century, if the Argentine officers were formed into units, it was necessary for an officer candidate to have solid family recommendations. For those who were well off, the military profession very often was not a permanent position. Armies were dissolved after the campaigns and the notables who were involved then considered that occupation as an honorific service rather than as a profession. Elsewhere, in more fluid and disturbed societies with no defined ruling class where "barbarian caudillos" succeeded one another, militarism was a genuine process of social mobility. Thus in Bolivia, the popular Tata Belzú,[18] a mestizo of very humble origin who at the age of fifteen had joined the revolutionary army of Upper Peru, was a fighter who came to the presidency in 1848. Melgarejo, who was said to have become a member of the infantry at the age of nine and was a clerk for a notary before becoming a "general," seems to have been characterized more by his personal excesses than by his popularity among the Indian masses. But this alcoholic old soldier, who was assassinated by his brother-in-law, was also a mestizo whose courage resulted in rapid military promotions and brought him to the summit of power. It is not certain, as is said, that he had his shirt executed or that he declared war on Prussia in 1870, or that "Let me enjoy life" was his political program, but the anecdotes remain in the mythology. In power for seven years, sensual and violent, perverse and unscrupulous, always ready to sell the territories belonging to the Indian communities and tracts of nationally owned land, he gave birth to a word in the Bolivian political vocabulary, *melgarejismo,* meaning a mixture of debauchery, excess, and militarism. It is a word that has been in frequent use since his time in the *altiplano.*

Even what is called the period of *militarismo* in Uruguay— that is, the dictatorial governments of Lorenzo Latorre, Maximo Santos, and his confederates, between 1876 and 1886—only involved soldiers of fortune and professional warriors. This kind of militarism is different from that of the praetorian dictator. Power is in the hands not of an institution but rather of "military heroes." Before becoming captain-general, Santos was a cattle driver. However, it was as a result of this that the Uruguayan army as a body developed an interest in becoming professionalized. In 1885 the Military Academy was founded for the educational formation of officers, and thus began the process of technification and modernization of a permanent army.

It was an army with special and somewhat contradictory characteristics. While it was a military institution that was politically partisan and therefore in this respect prestatist, nineteenth-century Uruguayan "militarism" did not resemble the violent and destructive anarchy of some of its neighboring countries where the "military" made (and unmade) the law. Latorre and Santos established order in the country, guaranteed the security of trade and property, and forbade vagabondage at a time when the large landholders needed a period of peace in order to produce meat and wool for the European market. Along with the introduction of the telegraph and the railroad, those governments presided over "the death of the gaucho" and a revolution in the countryside that involved enclosure of the fields, thanks to the introduction of barbed wire, *el alambrado*. Centralization of power thus was linked to integration in the world market. Militarism here seems to reinforce the state rather than acting as an obstacle to its establishment.

It is evident that a true militarism requires a stable and efficient state, and it generally follows the establishment of the state in Latin America. In Uruguay, however, the two phenomena appeared at the same time, which is why the militarism of that country was not destined to last long. This was especially true because from the time of the civil wars that produced that buffer state, the military forces were linked to the two parties—the Colorados and the Blancos or National party that were born on the field of battle in 1836. Until the war with Paraguay, the first foreign war in which Uruguay participated (1864–1870), a national army practically did not exist. The caudillos who fought for power in the course of the interminable civil wars were linked from the beginning with one or the other of Uruguay's large neighbors. Brazil and Argentina coveted their "La Plata" or "eastern" province, respectively. The Colorado party was allied with the first, the Blancos were supported by the other. However, for historical reasons that we cannot discuss here, the national army after 1850 was largely Colorado while the national guard in Montevideo and the coast was Blanco. The political preponderance of the Colorados led to armed uprisings by the Blanco National party, the last of which took place in 1904 and ended with the death of the Blanco caudillo, Aparico Saravia. The Blancos subsequently agreed not to engage in armed struggle against the dominant Colorado party. The agreement also contained military provisions concerning the rights of the officers of the "revolutionary army"; these did not change the political coloration of the institution but demonstrated its lack of autonomy with respect to the system of political parties.

In all the cases we have described, however, military control and the development of the coercive apparatus did not, as in the case of Europe in the classic age, increase the possibilities of state building. If, as Samuel Finer says, large existing or emerging standing armies reinforce the extractive and coercive capability of political power, thus enabling dominant forces to build a state,[19] in dependent nations with externally oriented economies the extraction-coercion cycle did not occur. Except for its role in the budget, the army had no fiscal responsibilities, since government revenues came principally from customs and international trade. The significance of this lack should not be underestimated.

THE MILITARY WITHOUT MILITARISM: THE BIRTH OF THE ARMED FORCES OF THE STATE

The movement from temporary ad hoc armies to the standing army, from the private armies of the caudillos to the army that is the monopoly of the state, did not take place everywhere in Latin America. The transfer of allegiance from the leader to the impersonal figure of the state is not a simple or spontaneous process. It involves many convergent factors. For one, the needs of the economy seem to have been decisive in determining the degree to which the skeleton of a state apparatus emerged. The growth of externally oriented social forces integrated into the world market at the end of the century presupposed political and social stability, and the establishment of the state conformed to the interests of the exporting ruling classes. The need for socioeconomic organization, for the establishment of an infrastructure, and for the expansion of services and of the public administration combined to build the state. On the other hand, in the nations that did not succeed in integrating themselves into international trade at this period, and therefore lacked export products that would permit the rise of a strong bourgeoisie and the appearance of an established social power, the crystallization of the state was slow in coming. In such nations civil convulsions were more prolonged and a national army never developed beyond the stage of a private garrison with a state facade. The case of Nicaragua from the nineteenth century until the era of Somoza illustrates that pattern, as does that of Honduras at the beginning of the twentieth century and down to the establishment of the banana enclave.

The economy was not the only influence in this direction.

In some countries the most professionalized sectors of the officer corps demanded the establishment of a regular army that was large and well equipped and possessed a monopoly on the control of violence. Corporate values and the military ethic gradually opened the way. The numerous disagreements between neighboring republics required armies that were conventionally trained and equipped and benefited from qualified recruitment. The European models (and their fellow travelers, the arms merchants) impelled them in the same direction. Nationalist feeling grew within the armies at the same time that it was declining among bourgeoisies that had become cosmopolitan and directed toward the outside world. In addition, the utilization of the military forces to wipe out major internal dissidence among the civilians, as in Brazil in 1896 and 1914,[20] made the officers aware that they were the guarantors of the status regni—that is, of the state—and that therefore they deserved special budgetary and legislative provisions. As symbols of national identity, the armies—whether victors or vanquished—acquired a special significance in the foreign wars in which they participated, few as they were.

The long war with Paraguay (1864–1870)—murderous as it was because of bad logistics and the deplorable equipment of the units—marked a turning point in the history of the Brazilian army. Henceforth the army leaders, having become the "defenders of the fatherland," had an important influence. The War of the Pacific (1879–83) had similar effects in different contexts in Chile, Peru, and Bolivia. The demands of enlightened officers went from the reorganization of the units to the establishment of universal military service, and included the purchase of modern arms and increased institutional independence.

The first state armies that emerged in the second half of the nineteenth century were very dissimilar, but they possessed a certain number of common elements that distinguish them from the modern armies that succeeded them. These included mediocre quality and difficulty in recruitment, a lack of professional formation of the officers, and promotion of officers still largely based on personal discretion. The true size of those standing armies was generally well below the theoretical figures cited by the bureaucracies and in the budgets. The enlisted men, again in theory, were volunteers under contract for variable—generally long—periods. In fact, the normal practice was forced recruitment (by lasso, it was said, in Brazil). Most of those engaged were the product of impressment. The armies thus drained off the social scum of the country, the unlucky ones who had been taken in the roundups by the recruiting sergeants, the unemployed, and the victims of natural catastrophes, such as the *nordestinos* fleeing the drought in northeastern Brazil. Men were sent to military service as if to prison if they displeased the social or political authorities, or lacked a "master" who was responsible for them. In some countries even the common-law criminals were put directly into the army, as was the case in Uruguay and Argentina.

Discipline was imposed on the enlisted men by corporal punishment. The officers were more prison wardens than intellectuals in uniform. In Brazil, under the Prussian disciplinary code of Count von Lipp dating from 1763, whippings were imposed for the least infractions. These punishments were abolished in principle in 1874 but they continued to be applied in the army and navy down to the twentieth century. In 1903 the soldiers in the fortress of Santa Cruz in the bay of Guanabara revolted against these conditions and massacred the officers responsible for their sufferings. In 1910 a revolt of the crews broke out in the navy against the severity and inhuman character of the disciplinary system. The atrocious situation of soldiers was identical in other countries. A Uruguayan wrote, "I deplore as much as anyone the terrible necessity of corporal punishment which is prescribed by our military laws . . . but take a look at the enlisted personnel of our army. They include a large number of African slaves [this is written in the 1850s] who are lazy and used to harsh rules . . . and still worse, fugitives from the gallows, drawn from the jails. . . . I wish we could abolish corporal punishment as a measure that is just and very appropriate for the level of freedom and civilization that our republic has achieved, but first let us reform the personnel of the army by purging it of criminals and the dregs of society."[21]

Revolts, "military crimes" (the term used by the press for a high level of criminality not always limited to the barracks), and a large number of desertions all characterized the most advanced Latin American armies at the beginning of the century. The people avoided military service by any means and cases of self-mutilation were not unusual.[22] In Brazil in 1862 the minister of war estimated that in time of peace the army lost a third of its membership every year. Even after the introduction of conscription by the drawing of lots the number of draft evaders remained very high, amounting to about one-fifth of those subject to the draft.[23] Draft evasion still exists today in countries where military service is obligatory in theory but where in practice roundups of young men of military age (*la recluta*) supplement the voluntary appearances required by law. This was the case not long ago in many rural areas of Peru and Colombia. It goes on in the same way today in several countries in Central America.

The procedures of "reverse selection" and the avoidance of "military obligations" affect the place of the army in the nation and the social status of the officers. Only those who cannot avoid it serve as enlisted men or in the navy. A Brazilian writer spoke at the beginning of the century of "the monstrous divorce between the army and the people." The type of recruitment is reflected in the racial composition of the armed forces: the enlisted men are largely Indian in the Andean countries, and they speak Quechua or Aymara in Bolivia and Peru. In Argentina they are mainly mestizo, and in Brazil the navy crews were 50 percent black and 30 percent mulatto at the beginning of the twentieth century. The war with Paraguay was a massacre of Africans. Although slaves had been exempt from military service up to that point, the slavemasters of the northeast sold their slaves to the army as cannon fodder. It is said that Argentina was "whitened" by that war since it sent the battalions of *pardos* to the front lines, thus permanently solving its black "problem."

The recruitment of officers by recommendation or family connections, even according to aristocratic schemes that were more or less respected, as in Brazil, created an enormous gap between the officers and the enlisted men—a veritable abyss that was not only hierarchical but also social, ethnic, and sometimes linguistic. Added to the particularistic and nonmeritocratic nature of access to the officers' ranks, that social distance increased civilian control over the army. The officer in the majority of the "old armies" of the continent—a misbehaving son, the castoff of a penniless notable, or the humble protegé of a powerful man—was generally trained by the head of an army corps. Badly educated and without great theoretical foundation, he owed his promotions not to his professional qualities but to personal connections, to the favor of a civilian politician, or to the vagaries of political life in which armed action often played a decisive role. The division between the dominant civilian groups and the military corps had not yet occurred. The institutional autonomy of the Latin American armies was still very weak. The military were still very civilian and thus in a subordinate position. Professional esprit de corps played a much less important role than loyalty to political networks. It was the professionalization of the military that was to permit it to regulate itself as an institution and that freed the officer corps from control by civilian elites.

In particular, the creation of a system of military education increased the homogeneity of the officer corps, creating a separate institution and developing a sense of military identity and later of military superiority. The instruction of commissioned and noncommissioned officers in specialized schools, cut off from civilian surroundings, values, and references, both raised the level of knowledge and diffused the military ethic. The existence of a specialized military educational system also introduced methods of recruitment in which civilians had no part. The military school officer is chosen by his peers, and political recommendation hardly has any role to play. Under the traditional system of recruitment the officers did not form an autonomous group that was socially distinct from the ruling classes. Lacking the cohesion that results from passing through the same common experience, the military was part of the established elite and shared its divisions, with corresponding limitations on its power. The civilians had no difficulty in exercising control. The obligatory passage of officers through military schools of good quality, therefore, was to give military society the moral, ideological, and institutional resources to shake off civilian tutelage. But that process was to be a slow one, even in the countries that had long-established military academies.

The dates of the creation of the officers' schools in the nineteenth century range from 1840 in Brazil to 1896 in Peru. In Bolivia the Military College was founded after several attempts in Sucre in 1891, while Uruguay had its Academy in 1885 and the Polytechnical School in Guatemala dates from 1873. Argentina, for its part, created a Military College in 1869 during the presidency of Sarmiento, but the majority of officers did not attend that institution until the great military reforms of 1891. The same was true in Brazil, where a distinction was made between officers who had graduated from the school and the *tarimbeiros* formed among the troops and on the field who had not received any theoretical education. These field officers criticized the book learning that the cadets at the school of Praia Vermelha had received, especially after the positivist educational reforms introduced in 1890 by Benjamin Constant Botelho de Magalhaes. The new study plan was attacked for its encyclopedic dilettantism, for teaching sociology rather than military subjects, and for creating "lawyers in uniform" rather than developing a martial spirit.

CIVILIAN PREPONDERANCE AND MILITARY MODERNIZATION

The eclipse of the warriors in the countries in which a coherent leading group imposed its hegemony began a period of civilian domination and political stability. The caudillos were brought under control because of the requirements of capitalism; the modern armed forces that resulted had not yet acquired the institutional resources necessary for them to intervene. Military men had power, but the military were not in power. This did not prevent strongmen of a more or less military background in some countries from taking control of the state and establishing themselves as dictators or irremovable patriarchs for life, such as Cipriano Castro (1899–1908) or Juan Vicente Gomez (1908–1935) in Venezuela, or Porfirio Díaz (1876–1911) in Mexico—to mention only a few.

In Argentina the army was involved in containing or pacifying the rebellious Indians to the south of Buenos Aires until the "campaign of the desert" ended that threat, and beginning in 1880 opened up immense territories to cultivation. The civil wars and the rules for recruitment did not separate the officers from the national elites, and still less made them independent of those in power. General Roca, who was president twice after having been the hero of the conquest of the southern territories in 1879, exhibits in his career the typical profile of an old army officer. While he was still in secondary school he joined the national troops fighting the secession of the province of Buenos Aires, won his lieutenant's bars at Cepeda (1859), and took part in the battle of Pavón two years later—two important events in the history of the Argentine civil wars. He became a colonel at the age of twenty-nine as a result of his action against the uprising of a provincial caudillo, and a general following his victory over a rebellion led by "General" Mitre, a former president. Yet until 1880 the civil wars that established the political physiognomy of the country were struggles among civilians, and from 1860 until 1930 Argentina experienced an uninterrupted succession of civilian governments.

In Chile the order created by Portales lasted until 1891. The short civil war between groups within the oligarchy that led to the suicide of President Balmaceda did not interrupt the continuity of civilian rule. The army remained loyal to the president despite the desertion of groups of officers, while the navy supported the Congress, the banks, and the English interests that were hostile to the nationalist policy of Balmaceda. However, the military did not have the initiative and the crisis only resulted in the weakening of the executive and the establishment of a parliamentary regime.

In Bolivia the defeat in the War of the Pacific totally discredited the military who had been more interested in controlling political life than in guaranteeing the sovereignty and territorial integrity of the country. A civilian era began that extended from 1884 until 1934 during which period the parties of the oligarchy and regional interests fought for power, sometimes with arms; however, the army as a corporate body remained outside of politics. While the mining economy spurred by the demand for silver and tin in the twentieth century guaranteed the prosperity and power of the local bourgeoisies, the Conservative, Liberal, and Republican parties succeeded one another at the head of the state. Thanks to the mining revenues, the army that had been demobilized and substantially reduced in size was to be transformed from top to bottom, as one of the measures that modernized the state apparatus. It remained, however, aloof and bitter, not far from power but not participating in it in an institutional way.

Brazil, with its continent-wide size and its distinctive independence process, should be given special mention since the decisive participation of the military in the fall of the empire and the establishment of the republic in 1889 seems to run counter to the demilitarization of Spanish America at the time. In fact, the establishment of the republic was preceded by a "military question" that the empire could not resolve, but which was more an indication of the discontent of the military than of its political strength. Under the empire the army was a second-rank military organization since it did not possess a monopoly of arms or of legal violence, thus demonstrating the weakness of the federal state. In internal matters the central power essentially exercised the function of an arbiter;[24] the dominant local groups enjoyed power that they were not willing to share. For them the central administration was suspect, especially the army. The 1891 constitution, which was made to measure for the provincial oligarchic groups, gave great autonomy to the states and limited the possibilities of federal control. Brazil at that time was a federation of twenty nations, to the disgust of the military defenders of the state who were hostile to centrifugal forces. The landed oligarchies who governed the country were distrustful of the army. Only the National Guard, which was not dissolved until 1918, had the rulers' confidence—since they largely controlled it. This taxpayer-based force that recruited its enlisted men from among the active and productive citizens and its officers from the upper classes appeared in many ways to be a counter-army. In fact the army drew its membership from marginal groups, the elements that were excluded because of their income level from service in the National Guard. The officers of the guard who bought their commissions and for a time were even elected by their men were always those with local social authority. The large landowner was often a doctor (in law) and a colonel (in the national guard) to the point that the word *coronel* became synonymous in the northeast with a notable landowner. That bourgeois army, serving as an electoral militia when needed, was an important element in the establishment of the Brazilian political system—it provided the forum for an exchange of services between the state and private power.[25] The army itself continued after the dissolution of the national guard to be a secondary organization that was counterbalanced by the public forces of the states.

These militarized police forces, which sometimes possessed artillery and aviation and were trained by European military missions (as was the case with the public forces of São Paulo at the beginning of the century), did not depend on the federal government. The governors could use them as they saw fit and sometimes they did not hesitate to employ them against the national government. The central government only took control of these petty local armies very gradually. In 1937 the military police were placed under the command of army officers, and in 1964 they were finally subordinated directly to the army general staff. But in spite of the insistence of the officers, the army was long numerically inferior to the police forces of the various states of the Brazilian federation.

In order to establish the superiority of the army, the Brazilian officers demanded the strict application of the law requiring universal obligatory service which they had finally obtained in 1916 as a delayed compensation for having participated in the overthrow of the empire. However, the local potentates continued to interfere in the functioning of the institution, blocking the recruitment of the men, and influencing the selection of garrison commanders. In addition, political influence and favoritism were heavily involved in promotions. To advance in the hierarchy it was necessary to have good "connections," and merit or professional qualifications still counted for very little at the beginning of the century.

Badly regarded, badly paid, badly equipped, and badly trained, the Brazilian military, which under the empire had been far from the corridors of power and had held unpopular views— it was opposed to slavery and in favor of republicanism—

TABLE 1
APPROXIMATE SIZE OF THE BRAZILIAN FEDERAL ARMY AND OF THE LOCAL
POLICE FORCES (THOUSANDS OF MEN)

	1909	1917	1921	1927	1932	1937
Army	19	22	29	38	58	75
States	18	28	29	28	33	38

Source: Robert M. Levine, *The Vargas Regime. The Critical Years: 1934–1938* (New York, 1970), p. 157.

little by little acquired influence, although they still thought of themselves as mistreated and neglected. Since a career in the military was not attractive, recruitment became more and more internalized; this in turn increased the separation of the military from the civilian elites and also contributed to the development of the esprit de corps that shaped military education. The officers who had graduated from the military schools began to look down on the civilian *bachareis* who dominated the administration and political life. Besides demanding a military institution that was numerically and technically strong, they also expressed the desire for autonomy that is the mark of increased professionalization. After the war with Paraguay and the fall of the empire had enlarged the arena for those previously despised soldiers, it was the leaders of the army itself who demanded the reform and modernization of their institution in accordance with the most prestigious models of the moment.

In other countries when the officers expressed such desires, the army was often reformed and modernized as a result of political considerations. The desire of the civilians to depoliticize the military by professionalizing it and separating it from conflicting factions and parties motivated the reorganization of the armed forces. The result most frequently did not correspond to the original intention: placing an autonomous army above the parties helped to provide it with the means to intervene, on its own, in politics. Nevertheless, depoliticization was the intent of the legislator. It was the "civilianist" Piérola in Peru who, after defeating the military, felt obliged to reconstitute a technically oriented and professional national army that was concerned with its military duties far from the political scene. In Colombia, after the War of a Thousand Days (1899–1902), the government of Rafael Reyes tried to create a regular army that in theory was free of party loyalties. The governments that followed, all of them conservative, introduced compulsory military service, created or reestablished military schools, and brought in foreign missions in order to end party-related armies and give the state an apolitical defensive institution. In Bolivia, the "domination of tin" and the establishment of a national army went side by side. Beginning in 1904, the country created the defensive arm of the state in order to guarantee order and stability in the new and prosperous mining enterprise.

Most of the time the transformation of the army was accompanied by the establishment of compulsory military service. In that period countries like Uruguay, which modernized its army but retained "voluntary" recruitment, were rare. In the Uruguayan case several factors were involved: the pacifism of the Colorado party but especially the refusal of the Blanco party to allow conscription of the youth from the Blanco-controlled countryside into an army that was believed to be loyal to an opposing party. In Argentina, on the other hand, compulsory military service operated to justify the great reforms of 1901. The establishment of conscription and the increased professionalization of the officer corps prescribed in the reform law were part of a vast effort to modernize Argentine society which would justify the predominance and legitimacy of the ruling group. In a country with massive numbers of immigrants conscription was also an antidote to cosmopolitanism. The army was to be the melting pot, the institution that would "Argentinize" the foreigner and produce Argentinians. This was a serious and delicate responsibility that involved a broad program and did not argue for the irreversible depoliticization of the military institution.

3

MODERNIZATION
BY THE ARMY

At the beginning of the century the national armies of the majority of South American countries experienced a qualitative leap. As a result of many factors, the "old army" gave way to a "new army." The overall military modernization began with the "professionalization" of the officer corps. This was an ambiguous formula that was to be cited often by the civilians when they were confronted by armies in revolt in violation of the constitutions that described them as "professional, apolitical, and non-deliberating." In Europe in 1973, because we had heard it said so often by the leaders of Popular Unity, we believed that the Chilean army was a professionalized and not a draft army. Alas, it was just the opposite. However, that misunderstanding is symptomatic of the change that involved making officers true professionals at arms with the understanding that they would then be concerned only with their profession. In a word, a reform that was aimed at organizing "the nation at arms" resulted in making military life a permanent full-time paid profession that required study, lengthy physical and intellectual preparation, and was subject to strictly codified bureaucratic rules.

That profound and dramatic transformation in relation to what preceded it could have appeared trivial to someone analyzing military power without considering the history and structure of the army. But if you wish to explain *how* in order to answer the question of *why*, it is difficult to overlook the specific characteristics of the modern army. Nor can one forget national differences. The permanent—even overwhelming—political role of the armies of the continent, as well as the praetorianism that appears to make them less concerned with things military, may lead us to underestimate their military nature. From there it is only a step to considering them simply as political forces in competition for power like the others. To reach that conclusion is certainly to be ignorant, not only about the "military parties" but about the functioning of the Latin American political systems for the last half century.

Therefore, we are going to examine the organization and composition of those armies that have such importance for the future of the continent. We will also look at how the officers become politicized, since the paradox of modernization, that—avowedly or not, was aimed at removing the military from politics—was that it marked the end of civilian hegemony in nearly every country in the region. Measures that were aimed at defending and stabilizing political life and regulating the harmonious functioning of the state produced, on the contrary, institutional ruptures and military usurpation. The armies, in emancipating themselves from civil society and the ruling class, became repoliticized on a different basis according to their own organizational logic.

MILITARY ORGANIZATION AND "PROFESSIONALIZATION"

Armies are all organized along the same lines. The degree of militarization of defense institutions varies, but the similarity in behavior and attitudes of military organizations that are separated in time and space is surprising. It is not necessary to postulate a common set of essential characteristics of the military, but rather to recognize that armies are institutions that act in accordance with their own manifest functions.

As complex organizations of a particular type, military forces always have as their objective, if not their reason for existence, the legitimate exercise of violence. From that defining mission follows a system of organization and norms. These values are linked on the one hand to the operation and on the other, to the functions of the institution—that is, to the goals that it has espoused. The institution's organizational values follow from the pyramidal structure and centralized command required for decision making in combat. Its operational values provide an answer to questions regarding the purpose and need for combat. "Why are we fighting?" "Why are they our enemy?" Those two sets of values overlap, but one can weigh more than the other in specific circumstances and armies can be divided in accordance with the relative importance of each complex of norms.

In addition, armies differ from other institutions in that they are "total" organizations, or nearly so. Even if military men are generally drawn from the civilian population, the specialty of arms is not a profession like the others. The distinction between civilians and the military involves something far more significant than the separation and sense of unity produced by wearing a uniform. Armies are coercive organizations in which authority is based on a constraint that is both physical and symbolic. They are bureaucracies to which the formalized mechanisms of checks and balances and limitations on the central authority do not apply. In short, the autocratic concentration of command is in conformity with the exigencies of combat, and it is this rationale that requires commissioned and noncommissioned officers to ask the permission of their colonel to take a wife. The self-sufficiency of the armies, their independence of society—demonstrated by the existence of "military" chaplains, doctors, musicians, barbers, and veterinarians—works in the same direction. Indeed, that special quality, the voluntary isolation that is supposed to anticipate the autonomy of armies on campaign, also has another function that is symbolic in character—that is, to produce an acceptance through rituals and myths, images and identification procedures, of the monopoly of violence and the need for a defensive apparatus.

Those *organizational* values may appear to be universal. The norms that we have called *operational*, that is, the military ethic or "symbolic system,"[1] however, are affected by the sociopolitical environment. More precisely, they are related to the type of recruitment, armament, and strategy of a given period and civilization. Thus a mass army recruited from rural groups with a low level of culture produces the glorification of heroism, honor, and self-sacrifice that promote obedience and discipline on the part of the foot soldiers. These were the dominant values among the Western armies when the Latin American states emulated them. The importance of the formation of character and "military drill" that was an expression of the deep division between the troops (the men) and the commanders (the leaders) resulted from the same requirement.

This was the model that the Latin American countries were to attempt to adopt—or, as their critics would say, to ape. Most of this activity took place in the absence of any imminent likelihood of armed conflict, and this contributed to an increase of institutional rigidity and to the development of a heroic rhetoric justifying these particular bureaucracies. The establishment of organizations of this kind required a high level of self-sufficiency, intense socialization of its members, and the institutionalization of the military career through continuing technical formation in a network of special schools. All these elements guaranteed a normative isolation, which, as we shall see, closed the army to society, only to open to it a more direct access to power.

We have seen in the preceding chapter how modernization responded to different needs in each country. But it is clear that in all cases—even when, as in Brazil, the dominant groups needed a great deal of persuasion—the formation of modern armies developed in response to Latin America's new role in the world economy. The modern armies were state forces that guaranteed internal order and the uninterrupted exploitation of the mineral and agricultural riches desired by Europe. As modern institutions with a technical level that was advanced by international—that is, European—standards, they projected an image abroad of seriousness and competence that reassured investors. In a way they were the complement "for foreign consumption" of the Westminster-style parliamentarianism that seemed to delight the Latin American elites at the turn of the century.

It is not true, however, that these armies were created by the metropolitan economic powers in order to control the sources of their primary products. The most important economic power and the primary investor in the subcontinent at the time of that change, Great Britain, was not a military model and only incidentally sold armaments. France, on the other hand, which shared with Germany a quasi-monopoly of the export of military technology, had only a modest place, apart from the sale of arms, in the foreign trade of the Latin American countries. Since the European countries were in constant rivalry, it is also difficult to believe in an agreement or division of labor that would be of primary benefit to Great Britain. In fact, we are discussing a process that was dependent, it is true, but was nevertheless directed from within Latin America in response to internal necessities. The modern army was both a symbol of progress and an instrument of centralization which promoted the building of the state. As national armies, the military establishments required a unified ruling class for their improvement and expansion. Thus the later that unification took place, the more the process of professionalization was delayed—sometimes to the benefit of an unstable civilian power, and sometimes to give way to the de facto power of a dictator.

Since the prestige of a well-organized and well-trained army reflected favorably on the state itself, it is not surprising that externally oriented nations should call upon instructors from the two most prestigious armies in the world between 1880 and 1920—the armies of France and Germany. These two enemy countries, victors and vanquished in two successive wars, made their services available to any nation that wished to reorganize its defensive apparatus. At stake were both diplomatic and commercial influence, and also the expansion of the armaments industry. Their transatlantic rivalry was a form of "warfare" pursued by indirect means, and in that context of bitter military-commercial rivalry any actions were justified. Secret agents inspired campaigns in the local press and gathered intelligence about the "enemy."[2] In Brazil the Germans did not hesitate to discredit French war materiel while the French denounced the racism of the German officer as being out of place in a nation of mestizos.[3] The struggle for influence and military preponderance put the Latin American states in a position of privilege and choice that they utilized in accordance with their own geostrategic characteristics. Nevertheless, we should note that externally oriented modernization through the purchase of technology and armament produces a narrow dependence. Those armies that were the symbols of independence and the emblems of sovereignty thus only seemed to be "European-style" armies. Without heavy industry of their own, they secured everything from Krupp or Schneider. Thus they were involved by necessity in the diplomatic game and participated in political decisions relating to foreign trade. This is why the military in the richest countries of the continent often took the lead in industrial expansion in order to diminish the "critical dependence" that might undermine the operational capacities of these imitative armed forces.

An Externalized Modernization

The three adversaries in the War of the Pacific—Chile, which was the winner, and Peru and Bolivia, which lost—were, if not the first states to turn to Europe in order to reorganize their armies, undoubtedly those that emulated the Continent most completely. In Chile, which learned from the Germans, Prussianization left traces that are still visible today. While the officers have stopped wearing the Prussian uniforms and the mustaches and monocles of the Kaiser period, the cadets in the military college still wear the pointed helmet and parade with the goose step. In 1885 the Chilean government decided to hire a German mission to professionalize its army. The victory in the war had revealed weakness in the national military structure and the dangers were far from over. Chile felt surrounded by enemies. Peruvian and Bolivian irredentism disturbed Santiago. Peru had not yet accepted the loss of the province of Tarapacá and the occupation of the ports of Tacna and Arica. Landlocked Bolivia kept an eye fixed on its lost maritime outlet, the port of Antofagasta on the Pacific, while Chile's large Argentine neighbor appeared hostile to the narrow nation confined behind a *cordillera* lacking clear boundaries. Colonel Körner, chief of the mission from 1886 until 1910, was to transform an army of veterans of the War of the Pacific into a modern force with a high-level Prussianized officer corps that enjoyed great prestige throughout the continent. While the *Libertador* O'Higgins had created the first military school in Latin America immediately after independence (1817), Colonel Körner founded a *Colegio Militar* in 1886 modeled on the Kriegsakademie with a three-year program of study. The best students were sent to German regiments and even to the imperial guard. More than thirty German officers were working in Chile by the beginning of this century. In 1906 a program of reform of the army's organization and internal regulations was completed that transformed the Chilean military into a veritable reflection of the German army. Colonel Körner, now a general, was a member of the Chilean army, having been named chief of the general staff in 1891. During the confrontation between the nationalist president Balmaceda and the parliamentary oligarchy, Körner and his followers supported the adversaries of the president while the army as a whole remained loyal to him. This has been cited as proof of Körner's antinationalist orientation and predisposition to European interests. It is undeniable that the German mission did much for German industry and for Krupp in particular. Under the influence of Körner the government contracted a large loan in 1898 in order to buy arms; in the course of the arms race that then ensued in the Southern Cone, the Chilean government did not hesitate to pledge the customs revenues of the country to its creditors.[4]

Almost at the same time, no doubt in response to the Chilean challenge, Peru hired a French military mission. The first team under the command of Captain Paul Clément arrived in Lima in 1896. The French organized and instructed the Peruvians until 1940, with an interruption between 1914 and 1918. In contrast to the Germans in Chile, the French did not become involved in the political life of Peru, but their influence was no less important. The French army, which at the time emphasized defense and fortifications, was of particular interest to the Peruvians because of desired assistance in the area of military engineering. In reports and instructions that were influenced by their colonial experience, the French gave special emphasis to transportation and communication, the military presence in the population, and their knowledge of the country. Some have argued that French influence was one of the causes of the "populist" and social orientation of the Peruvian officers, an attitude that was demonstrated in the 1960s.[5] A direct relationship cannot be proven, but the French influence produced a very different result from that of the Prussian officers in the hostile neighboring republic.

Bolivia, reacting later to the shock of the war, was more eclectic in its choice. A private French military mission reorganized the programs of the Military School and the War College in 1905. Beginning in 1910, however, La Paz imitated Santiago and hired German instructors. The director of the mission, Colonel Hans Kundt, was soon named head of the general staff. With a team of a dozen commissioned and noncommissioned officers from Germany, he initiated a German system of instruction of officers and enlisted men and introduced the regulations of the German army. His initial contract was extended until 1914. In 1921 Kundt, now a general, returned to Bolivia and became a naturalized citizen; subsequently he became deeply involved in the country's political life as one of the principal supporters of the Republican party. That old-style "politicization" of a military notable seems to have interfered with the strengthening of the war machine. When Bolivia faced Paraguay in the Chaco affair (1932–35), Kundt's army was beaten by the Paraguayans just as the old army had been beaten by the Chileans on the Pacific. That defeat and the difficult mixture of young academically trained officers with old-style generals, of veterans with politicians, had a long-term impact on the Bolivian military.

In cosmopolitan Argentina, which had attempted very early to professionalize its officer corps, eclecticism at the beginning dominated the choice of foreign connections. The Military College, which was responsible for the formation of officers and was created by Sarmiento in 1869, had as its first directors an Austro-Hungarian colonel and a French cavalry commander. The French army was the model for the Argentine army until 1904, but the armament of the old army was German Krupp cannons and Mauser rifles after 1884. In 1900 the prestige of the Imperial General Staff carried the day, and the Superior War School was created under German patronage. The teaching staff was made up of German officers, and the school, which certified members of the General Staff, remained until the eve of the Second World War a bastion of the German military tradition. For the Argentine admirers of the German military machine who continued after 1914–18 to analyze the 1870 war from the German side, it was as if Germany had not lost World War I.

The process of Germanization was completed after 1904 when Argentine officers were sent en masse for training in the regiments of the (German) Imperial Army. A Brazilian military attaché claimed in 1921 that "half the Argentine officers have gone through German schools or the German army."[6] The influence of the *Offizier Korps* penetrated Argentine military society profoundly. Half of the twelve books published between 1918 and 1930 by the Officers' Library series of official military texts were translated from German. Admiration for the German model was unbounded. Thus, few of the Argentine officers thought in 1914 that the most formidable war machine that had ever existed could be beaten. It is reported that General José Uriburu, who in 1930 would become the first military president of modern Argentina and had kept since his training in the Kaiser's guard the evocative nickname of "von Pepe," pointed to the map during the war and announced to the Military Club that the victory of the imperial armies was inevitable. This is why the few isolated voices that denounced the danger inherent in a mechanical imitation of the German model were justifiably disturbed.[7]

In Brazil it was the officers who tried to strengthen the national army. Some civilians did not share the fears of the regional oligarchies that a strong army could be the instrument of the central government. The poor performance of the army in the face of the peasant revolt of Canudos, and the distrust of Argentina, Brazil's traditional rival in the subcontinent, argued for a reorganization and an effort to modernize the equipment of the military. In order to accomplish this it was necessary to call upon Europe. The Germans and French could not have asked for anything better: from the end of the century the two countries competed to furnish cannons to Brazil. A French mission was hired by the state of São Paulo in 1906 to reorganize and train the Public Force so that it became a formidable local army. Nevertheless, thanks to clever propaganda, the Germans generally dominated. From 1905 to 1912 thirty Brazilian officers were sent to the German army for instruction, and in 1908 Marshal Hermes da Fonseca, the minister of war and the most prestigious and influential Brazilian general, was the guest of the imperial government. He participated in the grand maneuvers and agreed to open negotiations concerning the establishment of a German military mission. However, in 1910 the same marshal visited France and buried the German proposal, but without agreeing to a French mission. The competition between the two nations was for high stakes: the orders for the war industry included the rearming of the artillery, a program of coastal defense, and the creation of an air force.

Those who had been trained in the German army formed a "home mission" that instructed the cadets in the military school according to the German model. The oldest officers, whose promotion had owed more to political patronage than to their education or military capacity, were hostile to all foreign missions. They feared innovation for career reasons and did not always feel capable of adapting themselves to a European model. Nevertheless, the victory of arms was decisive between France and Germany, and in 1919 a French mission was hired. Directed by General Maurice Gustave Gamelin, it was to transform the Brazilian army from top to bottom, and to last until 1939.

Arms purchases from France allowed Brazil to close the enormous distance between the Brazilian military and the forces of industrial countries. However, it was in the domain of organization, education, and careers that the French influence was particularly marked. The distribution of units throughout the country in the manner of a police force was followed by the formation of large units that could be easily maneuvered and coordinated by a general staff along the lines of a French plan. The officers, who up to that time had received a very theoretical education, now were exposed to a solid military curriculum under the guidance of French instructors at all levels, as well as in the military school beginning in 1924. A series of practical schools and auxiliary services was created. As a result of the French updating, the old army, modernized French-style, underwent a veritable revolution; this was especially marked in the area of advancement, which from that time was strictly codified by law and removed from local political influence. Merit and professional accomplishment governed all careers.

The French impact was profound and lasting. In 1937 every member of the infantry High Command had been educated by the French as were all the successive ministers of war from 1934 until 1960. General Goes Monteiro, who dominated the military scene from 1930 to 1946, had ranked first in the advanced course organized in Rio de Janeiro by the mission in 1921. The Brazilian disciples of the French army did not lack opportunities to recall the debt that they felt toward their instructors and their admiration for the prestigious officers who commanded the mission. Thus, the image of General Gamelin is very different in Brazil from his image in France, where he is known as chief of the general staff that directed the "debacle." In 1926 a Brazilian military journal stated, "He was the founder of our military doctrine. He established its principles in our basic regulations and he familiarized us with genuine knowledge of it through the superb practical and theoretical lessons that he taught us on maneuvers and in the lecture halls."[8] Again in 1940 General Gaspar Dutra, the minister of war, declared in a speech given during the Third Region maneuvers in the presence of President Vargas, "I remember the great maneuvers of 1922. They were headed by the exceptional figure of General Gamelin, a universally admired name today that we always mention with nostalgia and veneration."[9]

The Gallicism of these admirers of the army of Foch and Pétain impressed contemporaries. Parallel to the Argentine "von Pepe" and just as real is the caricature of a Francophile general that appears in a scene in one of the novels of Jorge Amado. A self-important old fogey and a candidate for the Brazilian Academy, he had been a distinguished student of the professors in the French mission, and invincible in military maneuvers. The general, Waldomiro Moreira, nicknamed "Maginot line" by his enemies, wrote in the press that during the Second World War Hitler's *Panzer Divisionen* "had no respect for the established rules of military science, and every evening the Panzer Divisionen contradicted his predictions of each morning."[10]

If we leave aside—to return to them in a future chapter—

the neocolonial armies created by the United States, we find the same efforts to learn from Europe in nearly every country under different conditions and with different parameters depending on the level of development, the geopolitical situation, and the degree to which a national state had been established. Obviously not all countries hired expensive military missions. We should mention in this context the curious phenomenon of "second-hand" Prussianization carried out by the Chilean army in several countries of the continent. In Ecuador, Colombia, El Salvador, and Venezuela, Chilean military missions were called upon to reorganize and to "Europeanize" the national army. In Colombia a team of Chilean officers created the first military school worthy of the name in 1907. The same thing happened in Venezuela, but at the same time officer candidates went for study to Peru, and in 1920 a French mission established the air force and instructed the infantry.

The foreign presence was not without its problems for the host armies. First of all, the European missions aroused genuine resistance from officers who favored a different military influence—the pro-Germans in Brazil, for example. Also, the old officers of the earlier army were not happy about returning to school or having subordinates more knowledgeable than they were, and especially about allowing foreigners to come into direct contact with the internal mechanisms that guaranteed their power in the institution. The "missionaries," on the other hand, wanted to transform and regulate everything, indeed to exercise direct command so as to implement their reforms more effectively. There is no other way to explain the complete integration of the German missions in Chile and Bolivia. General Gamelin complained about the head of the infantry general staff that he "does not support our *tutelage* [sic]" and "dreams of a French military mission that is completely subordinated."[11] The responsibilities of a foreign mission were not limited to the transfer of technology and expert consultation; other functions, such as defense, the preparations and the development of military doctrine, related to the area of politics. Also, there were frequent conflicts and the admiration for the mentor army was not without a certain impatience on the part of its disciples. This is one of the paradoxes of externally oriented modernization that was perhaps too quickly forgotten when the armies of the continent changed masters.

RECRUITMENT AND FORMATION OF OFFICERS

The reform of the system of recruitment of officers is central to the modernization of the military. In order to accomplish this it is necessary to produce more educated officers and to raise the professional and technical level in all the grades. In most cases this required a single source of recruitment. Graduation from military school became obligatory in order to obtain an officer's commission. The ideal desired by all the armies, even if they did not always achieve it, was formation according to a single pattern aimed at increasing the homogeneity and esprit de corps of the officers. It was precisely this desired homogeneity that the Argentine military reformers admired in the Offizier Korps. "Their officers have one and the same origin, they belong to the same social class, and to be admitted must pass the same tests. Today they constitute a veritable family,"[12] said an Argentine general about the German officers, despite the fact that he was defending the "old army." But alternative sources of recruitment were not eliminated everywhere. A Brazilian officer, in a report to his minister concerning the Peruvian army in 1922, deplored the fact that by a law passed in 1901 a third of the officer positions in Peru were reserved for promoted noncommissioned officers because of the insufficient number of candidates for the military school. "This is a source," he commented, "of a lack of homogeneity that gives rise to a certain [internal] rivalry."[13]

The early methods of recruitment of officers were terminated or abolished more or less slowly. In Guatemala up until 1944 it was not uncommon to find officers who had risen from the ranks rather than graduating from the Polytechnic School that was established in 1873. The continued presence of field-officers was a source of internal division within the institution.[14] Similarly, the barrier between commissioned and noncommissioned officers was more or less unbridgeable depending on the country. It was permeable in Bolivia, but totally airtight in Argentina. In most cases after a transition period noncommissioned officers either could not receive a lieutenant's commission or they were required to take the entrance examination for the military academy, as in Peru. In Brazil, that possibility was ended in the 1930s, producing frustration among the sergeants. The officers, for their part, acquired a feeling of belonging to an elite or a superior caste. In these highly bureaucratized peacetime armies internal social stratification was therefore very pronounced and the myth that every soldier carried in his knapsack a marshal's baton was no longer applicable.

These reforms, however rigorous their application, had a further consequence. Besides the new cohesion of the officer corps due to a common military education, the recruitment process became in principle free of direct political pressure. The requirement of a unique type of education implied a system of selection based on standards that in theory were objective and universal. Thus, the cadets were chosen by their peers in accordance with an ideal image of an officer and the needs of the institution. The control by civilian "patrons," recruitment on the basis of support by "distinguished soldiers," or "promoted officers" became a thing of the past. The reform in recruitment, by increasing the independence of the military as a corporate group, established the basis of military power.

The force of the specific socialization and resocialization carried out by the institution not only increased esprit de corps among the officers but also enhanced their sense of belonging to the military branch of the state. This influence was all the more complete because the training process was carried out with young recruits in relative isolation and lasted for a considerable period. In Guatemala, for example, future officers enter the Polytechnic School at the age of fourteen and remain for five years.[15] In Argentina the cadets join at between fourteen and eighteen years of age. In most countries they are around sixteen or seventeen, whether or not a secondary school diploma is required. In these conditions a strong internalization of the proposed values and models takes place that assures a specialized socialization and a deeply rooted corporate spirit.

Who can become an officer and who in fact becomes one? The educational entry requirements for the military school seem to be the only limitation on an apparently open system of recruitment. If the completion of secondary school is required, we can assume that the cadet's family has a relatively high income. And in fact in countries in which nearly a majority is illiterate (Guatemala, Peru, Bolivia, etc.), the simple fact of access to secondary school is already strongly discriminatory. The lower classes are very poorly represented in those military schools, especially in the societies where those classes are the most impoverished. It is true that many officers choose a military career for economic reasons, since military studies are short and generally free. This does not mean, however, that officers are therefore recruited among the poorer classes, or that the army provides a clear means of social mobility in all countries. The closed selection system permits the application of social or even of ethnic requirements that are not democratic. Thus the height requirement (5 feet, 4 or 6 inches) is met by only 16 percent of the enlisted men in Peru, and practically eliminates the children of Indians in all the Andean countries. In Bolivia the seemingly vague and harmless requirement of belonging to a "distinguished family" implies a strict social selectivity.[16] Similarly, the investigation carried out in Argentina as to moral character of the family of the candidate is not limited to the elimination of illegitimate children or those whose families are not well thought of in their neighborhood. In addition, candidates are rejected as a result of medical examinations from which there is no appeal where appearance and skin color are more significant than size or chest capacity. Thus the military elite preserves its image. Not all regimes are as frank as the *Estado Novo* (of Brazil) which decided officially in 1942 to deny military school access to non-Catholics (especially Jews) and blacks, and also to the children of immigrants, political opponents, and divorcees or concubines.[17]

Much has been written about the social origins of the officers. Observers and publicists have tended to put too much emphasis upon it, even trying to explain the political attitudes of the armies solely through that much-misunderstood variable. The twofold relationship of the military to society and to the state, as well as the importance of specific patterns of socialization, should permit us to put this aspect of military society in proper perspective. As a result of the authoritarian training that he has received and of the specific characteristics of the institution that has formed him, the officer is determined less by his family origins than by his relation to the army. This does not mean that we should neglect family origins. These affect the relation of the officer to civilian society in the sense that since he lives in symbiosis with the institution that he has chosen as the organizing principle of his existence, his family (including in-laws) constitutes his main, and sometimes his only, source of contact with the civilian world.

The social and professional characteristics of the officers' parents are not the only significant elements especially in societies that are "dualistic" and contain very pronounced regional differences. Social and sometimes political coloration can result from geographical and ecological divisions. The opposition between the urban and rural areas has often been emphasized— and sometimes overemphasized. Thus, one author, noting the largely urban origin of a multinational sample of Latin American officers that included some who came from less urbanized countries (Honduras, Nicaragua) concluded that recruitment in the "modern" sector of society implies "reformist" or progressive attitudes on the part of the armed forces. There is no proof that the urban environment produces liberal or reformist behavior, even if the equation of rural and conservative is, with some reservations, more accurate.[18] Nevertheless, it is important in understanding the Peruvian army to know that fewer and fewer officers come from Lima and the dynamic cities of the coast, and increasing numbers of officers in the course of this century have come from small urban centers in the interior and even from the depopulated Indian sierra.[19] Between 1955 and 1965, among the infantry generals who were officer candidates in the 1930s, only 18 percent came from Lima and 56 percent came from the *sierra* or the Amazonian *selva*, while, as Luigi Einaudi notes, 94 percent of the most important leaders of Peruvian society were born in Lima or on the coast.[20] In 1968, two-thirds of the members of the governing junta were of provincial origin.

In Brazil, where the garrisons are unequally distributed and concentrated mainly on the southern frontier and in the coastal cities, it is not surprising that there are many officers who come from Rio Grande do Sul, which is next to Uruguay, while São Paulo, the economic capital, provides very few military men. In 1930, eight of the thirty divisional generals were *gauchos* (that is, they were born in Rio Grande do Sul) and none was a *paulista*.[21] The poor and economically depressed states also provide a strong contingent of officers. A military witness noted that at the beginning of the century the cadets at the Realengo Military School (Rio) were organized by place of birth and that the largest groups were those from Sergipe and Alagoas, two of the weakest and poorest states in the country.[22] A French diplomat who was chief of protocol at the Quai d'Orsay noted on the occasion of a reception in 1945 in honor of the general staff of the Brazilian expeditionary force that fought alongside the Americans in Italy, headed by the future president Castello Branco:

> I enjoyed meeting those fine officers, discreet in their bearing, and ferret-like in their appearance with their skulls flattened in the back (*cabeça chata*) which was evidence of some mixture of Indian blood. Almost all of them came from the states of the North (Piaui, Ceará, Pernambuco); they are the traditional efficient and able leaders of the Brazilian army. As former students of General Gamelin and Hutzinger in our educational mission, they have just fought with intelligence and modesty in Italy.[23]

Whatever the value of his anthropological theory, the statistical observation is less debatable. Politically, the fact that the officers come largely from the smallest and poorest states (Alagoas, Sergipe, Ceará, Pernambuco, Piaui) or from a more prosperous state that is far from the axis of power represented by the alliance of São Paulo and Minas Gerais is of primary importance.

Corresponding to the preponderance of these two geographical areas in recruitment are two different social backgrounds. In the south, which is an active area of cattle breeding and agricultural development with a considerable Italian population, many children of immigrants are attracted by the prestige of the armed forces and enter the military school in Porto Alegre; thus, the military completes the process of assimilation in the country that has received them. In the northeast, which was the economic center of gravity when sugar was king, it is the families of the ruined rural aristocracy that, in order not to lose standing, send their sons to the army. The *menino de engenho*, the grandson or great-grandson of the sugar baron, enters the military school when the family cannot pay for his education, since a broad range of acceptable professions is not available. Thus two opposite paths lead to the Brazilian officer corps.

In Argentina, as we have demonstrated elsewhere, the geographic origin that seems to have predominated since the great transformation at the beginning of the century is from the urban and economically modernized areas. The upper-level Argentine officers, for example, rarely come from the families of the rural squires of the old colonial provinces of the north. In that country the percentage of children of immigrants who reach the highest military ranks is very high. A desire to establish one's roots in the national society by choosing a patriotic profession also seems to have played a role here, since social mobility could have been achieved in many other more reliable careers in the economically expanding areas. Thus, the officer corps is an open group and not a hereditary caste that is reserved for the old families of "military" or political background. Let us now see to whom that profession is open.

The lack of documentation, as well as the social heterogeneity in nearly all the armies of the continent, has resulted in the commonplace that a majority of the officers in Latin America come from the middle classes. This is both true and of dubious utility. A universally applicable residual category, the concept of middle class(es) is too vague to aid our understanding. A few undoubtedly insufficient facts will provide better guidance.

In general, few representatives of the lower classes are members of the officer corps, for reasons that we have discussed earlier in this chapter; however, the lower classes are not absent. The social position that the officers adopt officially in society varies depending on their political role and the social prestige of the army, but most of the time they identify with the upper strata. The idea that hereditary social authority predisposes one to exercise command is generally well received, even though the dominant national groups refuse to send their offspring to the barracks. Nevertheless, the general staffs try to make the social profile of the future officers coincide with their social aspirations. This does not mean that they always succeed in doing so. In Argentina before 1945 only one prestigious colonel came from a working-class background—a friend of Perón who was the son of a railroad worker. A study of Argentine cadets at the end of the 1960s showed that 2.4 percent were the children of industrial workers, but if those who came from categories of the lower middle class (technicians, petty civil servants, tradesmen) were included, the working class amounted to 25 percent of the enrollment in that same period.[24] These figures demonstrate an undeniable democratization of access to the officer ranks.

In Brazil industrial workers and artisans provided 3.8 percent of the enrollment in the military academy in 1941–43,[25] and 15 percent in 1962–66. For Chile the only existing investigation based on a very small sample of thirty-seven retired generals indicates the figure of 9 percent for the children of employees.[26] We know that in Peru, where the recruitment has always been more open than in other South American countries, the officers have been recruited less and less from the quasi-white classes at the top of the social pyramid, and more and more "in the lower and darker-skinned classes."[27] At the end of the sixties, it was noted that among those who initiated the revolutionary-military movement of 1968 were officers of clearly lower-class background: the son of a schoolteacher (Leonidas Rodriguez), sons of peasants (Hoyos and Gallegos), and the son of a telegraph operator (Fernandez Maldonado).[28] Velasco Alvarado, who was obviously mixed in his racial background, came from modest origins in the distant northern city of Piura.

The traditional upper classes do not always leave the military career to the common people. Even in Peru they were present in the "revolutionary" junta of 1968, two of whose fifteen members came from prominent families (including the grandson of a former president who became president himself in 1975, Morales Bermudez).[29] In Brazil the traditional upper classes (the large landholders, the members of the liberal professions, upper-level civil servants) provided 20 percent of the enrollment in the military school between 1941 and 1943, and still constituted 6 percent in 1962–66.[30] The Chilean sample produces the figure of 66 percent who were children of professionals, business-men, or farmers, but these categories are very vague.

In Argentina well-known names abound in the upper ranks, and they are not absent in the graduating classes of the military college. Alongside the children of the immigrants, the local and national aristocracies are well represented in the up-per ranks in the recent period. In fact, composition of the re-cruits has changed depending on the political role of the mili-tary at various times. After 1930 the "aristocratic reaction" pushed the children of the oligarchy toward the military col-lege. At the end of the 1950s, on the other hand, Perón tried to democratize access to the military schools, with mixed results.

Internal recruitment and an increase in the number of the sons of military men are worldwide phenomena that are also evident in Latin America. Family values facilitate the choice of a profession that appears to contradict the evolution of society as a whole. For that reason, the increased difficulty of recruiting civil-ians, and even at times the disaffection of the sons of the officers with the military career, leads to the opening of the officer corps to the sons of noncommissioned officers for whom it constitutes an avenue of social mobility. The percentage of sons of military men among the students in the military schools was nearly 42 percent in 1967–68 in Argentina, and 35 percent in Brazil during the same period.[31] Families in which one can demonstrate a military tradition for three or four generations can be found in these countries as well as in Peru and Chile. Internal recruitment could produce a homogeneous military society, the formation of a military caste, if access to the military profession did not re-main open. Such a recruitment process at least results in accentu-ating the militarization of military life, and an insularity that is accepted, encouraged, and socially approved.

The unwritten code of the Chilean army disapproves of re-lations with civilians. The observation, "associates with civilian elements," written in the evaluation file of a young Argentine officer, was at the least a bad omen for his career. In the sample of Chilean officers already cited, seventeen out of thirty-seven had no civilian friends during their last year of active duty and seven of them had only one.[32] The emphasis on grades in examinations, practical training, and advanced courses—central to promotion in the absence of war—was modified at the time of the reforms at the beginning of the century in the direction of a military curriculum and a disdain for civilian subjects. Education that had earlier been very general and encyclopedic—as in Brazil—now became specialized, and civilian areas of specialization were not well regarded. In Argentina it was not until the 1950s that a university diploma would help an officer to be promoted rather than be held against him. Today, however, in the most militarized countries courses include such nonmilitary subjects as political economy and public administration—subjects that are related, it is true, to the actual responsibilities of an important sector of the officers.

In summary, except for the countries in which the prestige of the military is very low for historical reasons that we will discuss later (Mexico, Bolivia), the officers come essentially from the intermediate sectors that are comfortably off, the upwardly mobile lower-middle class, and the declining upper classes; however, the upper and lower classes are not absent—although those from the upper classes find it easier to be promoted to the higher ranks than do the members of the lower classes. Some specific examples will suffice to illustrate these social backgrounds.

First, we will consider two active Brazilian officers who opposed each other—General Goes Monteiro, the Minister of War and Grand Constable of the Vargas regime (1930–45), and Lieutenant Luis Carlos Prestes, who left the army to become general secretary of the Communist party. The first was born in the state of Alagoas, the son of a doctor who died young, leaving nine children who belonged, to use his own description, to the "decaying Northeastern rural plutocracy." He was born "in a period of the increasing impoverishment of his family."[33] He entered the military school of Realengo in 1903 and subsequently that of Porto Alegre without a vocation to military life; but this did not prevent him from having a brilliant career as an officer involved in politics. Prestes, the future "knight of hope" and the leader of the Long March across Brazil in 1924 that marked the military revolt against the power of the established order, came from the bourgeoisie of Porto Alegre, the capital of Rio Grande do Sul.[34] His paternal grandfather was a judge; his maternal grandfather was a rich merchant who had lost his fortune before his grandson was born. The father of Luis Carlos Prestes who was born in 1908 was an officer of the infantry. He died in 1908, leaving his widow with five children and a meager captain's pension. Luis Carlos, as the son of an officer, received a scholarship to attend the military preparatory school of Rio de Janeiro where his mother took up residence in a working-class area. She made her living by giving courses in music and French, and sometimes, it was said, doing sewing in her home. This is the basis of the legend of a Prestes arisen from the people, the son of a seamstress.

The biography of Roberto Viaux, the author of a coup in Chile who had his hour of glory at the end of the 1960s is rather significant. He was born in 1917 in Talca, the son of an infantry commander, and studied at a German preparatory school in Santiago that prepared him to enter the military school after his fourth year. He graduated in artillery, and married the daughter of a colonel—something not unusual in Chile—who was also well known for his antidemocratic ideas.[35] Last but not least, we should recall the mysterious family background of Perón, that, despite his unusual career, seems typical of the family background of Argentine cadets. Juan Domingo Perón belonged to a "good" family from the province of Buenos Aires. His grandfather, Tomás, was a doctor and well-known conservative politician. His father, who did not attend the university as his family wished, was unsuccessful in agriculture, and in his marriage. His son preferred to talk of his grandfather, rather than his father and mother,[36] which led to the rumor that he came from very humble origins (the son of a steward and a half-caste servant). After some years spent with his family in distant Patagonia (Chubut), with the help of his paternal grandfather he enrolled in a distinguished private secondary school in the residential suburbs of Buenos Aires. Thus he came from a good family in decline—one of the classic methods of access to the Argentine middle class and perhaps to military vocations in Argentina and elsewhere.

THE ESTABLISHMENT OF OBLIGATORY MILITARY SERVICE

Paradoxically, in these supposedly "professionalized" armies, the enlisted men were civilians. While in the old army the soldiers were professional military men and the officers were very often amateurs, in the new army the opposite was the case: permanent professional officers and transitory and civilian enlisted men. The military were those who most often called for the establishment of universal service. The ideal of "a nation in arms" was always under the surface in the reforms of the military structures at the beginning of the century. A universal defense obligation—at least in theory—was therefore a basic part of the reforms initiated at that time. For the officers and the heads of the general staffs who were aware of the mediocre quality of the human "materiel" secured by enlistment, the way to improve recruitment was to enlarge it, thus permitting an increase in both quality and quantity. With enlisted men drawn from marginal elements, the army remained at the periphery of society and of the nation. The modernizing military demanded that "society be opened to the army," in the words of José Murilho de Carvalho.[37] However, forming a citizen army is not a simple technical problem. The social and political implications of universal service are evident. An army through which, in principle, all citizens pass then aims at being the school of the nation, the crucible of national sentiment.

The role of military service in civic and moral formation has often been noted. The officers of the new Latin American armies love to speak of it. Very recently a Brazilian general in a high political position observed that it was in the barracks that a good number of Brazilians learned to use a toothbrush! Under a system of conscription, the role and responsibilities of the officer take on a national—and therefore clearly political—role. In heterogeneous societies the army acts to promote national integration and to form the citizenry. It was not by accident that during the discussion of a conscription law in 1901 in Argentina, a maladroit but sincere deputy exclaimed that it would be "a universal suffrage army" at a time when universal suffrage was part of the program of the opposition and ten years before it was adopted. In the mind of the legislator and thus of the ruling group a conscript army was clearly responsible for molding the mentality of future voters. The citizen-soldier would be *miles* [soldier] before he became *civis* [citizen].

Compulsory military service began in Chile in 1900, Peru and Argentina followed in 1901, Ecuador in 1902, Bolivia in 1907, and Brazil only in 1916. The delay in Brazil deserves some attention. The weakness of the central government and the combined opposition of the lower classes and the local oligarchies to the federal army prevented draft lotteries from being applied. An intense campaign organized by the officers and prestigious civilian leaders, as well as a world war, were required in order for compulsory service to be imposed and for the abolition of the National Guard—which offered military service to the privileged few—in 1918.

The civic and military arguments used by the League for National Defense in support of universal service are not without interest. In the writings of Olavio Bilac, a patriotic poet and Brazilian right-wing nationalist who lent all his literary prestige to the propaganda in favor of "a national democratic, free civilian army for defense and national cohesion," an army of "citizen soldiers, . . . that is the people,"[38] one finds the grandiose flights and sociopolitical reasoning that are still used by the contemporary military. Bilac believed that conscription would produce "the complete triumph of democracy, a leveling of the social classes"; it would constitute "a school that imparts order and discipline . . . the laboratory of individual dignity and patriotism." Military service, according to the poet,

> means obligatory civic education, cleanliness, and hygiene,
> as well as psychological and physical regeneration. The
> cities are full of idle men, shoeless and in rags, who do not
> know the alphabet or the bathtub, animals who have only
> the appearance of human beings. For those dregs of
> society, the barracks will be their salvation.[39]

During the same period the promilitary sectors of the Argentine political class spoke in the same way. A civilian professor of the military college declared in a lecture in 1915 that the officers were committed to the "redemption of the uneducated ignorant and perverse conscript . . . Argentine by birth but barbarian in condition, who constitutes a danger to social stability and a menace to our culture."[40] Such descriptions demonstrate that the officers felt that they had been given certain special rights in relation to the national community and that the social control involved in military service had political importance in the larger sense.

The introduction of obligatory military service, even with a lottery and many exemptions, led to a rapid numerical increase in all countries. Chile tripled the number of those in the army when the law went into effect between 1900 and 1901.[41] The Brazilian army went from 12,000 men in 1889 to 43,000 in 1920. Nevertheless, military service was by no means universal and it was only obligatory for those who could not find a way to escape it. The social selectivity of the system was part of the logic of its moral and civic function: the less well-off classes were the ones that needed to be educated and integrated into the nation, not the sons of the rich. The number of exceptions was high in every country: a diploma here, enrollment in a rifle society or gymnastic group there, a pilot's license in another country, were sufficient to allow exemption from a year in the barracks. Students in most countries were enrolled for a few months in the officers' reserve. Exemptions thus were made on the basis of social criteria, often against the will of the officers. The exemptions were abolished in Argentina to a significant degree when the army as an institution was in power. In that country the head of a corps who objected to the social discrimination would exclaim as each new contingent was incorporated, "How curious, only the poor had children this year."[42] No doubt because of this institutionalized social discrimination and the type of discipline that resulted from it, the level of desertions remained high, despite the fact that budgetary limitations allowed only a small percentage of each cohort affected by the obligation to enter the barracks. For the same reason recruitment of conscripts continued, and in certain countries a type of local recruiting sergeant became institutionalized (as with the comisionados militares in Guatemala).

All of this produced a considerable separation between the enlisted men and the officers that, along with the manifest goals of military service, brought with it political and social consequences, especially in multiethnic societies. A study of the literacy program of the infantry in Guatemala revealed that 62.5 percent of the conscripts in the service in 1960 were illiterate, and that 30.6 percent did not speak Spanish as their mother tongue, while 14 percent of the soldiers did not speak it at all.[43] The number of those who spoke only an Indian language in the Andean countries led one commentator to say that the Bolivian army resembled a colonial army with its short Indian enlisted men and tall white officers.[44] The officers retained an undeniable feeling of superiority as a result of their contact with the populace in the enlisted contingents, which tended to incline them in the direction of the ruling classes and of the elements that are hostile to political equality and representative democracy. A survey of cadets at the Military School in Guatemala showed that more than half of them considered Indians to be inferior.[45] However, we should not believe that the establishment of compulsory conscription of the poor into military service had only one effect on the officer corps. The contact each year with a new contingent of troops also enabled the officers to appreciate the socioeconomic developments in their country, and to discover misery and oppression, giving a professional and corporate aspect to their social concerns. This in turn is related to the ambiguous nature of military behavior and to the often quite noticeable pendulum in the character of their interventions.

To complete this overview of the modern state armies, we should touch upon the condition of the noncommissioned officers, totally subordinate to the officers. In Brazil, for example, their status is precarious and their term of employment is contractual. The slow pace of officer promotions at the beginning of the century and the bottlenecks in the pyramid of grades—and that did not change markedly after the reforms. Finally, we should say something about the navy, that unknown force that intervenes in political life only late in the evolution of the Latin American military. Sailors are removed from military society, more civilian in outlook and more cosmopolitan than the soldiers. Initially they took their models and structure from Great Britain, and later from the United States. However, their significance to the power of the military remains slight except in certain countries, such as Argentina, where they began to participate in the 1950s.

4

THE RISE OF
THE POWER OF
THE MILITARY

With their new civic and national responsibilities
and the measure of autonomy that they had acquired with reorganization and modernization, the new state armies of the continent were not inclined to play the role of silent partners. Both
their functions and their history impelled them to influence public affairs. Henceforth, the military sector of the state bureaucracy believed that it had a threefold responsibility: to centralize
state power by ending its geographic dispersion or impotence in
the face of Indian resistance; to control the entire territory with
garrisons that represented the sovereignty of the nation state;
and finally, to integrate the different ethnic, social, and regional
elements by giving them a feeling of common membership. The
three tasks did not incline the military to neutrality and civic
indifference. In addition, the tradition of political involvement
by party-based armies and the period of civil war was not long
past, and the immediate day-to-day functions of the armies were
not limited to the frontiers. The importance of internal defense in
nations that were rarely involved in international conflicts made
political intervention appear more normal and less a dramatic
perversion of roles; instead of suggesting excessive politicization
of the institution, political activity by the military seemed to be
an extension of the armies' routine activities.

Indeed, the armies of the subcontinent did not have to wait
for the Pentagon or the orders of a MacNamara or Kennedy to
give special attention to the internal enemy. Rather than the
European models of national defense—the protection of frontiers and an orientation toward an external enemy—internal

problems and domestic social and political dangers were the object of the specifically military actions of the Latin American armies. In Brazil, which had not had a war since the conflict with Paraguay in 1870, it was the army that—with some difficulty—crushed the peasant uprisings of the Contestado and of Canudos. The only enemies of the Argentine army were the Indians who were pushed back in the south and pacified in the north down to the 1930s, the metal workers of Buenos Aires in 1919, the seasonal workers of Patagonia in 1920, and the anarchists who had immigrated from Europe. In Chile, the battalions of the Prussia of South America could only apply the lessons of Moltke and Scharnhorst to the 1907 nitrate strike in Iquique and the some three hundred strikes that marked the first stages of the Chilean trade union movement between 1911 and 1920. We could multiply examples. Those armies were not a resource for diplomacy and external power, but rather an essential instrument for the maintenance of internal order and social peace.

It has been asserted that the influence of the European armies had much to do with the political activism of their transatlantic disciples. The French army is supposed to have transmitted to the Brazilian and Peruvian military its aristocratic tradition and its distrust of the representative system.[1] The Offizier Korps is suspected of having transmitted to the Prussianized armies of Latin America its caste spirit and a Junker mentality that was opposed to democracy. In fact, we have no proof of a correlation on the individual level between French or German influence and activism. On the collective level one example will suffice: the Chilean army, which had been deeply affected by German influence twenty years before the armies of Argentina and Bolivia, remained outside of politics from 1932 until 1973. This kind of reading by juxtaposition is not the way to analyze the influence and political importance of the European models. We must look elsewhere.

The prestige of the formidable German war machine was reflected by its South American disciples. For the Frédéric Thomas Graindorges or Prudhommes of that period the great German General Staff was one of the highest summits of European civilization—along with, of course, the House of Lords and the French Academy. The recognized excellence of the model was a source of pride and group cohesion. The mirror reflected a flattering image. In addition, the adoption of certain specific characteristics of the German army—the ritualization of military life, the emphasis placed upon the external signs of discipline and upon corporate unity—tended to exaggerate institutional values and to increase internal and external social differentiation. Thus it was the "Teutonic knight" aspect—the "order" in a religious sense—and the mystique of honor that was transmitted rather than Junker authoritarianism. This was not without importance.

The French army drew upon its recent colonial experience in its impact upon the South American armies. In Peru the insistence on the civilizing mission of the military institution in a country of unintegrated Indians was related to the influence of the French mission. The great concepts of the French overseas army were also presented in Brazil. Lyautey was their teacher. Even in 1937 a Brazilian officer raised the question in the pages of a military journal as to the applicability of the program developed by the "great African" concerning "the social role of the officer," concluding,

> Because of the extent of its territory, the abandoned children in the provinces of the interior, the low intellectual level of its populace, the problem of lack of unity, the immense effort which will be necessary for it to transform itself into a country made up of healthy and literate men which is economically sound and politically educated, and for the sake of the peace of the continent, Brazil perhaps more than any other country has the right to demand that its army should exercise an educational role.[2]

We might therefore think that the influence of France was to open the army to sociopolitical problems, while the Prussian model tended to close it in upon its own norms and rules. In fact, in different ways the two models established the prestige, cemented the cohesion, and reinforced the influence of the military apparatus in national life. But imitation of foreign models does not suffice as an explanation of the new political resources that the reformed armies acquired.

ORGANIZATIONAL FACTORS AND MILITARY
POWER

Modernization and the tasks assigned to the military gave the
institution a certain prestige and authority in the state and society. One of the peculiarities of the political development of Latin
America—with the exception of the Central American and Caribbean semiprotectorates—is the nonsynchronous modernization
of the state in which the military played the conscious role of
pioneers. Indeed, in many cases, the movement originated from
the needs of the army. In a word, the state began to modernize in
its military sector, and the rest did not always follow. Military
service was established before literacy and universal suffrage.
Military strategic doctrines were developed, but no one yet studied the problems of economic growth or the administration of
the territory. The increase in military expense with the reorganization and equipment of the army in every country that transformed the institution enlarged the role of the state. The militarization of the state was part of the same process.

Furthermore, the meritocratic procedures used in the selection and promotion of officers gave them a privileged place in
the state apparatus. In societies in which the liberal tradition
and the interest of the elites had kept the state weak and little
respected, and in which the "spoils system" made public service an accidental political reward rather than a career for which
one was obliged to prepare, the military now represented a
group of stable functionaries—in a way, more or less enlightened professionals among the amateurs who manned the administration. In other words, the "professionalized" corps of
officers formed a hard nucleus in a soft and unformed body.

In contrast with the interchangeable civilian bureaucrats,
the officers were well-educated elites who were seen as continually improving their capacities through a network of schools
and the intellectual and moral challenges of their careers. In
the majority of countries the officers were now very proud of
the high level of military education.[3] The Peruvians noted not
long ago that in that country a superior officer could spend a
third of his thirty-five years of active service in schools and

refresher or specialized courses. In the absence of war, therefore, the armies were transformed into bureaucratic bodies in which institutional rather than "heroic" values predominated. The life of the officer was filled with the application of the "regulation." One of the principal tasks of the foreign missions was to furnish the armies of the continent with a complete panoply of prescriptions that left nothing to chance. Finally, the codification of promotions as a major bureaucratic mechanism formed the mentality of the military officers and distinguished them from the civilian bureaucrats of the same period. The promotion table provided a rhythm for the career aspirations of the personnel. The scale of grades stipulated exactly the degree of seniority required; the promotion councils made up of superior officers deliberated each year concerning individual promotions. Henceforth, officers who were evaluated by their superiors throughout the length of their period of active service no longer depended in principle upon the capriciousness of political authorities—and they were very conscious of that fact. In order to safeguard this cherished meritocracy, the bureaucratic independence of the military institution was carefully protected by its members. Military society was hostile to outside intervention even when it was a constitutional requirement for promotion to the higher ranks.

The feeling of superiority that was produced among the military officers by their consciousness of being an elite group in the state was reinforced by other factors. The creation of a system of high-level technical and scientific education in order to produce certified arms experts and military engineers, as well as access to the modern technology represented by the equipment imported from Europe, gave the military experts in those nonindustrialized countries a clear awareness of their competence. These officers, who had not long ago been ignorant, no longer felt inferior in relation to the *doctores*—the lawyers and medical men of the political class. What is more, the procedures of recruitment and promotion based on universal criteria made the army a veritable ideal countersociety where, in the eyes of its members, justice, legitimated hierarchy, and organic solidarity ruled. Thus in 1944 Colonel Perón justified the intervention of the Argentine army against the corruption

of civilian society and the state by referring to the perfection of
military society:

> The internal organization of the army . . . provides an
> instructive example of discipline, comradeship, patriotism,
> hierarchy, and respect. In the army there are no unmerited
> promotions or unjustified punishments. The promotion
> table [*escalafón*] is respected with no exceptions or special
> considerations, in conformity with a very strict sense of
> justice—something which is not and should not be to the
> exclusive benefit of the armed forces but should be
> considered as a social conquest for all Argentines.[4]

The fact that the army knew the country better than any
other institution, thanks to the distribution of the garrisons
throughout the whole of the territories—these being generally
underadministered by the civilian government—reinforced the
sense of social responsibility that had resulted from universal
service. Not only was the army the school for the nation, since
its youth were entrusted to it, but its officers knew the problems of the people and therefore of the nation better than the
politicians or propertied groups. Here again we find confirmation in Perón's speeches. A year after the 1943 coup, Colonel
Perón declared, "We do not speak of the workers on the basis
of merely theoretical knowledge. We receive your sons and
brothers. We know your pains and misfortunes. We know how
the men in our country live."[5] This kind of feeling does not
necessarily produce advanced social views or a revolutionary
attitude, but it may assume a messianic dimension. An army
that is responsible for the education of a sovereign people and
for inculcating patriotism in them can only be made up of citizens who are pure, vigorous, and patriotic, confronting a civilian society that is—alas—corrupt, effeminate, and cosmopolitan. The duties of a military life that lacks heroic grandeur, and
the simplicity of an occupation that is oriented toward "action,"
predispose the military to the rhetoric of purification. The officer is "the priest of the cult of the nation" and consecrates his
existence to it. He is ready to offer himself to "regenerate" the
body of society, but he is unrecognized and feels neglected by
those in power. In these externally oriented economies the cosmopolitanism of the elites who make money in English and

amuse themselves in French helps to produce a feeling among the officers of spiritual and moral superiority that sometimes compensates for an inferiority of status.

The combination of isolation from the society as a whole and the cohesion and prestige of the group produces a haughty, closed quality in military life, a proud withdrawal into the institution that limits one's horizon at the same time that it produces a consciousness of having an important role to play. The overestimation of itself as a special closed group increases the autonomy of military society in the face of government power and at the same time increases its ability to intervene in political life. The professionalized officers of the new armies direct their loyalties to the institution of the military while believing that they are serving the state. Militaristic usurpation is the result of this kind of conduct. For these state armies the seizure of power by the military branch of the state apparatus is only a sort of internal adjustment. The military coup d'état, then, is only an intervention of the state within itself, producing a rupture in which by a sort of metonymy the part is taken for the whole—a sector of the bureaucracy acts as the "universal class" and becomes the government. This is why the corporate problems of the military often become inextricably mixed with social and national considerations. Whatever else it may have been, the modernization of the military was the source of a new militarism whose first manifestations reveal to us its mechanism and purposes.

THE NEW ARMIES TAKE THE STAGE

The relations of the military to politics can take varied forms. Military problems are always political problems, and at the most basic level group pressures are an expression of the power of the army. What interests us here is something else—namely, the extramilitary, and therefore antidisciplinary action of the army that is aimed at achieving political objectives and especially a break in the institutional order. In this context it is important to distinguish the initiatives that are properly military from the support that is given by certain units or officers to civilian movements that they do not direct. The new militarism obviously falls into the first category. The army intervenes as an institution that is above parties and even is antipolitical. However, in at least one case, that of Argentina at the beginning of the century, the first political activities of the educated officers aligned them with a civilian opposition movement. This would not merit our attention but for the fact that their orientation prefigures that of the coup-makers ("putschists") that shook several countries in the continent during the mid-1920s.

At the end of the last century in Argentina and up to the establishment of universal suffrage through the secret ballot in 1912, the Radical Civic Union saw its task as ending an "exclusionary" oligarchic state and broadening political participation. This party did not refuse to resort to the tactic of insurrection. The "Radical revolutions" mobilized groups of armed militants who tried to use arms to open the way to freedom of suffrage. The career military and the army in general participated in those *puebladas* (popular coups) in increasing numbers over the years. In 1890, 1893, and even in 1905, many young officers took part in the "democratic coups." According to Hipólito Yrigoyen, the head of the UCR, a thousand officers took part in the first coup after the reform of the military.[6] One of the participants later claimed that two-thirds of the army was involved in that revolutionary movement.[7] Let us not forget also that the Radicals were the ones who demanded that the establishment of electoral lists in 1912 be entrusted to the army in order to ensure the purity of the vote. This is why a Radical leader could write in 1915, "The Radical Party had two forces—the youth and the army—since both wanted to maintain their integrity in the midst of the general collapse."[8]

However, in the Radical coups the military remained subordinated to the civilians. A notable Radical was correct, therefore, when he noted the special quality of that military participation:

> The military action in support of Radicalism . . . differed
> fundamentally from the [revolutions] that have overthrown
> so many Latin American republics. Far from being barracks
> rebellions they were inspired by the demands of public
> opinion . . . they were directed by civilians; the people

> fought at the side of the army for common civic ideals. . . .
> It was not ambition that inspired the army, and still less the
> prestige of some presumptuous general."[9]

However, when the armies entered on the scene in the other countries of the continent fifteen years later, they did so through "barracks rebellions" that marked the beginning of a new militarism in which ambition or the prestige of a presumptuous general had less of a role than the demands of public opinion and questions relating to the army as a corporate group. In the twenties the military issued pronouncements in a more or less romantic or spectacular way against the status quo in Brazil, Chile, and Ecuador.

In Brazil, the uprisings of the junior officers, the *tenentes* (lieutenants), who were very small in number, represented an armed opposition the significance of which far surpassed its size, effectiveness, or immediate causes. The heroic gesture of a group of idealistic lieutenants who revolted in the fort of Copacabana in Rio on 5 July 1922 rapidly became a political myth. The direct cause of the revolt was a confused and disputed presidential succession, and an alleged "affront" to the army attributed to the president-elect. The tragic deaths of the young *tenentes* and the weakness of their organization and motives were forgotten. An uprising of *tenentes* in São Paulo in July 1924 took up the cause of the *paulista* opposition; although it appeared more serious than the Copacabana disturbance, it too was defeated. The political program in this case, although confused, was relatively explicit, demanding the application of the constitution against the usurpation by the executive. One of its manifestos declared that "the armed forces" had taken up arms to "defend the rights of the people, re-establish respect for justice, and limit the power of the executive."[10] Another unsuccessful *tenentista* uprising in Rio Grande do Sul, headed by Luis Carlos Prestes, supported the *paulista* rebels. The troops fought a long retreat in the famous Prestes-Costa column that marched from Rio Grande do Sul to the northeast and ended in Bolivia nearly three years later. The rebels therefore covered two thousand kilometers while being pursued by the army without having succeeded in involving the *caboclos* of the interior or producing the "regeneration" of Brazil.[11]

Based on a vague political and military dissatisfaction, *tenentismo* never threatened the oligarchic regime of the Old Republic, but because it provided heroes, tragic symbols of the possibility of a rebirth and of a purification of the narrow and corrupt life of politics, the movement of the young officers channelized the aspirations for change of all the socially discontented sectors. It prepared the way for the end of the First Republic and profoundly influenced the twentieth-century history of Brazil by its influence on the conservative authoritarian sectors as much as upon the revolutionary left. Luis Carlos Prestes, the "knight of hope," to use Jorge Amado's description, left the army and became secretary general of the Communist party, while other former *tenentes* were to inspire and direct the military regime that was created in 1964.

In Chile the sound of the military jackboot was heard for the first time in the corridors of the Congress in September 1924. A military committee made up of young officers demanded that the Congress immediately adopt a series of legislative proposals that it had been considering for months. This is how laws were adopted covering accidents on the job, retirement funds, and wage contracts. Once this had been done, the military called for the dissolution of Congress. President Alessandri left the country when he perceived that the officers with whom he had been cooperating to secure the approval of the social legislation by a reluctant and conservative Congress were no longer obedient to him. A military junta took power. A period of agitation, instability, and reform began that would not be ended until 1932.

The junta, made up of two admirals and a general and supported by the navy, soon began to represent the interests of the oligarchy. On 23 January 1925 the young officers took over the presidential palace, imprisoned the members of the junta, and recalled President Alessandri so that he could finish his term of office. However, it was Carlos Ibañez who was to embody the reforming spirit of the officers who had carried out the coups of 1924 and 1925. After participating as a commander on the military committee that was formed following the *pronunciamento* of September 1924, he became a minister of the government of Alessandri and his putative successor, after which he played the role of true head of government before being elected president by plebiscite with 98 percent of the votes in 1927. As general and war minister under two presidents, Ibañez removed the more conservative elements from the army and favored the reformist officers, but his "iron fist" and the authoritarian measures that he adopted regarding popular movements made him appear to the conservatives as the last bastion of order.

Supported by the civilian and military left, Ibañez governed with dictatorial powers, to the great relief of the right. It was in this climate that he organized the corps of *carabineros*, a kind of national police under the control of the Minister of the Interior. They replaced the local police who were regarded as too responsive to localized political interests. Added to that centralizing institution was the statist economic policy of Ibañez's minister, Pedro Ramirez, which was not well received by the Chilean oligarchy. Ramirez undertook to reform the treasury and the customs; he also sought to give the state the means to intervene financially in the areas of mining and industry while initiating an innovative public works policy. The economic difficulties resulting from the Depression ended these expenditures and led to the resignation of Ibañez in 1931 as a result of a wave of demonstrations by students and members of the middle classes calling for the restoration of civil liberties.

Military agitation did not cease and Chile entered a brief period that conservative historians have called "the anarchy."[12] The coup d'état against the parliament in 1925 was the result of the dissatisfaction in the ranks of the army with inflation and the delay in the payments of military salaries due to the length and lack of seriousness of the budgetary debates. In 1931 the decision of the provisional government that succeeded Ibañez to cut all the salaries of the civilian and military government employees by 50 percent produced new uprisings. The fleet anchored at Coquimbo mutinied in September 1931 under the leadership of its noncommissioned officers. But these imitators of the cruiser Potemkin were quickly forced to surrender by the army and by the air force, which bombed the mutinous units. On 4 June 1932, air force planes dived over Santiago and dropped leaflets on the presidential palace announcing the Socialist Republic of Chile, "which will end the crisis and aid the poor who are exploited by the national oligarchs and foreign imperialists."[13] Various groups of civilian and military socialists, partisans of Ibañez and populists linked to freemasonry (as was Ibañez himself), gave their support to former Air Force Commander Marmaduke Grove in an effort to overthrow the elected civilian president, Montero. The army did not act, and the carabineros regarded the movement with sympathy.

Thus, the Socialist Republic was born. Its slogan, *Pan, Techo, y Abrigo* (Bread, a Roof, and an Overcoat) emphasized social assistance to the masses who had been impoverished by the world depression. Its leaders, who rejected both capitalism and communism, proposed to relieve the misery of the populace by reducing unemployment and enlarging the role of the state under a system of economic planning. However, the technocratic and military socialism that "emphasized planning rather than the class struggle"[14] was only to last thirty days. While a part of the middle class gave quiet support to the new regime, the great interests were against it, as were the international powers, including the Communist party and the United States, which was concerned about its investments. The infantry, convinced that the government had been infiltrated by Communists, once again seized the presidential palace, La Moneda, and deported Grove to the distant Easter Island. A new junta was formed under the presidency of the *Ibañista* journalist, Carlos Davila, which vigorously repressed the demonstrations and protest strikes against Grove's overthrow. Davila, who announced that the Socialist Republic would be continued, remained in power for only one hundred days. Because of his dictatorial tendencies, the military replaced him with General Blanche Espejo, who promised to respond to the "socialist aspirations" of the people pending the organization of elections after which the military were to return to the barracks—for good, according to the members of the general staff.

The banner of socialism, therefore, was undoubtedly well received by the armed forces. Despite its brevity the Socialist Republic of Commander Grove was more than a tragicomic interlude in a period of intense but transient convulsion. In one year Chile had experienced four coups d'état and seven governments in succession. The Socialist party of Chile, with its peculiar mixture of nationalism and populism, was established as a lasting result of these convulsions. Grove, for some of his admirers the Luis Carlos Prestes of Chile, and an unsuccessful candidate in the 1932 presidential elections, was one of the founders of the Socialists in the following year. Good relations between the party—which played the game of democracy without rejecting the seizure of power by force—and certain sectors of the army continued until 1973. In addition, when faced with rightist parliamentary obstruction both Pedro Aguirre Cerda, Popular Front president in 1938, and Salvador Allende, Popular Unity president in 1970, were happy to resurrect legislation from the fleeting Socialist Republic that would permit them to carry out the reforms contained in their programs.

Reformist militarism also affected Ecuador in 1925. The export-oriented financial bourgeoisie of Guayaquil, weakened by the cocoa crisis in the immediate postwar period, imposed harsh repression on societal reactions to the recession. In 1922 the liberal government used the militia—the army was not sufficiently reliable—to repress the strikes in Guayaquil against the misery and inflation, killing a thousand people. In the Ambato highlands peasants dispossessed of their lands by a large company resisted and were massacred by the army in 1923. The manipulated elections in 1924 and the weakness of the president finally impelled the young officers to intervene.[15] As in Chile, the refusal of the military to be used to impose a repressive solution to social problems that those in power could not resolve was an important factor in their decision. On 9 July the League of Young Revolutionary Officers deposed the president and formed a junta before handing over power to an enlightened member of the upper bourgoisie of the coast, Isidro Ayora. Thus began the period that Ecuadorean historians call the *revolución juliana* (from *julio*, July).

For six years power was not in the hands of the Guayaquil *bancocracia* that had dominated the liberal regimes. For the first time in Ecuador laws were adopted that favored labor and allowed the state to intervene in economic and social life. The first coup d'état in Ecuadorean history that was not dominated by a *caudillo* and that proclaimed as its goal "equality for all and protection for the proletariat"[16] created a Ministry of Labor with a corps of inspectors who were responsible for seeing that the social legislation was observed. The first retirement funds were created at that time, as well as the central bank. Fiscal reforms were also initiated, especially the adoption of an income tax to cover the increased expense of the new policy and the expansion in the number of public servants. Through the introduction of habeas corpus and the recognition of illegitimate children the whole nation was modernized at the same time that measures for the protection of industry produced the beginning of a national development policy.

However, the reformism of the July revolution was timid and only benefited the stable urban workers and the middle classes in the broadest sense. It did not touch the essential areas. In Guayaquil the "golden calf" was still intact. The Bank of Commerce and Agriculture, which was despised by the young officers and which had made and unmade governments in the liberal period, was not affected even as it boycotted the new government. The Indian peasants, comprising more than half the population and reduced to a state of semiserfdom by the "hacienda system," were unaffected by the reforms; the oligarchy of the highlands actually participated in the revolutionary governments. The great Andean landowners were present everywhere from the central bank to the committee that drew up the constitution of 1929. Once the "July officers" had handed over power to the conservatives in order to get rid of the liberal plutocracy, a new military coup d'état in 1931 ended the reformist experiment to the benefit of the most reactionary forces of the highlands.

THE AUTONOMY OF THE MILITARY AND THE LIBERATION OF THE STATE

We may be surprised today that the military entered the scene on the left. However, the reformist tone of the new militarism is undeniable. While the intervening arms were not—as a Brazilian officer claimed in 1931—the "avant garde of the people," the military activists of the first part of the century defended democratic measures, took the part of the workers, fought for representation and justice, and forced the adoption of social legislation. Their progressivism is explained by some as reflecting the role of the army as the political representative of the middle classes, incorporating them into the political system.[17] This hypothesis enables one to explain the changes in the conduct of the military in a direction opposed to the lower classes once the participation of the middle classes had been assured.[18]

This interpretation, when rigorously applied, can account for the military participation in movements of civilian opinion aimed at establishing a broadened democracy in Argentina. However, it does not explain the independent and strictly military intervention of officers who distrusted civilians and had little relation with them, and were far from sharing the liberal values of the middle class. Antiliberal, centralizers, authoritarians, and nationalists, the reformist officers were not in ideological agreement with those classes that they were supposed to be representing.[19] Their character as salaried members of the public service—which made them part of the middle social sectors—was not restricted to the junior officers or to the reformers alone. In addition, it is well known that *tenentismo*, like other progressive military movements of the same period, involved only a minority of those "middle classes" in uniform. In fact, while they are indeed salaried, one too often forgets that the principal allegiance of the military is to the state and that the reformist interventions of these young officers had institutional motives that were not very different from those of the conservative coups that ended or succeeded them.

We have discussed the corporatist motives that set off the coups of the 1920s. Certain variables among the different nations ought to be identified. Thus in Brazil, the military were evidently very aware of the role of the army as the guardian of the republican institutions that it helped to establish. We may also believe that the younger officers were more responsible than the others. However, apart from individual differences, the resources provided by modernization and the normative attitudes that were transmitted influenced structures and produced attitudes in ways that transcended frontiers. Military intervention occurs in the space in the state and the nation that is occupied by the modern Latin American armies. However, its meaning is not predetermined; above all, it relates to the stabilizing role that the armed forces believe they have and that follows as a consequence of their formation. "Today," writes an Argentine colonel in 1915, "the army is the nation. It is the external armor that guarantees the cohesive operation of its parts and preserves it from shocks and falls."[20] Twenty years later you could read in the *Revista Militar* of Buenos Aires that "the mission of the army is to maintain the collective balance against wind and storm."[21] In Brazil the editors of the influential journal *A Defesa Nacional* defined the responsibilities of "the military class" in its first issue, published in 1913: "The army needs to be ready to preserve and stabilize the social elements in action. It should be prepared to correct the internal disturbances that are so frequent in the tumultuous life of developing countries."[22]

If we read these texts carefully we see that they describe projects that are to be carried out by an enlightened elite that is dedicated to the state. They do not express a political orientation. The attitude of messianism, above and beyond society, that they reveal does not involve an emphasis on law and order. Rather it demonstrates a clear desire to defend what exists, not as a response to the directions of the society, but in order to preserve the interests of the nation as the military see fit to interpret them. That can mean opposing the participation in power of a group or class that could endanger the collective equilibrium, or on the other hand taking action to save the system from its own beneficiaries. The role of the military is seen as closing or opening the system, imposing necessary reforms or rejecting them, all in the name of national cohesion and therefore of defense.

The reformism of the military is also included among those imperatives. In a way the Latin American armies try to "liberate the state from the burden of social class" so as to make it more autonomous and better able to carry out its mission.[23] This is the objective of the new antioligarchic militarism that we have described. But the state is neither as neutral nor as autonomous as the military bureaucracy believes and hopes. The witness of history argues against that bureaucratic illusion. Indeed, we

only need to see how the reformism of the military was eliminated or absorbed in the period of economic crisis that began in
1930 to understand that the state is not above class, but is rather
a synthesis of the relation of forces subject therefore to changes
in which all classes are not as equal as the organicist thinking of
the professional soldier assumes.

We have seen how the revolution of July in Ecuador died.
In Chile events proceeded more democratically but no less
clearly. Normal elections were held in 1932, resulting in the
victory of former president Arturo Alessandri, who was supported by the traditional parties. This time the former leader of
leftist liberalism, who had been called back to power by the
progressive military in 1925, was to govern on the right. His
second presidency (1932–38) marked a return to conservatism.
What is more, Alessandri utilized the *Milicias Republicanas*, a
kind of paramilitary white guard, against the danger of a possible resurgence of military leftism, thus effectively demilitarizing the Chilean political system. He was so successful that from
his presidency until 1969 Chile appeared as a democratic and
civilian-dominated exception in the unstable panorama of the
continent. The myth—supported by dominant interests—of an
army that was apolitical and "professional" was thus established in order to eliminate the radical activism of the socialist-
oriented officers.

While Brazil, as we shall see, presents a certain distinctive-
ness in the timing of the emergence of progressive elements—
and in their conversion to genuine conservatism—restorationist
or simply antipopular militarism was at work in 1930 in many
countries of the continent. In Argentina under a democratic
system in which the army had been out of politics since 1905,
President Hipólito Yrigoyen was overthrown in 1930 by General José Uriburu. The new leader wished to reestablish against
the parvenus of the Radical party the traditional elites of proven
capacity because of their family experience in public life.
Against the general will and "electoral arithmetic," he wished
to hand over power to the "collective reason" of the more enlightened. The new authorities took the direction of the national economy into their own hands, ignored the workers, and
cut back on the government programs that, under the demo-

cratic regime, had been an important way to redistribute the revenue of the nation to the middle classes. The new regime also intended to reduce the expenditure of the state and to reform the political system so as to prevent the "plebeians" and demagogues from ever taking power legally.

In Peru, where the army—which was despised by the ruling circles—had never been involved in reform, a coup d'état by Colonel Sanchez Cerro which overthrew Augusto Leguia after eleven years in power seemed to be another example of traditional military caudillismo. However, in the face of the disturbing rise of Alianza Popular Revolucionaria Americana (APRA),[24] the violent popular revolutionary movement, the ruling classes that had long been civilian in their orientation put aside their distrust of the military and supported the colonel's coup. The massacres in Trujillo in 1932 involving the army and the APRA were to establish a long-lasting defensive alliance between the military and the upper bourgeoisie. The Peruvian army clearly appeared at that time as "the watchdog of the oligarchy."[25]

The situation was more complex in Brazil where outnumbered *tenentes* who had been defeated in the 1920s seem to have had their revenge in the 1930 revolution that put an end to the Old Republic and brought Getulio Vargas to power. The victory of the revolution in 1930 that began as conflict within the oligarchy was due to a series of military factors among which the *tenentes* only played a minor role. A disparate coalition was produced by the participation of the antitenentista sector of the army in the uprising; the last-minute defection of the military hierarchy that took the side of the dissident states of Rio Grande do Sul, Minas Gerais, and Paraiba against the attempt of President Washington Luis to appoint a paulista successor; and, finally, the unnatural alliance of a part of the *tenentes* with the leaders of the old political class, their former adversaries. In the disparate political climate that resulted, *tenentismo* was swallowed up. Getulio Vargas, relying upon the support both of the reformist centralizing authoritarian *tenentes* and that of the local politicians, "in order thus to avoid a return to the oligarchical state and to militarism,"[26] moved quickly to discipline *tenentismo* and to take over its political goals. It is still not clear today whether the Mussolini-inspired *Estado Novo* that Vargas established in 1937 involved the realization or the final liquidation of the confused ideas of the young revolutionary officers.

Out of that unusual set of events two elements were to remain—one of them inherent in the character of the continent and the other without doubt the direct result of the recent modernization. One is struck, first, by the tendency to strengthen the state that is common to all the experiences of reformist military. This was true, in fact, both for the socializing military and for their equally activist opponents. Leaning more toward totalitarianism than to populism, a Brazilian officer who was hostile to *tenentismo* summarized its political goals as follows: "The state should have the power to intervene, to regulate every aspect of collective life, and to discipline the nation."[27] The worship of the state is thus one of the constitutive elements of military ideology at the beginning of the century.

In addition, another striking characteristic of the military of this period, without being universally true, was the generational and hierarchical divisions in the internal politics of the coups. This phenomenon practically disappeared in later periods, not because the captains and the generals always thought in the same way on current problems but because the later interventions that were usually institutional in character did not permit such hierarchical conflicts to develop, and because organizational and technical changes made pronouncements by young officers more and more unthinkable. Henceforth, as one Brazilian general who boasted of his strict "professionalism" clearly stated it: "It is necessary to make the politics of the army, not politics in the army."[28] In any case it is from this period that the belief arises (now discredited in this age of counterrevolutionary warfare) that generals are always more conservative than captains and that the junior officers, since they are not part of the establishment, have a certain tendency to question the status quo.

5

THE SIXTH SIDE
OF THE
PENTAGON?

So far we have discussed the armies in the independent nations in the continent and omitted the semiprotectorates that were directly influenced by the United States. While the American authorities until World War II did not press to participate in the training of the South American military,[1] this was not the case for the Caribbean and Central America. The neocolonial armies that were organized there by the United States and most often trained by the U.S. Marine Corps deserve special treatment, not only because of the nature of their creation and the states of which they are a part, but for two more decisive reasons as well. First, the military in these areas deserve our attention because of their political impact and praetorian role, which is symbolized by the two infamous names of Trujillo and Somoza. Second, armies in the semiprotectorates are important because of their role as formative agents for the United States as it became the giant world power that we know today.

In fact, the rise of United States imperial power that paralleled the decline of Europe, beginning with the Second World War, contributed in a major way to the limitation of the sovereignty of all of its southern neighbors. There is reason to believe that the United States, in extending its security frontier to the whole continent, attempted to impose on all the countries of the region a military tutelage that was similar in its objectives to that which existed in its Caribbean defense perimeter. In any case, beginning in 1945 the other states in the continent that had previously been in different situations of dependence and not always upon the "big brother" of the north now found themselves in the same situation as the micronations of the Caribbean—dependent economically, culturally, commercially, and militarily upon a single metropolitan power in the world. Understanding the characteristics and the consequences of the military presence of the United States in the "protectorates" of its strategic southern frontier will enable us to have a better appreciation of the realities and limits of the control by the Pentagon of the armed forces of the subcontinent after World War II, while avoiding hasty schematizations and conclusions. To do this we must recall certain historical aspects of the relations among the Americas.

If the defensive declaration of the Monroe Doctrine in 1823 (America for the Americans) seemed to establish the principle of a special responsibility of the United States for the former Spanish and Portuguese colonies, the Americans were very busy extending their own territory and did not become interested in the rest of the continent until the last quarter of the nineteenth century. Their "Manifest Destiny" was, first of all, the Pacific. However, in 1880 the industrial production of the United States was equal to that of Great Britain, which it surpassed in 1894.[2] At that point, an economic power was born. In 1889, as American imperialist groups developed their colonial projects, the United States convened the first International Conference of American States in Washington. The arrogance of American prosperity impressed the "Latin" delegates; however, proposals for an arbitration tribunal and a customs union were not adopted. Senator Beveridge continued to call for the opening of the Latin American market to Yankee products as their natural outlet. The ease with which the United States defeated a decadent Spain in 1898 and "liberated" Puerto Rico, Cuba, and the Philippines initiated an era of external expansion. The first Roosevelt, a brutal devotee of the "policy of the big stick," not only "took Panama" where the United States imposed its colonial enclave for a canal in 1903 but established the policy of the application of force to the southern nations as a principle. Through the "Roosevelt corollary," which the president added to the Monroe Doctrine in 1904, Washington officially gave itself an international police power in the neighboring countries.

Just as the United States considered the Caribbean region as an internal sea, the control of which was indispensable to the national interest, so also the Central American isthmus was viewed as an internal line of communication between the Atlantic and Pacific coasts of the United States from the period prior to the construction of the Panama Canal. In addition to these geopolitical considerations the United States also had important economic interests that had replaced those of the Europeans in some of the countries of its southern preserve. The United Fruit Company and the National City Bank became symbols of that economic domination. Establishing themselves as the gendarmes of *mare nostrum,* the Americans reserved the right to intervene militarily in that "vital security zone" any time that, in the words of Theodore Roosevelt, "repeated misconduct and a failure of power results in the general relaxation of the bonds of civilized society."[3] The principle of intervention was even written into the Constitution of Cuba after it was freed from Spanish domination.

The American occupation troops did not withdraw from the island until the Platt Amendment had been accepted, providing among other things that "the government of Cuba agrees that the United States may exercise the right to intervene to preserve the independence of Cuba, to maintain a government capable of assuring respect for life, property, and liberty" and observance of its international obligations.[4] The overthrow of a conservative pro-American government in 1906 produced a second occupation of the island by the marines that was a prelude to a series of military interventions; these, in turn, were followed by occupations of more-or-less lengthy duration and the direct exercise of administration by the United States in other countries in the region—Nicaragua in 1912, Haiti in 1915, Santo Domingo in 1916. In fact, the Dominican Republic was occupied from 1916 until 1924, Nicaragua twice (1912–25 and 1926–33), and Haiti was "protected" by the marines from 1915 until 1934.

Whatever the date of the withdrawal of American troops, it

was carried out under the same conditions. Before departing, the United States created a force of military police to replace the marines and to defend order, peace, and U.S. interests. These new-style armies were responsible for maintaining Yankee hegemony while sparing the tutelary power the substantial political and diplomatic costs of direct military intervention. In addition, these forces, gratuitously imposed on nations of limited sovereignty, gave rise to a militarism that had special characteristics.

FROM YANKEE OCCUPATION TO SUBSTITUTE ARMIES

An undersecretary of state wrote in 1927,

> The territory of Central America, including the isthmus of Panama, constitutes a legitimate sphere of influence for the United States if we take our security into serious consideration . . . Also we really do control the destiny of Central America, and we do it for the simple reason that the national interest dictates such a policy to us.[5]

The withdrawal of the occupation troops that was carried out in response to pressure from South America and in the face of the destabilizing resistance of guerrillas (Sandino in Nicaragua, the Cacos in Haiti, and the Dominican *gavilleros*) did not change anything with respect to the continuing American interests in the area. The Good Neighbor Policy adopted by the administration of Franklin Roosevelt in 1933, which involved the tactical abandonment of direct intervention and attempted to reduce tensions in the hemisphere by promoting peaceful penetration within the "Panamerican" system, was to use other means to achieve the same regional objectives. The departure of the marines was not meant to open the door to "revolution" or disorder. The creation in the occupied countries of "constabularies" (a kind of gendarmerie that for a long period in Nicaragua had the Spanish name of *constabularia*, so visible was the foreign hold) had two purposes: first, to suppress the national armies that were considered by Washington to be a source of instability,[6] and second, to establish nonpartisan military forces—that is, forces that were independent of all the national actors, but loyal to the former occupier.

In Cuba, "which had become a nation without having an army,"[7] the American military administration that departed from the new republic in 1902 left behind a rural guard on the Mexican model, as well as the Platt Amendment as a kind of insurance and reinsurance. The mission of the rural guard was to protect the sugar cane plantations. The Damoclean sword of the amendment strengthened the power of conservative governments against any "revolutionary" attempts by their liberal adversaries. Nevertheless, the liberals rose up in 1906 and the United States considered it its duty to intervene. The marines landed a second time and occupied the island, which they "pacified" by disarming the insurgents. The occupation had no popular support, and the American authorities became aware that the application of the Platt Amendment would lead either to the annexation of Cuba, or to repeated interventions that could involve the American troops in an extended conflict in which the United States had much to lose, especially in terms of its international prestige. An alternative solution was to Cubanize the intervention so that with the help of the United States Cuban nationals would maintain order and internal security and put down any attempt at revolution and social agitation. Thus, a Cuban standing army was created as a result of the "bilateralization of the Platt Amendment,"[8] which became a treaty with the metropolitan power and in fact the real constitution of the island until 1959.

The protection of foreign property and of a stable government that could defend it was therefore entrusted from that time forward to a national army trained by American advisors. Its officers received education and advanced training in the United States. All their equipment was provided by the protecting power, which obviously attached political conditions to its deliveries. By nature a counterrevolutionary force, created by an American occupier obsessed with the need for stability, a product of a broadened interpretation of the Platt Amendment, the Cuban army was basically conservative and hostile to any political and social change. It represented the guarantee of a sociopolitical order acceptable to the United States, and in that sense it had almost no national legitimacy. As an outpost of the United States and the representative of Washington in Cuban politics, that military institution appeared to be a neocolonial force before it developed its own bureaucratic and professional interests. It was despised by all classes of society, therefore, because it did not correspond to the national will or to national desires but rather to the needs of a foreign power. Its political role for thirty years, up to its collapse in 1959, was antinational in character.

While in Cuba late decolonization at the end of thirty years of liberation wars resulted in a precarious and unstable government, Nicaragua at the beginning of the century appeared to be at the point of developing both a modern leading class and a modern state. Long a battleground between the Liberals of León and Conservative caudillos of Granada, Nicaragua had been late in developing and owed to coffee its belated participation in the dynamics of agricultural export prosperity. The Liberal reform of 1893 appeared to be a typical example of modern agricultural capitalism. The Liberal president, Zelaya, had the communally owned lands sold, expropriated certain foreign interests, and undertook to create a modern army. He established a legal military obligation for all citizens, and created an *Escuela Politecnica* with Chilean military men to educate officers. The results of his program were modest. The generals became primarily political leaders whose rank depended on "their abilities to raise a local army of partisans."[9] As to military service, while it was universal in theory, it did not replace forced recruitment—as the following telegram sent by a *jefe politico* to Zelaya demonstrates: "I am sending you three hundred volunteers by train this morning to Managua. Please send the rope back to me since there still many here who want to sign up and their enthusiasm is great."[10]

Nevertheless, the country changed. Thanks to the tight control of the Liberal dictator, the state began to be established. The traditional oligarchy of tradesmen and cattle raisers, which was expressed politically in the Conservative party,[11] gave way to a new class of entrepreneurs who were oriented toward the international market. But the nationalism of Zelaya and his sympathy for Great Britain disturbed the United States. That country saw a strategic value in Nicaragua because an inter-ocean canal could be built there. Washington therefore needed a friendly government in control of a country that was the key to an isthmus vital to the defense and expansion of the imperial republic. In 1909 Zelaya was overthrown and the Liberal re-forms were ended with the conscious blessing of the United States—as a result of several carefully orchestrated interna-tional incidents and of a Conservative uprising. With the con-sent and obvious complicity of Washington, the Conservative pro-Yankee oligarchy was put into power. Adolfo Díaz, a former employee of an American company in Bluefields on the Atlantic, became president. However, the Liberals gave him no respite. Ignoring his patriotic instincts, Díaz sent a note in 1911 to the American chargé d'affaires appealing for a military inter-vention "like the one that had such good result in Cuba."[12] At a time when the nationalist rebels were gaining territory and con-trolling the principal cities in the country, the marines landed. In 1912 they amounted to a force of three thousand. The U.S. supervised elections that gave power to Díaz and signed the Bryan-Chamorro Treaty with him ensuring the possibility of constructing an interocean canal over the Grand Lake.

The military occupation gave power to the Conservatives, who were a minority in the country. By 1924 the United States believed that the status quo and the constitutional order were sufficiently assured for them to withdraw their last troops. However, Liberal uprisings broke out against a new Díaz gov-ernment. The revolutionary government of Calles in Mexico supported the Liberal, Sacasa, who had established a govern-ment at Puerto Cabezas in the northeast of the country. Wash-ington, fearing Communism, sent two thousand marine guards to the rescue. This time the Yankee intervention ran into a strong armed opposition of a new type that had a popular base and deeper roots than the troops raised by oligarchic clans. A Liberal "general" led this "national and anti-imperialist" resis-tance. His name is a symbol and a banner, César Augusto San-dino. The "Bolivarian" hero from Las Segovias, head of a "crazy little army," he gave a continental dimension to his struggle. This "general of free men," who was admired by Barbusse and Gabriela Mistral, by Ugarte and Vasconcelos, whose troops drew volunteers from all the neighboring countries, carried out an exhausting and relentless war for six years and laid down his arms in 1933 only after the marines had departed.

He did not accept the agreement between the Liberals and Conservatives which had been adopted under the aegis of the United States and which permitted the Liberal Moncada to be elected president in elections that were supervised by the American general McCoy. Those accords, conceived by the signatories as a way to check a social mobilization that was dangerous for the established order, would in the view of the occupying force permit the disarmament of the differing contending factions and the demilitarization of public life. To that end, the United States pressured for the creation of a *Guardia Nacional* (National Constabulary) that was nonpartisan and was led by American officers with a marine as *jefe director* until 1932. The guard, which was an army and a national police force commanded by foreign officers that enjoyed the privileges of juridical extraterritoriality, had a colonial and anticonstitutional character that was denounced from the moment of its creation.[13]

While the United States took great care to eliminate party politics from the ranks of the Guard, requiring the recruits to swear that they had given up any political affiliation,[14] it made less effort to give the new military force a national character. In 1930 there were only 15 Nicaraguan officers in a total of 120. Engaged in the struggle against the Sandino forces at the side of the American occupation troops, the National Guard was an antinationalist and antipopular force from the beginning. The United States had replaced the private armies of the civil wars with the private army of the United States. Its pro-American tendency continued to the 1970s. From 1956 until its dissolution in 1979 the National Guard was commanded by West Point graduates and the cadets of the military academy founded by the Americans in 1930 spent their fourth year of study in an American school; this was especially true beginning in the 1960s with the establishment of the School of the Americas in the Canal Zone.[15]

Furthermore, when the marines sought a Nicaraguan *jefe director* in 1932 who would be useful for their purposes, they found a man who was not too deeply involved in politics although he had participated in the first Liberal uprisings. He was also a nephew by marriage of then-president Sacasa, and in particular he knew English and the United States well, having studied in Philadelphia. Anastasio Somoza García, this improvised general to whom the guard was entrusted, did not stay there long. The last of the marines and the chief of their Nicaraguan janissaries, he knew how to exploit both the unusual social autonomy of the guard and his ties to the metropolitan power. The bloody dynasty that he imposed on the country for forty-five years was indeed the fruit of the intervention.

In the black republic of Haiti, the American occupation was also extended by the creation of a "native gendarmerie" equipped and trained by the U.S. Marine Corps.[16] The United States, disturbed by the economic interest of the European countries, especially Germany, in a country whose coasts had a key position on the sea lanes to the Panama Canal, followed Haitian developments closely. The government's need for money and the instability of a country that had had six presidents in four years allowed the United States, as part of the dollar-diplomacy policy, to intervene militarily to take control of customs, the national financial system, and then the administration of the country. The Roosevelt Corollary justified this action: were not property and persons in danger because of the Haitian anarchy?

There, too, the occupation troops were to find a very tenacious popular resistance in the Cacos Rebellion that successfully mobilized fifteen thousand partisans under the leadership of Charlemagne Peralte with the objective of "throwing the invaders into the sea." With racism as a contributing factor, the repression was a terrible prefiguring of other American colonial "pacifications," especially in its use of relocation camps for the population. After the assassination of Peralte by the occupiers in 1919, the movement ended in surrender. In two years of fighting the Cacos had lost two thousand two hundred and fifty Haitians, compared to the marines' twenty-seven.[17]

To complete the pacification and to prepare for the future, the occupation forces after the dissolution of the existing army created a public force in 1916 called the "gendarmerie of Haiti." This force later became the guard (1928) and finally the army (1947)—and it was involved alongside the marines in the "campaign of extermination of the Cacos guerrillas."[18] From its initiation the gendarmerie played the role of "indigenous occupation troops."[19] It is true that in 1930, 60 percent of the officers of that body were Americans. The Haitianization of the military forces was to be slow and uninterrupted. The military academy, founded in September 1930 on the model of the U.S. Naval Academy, was also directed by American officers. However, the Guard was to remain a relatively weak institution in Haiti.

In the eastern and Spanish-speaking part of the island of Hispaniola, the Dominican Republic was also occupied by the Marines in 1916 under similar conditions to those of its French-speaking neighbor. Instability and bankruptcy were the two pretexts for intervention. In the seventy years of independence since the end of Haitian control of that part of the island in 1844, the Dominican Republic had had twenty-three victorious revolutions. Civil war was the sole functioning mechanism for the transfer of political power. An elite of large landholders fought for control of the government by force of arms without establishing either a stable democracy or a permanent and effective dictatorship. The specialization of agricultural production seems to have been the cause of the fragmentation of the ruling groups. One spoke of the cocoa oligarch, the sugar imperialist, and the tobacco democrat.[20] The governors of the provinces were actually local military leaders.

Faced with the anarchy produced by the warlords, who with their military uprisings and civil wars helped to increase the national debt, the United States here as elsewhere dictated the establishment of a "neutral" police force in 1916. However, in the Dominican Republic it was not content to prop up a government or to place it under tutelage. The United States simply abolished the local regime and replaced it with a military government with American officers as members of the cabinet. The principal direct consequence of foreign occupation was to destroy the military power of the semiindependent caudillos and to centralize the administration of the country.[21] The National Guard created by the marines thus became the first regular standing army in the history of the Dominican Republic.

While the resistance to the invader was more localized and less widespread than in the other occupied countries in the area, the new National Guard was seen as a substitute army for the occupiers and a foreign body. The Dominican bourgeoisie was largely hostile to the United States, and leading families refused to allow their offspring to become colonial officers. Also, the American authorities who recruited enlisted men among the lower-class elements in the cities were unconcerned with the past conduct of the future officers, who were publicly denounced in the press as traitors to the nation.

Thus it was that a former telegraph operator and later chief of the private police force of a sugar plantation joined the gendarmerie of the marines. His rise was meteoric—lieutenant in 1919, captain in 1922, commandant in 1924, and chief of the general staff in 1928. The man with this less than brilliant background, Rafael Leonidas Trujillo, would soon be a generalissimo. The future "satrap of the Dominican Republic," the "little Caesar of the Caribbean,"[22] had the confidence of the marines. His dictatorship was again the poisoned fruit of the Yankee occupation.

The United States would have liked to establish national guards on the model that we have described at least in all the five states of the isthmus, as well as in Panama. However, except for the occupied countries, Washington did not achieve this goal except to a degree in Panama. In fact the new republic established a National Guard shortly after independence without the aid of the United States, although under its watchful gaze. Part police and part army in its character and development, it greatly resembled the similar institutions in neighboring countries. It is understandable that the United States should wish that nations located in areas of importance to its national security should possess military forces that were trained by it, and were therefore responsive to it. But in fact the motivations of Washington were characterized by a combination of Machiavellianism and naiveté. Analysis by responsible Americans, officially at least, was the product of a schematized and superficial view that instability and chronic militarism in the region were simply due to the partisan character of the armies. To remedy this it was only necessary, therefore, to establish armies that were nonpolitical and above parties, professionalized and disciplined. Then you could kill two birds

with one stone, both assuring that the country would be demilitarized, and securing useful internal allies.

This was to forget that in the chaotic and unstable countries in which the constabulary model was put into practice the
state was either practically nonexistent or else a notorious
anachronism with no social group powerful or dynamic enough
to triumph over its rivals and to take in hand the modernization
of the administrative and political structure. Thanks to the
United States not only did the modernization process begin
with the army, but it was imposed by a foreign invader that at
the same time removed or crushed the emerging ruling classes
and destroyed what remained of traditional institutions, thus
eliminating the possibility of constructing a national state.
While the external orientation of the military was carried to an
extreme, these modern centralized armies, designed only to
maintain internal security, only possessed legitimacy in the
eyes of the occupying power with whom they maintained relations of more or less strict loyalty. By their nature, these
antinational enclave armies could not form the nucleus of the
state that they had replaced in the institutional no-man's-land
left by the invader. They were thus available for adventure, or
were at least ready to re-create the instability that they had been
created to prevent.

THE PAX AMERICANA AND THE ORDER OF THE PENTAGON

The Good Neighbor Policy that ended the military occupations
of the Caribbean and Central America guaranteed that the
United States would be able to get support for its policy from all
of its southern neighbors when the war broke out in Europe.
Prepared by a series of consultations among the foreign ministers of the Americas, the entry of the United States into the war
following Pearl Harbor in 1941 was supposed to result in the
abandonment of neutrality by the Latin American states. The
United States promoted this alignment, offering under the
Lend-Lease Program to deliver arms to friendly countries while
at the same time pressuring those who refused without regard

for their national interests. Thus Argentina, traditionally linked to the British market and a country for which neutrality was a vital commercial necessity, was outlawed by the rest of the continent and its governments were accused of "neo-fascism" by the Department of State.

In the area of economics, the United States demanded that its Latin American allies participate in the war effort by agreeing that the price of commodities be fixed unilaterally and by accepting payment for exports in dollars that could not be used until victory. Some countries, such as Brazil, drew their pound of flesh as a price for closer collaboration with the cause of democracy. Getulio Vargas, although he had created an authoritarian regime on the European model, offered the United States air bases in the northeast, sent a division to fight in Italy alongside the U.S. Army (the *Força Expedicionaria Brasileira*) and obtained in exchange and contrary to all expectations a considerable loan from the Export-Import Bank for the construction of a national steel industry.

Generally, the war increased the economic dependence of the Latin American countries on the large nation to the north, as well as the political influence of Washington over the future of Latin America. In 1945 a new epoch opened in hemispheric relations that was to result in different relationships among international forces and changes in the structure of financial and economic dependence. In fact in the interwar period and especially after the Depression, the United States had replaced the European countries that were in serious financial difficulties as the principal source of investment throughout the continent. Great Britain retreated. Its investments fell from 754 million pounds in 1938 to 245 million pounds in 1951.[23] The United States, which had only $300 million in Latin America in 1897, increased its investments to nearly $2 billion in 1920, reaching $3.5 billion in 1929, $4.7 billion in 1950, over $6 billion in 1953, and more than $12 billion in 1963.[24] In 1914, the direct investments of the United Kingdom were three times those of the United States. The two countries were practically equal in 1930. In addition, the American influence was extended beyond the "Caribbean Mediterranean" to the large states in the south of the continent. In 1897 Mexico and Central America absorbed

72.8 percent of those investments and South America only 12.4 percent; in 1929 Cuba received 24.3 percent (almost as much as Mexico and all of Central America combined), but South America accounted for 47.2 percent. The share of the Caribbean and Central America dropped from 86.1 percent in 1908 to 52.8 percent in 1929. Trade between the northern and southern parts of the continent followed the same pattern of expansion. U.S. imports from Latin America averaged $553 million a year from 1936 to 1940; they represented $2.35 billion in 1948.[25]

Dollar diplomacy proved itself. The principal foreign investor, often the principal or only customer, was no longer a distant European country but a metropolis located in the same continent as its vassals—a giant next door. Thus, the United States was not only both the primary world economic power but also the primary military power, while Europe in the process of economic recovery had difficulty avoiding complete military subordination and the dangers of the cold war forced it to seek shelter under the American "umbrella" and Atlantic integration. Thus, for several decades, at least, the Latin American states were to find themselves alone or nearly so with their enormous protector—a country that represented 6 percent of the world population but consumed nearly half of the resources of the planet, the primary consumer and producer in the world.

Once peace returned the United States began to establish a system of hemispheric security through a complex network of multilateral and bilateral pacts. The overall idea that was to inspire that Inter-American system was expressed during the presidency of Harry Truman as "a closed hemisphere in an open world."[26] Universalism, of course, but only up to the shoreline. The "zone of vital interests" of the United States now extended to Tierra del Fuego. Yalta had led to this.

The bases of the military system were established during the war with the creation of the Inter-American Defense Board (or *Junta Interamericana de Defensa*). In 1947 the Inter-American Treaty of Mutual Assistance signed at Rio de Janeiro established the principle of collective security in the face of extracontinental aggression. In 1948 the Charter of Bogota that created the Organization of American States (OAS) set up the mechanism for the peaceful resolution of the conflicts that might arise within the inter-American system. The OAS charter empha-sized the principle of nonintervention. But Article 6 of the Rio Treaty provided for the case of an "aggression which [is] not an armed attack but [is] capable of endangering the peace of the Americas," a concept that expanded the notion of hemispheric defense in the opposite direction.

This relatively easy and loose multilateral arrangement was based on the principle of a harmony of interests among the coun-tries that were members of the "family of the Americas" in accor-dance with the paternalist conception of the U.S. Department of State that was accepted without too much disagreement by the governments of the "client" countries. It seems, however, that the American government actually wished to go further in the area of continental defense. A bill for an Inter-American Military Cooperation Act was introduced in Congress in 1946 but was not adopted. It aimed at standardizing equipment, weapons, and organization in order to "make the Latin American armies com-pletely independent of European sources"[27] since, according to the secretary of war at the time, the United States had "learned during the Second World War that the introduction of foreign (sic) equipment and foreign training methods represented a dan-ger to the security" of the country.

Despite the interest shown by many civilian and military leaders in a military integration similar to that in the North Atlantic, when the Korean War broke out the United States was content to sign bilateral military assistance treaties with twelve Latin American countries within the framework of the Mutual Security Act adopted by Congress in 1951. Latin America was not a defense zone of high priority. Despite the Guatemalan warning of 1954,[28] Communism did not appear to the American administration as a pressing danger. Military assistance that included training of the Latin American military, grants of used or surplus materiel, and credits for the purchase of equipment represented less than $450 million between 1953 and 1963, ris-ing to $448 million for the four following years.[29]

In the meantime the situation in the hemisphere had changed. The Cuban challenge had modified the strategic con-ceptions of the United States. The appearance of a socialist state one hundred twenty miles from Florida was seen as a serious threat to the American hegemony over the continent. Therefore, under Kennedy the mission of the Latin American armed forces was redefined. Internal security and the struggle against subversion replaced the policy of a common defense against external aggression. The content of aid also changed. Counter-revolution does not require cannons and bombers, but rather light arms and a firmly anti-Communist ideology. The shift under Kennedy was to tighten the links between the Pentagon and the Latin American armies and to give their collaboration a strongly political coloration.

In emphasizing the "defense of the internal front" against communist subversion and the responsibilities for "civic action" by the armies in order to prevent it, American military aid, beginning in 1962, became more intensive and better institutionalized than before. American military planning became more structured and the relations between the Latin American armies and that of the metropole grew closer. The U.S. Army had military missions of varying importance in nineteen countries of the subcontinent and their presence was often an integral part of the agreements for the sale or loan of military equipment.

The Military Assistance Programs (MAP) of the United States were coordinated by the Southern Command, one of the four large military commands of the United States, which was transferred to the Panama Canal Zone in 1963. The Southern Command (or "Southcom"), the establishment of which was linked to the Cuban situation, was responsible in principle for the defense of the canal. However, that "miniature Pentagon," with ten to fifteen thousand men from all three services who were capable of rapid intervention in case of necessity, represented the military assistance and influence of the United States throughout the continent. Annual conferences of the commanders of the armies of the American states focused on the situation in the continent and on the division of defense responsibilities among the Latin American states. Joint maneuvers such as *Operation Unitas* of the navies and regional integration agreements such as the one that led to the formation of the Central American Defense Council (ODECA) proceeded directly from the overall defense planning of the American military authorities.

TABLE 2
U.S. MILITARY ADVISORS IN RELATION TO NATIONAL ARMED FORCES, 1964–68

Argentina	1/2034	Guatemala	1/300
Brazil	1/1760	Nicaragua	1/323
Chile	1/1250		

Source: Geoffrey Kemp, *Arms Traffic and Third World Conflicts* (New York, 1970), p. 7.

In the case of the navy, the loan or rental of ships by the U.S. fleet facilitated the pressure for close cooperation.

This elaborate network of military collaboration varied in intensity depending on the country. Likewise, for the military mission, the amount of financial aid and the percentage of officers and noncommissioned officers trained in American schools varied perceptibly according to the country. As we see in table 3, the overall amount of financial aid (grant aid program, credit sales, and excess stock program)[30] is unrelated to the size of the armies except perhaps in the case of Brazil; however, aid can perhaps be linked to the capacity of the country to finance the increases in defense expenditures as well as the Pentagon's estimate of the potential threats to that country. The first factor can explain the low level of aid received by Argentina, but the second would explain the relatively large amounts of aid received by Colombia and Peru where guerrilla movements emerged in the 1960s, as well as the place of Chile and Uruguay.

For a serious understanding of the direct and indirect political consequences of that aid, we must examine how it changed over time. In table 4, we can see that in the years 1962–66, aid is

TABLE 3
U.S. FINANCIAL ASSISTANCE, 1953–72*

Argentina	129.5	Ecuador	63.8
Brazil	365.2	Peru	120.2
Colombia	131.3	Uruguay	58.5
Chile	160.7	Venezuela	53.9

Sources: U.S. Agency for International Development, Statistics and Reports Division, *U.S. Overseas Loans and Grants and Assistance from International Organizations: Obligations and Loan Authorizations, July 1, 1945–June 30, 1972* (Washington, D.C.: U.S. Government Printing Office, 1973).
*Millions of dollars, minus interest.

TABLE 4
THE EVOLUTION OF AMERICAN MILITARY ASSISTANCE*

	Argentina	Brazil	Chile
Postwar relief, 1946–48	—	—	—
Marshall Plan, 1949–52	—	—	—
Mutual Security Act, 1953–61	3.0	170.6	47.4
1962–65	56.1	109.1	69.5
1966	27.3	30.6	10.2
1967	15.6	32.6	4.2
Foreign Assistance Act, 1968	11.4	36.2	7.8
1969	11.7	0.8	11.7
1970	0.6	0.8	0.8
1971	16.4	12.1	5.7
1972	20.3	20.8	12.3
	162.4	413.6	169.6

Source: U.S. Agency for International Development, Statistics and Reports Division, *U.S. Overseas Loans and Grants and Assistance from International Organizations: Obligations and Loan Authorizations, July 1, 1945–June 30, 1972* (Washington, D.C.: U.S. Government Printing Office, May 1973), p. 35.
*Credit sales, grants, and surplus, in millions of U.S. dollars.

concentrated on two countries, Argentina and Chile, which at that time were undergoing changes that were decisive for the situation in the continent: the election of a Christian Democrat as president against a "Marxist" in 1964 in Chile, and a Western and pro-American coup d'état in Argentina in 1966.

The number of military men who took courses in schools or training centers in the United States is a still more direct indication of the degree of American influence. Again the variations in time and space are sufficiently significant that one cannot yield to the temptation to draw definitive overall conclusions. The figures on the total number of the Latin American military who passed through U.S. bases shows a decided increase after the Cuban crisis. From 1950 until 1965, 31,600 Latin Americans took courses in the United States or the Canal Zone. That number rose to 54,270 in 1970 and 71,570 in 1975.[31] As table 5 indicates, the different countries show interesting disparities. Thus Argentina, with the second largest army in the continent, sent substantially the same number of personnel to school in the

TABLE 5
MILITARY PERSONNEL TRAINED AT U.S. FACILITIES FOR SELECTED LATIN
AMERICAN COUNTRIES

	1950–65[a]	1965–70[a]	1950–65[b]	1965–70[b]	Total	Size of armed forces in 1970
Argentina	1375	1007	256	170	2808	137,000
Brazil	3632	2377	366	481	6856	194,300
Bolivia	208	202	1065	1183	2658	21,800
Chile	2064	489	549	1272	4374	61,000
Colombia	1694	432	1180	1323	4629	64,000
Ecuador	1222	316	1506	1240	4284	20,000
Peru	2306	584	1080	1037	5007	4,650
Venezuela	749	562	982	1785	4078	30,500
Guatemala	491	135	678	976	2280	9,000
Nicaragua	329	286	2494	855	3964	5,400

Sources: U.S. Department of Defense, 1967 and 1971, and Robert P. Case, "El entrenamiento de los militares latinoamericanos en los Estados Unidos," *Aportes* (October 1967); and "La asistencia militar de los Estados Unidos a America latina," *Marcha* (4 July 1972).
[a]Training in the United States.
[b]Training at bases outside the United States.

United States as did Bolivia, whose army was only one-sixth as large, or Guatemala whose army totaled nine thousand men in 1960, and fewer than Somoza's Nicaragua, which had around eight thousand men under arms. The military history, the economic capacity, the level of development, and the geopolitical situation of the different countries explains those not insignificant discrepancies.

As a real measure of the Americanization of the Latin American armies and of the political influence of the United States it is necessary to differentiate among the types of training and to know their respective programs and orientations. The schools that incorporate the Foreign Military Training (FMT) trainees are numerous and the curriculum varies in level and content so that it is difficult to gauge the impact on Latin American officers. Nevertheless, it is thought that the schools in the Canal Zone—especially the well-known U.S. Army School of the Americas (USARSA) at Fort Gulick where the courses are given in Spanish or Portuguese and are aimed at "giving the

Latin American military the formation that will make them better able to contribute to the security of their respective countries,"[32]—reflect most directly Washington's conceptions as to the military division of labor in the continent. These are the schools whose courses are the best at communicating an anti-Communist ideology and the philosophy of counterrevolution. The number of military men who have taken courses at American bases outside of the United States is worthy of note. Let us not forget that in 1974 the USARSA graduated its thirty thousandth student. If a maximum of ideological content is dispensed at Fort Gulick and appears to predominate in all the schools of the Southern Command (even in the Inter-American Air Force Academy at Albrook Air Force Base and the Inter-American Geodetic Survey at Fort Clayton where the emphasis is also placed on techniques of counterguerrilla warfare), the schools in the United States, because they are mixed and have more prestige, can also have an impact that is useful for the Pentagon. The infantry course at Fort Benning, Georgia, and especially the general staff course at Forth Leavenworth and the Inter-American Defense College with admission reserved for superior officers seem to have more attraction for the Latin Americans than the training programs in the Canal Zone. At the extreme, a course in counterguerrilla warfare mixed with simple and heavy-handed anti-Communist indoctrination can produce anti-American reactions, while an advanced technical course for experts in a U.S. military school that is not restricted to the training of foreign officers can create a boundless loyalty to, and admiration for, the American way of life.

In any case, it is undeniable that the USARSA, which is designed to train Latin American officers for internal warfare in accordance with the desires of the Pentagon, gives considerable emphasis to anti-Communism and pro-American indoctrination. Not only do the courses on counterrevolutionary warfare insist on denouncing the enemy, but even the technical courses (commissary, radio operation, etc.) emphasize the "Communist menace." Twenty percent of the officers' program is devoted to Communism. In addition, the students at Fort Gulick are inundated with blatant propaganda brochures in Spanish with titles such as "*Qué es el comunismo? Ilusión comunista y realidad democrá-*

tica; Expansión del comunismo en América Latina,"[33] in the best spirit of the cold war. There is no doubt about U.S. desire to influence the politics of the officers.

The purpose of the military aid program after the adoption of the Kennedy-MacNamara policies was to convert the armies of hemispheric defense into forces of internal order mobilized against Communist subversion, thus contributing to the security of "the free world." This was why the armies of the subcontinent were trained in counterguerrilla warfare and in civic action—that is, in nonmilitary projects that are socially useful. The civic action in which the French army was involved in Algeria with their soldier-builders was aimed at bringing the army closer to the most deprived parts of the population where the guerrillas might develop. In that action it was the counterguerrilla forces that were supposed to be integrated among the people.

For the United States all of its military investments were aimed at guaranteeing at the least cost the security of a continent that after 1959 had become a player in the cold war—a secondary player it is true, but one that deserved special attention. The new inter-American military planning, conducted by simply involving the military leaders of the continent, was to transform the Latin American armies into "national guards" amenable to the strategic perspectives of the United States and, at the extreme, capable of aligning their national interests with those of the country that was the leader of the "free world." The official evaluations of the Military Assistance Programs left no doubt as to their very positive results for the United States. A congressional committee concluded in 1970 that the Military Assistance Program had made a major contribution to "strengthening the defense of the free world," especially by "efficiently communicating anti-subversion thinking to several threatened countries" and that it had enabled the United States to "develop military influence in the recipient countries with a very low cost/benefit ratio."[34] However, for proponents of the program the interest in a policy of Good Neighbors in Uniform[35] went beyond the global defense of the capitalist world. Military relay diplomacy appeared to be a substitute for the direct intervention of the United States. This could be seen in the cases of Brazil under Joâo Goulart and in Chile under Allende. In Brazil prior to 1964, as well as in Chile at the beginning of the seventies, in addition to establishing an "invisible blockade" around governments deemed hostile to American interests the government in Washington had been careful to maintain and even increase its military aid (see table 5). Ambassador Lincoln Gordon, in the embassy in Brasilia at the time of the Brazilian Labor party government of Goulart, recognized that military aid was "a major way to establish close real relations with the personnel of the armed forces" and "an important element in influencing the Brazilian military in a pro-U.S. direction . . . an essential factor in limiting the leftist excesses of the Goulart government."[36]

According to the Department of Defense itself, military assistance is not solely aimed at raising the professional level of the Latin American military in the interest of the common defense; in particular the training carried out by the United States is supposed "to prepare those who receive it to share its benefits with their compatriots when they return home to occupy positions of responsibility and increased influence."[37] It is easy to understand that the Latin American policy of the United States in the period of the Rockefeller Report (1969) and throughout the Nixon era could at least rely on the power of the military as "a progressive force able to carry out social change in a constructive way,"[38] that is, in an orderly fashion.

MILITARY DEPENDENCE AND ITS LIMITS

That American military aid had a political dimension no one will deny, even if there is no direct and mechanistic relationship between the political ends pursued and the real impact of the aid on the armies of the subcontinent. In the United States itself there was no lack of criticism of the antidemocratic political character of that military aid. Public opinion is disturbed to see World War II surplus Sherman tanks breaking down the gates of the presidential palace in the pale dawn of a military coup. In Senate hearings the witnesses and political authorities denounced anti-Communist and counterrevolutionary indoctrination as a source of the aggressive conservatism and inclination to coups of the Latin American military.[39]

It is undeniable that an anti-insurrectional military theory reinforcing the alarmism that is characteristic of the military leads to a predisposition in favor of the intransigent maintenance of the status quo. The crusading spirit fostered by the tensions of the current situation led to the equation of every desire for change or reform with Communism. Between March 1962 and June 1966—the most intense period of the Cuban crisis—nine coups d'état took place in the continent. In at least eight of those cases the army took preventive action to eliminate a government that was felt to be too weak to take action against popular or "Communist" movements or that was even accused, as in the Dominican Republic or Brazil, of desiring to carry out subversive reforms itself.[40]

To talk about the denationalization of the armies of the subcontinent in that period is not an exaggeration. A combination of adjectives, occidental and Christian, seemed to have replaced the nation-state in the hierarchy of loyalties of the professional officer. It is true, as B. H. Liddell-Hart has remarked, that "in the majority of the professional armies, a nationalist feeling has become a secondary factor after the military spirit that is produced by training, camaraderie, and a sense of mission."[41] The French foreign legion is a very good example, of course. However, can one say that without the American influence similar attitudes would not have developed among the Latin American military, or that their conservative orientation was transmitted to them, even imposed upon them by the Pentagon? The most extreme versions argue, for example, that the Latin American military have received a narrow resocialization from the United States and are assigned political roles in conformity with Yankee interests. Fort Gulick, in this view, is the "school for coups" and the armies of the continent are all manipulated by the metropolitan power.

The global and nonhistorical evaluation of the political effects of Latin American military dependence that derives from an instrumentalist conception of contemporary militarism tends both to overestimate the success of "imperialist" policy and to deny national and individual differences. In addition to anecdotal evidence, such as the breakfast of the American military attaché with General Castello Branco the morning of the April

1964 coup in Brazil—or still unverified stories, such as the coordination of the military operations during the September 1973 coup in Chile by a "mysterious" U.S. Air Force plane[42]—the relation between Latin American militarism and Pentagon aid is based only on theories or personal convictions. There is no statistical proof of a relation between military coups and the level of military aid. The degree of democracy achieved in the various Latin American states seems to be independent of the size of U.S. military assistance.[43] The correlations between those two variables are of very little significance. For some countries an increase in military aid seems to have been accompanied by a deterioration of civil-military relations in the 1960s, but the opposite is true in other countries in the same period. Furthermore, despite the substantial increase in military aid expenditures at the end of 1961 and the change in the orientation of that aid, the results in terms of the relations of the army and the government are unchanged for the majority of countries between 1945 and 1961, and between 1962 and 1970.[44]

If we take budgetary dependence as a variable that is subject to measurement—that is, the percentage of the U.S. contribution to the military expenditure of each nation—we find that in 1965 Argentina, Venezuela, and Mexico all depended on the United States for less than 3 percent of their budget, and Brazil, Colombia, and Chile financed around 10 percent of their military budgets with American aid.[45] Argentina in the period between two military coups was in the same situation as the stable "democracies"; Brazil under military rule was in the same position as two civilian systems that were believed at the time to be very solid.

It is important not to mix countries and confuse different situations. The armies of the large, more developed nations are those that are the most "professionalized" and the least dependent. These also are the ones that are the least susceptible to the maximalist ideological influence of the USARSA at Fort Gulick. Brazil and Argentina, hardly stable democratic states, send only an insignificant number of military men to the Canal Zone, and even fewer to Fort Gulick (see table 3). On the other hand, the armies of the small Central American countries that are more directly under American control and lack high-level mili-

tary schools and a sophisticated system of defense send substantial contingents to the Canal Zone. However, there too it is
necessary to avoid a mechanistic conclusion. Even in Panama,
where between 1962 and 1970 more than half of the total membership of the National Guard was trained in the Canal Zone,
opposition to change and to social programs does not seem to
have been the dominant ideology among the military. The regime that was established in 1968 actually developed a socializing pragmatism whose slogans (*soldados, campesinos, machete y
fusil unidos*)[46] were not unanimously endorsed by the propertied classes. The specific history of the country, marked as it
is by the colonial scar called the Canal Zone, is important in that
evolution.

The ambiguity of the pro-U.S. indoctrination is even more
evident on the individual level. For one thing we know that
former students of religious schools are often the most virulent
anticlericals, and for another, at least in terms of brainwashing in
the clinical sense of the term, it is difficult to see how training
programs typically limited to four to forty weeks could profoundly modify the conduct and values of military men between
the ages of twenty-five and forty-five. To attribute their Manichean counterrevolutionary orientation exclusively to the influence of doctrines made in the United States is to demonstrate, if
not a lack of perspective, at least a tendency toward gross exaggeration. The Brazilian military have been officially anti-Bol-
shevik since 1935, the date of the abortive uprising directed
against military objectives that has now become a myth—the
intentona comunista, the annihilation of which is now commemo-
rated religiously every year by the armed forces. The Argentines
go back to the "tragic week" of 1919 as the basis for their
antirevolutionary obsession. The Pentagon was not involved. It
was also absent from the bloody repression of the Salvadoran
peasant uprising of 1932—called Communist by the dictator at
the time as a ruse rather than because of the real participation of
the Communist party—that ever since has justified the defense
of the interests of the oligarchy by the Salvadoran officers.[47]

We know that twelve of the fifteen generals and colonels in
Peru who initiated the nationalist revolution in 1968 went to
American schools. General Velasco Alvarado, the leader of that

military revolution—along with General Edgardo Mercado Jar-
rin, his foreign minister—was the primary defender of a policy
of national independence that did not respond to the desires of
the State Department and the Pentagon. We know the history
of the famous Guatemalan guerrilla leader who died in 1966 at
the age of twenty-four, "Commander" Turcios Lima. Before he
became head of the "Edgar Ibarra" Guerrilla Front, he was a
lieutenant in the Guatemalan army. Upon graduation from the
polytechnic school in 1959, he was sent in the same year to Fort
Benning, Georgia, to be trained as an antiguerrilla Ranger and
to take the marine infantry course. His participation in an uprising by junior officers in 1960 turned him into a Castroite revolutionary leader. How does one explain that conversion? He himself wrote in a letter to his mother, "It seems inexplicable that
someone like me who received such a reactionary education in
school, then studied for the priesthood and finally became a
military officer with good recommendations, should now adopt
a course such as this."[48] His supporters simply recall the poverty of his parents and his "great human sensitivity."

One of the few case studies that we possess arrives at
conclusions that are just as indecisive. John S. Fitch, working
with a small sample after the 1963 Ecuadorean coup against
President Carlos Arosemena, who had been denounced as a
Castro sympathizer by the United States, found that the proportion of officers who favored the overthrow of the president was
not greater among those who had been trained by the United
States than among those who had not. In addition, in discussing the political situation those who had been trained by the
United States did not give special emphasis to the "Communist
menace," as one might have expected.[49]

By way of hypothesis, one might assume that the military
who request or accept a training program in U.S. schools generally demonstrate a certain sympathy for that country. However, this U.S. training can stem from different, and even contradictory, motives: adhesion to extreme anti-Communism of
the McCarthyite variety, or admiration for the largest democracy in the world, the model for the constitutions of most of the
countries in the subcontinent. Those two ingredients can be
complementary or contradictory. The propaganda in the orien-

tation tours in the United States, and the gifts and brochures glorifying the American way of life have a limited impact: they are preaching to those already convinced. While one might observe that a great number of the military men involved in the overthrow of President Goulart in 1964 had been trained in the United States,[50] it should also be noted that most of the officers around General Castello Branco, who carried out the coup, had fought in World War II as members of the Brazilian expeditionary force in Italy alongside the American army.

The definition of the mission of the armies of the continent by the Pentagon aroused no more opposition on the part of the military than in the case of the Atlantic Alliance among the armies of Western Europe. In both cases, the alliance was more or less thoroughly discussed and accepted, and its objectives had unanimous support. The ideology of counterrevolution, sometimes developed as in Brazil as a genuine doctrine of national security, but most of the time rudely constructed, was not imposed from outside but was rather accepted, and even created, internally. United States military cooperation was consciously sought by the Latin American general staffs. Thus in 1962, with the aid of the U.S. Army, the Colombian military put into operation the Lasso Plan against the guerrillas without experiencing a spiritual crisis. And there are those who claim that the Chilean military hoped that the Camelot Plan, which woule be ordered by the Pentagon upon the advice of sociologists of the American University in Washington to "measure the potential for internal war," would be carried out; however, the scandal that was created when its existence was revealed did not permit its execution.[51]

While the hemispheric ideology of counterrevolutionary war and the quasi-dissolution of nationalist sentiment in favor of the concept of the defense of the West often weakened the nationalist reactions of the armed forces of the continent, the increasing Americanization of the armies also had unintended consequences that were greater and more varied than expected. The programs of military aid helped to reinforce the institutional confidence of the officers and to increase their consciousness that they possessed technical and organizational capacities that were superior to those of the civilians. In this respect the strictly professional and technical training programs acted to reinforce their counterrevolutionary ideological apprenticeship. Aid and loans, as well as the "demonstration effect" of a defense structure that benefited from a scientific defense system based on industrial production with advanced means of calculated destruction, frequently resulted in increased demands for arms purchases. Sometimes, as has been noted, the exposure during the training programs to the life-style of the American military produced a desire for a higher standard of living among the leaders of the most backward armies. This was the case, according to Richard Adams, of the military of Guatemala who received training in the Canal Zone where they received salaries during the programs there that were much superior to those in Guatemala.[52] The new aspirations of the officers, once they return, motivate them to find additional sources of revenue, whether by combining a civilian position with that in the military, or going into private life. This explains why there are so many businessmen-officers, and especially officers who are large landholders in the areas that are being developed by the state. The financial gap is also related to military involvement in business in several other countries in which an army that has been heavily influenced by the United States (especially Bolivia) clings to power in a spectacular fashion.

However, at the present time such subordination to the United States can be a two-edged sword. Given the policing role that is assigned to the military by the Pentagon in the name of internal security, a sentiment of frustration has emerged in certain armies. In fact, from the redefinition of hemispheric security until the presidency of Reagan—with only a few exceptions under Nixon and Ford—all American governments since 1962 have only been willing to sell the Latin Americans light arms and vehicles that can be used for limited operations to maintain order. The United States refuses to sell the classic heavy weapons—and it is supported in this by Congress and public opinion—because these can be used, in their view, to upset the Pax Americana and to weaken the rear areas.

This is why the Peruvian army, which felt itself underequipped in 1965 when it faced Castroite guerrillas, was unhappy, given its role in national life and its self-image, to be assigned subordinate functions in the "inter-American military division of labor." This policy produced a certain resentment of the United States, since, according to certain reports, it had even refused to deliver napalm to Peru for use against the guerrillas for fear that it might be used against a neighboring country. It is reasonable to suppose that, following this refusal of the United States and its subsequent insistence on attaching conditions to the provision of arms, the decision of the Peruvian general staff to go to Europe to obtain modern arms was the first step in a policy of nationalist self-assertion and military-directed development.[53] Paradoxically, besides the fact that Peru thus broke with a single source of arms, the purchase of the advanced weapons turned the army's attention away from internal security problems and helped to weaken the antisubversive obsession that had led it to identify its military objectives with the preservation of the status quo.

Under very different conditions in Argentina, with a military regime that was completely pro-American, the technical inadequacy of the U.S. military aid and its humiliating strategic-ideological content led the leaders of the general staff in 1969 to move away from the Pentagon. The provision of materiel that was often in bad condition; the control of the type and use of armament by its provider; the desire to transform the Latin American armies—even the most technologically advanced—into colonial police equipped for counterguerrilla warfare but lacking any sophisticated weapons, were also reasons for Argentine irritation with the United States programs of military assistance. As a result of these considerations Argentina also went to Europe for military equipment.

The Argentine problems began in 1967, when the cavalry, the pride of a regime whose president was a cavalry general, decided to replace its twenty-year-old Sherman tanks. Since the United States did not seem to be in a hurry to deliver Walker-Bulldog M-41 light tanks, a mission made up of members of the general staff went to Europe and made contact with the Schneider Company in France in order to buy sixty AMX 13s and later to have French arms manufactured under license in Argentina. This policy (Plan Europe) was aimed at giving Argentina freedom to buy modern arms and to break the American monopoly by developing a national armament industry.[54] Thus the two great powers of South America, Argentina and Brazil, have become important arms producers today. At the beginning of 1977, when the Carter administration wanted to demonstrate—in a maladroit fashion—its repudiation of the human rights situation in the two nations by reducing military aid, both countries immediately abrogated the military aid agreements that linked them to the United States, which they no longer needed. *Fabricaciones Militares* in Argentina and IMBEL in Brazil, thanks to their own technology or their European licenses, produce enough for national needs and for export, and in fact have developed a mass production system. We know that certain armies of the Old World have been equipped with Brazilian Xavantes planes and that Cascavel and Urutu armored cars that were sold to Iraq were used in the Iranian conflict in September 1980.[55] However, that military independence has not changed the political orientation of the military in the two countries, any more than orders for Soviet materiel placed by the Peruvian army under Velasco Alvarado altered the antireformist conservatism of General Morales Bermudez, who overthrew him in 1975.

The political reversal of military dependence can sometimes also result from excessive involvement. In Bolivia at the end of the 1960s, the obvious presence of American military advisers had something to do with the reinforcement of the nationalist sector of the army that involved the country in a progressivist military experiment in 1969. The discovery of the guerrillas in the first months of 1967 and the unusual interest paid to them by the security services of the United States because of the presumed presence of the famous *guerrillero*, Ernesto Guevara, was a cause of some discontent among the Bolivian officers. Forgetting, first that American aid permitted a rapid reorganization of the Bolivian armed forces that had been reduced to skeleton size by the purges following the 1952 revolution, and also that Bolivia was among the Latin American nations whose military expenses were most dependent on the United States,[56] the Bolivian officers were irritated—even wounded in their professional pride—by the involvement of foreign officers in operations that the national army felt it was quite capable of carrying out on its own.

The refusal to allow Bolivians to participate in a process of "military cooperation" of the Vietnam type was perhaps one factor in the arrival of the short-lived revolutionary regime of General Juan José Torres.

GLOBAL DEPENDENCE AND SECURITY

The obvious character of its military hegemony and the impulse to identify those who were responsible for its establishment have no doubt led to an overestimation of the military component of the American control of the continent. Besides, it is logical that official spokesmen in the United States should periodically deplore the arms race in Latin America—especially whenever the Latin armies turn to foreign providers to secure sophisticated arms. In fact, Latin America is a continent with a relatively low level of armament—as indicated by the figures on military expenditures in table 6. If militarism is measured by the percentage of the gross national product (GNP) that goes to defense, the European states allocate more to their armies than do the Latin Americans. It is obvious to the United States that Latin America, just because it is so close to the United States (and to the SouthCom), is not a high-security zone that has to be heavily armed.

In addition, in view of the secondary importance of the U.S. military for its tutelary power, the dependence of the Latin American nations on the United States is general and varied, and cannot be reduced to its military component. The nations of Latin America are involved in a network of influence and concern that far exceeds the operation of a military apparatus. There is no need to believe, moreover, that Wall Street, the Pentagon, and the White House always and everywhere present a monolithic front, for there is no doubt that it is in Latin America that the contradictions of North American policy have been most evident. Did not Kennedy's Alliance for Progress insist on the establishment of democratic reformist regimes at the very same time that military aid was educating the armies in counterrevolution?

The American omnipresence, the often-institutionalized ex-

TABLE 6
MILITARY EXPENDITURES AND NATIONAL ECONOMIES

	Per capita military expenditure (dollars)	Military expenditure as percentage of GNP	
	1969	1966	1969
United States	393	8.5	8.6
Soviet Union	164	8.9	8.5
Czechoslovakia	109	5.7	5.6
Great Britain	100	5.6	5.1
France	123	5.0	4.4
Greece	47	3.7	5.1
Portugal	35	6.3	6.1
Turkey	35	4.3	4.6
Sweden	138	4.2	4.0
Algeria	13	3.9	5.8
Iraq	32	10.5	10.0
Israel	400	23.3	25.1
Egypt	25	11.1	13.3
Burma	4	6.4	4.7
North Vietnam	—	—	21.3
South Vietnam	25	7.7	13.6
Nigeria	5	1.5	5.9
Argentina	18	1.5	2.6
Brazil	6	2.2	2.6
Chile	—	1.9	1.7
Colombia	6	2.0	2.0
Cuba	33	7.2	6.1
Mexico	—	.7	
Peru	12	2.6	3.2
Venezuela	—	2.2	—

Source: *The Military Balance* (London: Institute of Strategic Studies, 1970).

pression of its interests and decisions, invites one to place the military factor in a relative context. In these penetrated economies with bourgeoisies that are largely associated with American partners it is no doubt excessive to use the expression of the Dominican former president Juan Bosch, "Pentagonism is a substitute for imperialism."[57] The means of economic pressure available to the United States against unfriendly regimes are many and well-known, as is demonstrated by the pressures placed on Cuba after 1960 or the quarantine that choked the Popular Unity regime in Chile. The panoply goes from the suspension of economic aid in cases of the expropriation of American goods without "adequate compensation" (the Hickenlooper Amendment) to the suspension of imports and exports, including replacement parts for American industrial machinery and even cultural items.[58]

American interference in Latin American affairs has taken many forms, including selective economic aid to opposition elements, as was the case in Brazil, where the anti-Goulart governors received American aid that had been refused to Brasilia. More discrete assistance to the opposition forces was also provided in Brazil and in Chile under Allende, in the form of substantial support for the election of "good" candidates, not to mention the direct and often gross intervention of ambassadors such as Spruille Braden in Argentina at the beginning of the Peronist period, Ralph Dungan under Frei (1964–67)[59] and Edward Korry under Allende in Chile, and Lincoln Gordon under Goulart in Brazil. To be complete we should also add the omnipresent (and rarely effective) Central Intelligence Agency (CIA), some of the secrets of which have been revealed by Philip Agee. In that area it is clear that cooptation of the openly anti-Communist and pro-American military is less effective than the control of the trade union elements of the radical left by "the Company," such as took place in Ecuador before 1963.[60] Why speak of the armies as the only repository of United States ideology when we know that at least one Bolivian interior minister has confessed to being in a confidential relationship with "the Agency" (before becoming a correspondent of the Cuban government) and that there are strong presumptions that one foreign minister of the Pinochet government in Chile had been in the hire of the CIA.[61] In addition, the same suspicions were raised concerning a former president of Venezuela and his Mexican counterpart who both (despite this) were characterized by rather nationalist policies. To place the role of American military influence in its proper context it is necessary to recall how widespread is its ideological hold. How important in fact is the psychological orchestration carried out among the military by the United States in comparison with films, television, the press, and advertising that continually transmit everywhere the values of the American way of life?

This discussion is aimed at placing things in their proper

perspective, not reducing reality to easy ideological or philosophical schemes. That since 1945 the United States has tried to create a reserve force out of the Latin American armies in the service of its long-range interests—and not only its strategic interests—is evident. However, that military relay policy is not sufficient to explain contemporary militarism. Conspiratorial history reveals only the prejudice of those who engage in it. Neither the "hand of the foreigner" nor "revolutionary agents" who have come from outside achieve anything if the terrain is not ready. Neither the U.S. naval squadron near Rio de Janeiro in March 1964 nor the supposed U.S. plane over la Moneda on September 11, 1973, accounts for the fall of João Goulart or the overthrow of Allende. Rare are the armies that passively obey the commands of Washington, even in the protectorates of the Caribbean. As internal actors with specific corporate interests, the armies respond above all to a social dynamic in which external dependence is a conditioning, but not an explanatory element.

Part II

6

PRAETORIAN GUARDS AND THE PATRIMONIAL STATE

As we have seen, the dictator-generals of the nineteenth century in Latin America were rarely professional military men. We use the Latin American term "caudillo" for them, but it is more accurate to call them "political entrepreneurs" who made use of a variety of means—most often force, but also ideology—to further their enterprise of enrichment and personal power. The government belongs to the one who can seize control. The state is available for the taking because there is no state. The daring *hacendado* transforms his peons into soldiers, and distributes Mauser rifles instead of pickaxes; "he harvests wheat in time of peace, gathers in men in time of war."[1] A partisan chieftain calls himself "general" and if he is lucky he becomes one of the heavy-handed patriarchs whose picturesque tales loom large in the history of the continent.

In Venezuela in the twentieth century, "General" Juan Vicente Gomez waited for the right moment to seize power from his comrade Cipriano Castro after serving as his faithful second in command, and allowed the petroleum whirlwind to modernize the country and the state. This precocious native of the Andes administered his family's hacienda in Tachira on the Colombian frontier at the age of fifteen. He distrusted the army and only reluctantly accepted the foreign military missions, which he played off against each other. He seems to have

believed—correctly—that educated officers and semiautono-
mous institutionalized armed forces were in contradiction to his
rude personal style of government. Men who had a little bit of
power and owed him nothing were potentially dangerous. He
knew so well who his adversaries were that with the help of
petroleum he died in his bed in 1935 after twenty-seven years
as dictator.

However, the confusion, or least the customary identification, of dictators with generals does not come only from the fact
that civilian despots in the tropics don gold braid. It is true that
repressive and narrowly personalized tyrannies have used the
army as their instruments, and its officers have been their principal beneficiaries. The military pronunciamento has become a
modernized form of political entrepreneurship. The professionalization and bureaucratization of the army have made personal
uprisings more and more difficult, but nevertheless the coup
has made a deep impression on the collective memory. In addition a military neocaudillismo has appeared in certain national
and organizational circumstances, the analysis of which is helpful in comprehending the nature of military power.

We also tend to identify dictators with generals in the
apparently disorganized state of the politics of the continent
because there is no fundamental difference between the governing style of the caudillos in uniform and that of their civilian counterparts. The institutional element is almost absent in
a number of cases in the nineteenth century in which the
general-presidents seem to have deliberately ignored the impersonal objective norms that govern the functioning of the
civilian and military bureaucracies. Among the most flamboyant and baroque dictatorships were those that permitted the
accession to power through a coup by an officer who had
grown old in the military service. General Hernández Martínez in El Salvador and General Ubico in Guatemala in no way
yield to their nonmilitary colleagues in neighboring countries
or earlier regimes. The Salvadoran general who was responsible for the massacre of some thirty thousand peasants in 1932
governed that tiny republic of the Central American isthmus
from 1931 to 1944 to the profit of the large landholders, and

made notable contributions to the "unknown mythology of Central American tyranny."[2] Not sparing those who opposed him, this convinced theosophist claimed that in fact it was more criminal to kill an ant than a man, since the man could become reincarnated. At the time that Roosevelt was giving his fireside chats on the goals of the New Deal, this magician general initiated radio programs on spiritualism in which he responded personally to the questions of the listeners concerning the transmigration of souls and miraculous cures for all ailments.

We do not intend to focus on these more or less extreme examples of political despotism, nor are we trying to single out the most "uncivilized" tyrants in this century. However, we would like to use some of the more recent and politically significant examples to examine a certain type of authoritarianism. In a word, we seek to understand how the armed forces can support personal, and even family, dictatorships and the degree to which one can describe patrimonial tyrannies as military regimes. What are their real relations with the army? How do such dictatorships maintain themselves after having been established? What is the role of the military factor and of other power resources under their control? What is the degree of loyalty that the armed forces have to them, and how is their reliability assured? If the nation's military have become the praetorian guard of a despot, what are the causes of that transformation and what appear to be its limits?

We begin obviously with an analysis of the "Sultanates" of the Caribbean where archetypal tyrannies—some of which have only recently ended—arose within the guards or the "apolitical and nonpartisan" armies established by the American marines in the course of de facto protectorates. The Somoza dynasty in Nicaragua, the Trujillo despotism in the Dominican Republic, and the authoritarian presidencies of Batista in Cuba nevertheless possess relatively distinct characteristics and very specific military components. We will then see how certain personalist authoritarian regimes in South America illustrate the particular mechanisms of power characteristic of governments in which the army is strongly statist in orientation.

Nicaragua: The Dynasty and Its Guardians

Having recently become a politician in the Liberal party, Anastasio Somoza García—"Tacho" to his friends and protectors as well as to his enemies—became Jefe Director of the National Guard that had been set up by the Yankee occupier because he spoke English perfectly and knew how to please. Stimson, the representative of Calvin Coolidge in Nicaragua, described him as "open and friendly."[3] Tacho was, it is true, as jovial and optimistic as his son and successor, "Tachito," was sinister and irritable. As for the son, he was a genuine military man, having graduated from West Point. One of his enemies said of him, "Khaki is like a second skin for him."[4] In contrast, Tacho, the first Somoza, was an authentic civilian. When he received the command of the guard, the only activity of that substitute force was to hunt down the *libertador* Sandino, an action in which the first Somoza did not participate. Nevertheless, it was Sandino and the Sandinista menace that allowed him to assure himself the loyalty of that new army. With consummate ability Somoza was able to utilize the fear of the "general of free men" to unite that inglorious force behind him. And if—no doubt because of the pressure from his officers who feared the revenge of the head of the "crazy little army,"—he agreed to the traitorous assassination of Sandino without being aware of how unpopular that act would be for his future political career, it was no doubt because he understood that with the murder of the hero he signed a veritable blood pact with his officers and with the guard as a whole. By 1936 the way to power was open to him; his control of the guard was total, thanks especially to his enemies who denounced his crime and his ambition and identified him completely with his men. President Juan B. Sacasa, a relative of Somoza's by marriage, became involved in a veritable contest with the "Jefe Director" with the National Guard as the prize. The president tried in vain to control the guard as mandated by the constitution, while Somoza took pains to deflect and undermine him by placing reliable men in all the command positions.

The result of that confrontation was that Somoza, after removing Sacasa by a judicious use of force, became the only candidate in presidential elections that were supervised by the National Guard. He won the election despite the desperate appeals of the former president and his political allies to the American authorities, who nevertheless allowed the election to take place. The Department of State and the War Department had such confidence in their creature that they were not upset by the fascist-style populism that the candidate exhibited during his campaign. As paramilitary "blue shirts" raised their fists in the streets of Managua, the *Somocista* campaign speeches were happy to compare the Jefe Director to Hitler or Mussolini.[5] Rare, however, were the American diplomats such as Bliss Lane, who understood that the National Guard was not the apolitical gendarmerie that they had imagined, but rather an "American-Nicaraguan hybrid" that would henceforth constitute one of the "principal obstacles to the progress of Nicaragua."[6]

Thus the longest-ruling Latin American dictatorship was born. (The Somoza family reigned over the country for no less than forty-three years, from 1936 until 1979.) The death of the dictator, assassinated by an opponent in 1956, did not produce the end of the dictatorship; his oldest son, Luis, took over his father's responsibilities, with the aid of his brother, Anastasio (Tachito), who commanded the guard and then assumed supreme power in his turn until he was overthrown by the Sandinista insurrection—not without the hope that his son, an officer of the guard, would take over the family business. Thus, it is a family dynasty that we are discussing, and not politics in the modern sense.

The first Somoza, the founder of the dynasty, belonged to a middle-class family and inherited a badly managed coffee plantation. He himself had made his living in different ways, including as a used car salesman in the United States, as an inspector of public latrines (for the Rockefeller Foundation), and as a coffee grower. It was also said that he had tried his luck at gambling and at counterfeiting American currency.[7] In any case, his fortune was established in 1956 at some $60 million, and the family appeared to be the largest landholder in the country: 51 cattle-raising ranches and 46 coffee plantations belonged to him, as well as properties in nearby countries such as neighboring Costa

Rica and as far away as Mexico, not to mention 48 properties in Managua. It was rumored that 10 percent of the arable land in Nicaragua belonged to him and his industrial interests were already very diversified. The heirs of the first Somoza did not let the family empire decline. It is estimated that the Somoza fortune in 1979 was between $500 and 600 million and included a fifth of the cultivatable land in the country, the 26 largest industrial companies, and interests in 120 corporations. With the 8 biggest cane plantations in the country and several refineries, the Somozas were the largest producers of sugar and had a monopoly on alcohol; they had partial control of bananas, meat, salt, vegetable oils, and a monopoly on pasteurized milk. The Somozas, for whom there was no such thing as a small profit, were also the representatives of Mercedes and other European automobile companies in their fiefdom; they owned the only national air line (LANICA), the shipping companies, and had major shares in the textile and cement industries. Their holdings were in the hands of a bank that belonged to them and they controlled a savings and loan company that was concerned with building construction (CAPSA).[8] This list is incomplete. We should emphasize that the precise and full extent of the business of the clan is not known and note that certain American business groups frequently worked with the family companies. United Fruit and the eccentric billionaire Howard Hughes were often associated with the Somoza enterprises. However, one should add that because of the Somocista domination, many foreign countries preferred to invest in Nicaragua's neighbors.

More interesting, no doubt, are the methods used to acquire these riches. It is evident that it was not unremitting labor and savings that made it possible, but rather extortion, racketeering, violence, and fraud of all kinds. The origin of the family's control of national wealth was to be found in contraband in gold and imported products, the purchase at a low price of herds that had already been endangered, or of enterprises that had been put into financial difficulty by the government or by political friends of the dictator. Intimidation and bureaucratic or physical harassment evidently played a considerable role in the amassing of the family fortune. The first Somoza also had the custom of collecting personal commissions on foreign trade and on less respectable activities: gambling, prostitution, and smuggling. The war permitted him to seize the properties of German citizens, providing the initial nucleus of his landholdings.

In addition, the weakness of capitalist development in Nicaragua facilitated the control of Somoza. It was the state or its functional equivalent that, in a period when statism did not yet have a bad name, replaced a deficient private sector in the areas of banking and public services. Electricity, hospitals, railroads, and water companies were state companies in which the clan took care to place near or distant relatives, thus furthering the business interests of the group by putting public enterprises at the service of the private interests of the dictatorship. This confusion between the state and the interests of the family gave a certain foundation to the humorous claim of the last Somoza that since the time of his father Nicaragua had been "a socialist state."[9] In fact it was precisely the insatiable cupidity of the Somocista dynasty that produced its defeat.

The cotton boom in the 1950s and later the industrial opportunities provided by the Central American Common Market resulted in the formation of a local bourgeoisie that constituted several large groups, posing a threat to the clan.[10] Their relations with the hydra-headed Somoza enterprises deteriorated rapidly after Tachito came to power in 1967. The bourgeoisie did not appreciate the special privileges that the Somoza businesses enjoyed or the brutal and unscrupulous "dynamism" that limited their own development. The dynasty's administration of the international aid that was given to the country after the 1972 earthquake increased that separation. Rather than dividing the bonanza and aiding private groups in difficulty, Somoza took total control of the aid and diverted the funds for his own profit, thus allowing the rewards of international solidarity to be pillaged by his friends and concealing the corruption imposed on his people. From then on the bourgeoisie joined the opposition; the dynasty no longer guaranteed the overall interests of the propertied classes. Despite its traditional capacity to maneuver, the family became isolated due to its excessive voraciousness and thus gave the Sandinista insurgents the leverage they needed to emerge from their marginal situation.

If the first Somoza had had some justification for saying,

"L'état, c'est moi," his personal control over the National Guard was not an inevitable result of the weakness of the organization of the Nicaraguan state. In fact the loyalty of the guard was assured by various factors that often had little to do with the military ethic. In the first place, ever since the assassination of Sandino had produced the image of the guard as a repressive and illegitimate body in national terms, the military forces and Somoza had locked themselves into a situation of reciprocal guarantees for mutual benefit. In addition, two sources of the guard's loyalty lay in its paternalism and the corruption of the officers. That army, so little statist and lacking in tradition, supported the family's power because the leadership enjoyed their privileges and benefited from the enrichment of the dynasty. There is no need to recall that since the time of the first Jefe Director family members were always at the top of the chain of command, and the Somozas never gave the direct and indirect control of the army to others. Tachito, son of the founder, did his military studies at West Point and it could be said that he was the only cadet to receive an army as a graduation present. Once he became dictator, his half-brother, José, supervised the guard command directly, while his son, Tachito II, a graduate of American schools who had been promoted to the rank of captain for "services rendered to the country" after the 1972 earthquake, commanded the elite antiguerrilla troops.

Beginning in 1967, the year when the last Somoza actually became president, the government appeared to be simply an extension of the army. The dictatorship, faced with internal and external difficulties, became militarized, but in its own special way. As a symbol of the times, the presidential palace, which was perched on the Tiscapa Hill, became a barracks of the guard overlooking Managua in a quasi-feudal manner. The government, the army, and the family became one. Private apartments, offices, and military encampments revealed the nature of power. While denunciations and mutual espionage were abundantly utilized to prevent military conspiracies, loyalty depended on extrainstitutional factors. The Somoza who directed the guard acted more as a "godfather" than the head of the general staff. The army that was also the police force and administered the customs, borders, and prisons saw its functions multiply in the course of the years. In addition, all the commands had additional revenues that the dictator ignored. Appointments to the most lucrative posts and illegal revenues completely out of line with modest officers' salaries were common within the guard, depending on the loyalty and servility of the officers. The military command of each city had its price. The commander of Chinandega was required to collect some $20,000 a month for the protection of bars, night clubs, gambling halls, gun permits, and various violations and fines.[11] The head of the immigration service could make four times as much, as could the head of the central police services, a post with good connections. The officers on active service rapidly became millionaires in cordobas and in dollars—thanks to these semiofficial sources of income that were known to all. Since the dictator was able at any point to retire an officer into the reserve, the corps' economic situation was a direct function of their support for the clan. Similarly, once in retirement loyal officers could benefit from civil positions with revenues equal to those that they had had in the military. The businesses of the dynasty and the public corporations swarmed with retired senior officers who, although without particular competence, occupied the high-level positions. One observer remarked a few days before the fall of the regime that half the members of the board of directors of the national bank were retired officers, "whose knowledge of banking would no doubt fit on the head of a pin."[12]

This complex network of military and bureaucratic factors, of economic interest and pure and simple gangsterism, all stimulated and controlled by the government, appeared to be one of the foundations of the Somoza system. The soldiers, a majority of them only semiliterate, were the first victims of the corruption of the officers: they were badly clothed and fed as a result of the "commissions" collected by their officers. An officer who deserted from the guard claims that they also had inferior military supplies because of kickbacks to those responsible for military purchases.[13] However, for the troops military paternalism took the place of equity and served to reinforce group loyalty. During the last campaigns against the Sandinistas, the boots worn by the guard fell apart in the first rainstorm. Somoza's son, Tachito II, as a captain, distributed new jungle boots made in the United States as a Christmas present! The Somozas knew the private and family problems of the soldiers, and on their part they could ask for personal assistance in case of need. There was nothing less bureaucratic and impersonal. These soldiers were assured that Somoza "would not let them down." Enlisted men and low-level officers had easy access to the services of the presidential "bunker" and to the head of the clan in violation of military hierarchy and etiquette, because they were assigned to spy on their superiors. Institutional orders or rules had no binding power over the president. The hierarchy that counted was not that of seniority and merit, but the links between the men and the person of the dictator and his family. Officers and politicians responded by denouncing the violations of the principles of discipline. This apparently "military" dictatorship thus demilitarized the army by corrupting it and by violating the hierarchical chain of command. The Nicaraguan National Guard was not an army like the others.

Still, it would be wrong to believe because of the bloody and indiscriminate repression that accompanied the last days of the regime in 1979 that the reign of the Somozas was only maintained by the terror imposed by the praetorian guards. Whereas it is clear that the dictatorship resorted to a high level of violence, it is not likely that one could terrorize a whole people for nearly forty-five years, and besides, repression alone does not explain why the dynasty was able to survive the death of the tyrant who created the system. This is true even though in 1956, after the assassination of the elder Somoza, the wave of repression that followed was particularly intense in order to discourage any hint of opposition. It was at this time that the patrimonial character of the system appeared most crudely. Not only did the two sons of the dictator carry out military repression, but the jails in the presidential palace were filled with distinguished prisoners who were subjected to torture in long interrogation sessions in which Tacho II, the chief of the guard, personally participated.[14] It can be said that official political violence never ceased from the time of the electoral campaign of 1967 in which the Somoza candidate (Anastasio Somoza Debayle, still in power in 1979) won a highly disputed election thanks to fraud and the utilization of paramilitary groups to massacre demonstrators who favored his opponent.

In fact, the dynasty made use of other political resources. The astuteness of the first Somoza undoubtedly played a role,[15] but specifically political and social methods should be mentioned. Despite his common origins and his seizure of power, the elder Somoza acquired a certain social legitimacy within the Nicaraguan ruling class by marriage. He was related in that way to the Debayle and Sacasa families, that is, to the Liberal oligarchy. In these societies, where patronage plays an important role, this was a valuable asset. Those under obligation to, or unconditional supporters of, the Debayle family thus supported the dictatorship for reasons that had little to do with its politics. In addition, the dictatorship knew how to utilize the traditional two-party system. Somoza, when he took control of the Liberal party with which he was allied politically and socially, acquired a network of followers and political control that was parallel to that of the army. Paradoxically, the fact that the Conservative party, the enemy of the Liberals, had been closely linked to the United States since Díaz helped to undermine the credibility of the opposition. That weakness, as well as the characteristics of the national ruling class, helped to produce a number of arrangements between the opposition and the dictatorship that periodically legitimized the power of Somoza. Indeed, the regime maintained a façade of constitutionality that was carefully preserved despite some problems of adjustment when the political course followed by the family was particularly irregular.

The first Somoza, who was assassinated while distributing free drinks during a workers' club festival in León, knew how to play the populist role in order to stay in power. After receiving the unexpected support of the Communist party at the end of the Second World War, after he had aligned his country docilely with the United States, Tacho overcame the serious postwar crisis that was fatal to his neighbors, Ubico and Hernández Martínez, by adopting social welfare measures that divided his opposition. At that time the government created official trade unions and decreed a very advanced labor code that was to be applied in particular to the enterprises owned by opponents of the regime.

Nevertheless, under pressure from the United States, Somoza decided to hand over power in 1947. Argüello, his carefully chosen successor, was removed four weeks later when the new president indicated that he wished to free himself of the control of his predecessor—who still commanded the guard. Argüello's puppet successor lasted three months, at which point Tacho changed the constitution and "elected" his uncle, Victor Román Reyes, who remained as president until his death in 1950. Tired of these maneuvers, the dictator again changed the constitution and had himself elected for six years by the Congress after an agreement with the Conservative party. At his death, Luis, who seemed to have some ability for politics, was elected president. When Luis died in 1963 it seems that American pressure—under the Kennedy administration in the period of the Alliance for Progress—prevented Tachito from ascending the throne in his turn. A confederate, René Schick, occupied the presidency. Schick tried to broaden the base of the family's power, bringing the country a period of liberalization. Waiting no longer, the impetuous general who had been the favorite son, it was said, of the assassinated patriarch, had himself elected president in 1967. Although he had fewer votes than his Conservative opponent, partisan vote-counters were sufficient under the Somozas to reverse the results.[16] In 1970 a new agreement with the Conservatives restored the facade of democracy to the system. Somoza was replaced by a provisional triumvirate without power until the December 1972 earthquake that led the general to place himself patriotically at the head of the National Disaster Committee and to use that occasion to achieve total power.

Everyone was aware of how much the clan owed to the United States. Tachito, after he was let down by his protector in 1978, said much about the services he had rendered in return for U.S. favor. Yet we should not believe that the successive dictators were puppets in the hands of the United States or simple instruments for its purposes. If this had been the case there is no doubt that a military coup d'état at the appropriate time would have deposed the unattractive U.S. partner. In fact, Somoza and the Somozas knew how to make use of the United States to maintain their power and to disarm their internal and external enemies. Besides, since relations with the great protector were a decisive political resource, the family itself made sure of the diplomatic representation in Washington. Ambassador Sevilla Sacasa, the son-in-law of Tacho and brother-in-law of Tachito, remained as the representative to the authorities of the metropole for practically the entire duration of the dynasty, and even became the dean of the diplomatic corps in Washington. In addition, to further defend their interests the Somozas maintained a lobby in Washington that was, however, more costly than effective. In 1975 the general spent an official figure of $500,000 to retain the favor of the Americans.[17] A former congressman from Florida, N. Cramer, and the former secretary of the navy, Fred Korth, were his principal lawyers, while representatives John Murphy of New York and Charles Wilson of Texas could secure the support, when necessary, of several dozen members of Congress. The United States ambassadors, far from acting as proconsuls in Managua, often appeared to be employees or business partners of the clan that they defended at the Department of State. The famous Ambassador Whelan, "Tom" to his friend, Tacho, and a "real father" in the words of Tachito, through his unconditional support for the dictatorship acted to undermine the Good Neighbor Policy of F. D. Roosevelt. More recently, Turner Shelton, ambassador to Managua under Nixon, gave unlimited support to the Somozas in open disagreement with the more prudent analyses of the State Department and the White House.[18]

The hereditary dictatorship of the Somozas thus seems to demonstrate more the structure and conduct of the Cosa Nostra in Sicily or New York than the values and mentality of the military. It is not without significance, however, that a certain type of armed force was able to produce this kind of regime and that it was not the only one of its kind.

THE DOMINICAN REPUBLIC: THE GENERALISSIMO AND THE LAW OF THE "PRIME COMBATANT"

The arrival in power of Rafael Leónidas Trujillo, head of the Dominican army thanks to the U.S. Marine Corps, was not very different in fact from that of Somoza. In the exercise of power he also acted in ways that were strangely parallel. Head of a clan and an entrepreneur, he too relied for support on the army from which he had come, and his regime was marked by the most obvious gangsterism. Having risen very rapidly from within to the head of the army created by the United States, Trujillo ran for the presidency and was elected in 1930 without opposition after a campaign of terror carried out by paramilitary groups that supported him. From that time on a single caudillo was to replace the many unstable caudillos of the period before the American occupation. Like them, the generalissimo had his own private army, but this time it was the national army.

Again like Somoza, Trujillo took pains to respect a certain constitutional legality, yielding the presidency to straw men and loyal servants. In 1938 Jacinto Peynado succeeded him and Manuel Troncoso completed Peynado's term after his death. Following a new direct election in 1942, Trujillo named his brother Hector to the presidency for a ten-year term. When he resigned in 1960 he was replaced by Joaquín Balaguer, a faithful follower who owed everything to him. When Trujillo retired from civilian power, he retained control of the military. He served as minister of war under Troncoso, and had himself named commander in chief of the armed forces by his brother in 1952.

Also like the Somozas, Trujillo had a sense of family and the upper ranks of the army were filled with his relatives, many of whom were picturesque if not eccentric. Among his brothers, Hector was chief of the general staff and minister of war, Aníbal was also chief of staff, Virgilio carried out the sensitive functions of minister of the interior, and Arismendi was divisional general. His brothers-in-law José García and José Román Fernandez, and his nephews José García Trujillo and Virgilio Garciá Trujillo, were generals or superior officers and held important commands. As to his sons, one can say that they were officers from birth. Rhadames was an honorary commander at the time when children play games, and the future playboy, Ramfis, was a brigadier general at nine years of age.[19] There were several dozen relatives of the Trujillo family in the upper ranks of the army.

The control of "the Benefactor" over the Dominican economy was no less complete than that of the Somoza clan on Nicaragua. Estimates suggest that Trujillo owned 50 percent of the arable land, and 119 enterprises representing 80 percent of the business capital of the capital city, renamed Ciudad Trujillo. It is necessary to allow for partisan exaggeration for argument's sake. But even allowing for overestimates on the part of his opponents, it is certain that Trujillo had a monopoly of the tobacco business (a state enterprise, but where does the state begin and the businesses of Trujillo end?), of pasteurized milk, a quasi-monopoly in sugar, and majority interests in two shipping companies. He had his own bank, and supervised the importation of pharmaceutical products. Around 1960, when the per capita income of the Dominican Republic was about $200 per person, the family fortune was estimated at between $500 and $800 million. Some observers have argued that this overwhelming domination of the national economy by Trujillo was an important means of political control. According to them, 70–75 percent of the salaried population worked in companies that were either owned by the state or by the Trujillo trust, and were thus at his mercy. The dictator could thus deprive any supposed opponent of his means of survival.[20]

The privileges enjoyed by the army for whom Trujillo was really, if not the "prime combatant" at least "the Benefactor," and the corruption of the superior officers guaranteed the loyalty of the military. The domination of the upper ranks of the officer corps by the family reinforced the isolation of the military who were despised by the traditional leading classes; the local aristocracy regarded the officers as collaborators and Trujillo as a parvenu with whom they did not wish to associate socially. The Caribbean tyrant thus lacked the social and political legitimacy of Somoza. Police forces, both secret and public, were well developed, as well as a number of paramilitary bodies.[21] In fact, the army was the creation of Trujillo and the opposition identified it with the despot. Trujillo's megalomania, his taste for large public works and gigantic infrastructure expenditures, did not displease the military, since they received their share. Nevertheless, the army was under a high degree of surveillance. He was not sure even of his brothers;

Virgilio and Arismendi, when they became too popular with the military or the police, were removed. Special inspectors spied on the barracks; and the army, which was organized for internal warfare against the opposition, was rigorously disarmed and its ammunition guarded in arsenals entrusted to reliable men. There were good reasons, it is true, for Trujillo to distrust his army.

Besides an impressive police apparatus and overwhelming domination of the economy, Trujillo had still other political resources at his disposal. The effectiveness of the cult of personality that he promoted among the inhabitants of Trujilloland (the capital and the highest point in the country bore his name) was dubious, as was the slogan, "Trujillo, you are our guiding star," and also the many titles of excellence bestowed on him by his adulators; however, the same was not true of nationalism. Trujillo used brutal methods and incessant propaganda to promote a feeling of national identity among inhabitants of the eastern half of the ancient island of Hispaniola against the mostly black and French-speaking citizens of the other half. For that purpose he did not hesitate to have fifteen thousand Haitian immigrants massacred in 1937. Clientelism in its modern and more traditional forms was also evident, not only among the elites, but also among the humble. The "loyalty days" organized by corporate groups were not only ritual obligations but also guaranteed Trujillo a certain audience of coopted leaders. Trujillo was also the godfather and patron of hundreds of children in the countryside whose families, by virtue of *compadrazgo*, felt under obligation to the dictator who also knew how to be generous to them on that occasion.

The existence of government trade unions from 1951 and an incipient single party that was actually an appendage of the patrimonial administration did not prevent this Caribbean version of oriental despotism from relying on the only coherent and permanent organization: the army. It was from within the army that the opponents came who on the night of 30 May 1961 were to assassinate the long-lasting tyrant. That assassination, which had the benefit of the technical collaboration of the CIA, was carried out by men close to Trujillo: businessmen, a senator and an ex-mayor of Ciudad Trujillo, generals and officers of the personal general staff of the dictator. Earlier there had been signs of discontent and agitation in the army, and especially in the air force because of its close relations with the United States. The assassination of Trujillo, around the time of the Bay of Pigs invasion that was supposed to put an end to the Castro regime, had the advantage in the eyes of the United States of maintaining an equal balance in the Caribbean between the two extremes, in accordance with the Kennedy policy. It is true that the activities of Trujillo in the region, notably the attempted assassination of the social democratic president of Venezuela, Romulo Betancourt, had led to sanctions by the Organization of American States, measures that were generally preliminaries to direct intervention by the United States.

The American political operation that had been almost too successful at the outset consisted in attempting to maintain "Trujillismo" without Trujillo, just as in 1979 Carter and his advisors tried in vain to establish a Somozaism without Somoza in Nicaragua. However, the election of a social democrat, Bosch, in 1963 produced a coup d'état by military elements loyal to the dictatorship who feared for their futures. This was followed by attempted countercoups by other sectors of the army and the landing of the marines in 1965. The intervention was ordered by Lyndon Johnson with the purpose of ending the civil war to the advantage of the pro-American forces and of a man who was a faithful follower of the United States after having been the same for Trujillo: Joaquín Balaguer. He had himself elected in 1966, was reelected fraudulently in 1970 and again in 1974, and would no doubt have succeeded in having himself reelected in 1978 with the support of the army, although the electoral verdict was unfavorable to him, if Washington, obsessed with democracy at that time, had not successfully threatened to take severe measures against such action. Had it not been for the intervention of the United States, Balaguer, the former minister of the dictator and Trujillo's vice president, was prepared to prolong the era of Trujillo in more "appropriate" forms—nearly twenty years after his death.

The army—divided in 1961 and torn apart in 1963 and 1965—was made up of strongly opposing tendencies: a neo-Trujilloist majority and a Castroite sector grouped around

Colonel Caamaño, the author of the 1965 uprising, who met his death after he landed on the Dominican coast in 1973. According to well-informed opinion,[22] the army created by the dictator still has no function other than politics today, and, being made up of "officer factions in competition for the spoils of power," is therefore little motivated by ideological consider- ations. They are military predators rather than military re- formers—as the about-face of the army chiefs between 1963 and 1965 proved—corresponding well with the nature of an army that antedated the state and was produced in the bosom of an unending tyranny.

CUBA: THE LAUGHTER OF THE SERGEANT

In Cuba, the American sugar viceroyalty and semiprotectorate, the army that had been established by the United States was related to power in a very different way. Late decolonization had at least the advantage of providing the country with a political class as a result of the war of independence against Spain. The army left by the marines was not the only coherent group. The legitimacy provided by the independence effort gave importance to, among others, the veterans of 1895. In addition, when the army was created in 1906 it was in the hands of the Liberal party—as in Nicaragua—which named its loyal members as the generals. This is how Cuba acquired its first strongman, who came close to putting himself in power for a long time. With "General" Gerardo Machado the army en- tered decisively into the political life of Cuba. This noted Liberal from Santa Clara, a former butcher and horse thief,[23] was named inspector-general of the army by President Gómez after the 1906 rebellion. After becoming a wealthy businessman— some say by acting as a front man for American companies—he was elected more or less honestly as president in 1924. His administration was characterized by great economic difficulties, but especially by its corruption and the suppression of civil liberties. Having promised the arrival of a golden age, Machado turned out to be a dictator who was inclined to assassinate his enemies, especially the leaders of the labor opposition. This disappointing president loved power, and despite his increasing unpopularity, convened a constituent assembly that re-elected him for six years in 1928. The establishment of the dicta-torship, coinciding with the Great Depression, produced a wave of social and political agitation in many forms that seemed likely to result in a revolution.

Machado responded to the popular demonstrations by es-tablishing repression and assassination as a veritable system of government. In 1929 he had the Communist leader, Juan Anto-nio Mella, assassinated. Between March 1930 and 1932, the left-dominated unions launched a series of strikes that were crushed; as a result, the university was closed, and the worker centers forbidden. The United States, where Roosevelt, who had just been elected, wished to change the country's Latin American policy, began to be disturbed by what appeared to be uncontrolla-ble revolutionary actions. The White House sent a mediator to find a moderate "Cuban-style" solution and to guarantee a peace-ful change of government. A high-level diplomat, Sumner Welles, was entrusted with this delicate proconsular mission. Welles, when faced with the terrorist actions of certain opposi-tion groups and the rebellion of Machado against his protector, seemed inclined toward military intervention by the United States. Roosevelt did not favor this. The negotiations with the parties undertaken by the mediator needed only the departure of the dictator to be concluded. Because of the imminence of a U.S. intervention against Machado, who was defying the Ameri-cans and appealing to the people against Washington, the army deposed him in August 1933.

The military under Machado had been the special beneficia-ries of the regime. The dictator gave them many civilian responsi-bilities, not hesitating to cite the army as an example for the whole Cuban administration. Defending himself against the charge that he was "militarizing the state" by placing military men in key posts in the civilian bureaucracy, Machado declared, "Supervision (by officers) of the administration does not repre-sent a regular practice of government but a need of the moment. One can even say that far from militarizing the administration, this has made clear the excellent civic qualities of our officers."[24] In this situation it is easy to understand that the army chiefs had an interest in avoiding an American intervention that would have placed them in an awkward position between their distant protector and their immediate benefactor. Machado's overthrow thus was a response to a need for corporate defense.

The ending of the *Machadato* in September 1933, far from pacifying the social climate, produced a quasi-revolutionary situation. The unions took more radical action under the leadership of the Communist party. A wave of occupations of sugar mills was accompanied by the establishment of worker councils. Soon the Bolshevik slogan, "All power to the workers and peasants, supported by the soldiers and sailors" was proclaimed by "revolutionary elements."[25] It was in this context—for corporate reasons, since there was a rumor that their wages were going to be cut—that the infantry noncommissioned officers rose up. Hostility and distrust of the officers that had been to the advantage of the earlier regime were not absent from the motives of the mutiny of Camp Columbia. At this point the leader of the sergeants, Fulgencio Batista, who was going to dominate public life for the next twenty-five years, appeared on the scene.

While the noncommissioned officers and the troops who supported them arrested the officers and a large number of them took refuge in a hotel in Havana where many American citizens, as well as their ambassador, were living, others, especially the younger officers observing the turn of events, hastened to support the uprising. The civilian revolutionary forces and the leaders of the opposition to the provisional government that had replaced Machado tried to give the sergeants' mutiny a political dimension that it did not have. A committee of five members (the Pentarquia) led by Ramón Grau San Martín, deposed the existing authorities with the support of the military in revolt: Students and university professors rushed to help the sergeants and their revolution. Grau San Martín assumed the presidency and formed a government that could not do less than promote Batista to the rank of colonel and give him command of an army that had been purged of a part of its officers and lacked a head. His mission was to name and put in place the officers needed for the proper functioning of the institution—which gave him enormous power.

Two questions arise immediately: Why did the officer corps collapse so completely as a result of the pressures of what was little more than a trade union demonstration? And, what was the extent of the transformation of the Cuban army which took place at that time? The breakup of the army leadership seems to have been due to many factors that are not unrelated to the later power of Batista. The upper levels of Machado's army was made up of officers who had risen from the ranks and had been promoted for political reasons. The educated younger officers were not promoted and had legitimate reasons for resentment, which explains why they rallied to the support of the revolutionaries. Nearly 56 percent of the officers under Machado had not graduated from the military academy and those who had received their diplomas between 1913 and 1915 were still only lieutenants in 1933, while those who began as enlisted men had had brilliant careers.[26] In addition to the absence of cohesion in the officer corps there were also social tensions in the military institutions. Since the period of the American occupation when the army was created, only Cubans of the white race had received officer's commissions. The continuation of this practice created a profound division between a white officer corps that came from the political class or was supported by it, and the noncommissioned officers who were for the most part of mixed blood. Batista himself was considered to be a mulatto in the socially accepted ethnic division of the time in Cuba. After the sergeants' revolt, a great number of Afro-Cubans became officers. According to the U.S. military attaché, the army was "darkened" considerably at that time, with blacks forming 40 percent of the total, and mulattoes 35 percent.

After the elimination of the officers who had tried to make a last stand at the Hotel Nacional the leadership of the army was completely reorganized: More than four thousand noncommissioned officers and some sixty civilians were named officers at all levels. These new officers, who were unconnected with the political and social elite, were totally lacking in the traditional power resources in Cuba; they could not claim that they were veterans of 1895, or members of the political oligarchy, or of the upper classes. Nor were they products of an autonomous military education. Before entering the army by choice or necessity they had been manual laborers, or unemployed. Batista, a sergeant stenographer in the army—which meant in terms of rank that he was semiliterate—had earlier been a cane cutter, a carpenter, and a railroad worker. If the ex-sergeant, quickly named general, used the army to take and keep power, he did this not as a military man, but as a civilian in uniform. Because he had black blood and favored the Afro-Cubans, Batista was to enjoy very great popularity that was not limited to the military. His personal charm as a *mulatto lindo,* which impressed the journalists, his contagious laughter and his captivating smile, would not have led one to predict at the time that this man of the people was a future dictator.[27] Thus a new military class was established. Paradoxically, this *Lumpenproletariat* in uniform, to use the words of Andrés Suarez, was the base of a government that was made up of revolutionary intellectuals.

This government was not to last long—a little more than a hundred days—during which Grau and his interior minister, the young and very popular Antonio Guiteras, who was supposed to be a Communist but was not, hastened to promulgate social reforms that were very advanced for Cuba (minimum wages for cane cutters, an eight-hour day). These policies produced an alliance of the traditional political forces with economic circles, as well as the increasing concern of the American administration. The reformist government was all the more certainly condemned because the parties of the left, especially the Communist party, were unceasingly attacking the, to them, lukewarm reformism of the Grau team.

The government of the United States, although urged to do so by the American interests in the island, refused to intervene. However, the wise diplomats of the Department of State understood all the while that it was possible to transform the newly reformed army that had emerged as the power behind the throne. When Grau fell and left the country in a state of anarchy and total instability, the head of the army, after brutally repressing the worker movement and the students in 1934, became the electoral decision maker with the consent of Washington. Under his aegis "do-nothing presidents" succeeded one another while the United States, following the new Roosevelt policy, abrogated the Platt Amendment that it had retained for possible use during the long crisis of 1933.

In addition to the discredited traditional parties, the new

anti-Machado groups (Ejercito del Caribe, ABC, OCRR, Joven Cuba), generally grouped around dramatic and violent figures such as Eduardo Chibás, appeared only as groups of uncontrollable activists who practised various forms of radical gangsterism at will. The army seemed to be the only institution that could both impose a certain order and strengthen the state. Still more, the new army, with its lower-class and ambitious leadership that was open to the advice coming from Washington was the only group that could put into place modernizing reforms that would limit the social atrophy from which Cuban society was suffering. In the absence of a party, therefore, the army under Batista was, in accordance with the objectives of U.S. policy, to play a modernizing role aimed at strengthening civil society that had been weakened by the neocolonial structure of the sugar economy.[28] In 1937 a plan for social and economic reconstruction was published called The Three Year Plan (nicknamed because of its ambitious and unrealistic character, the Three Hundred Year Plan) that was supposed to have been inspired by a team of researchers from the Rockefeller Foundation.[29] Its objectives were the improvement of the living conditions of the day workers in the sugar industry and especially the expansion of small property holdings and agricultural diversification. All his life Batista claimed to have been the author of this program of reforms that the army was charged with executing, at least in the social and educational areas.

Beginning in 1937, as had been the case under Machado, Cuba became militarized. A third of the national budget went to the army—or through it—to carry out the ambitious reform program. The head of the army created a kind of parallel government and established military cabinet posts that were in competition with the corresponding departments of the national government. Batista even organized a network of rural schools with sergeants as teachers that was run by the army. The process of modernization began with the military institution itself, which benefited from housing projects, recreation centers, hospitals, and orphanages for which there were no civilian equivalents. Everything seemed ready for the development of a military dictatorship—even the propaganda pointing to the exemplary role of the army.

Not the least of the paradoxes of the Batista era was the fact that this sergeant who aspired to be a dictator and acted like one, in fact from 1934 initiated the only period of representative democracy that the island had known, lasting until 1952, the date of his return to power. More flexible and more opportunistic than Somoza, this smiling army chief nicknamed by his enemies "Colonel Castor Oil" for the Mussolini-style treatment that he reserved for them, was a man who knew how to adjust to circumstances. Thus by small favors and able propaganda he took advantage of the Popular Front policy of the Third International to obtain the support of the Communist party that had a growing response in the labor movement. From 1938 he dealt with Blas Roca, the leader of the Communist party, and in 1939 with the help of the World War he favored the Confederacion de Trabajadores de Cuba—which was led by Lazaro Peña, a black tobacco worker, who was to carry out the same functions under Fidel Castro—over the other general labor organizations. Beginning in 1938, even before the entry of the USSR into the war, Batista was thus allied with both the United States and the Communists. Fortified by this support, he called a constitutional assembly in 1940 that adopted a socially advanced constitution, and then had himself elected president with the firm support of the Communist party, but also with that of the American interests and the agreement of nearly all social classes.[30]

As a civilian president Batista appointed two Communists to his government in 1942: Juan Marinello and the young Carlos Rafael Rodríguez. However, former comrades at arms who believed that the moment had come to receive the benefits of their loyal political actions gave him trouble. Faced with the attack of the ex-sergeants, now army chiefs, he made efforts, in fact, to demilitarize his regime and to give it a broader base. In 1944 he did not run for president and his candidate was beaten by Grau San Martín, despite the support of the Communists who regretted the departure, in their words, of the father of the Popular Front, "the idol of the people," and "the magnificent resource of Cuban democracy."[31] Batista may have declined to use fraud to win the election and govern through a frontman president as his neighbors did or as he himself had done in 1934 because he preferred for the moment to return to private life to enjoy in peace the fortune that he had amassed in power.

Grau succeeded him, but the revolutionary leader of 1934 became in 1944 a corrupt president. Partly because of economic difficulties the people longed for Batista, who was then living in the United States. Political gangsterism, which had been a distinctive feature of national life since Machado, developed in a disturbing manner. The politics of the university was also involved.[32] When Prio Socarras, the candidate of the Autentico party, succeeded Grau and followed the same practices as Machado, a flamboyant orator with a prophetic voice, Eduardo Chibás, head of the Ortodoxo party, electrified the middle classes with his denunciations of corruption and his attacks on the government before committing a quasi public suicide during a radio broadcast. It was in this deteriorating atmosphere as the 1952 elections were approaching that Batista prepared a coup d'état against Prio, who was suspected of being unwilling to give up power to the Ortodoxos who seemed likely to be the victors in the election.

Batista appeared as an alternative for the military and the lower classes. His democratic past seemed to augur well for his future actions. His initial intentions ("to deliver the island from gangsterism") appealed to public opinion. Soon, however, Batista became an idle petty tyrant who enriched himself lavishly and devoted himself to the good life. This parvenu did not wish to govern by terror as his neighbor Trujillo did, although he became one of the most cruel and bloody tyrants of the Caribbean after Fidel Castro launched his guerrilla war in the Sierra Maestra. This man of the people wanted to be loved. He encouraged the Afro-Cuban cults of the *santerías* and cultivated his popularity among the black population while at his side the very beautiful Marta Fernández played at being Eva Perón. Trujillo had only contempt, it was said, for the populist sergeant.[33] It is also true that apart from the atrocities committed under his regime, when confronted by the Castroite guerrillas, this "democratic" dictator did not exhibit the excesses and economic greed of a Trujillo or a Somoza. Would such a course have been possible anyway in the Cuban semiprotectorate?

As to the military, it was evident at the end of the regime

that the loyalty of the army was rather weak. The Cuban army defended first of all its own corporate interests and its extra-military role in society. Isolated from class interests, the military found themselves deprived of all legitimacy when the United States withdrew its support from the Batista regime. As in 1933 they reacted by trying to save the institution by remov-ing Batista—although too late—in the midst of a general effort at survival (certain units sold arms to the rebels) that coincided with divisions among competing cliques. The Cuban army did not constitute for Batista a praetorian guard on the model of the Nicaraguan National Guard under Somoza. Its special character-istics, which were partly influenced by the first Batista period and by the revolution of the sergeants, made it inappropriate for such a patrimonialist usage.

PARAGUAY: THE FORGOTTEN GENERAL

The regimes that we have just examined appear to be dictator-ships that were not very military in character. First, these ty-rants in fact enjoyed other political resources that permitted them to counterbalance or to supplement their military sup-port. Democracy, in the case of Batista, seems to have been used for this purpose. Second, they deinstitutionalized the mili-tary, either by creating chains of command and selection that were based on particularistic criteria and highly influenced by nepotism, or by the subversion of hierarchy and discipline, as in the case of the sergeants' revolution in Cuba. Nevertheless, the state-oriented armies of South America, even in the contem-porary period, have produced systems of power that involve continuing authoritarian and personalistic controls that are com-parable to those produced by the neocolonial armies.

Indeed, the oldest dictator of the continent is an authentic military man who has been solidly in power for more than a quarter of a century. In 1954 General Alfredo Stroessner seized power in a coup d'état. Since that time Paraguay, the unfortu-nate Arcadia between the rivers (the Paraná and the Paraguay), has been in the hands of a general whose primary concern seems to be that no one should talk about him or his country.

Every effort is made to ensure that the world is not too interested in this little, essentially rural country squeezed between
the two South American major powers, Brazil and Argentina. It
has even been said that to be more certain, the correspondents
of the major press agencies belonged to the official party; one of
them, the correspondent of Agence France Presse, was thought
to be a member of the government, and more specifically of the
office of the president. That desire to be ignored is not entirely
explained by the fact that it is a country that has been isolated
historically and shut in with its own language (*Guaraný*) and
culture. Cut off as it was from the world by the nationalist
autocrat, Francia, from the beginning of the nineteenth century, then blockaded by the Argentine, Rosas, before being
encircled by the armies of the Triple Alliance from 1865 to 1870,
the archaic society of Paraguay was never oriented very much
toward the outside world. However, that modest attitude is
also shared by a dictator who has been fortunate enough to be
able to break the records for longevity of his more prestigious
and colorful predecessors to whose memory he does not hesitate to appeal. Following the example of Francia, "El Supremo,"
who held power as dictator from 1816 until 1840, and of Francisco Solano López, "the Marshall," who succeeded his father
in 1862 and died on the field of battle against the armies of
Brazil in 1869, Stroessner at the beginning of his regime bestowed on himself the modest title of "El Continuador."[34] Nevertheless, he did not affront his powerful neighbors as did
López, or defy the metropolitan powers as did Francia, indeed,
he did the opposite.

Since the Paraguayan War decimated the country—only
half of its 1860 population and one tenth of its adult males
survived—Paraguay has had a tradition of military heroism and
valor that is recognized throughout the continent. In the twentieth century the country established a regular standing army
with obligatory military service for two years (in fact, selectively
applied, since it is sufficient to pay a tax to be exempted) and an
efficient system of military schools.[35] Its officers were very frequently favorably received for advanced training (especially before the establishment of the Superior War School to train the
general staff) in the institutions of neighboring countries, Ar-

gentina and Brazil. This warrior nation fought Bolivia between 1932 and 1935 when its military forces tried to encroach on Paraguayan territory. The army of Paraguay pushed the Bolivians back but found themselves unable to exploit their advantage at the foot of the Andes because of a lack of logistic support and economic capability. The two exhausted countries lost one hundred twenty-five thousand men. A treaty of peace was signed after three years of negotiations. All the states of Latin America expressed their sympathy for the victim of aggression and the rumor spread that international petroleum interests had something to do with the causes of the conflict. However, the war had unforeseen social and political consequences on both sides. Associations of veterans and war heroes led to an active, if not dominant, role for the army in public life.

Paraguay, and some of its neighbors as well, had experienced a very unstable political life since independence: thirty-two presidents and one triumvirate had been in power between 1820 and 1932. It could even be said that in the twentieth century it had a one-year presidency. Two large parties traditionally fought for power: the Republican or Colorado party and the Democratic or Liberal party. The latter party, having removed the conservative Colorados in 1904, dominated political life until the war with Bolivia.

On 17 February 1936 Colonel Rafael Franco, supported by part of the army and by the powerful association of veterans of the Chaco War, overthrew the Liberal party government, sent the old political class into exile and, openly following European authoritarian models, issued a decree that forbade all party activity. That "February Government," which gave rise to the Febrerista party that announced the birth of a "new Paraguay," appeared like many of its counterparts at the time throughout the continent at the same time reformist and authoritarian, fascist and progressive. It called for expropriation of the land to improve the condition of the peasantry and for social legislation for the workers. But the Liberals who were plotting against it did not give it time. Franco, less fortunate than his contemporary of the same name in Spain, was overthrown in a new coup d'état in August 1937. General Estigarribia, who replaced him, had a constitution promulgated in 1940 that was authoritarian, presidentialist, and vaguely corporatist, and granted the president discretionary power to declare martial law. That clause was to provide the basis of government for the country for twenty-five years after 1947. Some months after the adoption of the new constitution, the president and his wife were killed in an aviation accident, and his minister of war, General Morinigo, succeeded him following an election in 1943 in which he was the only candidate.

Morinigo and some members of the Colorado party, which had a certain following in the army, governed in a dictatorial way. In March 1947 the Febreristas, along with the Liberals and a group of young officers, organized an uprising, plunging the country into a six-month civil war. Despite the success of the insurgents and the division of the regular army, Morinigo and the Colorados won out, thanks to the assistance of the Argentine government and General Perón,[36] and perhaps some American support.[37] The victory of the existing government was followed by the "Colorado anarchy," during which, for a period of two years, a succession of presidents belonging to that party were overthrown by coups, one after another, while Paraguayans fled to Argentina by the thousands.[38]

By appealing to the old Colorado party, which had been kept from power so long, to provide a base for dictatorship, Morinigo produced the division, if not collapse, of the party. Each faction, too weak to govern by itself, sought the support of the military. This is how the commander in chief of the army, Alfredo Stroessner, in May 1954 took the party over for himself, had himself nominated as the only official candidate, was "elected" in July, and remained thereafter as "constitutional" president of Paraguay. Confirmed in the presidency by plebiscite in 1958, he has been reelected every five years with a clockwork regularity that is astonishing in that continent. Making use of some minor constitutional changes, on 12 February 1978 he accepted his sixth mandate for "order and peace" in Paraguay.*

Just as regularly every sixty days "the most anti-Communist government in the world," in its own words, extends

*Stroessner was elected to a seventh term in 1983. (Translator's note.)

martial law that is only lifted on election day. In those elections the real opposition parties are excluded but a "loyal opposition," promoted or in various ways tolerated by the dictatorship, is given an honorable place at least in the congress where it automatically has a third of the seats.[39] Respect for human rights is not a central concern of the artillery general who presides with a quasi-lifetime title over the destinies of the Guaraný nation. Agrarian leagues, the Communist party, dissident Colorados, and militant Febreristas are pitilessly beaten, imprisoned, or eliminated.

This blond son of a Bavarian German, who rules over a dark-skinned nation of Guaran Indians, leaves nothing to chance. While the dictator as well as his family have discretely acquired wealth, Paraguay has not been transformed into a Nicaraguan-style Stroessner fiefdom. Only the son-in-law, Dominguez Dibb, a prosperous businessman was discussed in the world press because of his rivalries with Somoza. The Paraguayan state has a tangible existence, and the army is not the personal property of the president. It is unlikely that a Stroessner dynasty will become established. The oldest son, an aviation officer, has no military base, and the marriage of the youngest son to the daughter of a powerful general, Andrés Rodriguez, did not produce the results that had been anticipated.[40]

This state army that enjoys an enviable historical legitimacy has sometimes posed problems for General Stroessner. In 1955 a group of young officers linked to a dissident sector of the Colorado party rose up against its leaders. The control of the army is one of the principal concerns of the dictatorship. Beginning in 1948, as a result of the civil war, all Liberal or Febrerista officers were eliminated from the ranks of the military. Henceforth it was necessary to be a Colorado to become an officer, and the cadets at the military school were chosen from families that were affiliated with the official party. To consolidate his power Stroessner was careful to remove from positions of command all the officers who possessed personal prestige, the heroes of the Chaco War among them, and he replaced them with men who owed much, if not everything, to him. But it is corruption and the possibility of enrichment offered to loyal officers that assure military tranquillity. Loyalty pays off, especially in a "contraband state" such as Paraguay where to a greater or lesser degree everyone, from the tourists to international smugglers with official protection, engages in that commercial activity. The discovery of the Ricord affair and "the Paraguayan connection" in 1972 revealed to the world that very high levels in the country were involved in the drug traffic. It was claimed at that time that a former French pimp who had worked for the head of the "French Gestapo" on Rue Lauriston in Paris during the German occupation enjoyed the understanding of high military personages in the immediate entourage of General Stroessner, including General Patricio Coleman, who was responsible for the antiguerrilla struggle,[41] and even General Rodríguez, number two man in the regime and Stroessner's possible successor.[42] In addition an admiral is said to control arms smuggling and each chief of a military region on the frontier has his specialty depending on the internal or external demand and on the decisions of the "godfather"—flour, television sets, automobiles, household machines, stolen cattle, and so forth. The fact that the Paraguayan frontiers are highly permeable explains why its historical tolerance regarding such commerce has become an instrument of government. It is the "price paid for peace," Stroessner is supposed to have said cynically, that leads him to sacrifice the domestic economy to his political longevity.

Under a veneer of institutionalized democracy the Paraguayan dictatorship also practices a police violence that is the underside of the generalized corruption of the leading civilian and military sectors. The terror exercised by the *pyragues*, spies with "winged feet" in the Guaraný language, whose informers are everywhere (one out of four inhabitants, it is said)[43] reinforces the recruitment, not to say total control, that is offered to the government by the official party. The conservative but nonclerical Colorado party has been totally taken over by Stroessner, who has purged it of all potential rivals and independent personalities who might offer resistance to him. All the public servants in the state and local government are obliged to be members of the party. A party membership card is required in order to receive subsidies or salaries from the state. It is not surprising that the organization claims nine hundred thousand members, which is the number of votes that it receives in elections in a country of three million inhabitants. The hereditary character of party affiliation gives still more force to party recruitment. The parties in Paraguay are above all social communities that are expected to provide service and protection. A survey in the 1960s showed that half of the members of the two large parties had relatives who already belonged to the same party.[44] Also, during the campaigns the police repression is carried out by Stroessner's party. Its representatives, the *mbaretes* or village caudillos,[45] are all-powerful and do not hesitate to carry out vengeance or to put pressure upon the peasants who are not Colorados. The Colorado exclusivism would appear to be totalitarian, no doubt, in a less rudimentary society. The party slogan "He who is not with us is against us" is indeed not much of an indication of political tolerance. "There should not be a single Colorado who is poor," preached the program of the official party in the 1950s, thus covering over its violence against political adversaries and a clientelist policy that had produced results. The local branches of the Colorado party are in fact very attentive to the needs of the membership that they provide with legal aid, assistance with funerals, and school supplies.[46]

The opportunism of Stroessner and his balancing act between Brazil and Argentina have facilitated his survival. His sensitivity to the pressures from Washington is only equalled by his desire to be well regarded by the metropolitan power in an area in which he is without rival—that of the anti-Communism that has always been used to legitimize his regime. This is why Stroessner sent a Paraguayan contingent to reestablish order in the Dominican Republic at the side of the marines in 1965, and why one of the most recent congresses of the World Anti-Communist League was held in Asunción.

As we see, this personal dictatorship is quite civilian in its essential base. While the army is not far from power, it does not govern, and Stroessner is not its spokesman. Rather he has succeeded in neutralizing it through various means, including corruption, that are legitimated and supported by a logic of party loyalty. The specific characteristic of this type of extreme "sultanate" or patrimonial regime—to use the terminology of

Max Weber—is that it corrupts representative institutions and the universalistic organs of the state.

PERSONAL POWER AND MILITARY POWER

The fact that power originates with the military is thus not sufficient to give it a specifically martial character. In the personal dictatorships that we have described the army as an institution does not delegate its power to a military leader; rather, power is wrested from it by the action of the dictator who establishes a network parallel to the disciplinary hierarchy founded on loyalty not to the institution but to his person, and sometimes reinforced by a party element as well. While these regimes, which are military in appearance, have in fact, become demilitarized, it is interesting to observe that the movement from a system of domination by the military to one or another type of personal power is marked by severe conflict. In fact, the history of what are in general terms called contemporary "military dictatorships" is a history of struggles by the general-presidents to emancipate themselves from those who have put them in power or from their institutional base, and to make their power permanent. Military men who have become heads of state for corporate reasons, because they were at the top of the hierarchy, rarely become autocrats of the traditional patriarchal type in the continent. General Stroessner successfully carried out that transformation. In Venezuela General Pérez Jiménez, who was a member of a junta that removed the social democrats of the Acción Democratica from power also achieved that goal for a while. After the assassination of Colonel Delgado Chalbaud and thanks to a favorable petroleum situation as well as the support of the United States, Pérez Jiménez became a petty and bloody dictator. Professionally educated and a product of a modern army, he knew how to purchase the silence of his peers by fabulous expenditures for the welfare and pride of the armed forces. But the army officers who were kept out of power were disturbed by the presence of police everywhere, while the air force and the navy felt that they were involved, with no benefit to themselves, in a regime that favored the clique of officers from the Andean region who surrounded the dictator. Military discontent grew and an uprising put an end to the regime. Pérez Jiménez gave up power and left Venezuela in January 1958.

In Argentina where military presidents, interspersed by occasional intervals of civilian rule, have succeeded one another since 1930, conficts between the high command and the presidents drawn from their ranks are standard fare, and the replacement of one general by another at the head of the state in a palace revolution has taken place at least five times. Officially the army deposes the provisional occupant of the Casa Rosada in order to prevent him from perpetuating himself in power and removing the military from government. Thus suspicion that General Juan Carlos Onganía, the beneficiary of the 1966 coup d'état, wished to extend his mandate when he stated that the armed forces did not "co-govern," was sufficient for the High Command to take action to overthrow him at the appropriate time. In Peru, General Juan Velasco Alvarado, who—thanks to the army—headed the "revolutionary nationalist" movement that began in October 1968, was deposed by his peers because he tried to acquire personal support through a populist policy and to extend his power beyond the time prescribed in the military regulations.

While not so long ago the *pronunciamentos* and the *cuartelazos* of ambitious generals produced highly personalized dictatorships, today the governments of the armed forces are above all bureaucratic authoritarian regimes. Brazil after 1964 with its orderly succession of general-presidents undoubtedly represents the most developed paradigm of the "impersonal power of the army" that characterizes and legitimates the military state. However, the personalization following the Franco model of the counterrevolutionary regime of Chile since 1973—although it is very far from the patrimonial dictatorships of the quasi-sultanates that we have analyzed—shows that this type of evolution is not excluded, even within one of the most state-oriented and professionalized armies of the continent.

7

MODEL
DEMOCRACIES
AND CIVILIAN
SUPREMACY

The social characteristics of the nations of Latin America do not seem to encourage the development of liberal democracy. It is argued that the peoples of Iberian America are not "mature" enough for the delicate balance involved in representative government, or at least that democracy is not universalizable and that it remains coextensive with the individualistic and Protestant values of the European West. Thus, what the contemptuous writers of the end of the last century called the "French sickness" is now rebaptized there as the "Latin sickness." The political monstrosities that we have just described would lead one to draw a similar conclusion. However there is considerable empirical evidence that refutes those who maintain the immaturity thesis. No people is fated to endure dictatorship or is naturally incapable of civilian supremacy, nor does a high cultural and economic level make a society immune to authoritarian, even totalitarian, deviations, as the history of Europe in this century has sufficiently demonstrated. Along parallel lines, here and there in Latin America there have been countries in which civilians have been in power for a relatively long time. Military men who do not intervene in politics are not an unknown species in the subcontinent, which means that we should come to an understanding of both the significance and extent of civilian supremacy and the proper definition of military intervention.

Is the Cuban regime born in the Sierra Maestra really civilian in nature, and are the *comandantes* of the Nicaraguan Sandinista FSLN really military? In mobilizing states on the road to socialism these distinctions are not appropriate. Like the distinction public/private, the distinction civilian/military is foreign to Marxist-Leninist models and proper to capitalist societies. In addition, civilian control of the armed forces is a question of degree. In no country are the military completely removed from politics; everything depends on the political space that they occupy. On a continuum going from corporate influence to military usurpation to the overthrow of the civilian authorities, we can identify two other levels: participation in decision making in areas that are not strictly military in the name of an expanded conception of the tasks of defense, and army control of the exercise of power that reverses civil/military relations without replacing the legitimate authorities. The term "intervention" can be used to apply either to the usurpation of power or to the two lesser degrees of involvement. If we keep to the classic definition according to which intervention involves the rupture by force of institutional continuity we can claim, nevertheless, that there are many armies in Latin America that do not intervene in politics. However, one cannot be too prudent. In 1970 we would not have hesitated to cite Chile and Uruguay as clear examples of demilitarized states. Keeping these reservations in mind, in the 1980s we can point to four countries that have had uninterrupted civilian rule and military subordination for over twenty years. We do not say that those countries are all paragons of democratic virtues, or that they have not experienced attempts at a coup. We simply state that Colombia, Costa Rica, Mexico, and Venezuela are the only states in which for the last two decades the relations between the civilians and the military have been of a non-praetorian type and coup makers, when they have existed, have had no success.

It has seemed useful to us to examine the methods and causes of that civilian supremacy as well as its limits and uncertainties over time. These civilian-dominated states, whether lasting or not, can also tell us something about the military state. And reversing the problem through studying the cases of armies that do not intervene can help us to perceive the processes and factors underlying militarization, although we must keep in mind the irreducible national differences and the danger of continent-wide generalizations.

COSTA RICA: THE WITHERING AWAY OF THE ARMY AND THE WELFARE STATE

Costa Rica is not only, to use the tourist description, a "Spanish-speaking democracy." This little peaceful country located in a region dominated by dictatorships and popular upheavals has not had a coup d'état since 1917 nor an army since 1948. The Costa Ricans are proud that they have twenty thousand schoolteachers and only eight thousand men in their police force. If, unlike its neighbors, Costa Rica has had only one military coup d'état between 1891 and 1948 and one brief period of dictatorship,[1] this is because its army has never been a powerful and prestigious defensive organization. In fact, it had already begun to disappear well before its legal abolition. Following Costa Rican independence in 1821—gained without conflict simply as part of the *Capitanía Géneral* of Guatemala—that neglected backland of the isthmus did not develop a warrior tradition or predatory caudillos during the nineteenth century. The nonexistence of a large Indian population and the importance of small peasant landholdings were the reasons for the low level of social conflict that in turn could explain the lack of interest by the ruling classes in the creation of a powerful and permanent military apparatus. From the beginning of the nineteenth century—some think that the importance of the banana enclave controlled by large foreign companies was a factor—Costa Rica relied on the mediation of third countries, especially the United States, whenever a conflict broke out with one of its neighbors, such as with Panama in 1921. In 1948, when political confrontations degenerated into civil war, the army had only three hundred men. Yet there were more than one thousand deaths because of the involvement of popular militias formed by the trade unions and the Communist party. The insurgent army made up of civilians had little difficulty in defeating the Costa Rican military.[2]

It is always necessary to go back to 1948 if we wish to

understand the political evolution of the country. The civil war was a point of rupture and nonreturn in its institutional history. Among the origins of the war were the particular political realignments that were only made possible by the climate produced by the Allied victory in the Second World War. A populist Catholic president isolated from the real forces in the country allied himself with the Communist party and secured the support of the church to maintain himself in power. That reformist regime of President Calderón Guardia upset the grand coffee and banking bourgeoisie because of his unsavory associations and his social reforms, and provoked the hostility of the middle class because of his corruption and his disregard for constitutional guarantees. The opposition concluded that the electoral route was closed to it since the government had annulled the results of presidential elections that had been unfavorable to it; in the climate of the cold war and with the approval of the United States, these forces launched a military uprising that had a social and political backing as heterogeneous as that of the "Calderón-Communist" regime. Allied with a group of modern entrepreneurs and urban middle sectors that desired reforms, espoused social democratic ideas, and wanted to rid the Caribbean region of its dictators were the coffee-producing oligarchy, financial circles, the large traders, and the traditional parties.

The Army of National Liberation led by José Figueres won the war. The official army, undermined by clientelism and amateurism, collapsed, and difficulties began for the "opportunistic alliance" that had overthrown the government of Calderón Guardia and his successor, Teodoro Picado. The upper bourgeoisie, with the coffee planters at the head, only wished to end the Communist threat while Figueres and his Liberacionistas and Caribbean Legion wanted to carry their democratic crusade beyond the frontiers of Costa Rica and refused to call into question the reforms that had been adopted by the defeated government. Neither the labor code nor the complex of social laws was repealed. In addition the victors, after outlawing the Communist party, nationalized the banks, imposed taxes on capital, and expanded the economic responsibilities of the state in the areas of prices and production. While

Figueres and his friends, under pressure from the United States, agreed to dissolve the Caribbean Legion and to abandon the international struggle against tyranny, they hoped to be able to institutionalize the army of "liberation" that had brought them victory. The upper bourgeoisie and the conservative groups, which were so weak politically that they had been forced to ally with the "newly arrived" groups to recapture power and lacked a military apparatus, opposed that view and desired to reconstitute the regular army. Since the conservatives dominated the Constituent Assembly that was elected in 1949 while Figueres and his Liberacionistas had force on their side, a compromise solution was found in the legal prohibition of any military institution. The abolition of the army was, first of all, aimed at disarming what was to become in 1951 the Party of National Liberation (PLN) while guaranteeing to the victors in the civil war that the oligarchy would not reconstitute a state military force that was directed at them.

There was a certain false symmetry about this too perfect solution. The "security forces," a kind of national gendarmerie that was established after the two armies were abolished, was actually dominated by the followers of "Don Pepe" Figueres, the charismatic leader of the Movement of National Liberation.[3] In addition the veterans of the Caribbean Legion did not disappear, nor did their weapons. Some even considered themselves to be a politico-military reserve force in the service of the Liberation party and its historic leader. And even today Figueres does not hesitate to confess that while his country has no army he does not lack arms and men ready to use them in case of need.[4] Therefore, we can ask why a military force was not reestablished after 1949 and what beyond the vagaries of history are the underlying reasons for that special situation.

In 1953, when the new Party of National Liberation elected Figueres to the presidency by a massive majority, a development-oriented group of modern entrepreneurs favorable to the industrialization of the country came to power. The objective of this group was to harmonize the interests of the different social sectors and to give stability to the renascent democracy through the active intervention of the state. Large public investments and the creation of numerous state enterprises in close liaison with private enterprise produced an "oversized bureaucracy" that, in the view of some observers, compensated for the narrowness of the market and the rigidity of the agrarian structures.[5] A welfare state was also established at the same time involving stabilizing transfers that, even if they favored the urban middle classes more than the rural proletariat, did not leave funds for military expenses. The commonplace that compares the numbers of policemen and schoolteachers is more than an ideological circular argument: it is the expression of a system of government that is called by one Costa Rican author, "welfare state capitalism."[6] Also, the abolition of the military that seemed in the first place to be merely the product of special circumstances is not likely to be reversed. No doubt because it corresponded to deeper motivations linked to the social equilibrium of the Costa Rican nation, a nonmilitary state has become today one of the bases of its democratic consensus. In the same way a firm and conscious commitment to the practices and the values of democracy is now a distinctive element in the identity of the nation after more than thirty years of orderly electoral successions and alternations in power between the PLN and its conservative adversaries.[7]

Internationally this unarmed republic draws strength from its very weakness. Its best defense is precisely its image as a disarmed country. However, the security of Costa Rica does not depend solely on the judgment of international opinion. The foreign policy of San José shows this in that it does not depart one millimeter from that of Washington. Officially the new regime that was established at the same time as the Inter-American Treaty of Reciprocal Assistance (1947) and the Charter of Bogotá (1948) claims that it relies on the arbitration and protection of the inter-American system for its security. But in doing so, Costa Rica gives a continuing legitimacy to the Organization of American States and to the diplomatic instruments that act more to cover armed American interventions than to protect fragile democracies.

In addition, the functioning of its institutions and the acceptance by the dominant party of an alternation in power have helped to prevent the reestablishment of a stable standing army while also proving by a negative example that the establishment of autonomous armed forces is actually one of the reasons for their involvement in politics. In fact, in Costa Rica the officers of the Civil Guard do not enjoy the meritocratic privileges of the majority of the armies in the continent. Their professional continuity is even rather less than that of the civil servants. In the absence of an agreement between the different political forces to make the security personnel really permanent, they are part of the spoils system. The organizational weakness that results from this does not encourage the transformation of a gendarmerie into an army. Both the leaders of the PLN and their adversaries fear that stability of personnel under the aegis of the other camp would lead to the surreptitious reestablishment of a party-dominated armed force. The year 1948 has not been forgotten. As distinct from the situations in South America where the army leadership, enjoying autonomy in recruitment and freedom from political interference, forms an administration made up of amateurs, in Costa Rica the civilian bureaucrats—"state bourgeoisie"—are more professionalized than the security forces, thus making their militarization practically impossible and civilian supremacy absolute.[8]

The orientation and the characteristics of the Costa Rican state in large part demonstrate that durable demilitarization. The structural elements that gave rise to its establishment merit some attention. It has been said and repeated that the absence of gold and of Indians made that isolated backwater of the Captaincy General of Guatemala, despite its name, a poor colony of the Spanish empire. One can undoubtedly assume that the absence of an indigenous population played a determining role in the formation of Costa Rican society. Not only was there no population available for forced labor, but labor was scarce throughout the history of the country. While in the north of the isthmus in Indianized Guatemala and overpopulated El Salvador there was an abundance of workers, here labor was lacking. The Spaniards who settled the country in the colonial period worked their land themselves and therefore, it was said, did not take more land than they could cultivate.[9] When coffee, which requires so much care to cultivate and harvest, became the dominant product, the scarcity of the labor factor became the chief characteristic of the economy. Seasonal workers came from neighboring countries. Even in recent years the dates of the school vacations were moved up in order to permit children to aid their parents in harvesting the precious berry. The development of a pioneer spirit and the existence of vacant land for all who desired it helped to promote a relaxed social climate tied to family-sized property and the preponderance of private values. Costa Rica is a sort of anti-El Salvador if we consider that that other Central American country is marked by overpopulation and the concentration of landholding in the hands of a tiny minority.

In Costa Rica, therefore, everything seems to tend toward compromise. The need for a work force has pushed the employer to make concessions. Agricultural wages are the highest in Central America, nearly twice those of Guatemala and three times Honduran wages.[10] The paternalism of the farmer working the land is fundamentally different from mediated relations with an absentee landlord. The welfare state is also one of the structural determinants, since the high cost of labor, by discouraging foreign investment for many years, left the field open to a "democratic welfare-state capitalism"[11] that supports the political institutions. It is true that the abolition of the army was the result of particular circumstances, but that decision translated and expressed the strong and attractive special character of Costa Rica—although it still has its problems.

PETROLEUM AND THE DEMOCRATIC COMPROMISE IN VENEZUELA

After the long primitive personal dictatorship of Juan Vicente Gómez, the archetype of all the tropical tyrannies, who presided over the first petroleum boom from 1908 to 1935, Venezuela entered into an uncertain period of democracy. However, when the democracy conceded by the "Gomezista" Generals López Contreras and Medina Angarita did not develop quickly enough in the eyes of the civilian and military opposition a group of young officers, and the Acción Democrática party overthrew the postdictatorial government in 1945. A junta headed by Romulo Betancourt and an elected president, Romulo Gallegos, tried for three years to establish an advanced democracy of a socializing orientation, but this effort was interrupted in 1948 by a conservative coup d'état. Eliminating his rivals, Colonel Pérez Jiménez established himself as dictator for a period of ten years. Venezuela had moved from caudillismo to praetorianism, only to return to a regressive personalism in power. In January 1958 a part of the army together with the navy and air force finally removed Pérez Jiménez. From then on civilian government has prevailed with orderly presidential successions that have permitted an alternation between Social Democratic and Christian Democratic presidents. Not a single military coup has broken the continuity of civilian control in a country that during the 1960s experienced violent political agitation. We may ask how this could happen, especially since the apparent architects of this democratic stabilization were the same men who had been easily removed from power by the army.

To answer, we must first discuss the army. At the beginning of the twentieth century the Venezuelan army was regarded in the whole continent as a military institution that was full of officers with much gold braid but little education. It is true that the civil wars that ravaged the country throughout the preceding century had produced very decentralized armed forces in which the indiscipline of "revolutionary" generals was combined with an astonishing inflation of rank. The 1873 census reveals that in the state of Carabobo alone in a male population of 22,952 inhabitants there were 3,450 officers, including 449 generals and 627 colonels.[12] Professionalization came late despite some cautious attempts by Cipriano Castro and later by Gómez. Playing one foreign mission against the other without ever entrusting the reorganization of the army to any of them, Gómez only succeeded in centralizing and unifying the Venezuelan military by resorting to local recruitment and favoritism.[13] Under his reign the hegemony of those from the Andean region was institutionalized. More than 80 percent of the members of the officer corps came from the three states on the Colombian border, and a large majority of those Andeans came from the state of Tachira, Gómez's native state. Thus General López Contreras, who became head of state after the death of Gómez, was a *tachirense* who had enlisted in the "revolutionary" army of Castro, the first Andean to come to power in 1899. His successor, Medina Angarita, became the first military school graduate to become minister of war in 1935. The change in the Venezuelan army took place between those two dates and men.

It is true that Pérez Jiménez was an Andean, as were many of the other officers, but in 1945 the Venezuelan army resembled its counterparts in neighboring countries more than it did the montoneras of the independence period. The 1948 coup d'état was not a resurgence of caudillismo, but was rather the result of an entirely new political situation. The emergence and immediate domination of the country by a Social Democratic party—whose leaders were viewed as Communists—transformed the Venezuelan political panorama. The beneficiaries of the 1945 coup d'état, who did not have unanimous support in the opposition, monopolized power by securing their support from large mass mobilizations that frightened moderate opinion. Intent on implementing their program without delay, they initiated a number of reforms at the same time, with the result that they increased the number of their adversaries. Thus the church, which was opposed to the secularization of private education, joined the traditional political elites, the foreign companies, and conservatives of every stripe in a common front against the new regime. The petroleum companies, on whom a fifty-fifty tax had been imposed, conspired against it. The overwhelming majorities that it had obtained in the elections to the constitutional assembly and in the 1948 presidential elections (78.4 percent and 74.4 percent respectively), far from increasing the legitimacy of the new government, contributed to its fragility.[14] The other parties attacked the sectarianism of Acción Democrática and their press openly called for a coup. The night of the coup against the novelist-president Romulo Gallegos, the Christian democratic leader Rafael Caldera and the leader of the center-left, Jovito Villalba, gave their support to the military authorities.[15] The overwhelming domination of the government by the *Adecos* was therefore their principal weakness while the "new government threatened too many established interests, both symbolic and material at the same time."[16] The experience was not to be forgotten. The return of democracy ten years later and its consolidation owed much to the lessons of that sad apprenticeship.

The lessons of the defeat of the *trienio* (1945–48) related both to the limitation of political conflict and the attitude that was to be taken toward the army. Acción Democrática (AD) and its democratic opponents understood that in 1948 democratic institutions had been the victims of the intensity and the in-eradicable and cumulative character of civilian conflict that opened the way to military intervention. Therefore the parties that met in New York signed the Pact of Punto Fijo in October 1958. This agreement, although it did not provide for a common candidate in the first presidential elections,[17] established a code of conduct and of coexistence. Coalition and compromise were the order of the day. All the political forces that signed the pact agreed to reduce the intensity of open party conflicts and to channelize and control them. Henceforth, for the Acción Democrática, negotiation became more important than ideology and program. To build a stable and durable democracy was the first priority. It was not possible at the same time to construct democratic institutions and to initiate profound social and economic reforms. However, an openness to compromise and to the lessening of ideological tensions was insufficient; it was also necessary for the opposition to refrain from turning to the military to resolve partisan differences.

Certainly the fact that the megalomania and the police methods of Pérez Jiménez had discredited military intervention operated in favor of democratic institutions, at least in the first years after the return to democracy, but favorable economic conditions undoubtedly helped to lower the political stakes. The search for "technical"—as opposed to political—solutions for problems would not have been possible without the petroleum resources. It was evidently less costly to draw on those resources than to alter the distribution of wealth, or to tax and redistribute it. As to the social cost of stability, there are various views on that subject. However, we can also ask about the social cost of change if it results, as it did in Chile, in a dramatic retrogression in both politics and society.

It would be wrong, however, to think that petroleum was the only explanation. In itself this kind of wealth is not stabiliz-

ing, much less democratizing.[18] Economic booms can just as well
have the opposite effect. In the Venezuelan case, we should not
underestimate the coherent structure of the party organizations,
especially of the two dominant parties, AD and COPEI (the Social Democrats and the Christian Democrats) who, despite the
multiplication and successive divisions of the parties, have received between 50 percent and 75 percent of the votes ever since
1958. The "passion for voting" that is attributed to the Venezue-
lans because of the high level of electoral participation since 1958
also demonstrated that the system enjoyed substantial popular
support.[19] Finally, we should mention the decisive role of prudent and strong leaders, especially that of Romulo Betancourt,
the president elected in 1958 who remained until his death in
September 1981 the guiding spirit of Venezuelan democracy.

Under his presidency from 1959 until 1964 there was no
lack of coup attempts by both right and left. The Castroite guerrillas and the personal vindictiveness of Dominican Republic
dictator Trujillo[20] did not make the task of the first constitutionally elected president an easy one. The right wing of the military that was favorable to the deposed dictator rose up at least
twice in a spectacular way: in Tachira in April 1960, led by the
former minister of war of the 1958 junta, and in Caracas in
February 1961. At the same time the parties of the left plunged
into armed struggle and on two occasions important contingents of marines led by Castroite officers revolted in Carupano
and Puerto Cabello.[21] Betancourt crushed the rebels, sometimes
with the aid of the civilian population, using a severity against
them that was uncompromising, but in conformity with democratic legal procedures.[22]

Romulo Betancourt, who had reserved for the president
the areas of relations with the army and with Washington, took
his title and role as commander in chief very seriously. He
participated in military ceremonies and never missed an occasion to visit their camps. Acting to isolate the seditious elements without provoking a corporate reaction, he made special
efforts to maintain contact with the officers. Taking care to demonstrate that the antimilitary sentiments attributed to him were
unfounded, President Betancourt exhibited an extreme solici-
tude for the corporate concerns of the armed forces (armament,

barracks, maneuvers) as well as for the personal conditions of the officers (housing, loans, etc.). In his speeches to the armed forces, the president lost no opportunity to remind them that they had been allies in the restoration of the constitutional regime and to emphasize the state of abandonment and neglect in which they had been kept by the dictatorship. In addition Betancourt knew how to exploit the guerrilla threat with consummate ability in order to secure support for the institutions of democracy from the former enemies of his party—the army, the church, and business. Against the possibility of the establishment of the Cuban model, this ex-Communist represented a lesser evil. For military consumption, it was not difficult for him to make effective references to the foreign origin of the terrorist threat and to the fate promised for bourgeois armies by Castroism.[23] Having been wounded in the attack organized against him in Caracas by the Dominican tyrant, he had a special right to denounce foreign aggression, especially when it was aimed in his view at Cubanizing Venezuela. This is why guerrilla activity, which is so often fatal to democratic governments because they are regarded as too slow and weak, helped to strengthen civilian institutions in Venezuela. The defeat of the guerrillas and their later reintegration into the democratic system through an amnesty of the parties of the left who had been involved in armed struggle also helped to consolidate democracy.

Under his two successors, belonging respectively to Acción Democrática and to the Social Christian party, a less agitated political climate seemed to accompany the continuing subordination of the military. In fact, the Venezuelan army, which did not lack power, remained nonpolitical, and the means of civilian control were not, on the evidence, exclusively constitutional. The Venezuelan army, which is well equipped and enjoys a substantial budget, is characterized today by a high level of technical organization. The military academies produce engineers and administrators. The social sciences and management are taught, along with professional subjects, and the officers are encouraged to earn civilian diplomas.[24] Of course, the official mission of the Venezuelan officer is the defense of the frontiers. The disputes with Colombia and Guyana in the Gulf of Maracaibo and Essequibo are serious enough to occupy them. But officers, as former president Carlos Andres Pérez recently recalled, "are not outside the social and economic life of the country."[25] Trained for functions that are extramilitary in the strict sense, the Venezuelan officers are particularly interested in problems of development. The political authorities provide them with opportunities for experience in that domain. The case of General R. Alfonzo Ravard, the head of the powerful Petroleos de Venezuela, is well known, but it is not an isolated case. Is this a utilization of skills or an ambiguous form of control? Upper-level officers are numerous in the nationalized sector; the management of development seems almost to be one of their essential tasks. The administration of the Guyana Corporation, the policy setting of the Price Control Council, and the education of technicians for the steel and aluminum industries are all dependent in varying degrees on a superior officer, if not on the army as a whole. The economic function of the military institution is therefore evident.

Besides involvement in decision making, which gives an important role to the army and can at the same time keep it out of political adventures, it is necessary to add the factor of its real organizational autonomy. The minister of defense is a superior officer. Carlos Andres Pérez reports that the general staff itself designated his military aides.[26] It is true that the former president presents that situation as the result of a concern on his part not to politicize the army, but another reading is possible that seems to be confirmed by the difficulties that the Christian Democratic president, elected in 1979, Luis Herrera Campins, experienced with General Castro, head of the infantry. Other facts would tend to suggest that the Venezuelan armed forces also have political preferences. The influence of the Acción Democrática party in the ranks of the officers was decisive in the period of Betancourt. The pro-AD demonstrations by retired officers, and the fact that certain well-known military chiefs belonged to the families of representatives or leaders of the party, could have given the impression that there was a dominant military faction that was favorable to the Social Democrats. This would be another method of civilian control that could pose serious problems for the Christian Democrats if they wanted to end that situation. Insofar as they succeeded in depoliticizing recruitment and promotions, this would contribute to an increase in the autonomy and therefore of the political resources of the Venezuelan army.

Civilian Authoritarianism and the Demilitarization of Political Life in Mexico

With a powerful president and a single-party democracy, post-revolutionary Mexico is difficult to define, indeed to understand: an anonymous dictatorship by a party that is dominant but not the only party provides a case of troubling rarity in the continent. For our purposes the sources of its stability and demonstrated civilian preponderance lie in the strength of the state and the legitimacy of a party that is mistaken for it. The well-named Party of Institutionalized Revolution (PRI) is the "party of the state."[27] It is all powerful and nothing escapes its purview; thus, it is not surprising that a system that controls everything should also control the military.

Since 1920, the year of the assassination of Venustiano Carranza and of his uprising against Alvaro Obregón, no coup d'état has been successful in Mexico. The presidents have been chosen by the official party since its establishment in 1929 and "regularly" elected. The last military rebellion of any significance goes back to 1940. At that time General Almazán, along with a considerable number of officers, rebelled against the result of the elections. The rebellion failed. Avila Camacho, elected in 1940, was the last general to occupy the presidency; his successor, Miguel Alemán, initiated the regime of the *licenciados* (university graduates) and civilian bureaucrats. It is true that Alemán was the son of a general, and his successor, Ruiz Cortines, had reached the rank of *comandante* in the armies of the revolution—thus both were known in military circles.[28]

References to the revolution are not merely an ideological or rhetorical device used by those in power. We must go back to that great upheaval to understand the fifty years of civilian supremacy observed by the official party in 1979. In the beginning, therefore, was the "revolution," a gigantic social and political upheaval. The federal army of the dictator, Porfirio Díaz, against which the liberal bourgeoisie, Indian peasants, socialist intellectuals and opportunistic fighters rose up, was dismantled in 1914–15. The reign of the "warlords" began at that time. Each caudillo was master of his army, and, through his army, of the land that he occupied. Victoriano Huerta, Venustiano Carranza, Pancho Villa, and Emiliano Zapata were the different competing leaders of the revolutionary troops. They had behind them hundreds of thousands of men—and indeed of women, for those *adelitas* along with the military trains in fact played a decisive role in those armies that had no commissaries or adequate medical services. With the exception of the counterrevolutionary, Huerta, all the leaders, generals, and superior officers were civilians. The toughest ones occupied the upper echelons of the hierarchy. Alvaro Obregón was a *ranchero* from Sonora, Pablo Gonzalez was a miller, and Zapata, as is well known, was a small peasant and Villa was a cattle-thief.[29]

It is not surprising that those improvised leaders who rose up against the police and the army of Díaz should for the most part demonstrate a violent antimilitarism that was never totally to disappear from the official ideology. Villa was always against a standing army. Carranza, one of the most "military" of all, refused to be called generalissimo and had himself addressed as "first chief." In fact, the warlords of Mexico were at the head of political parties in arms and not of military institutions. This did not prevent these more or less military amateurs from living on the country by the force of arms.

These predatory armies that were difficult to demobilize were very expensive for the budget. The multiplicity of centers of power and the violent political rivalries divided the state and weakened a nation that economically was in ruins. Reconstruction was carried out by gaining control of the turbulent "generals" and unifying the centrifugal forces. Obregón, and especially Plutarco Calles, the *caudillo maximo* whose shadow hung over Mexico from 1924 until 1935, established the bases of the modern Mexican system. To accomplish this, after the violent elimination of the war leaders who could not be assimilated or dealt with (Zapata was assassinated in 1919, Villa in 1923), he ended the power of the regional caciques while at the same time creating an army and centralizing political institutions. To demilitarize politics it was necessary in effect to militarize the military. Thus, the old military college was remodeled, an advanced war school was opened, and the careers of the officers were regularized. However, the essential thing was to force the "revolutionaries"—that is, the victors—to unite and to accept certain rules of the game. The first rule was to resolve differences through institutions and not by violent means. The unification of the "revolutionary family" was carried out by the Party of the Revolution.

That party, created by the state and not designed to win competitive elections, had as its first objective to unify and dominate the armed political factions. It was henceforth supposed to be the legitimate political arena where the revolutionary forces were to discuss their common interests. However, the transfer of power to the party only took place after the military had been disciplined by Calles, who made use of the army to impose his own control over the country during a period of ten years. Under his *maximato* the army seemed to be at the pinnacle of power and covered with honors. Whether president or not, Calles ruled the destinies of the nation through the instrument of the military. He went so far as to add a Festival of the Soldier to the calendar and the principal ministries were in the hands of generals of the revolution (Amaro, Cedillo, Riva Palacio, etc.).

Yet in fact Calles and his successors, including Lázaro Cárdenas, himself also a "general" who got rid of the mentor who had chosen him in 1935, institutionalized the revolution by putting an end to the confusion of roles each time that it seemed to be dysfunctional for the strengthening of the state.

Carried out by pseudo-military men, the triumph of the state over the centrifugal forces—in the view of some observers a continuation of the modernization carried out by Porfirio Díaz[30]—made the party preeminent over the army. The army, after having been dissolved, reorganized, and put back on its feet by the indefatigable General Amaro was incorporated into the National Revolutionary Party along the sectoral model of the totalitarian parties of Europe. When it became the Party of the Mexican Revolution under Cárdenas (1934–40) it had four sectors: peasants, workers, the popular sector—in fact, a catch-all—and the military. Thus, paradoxically, the military were politicized in order to demilitarize politics and to neutralize the military by involving them politically in a subordinate position.

The risk was minor. The modernized and professionalized armed forces were no more than a part of the state bureaucracy. Cárdenas, facing an incipient Catholic guerrilla effort (the last convulsions of the bloody Cristero uprising against the antireligious policy of Calles), as well as the hostility of the United States following the nationalization of petroleum in 1938, placed strict controls on the army. In addition, this was both justified and counterbalanced by the creation of a peasant militia. After 1940 "with the lessening of foreign pressures on Mexico it was no longer necessary to keep the military captive within the party."[31] Avila Camacho ended that situation. The political bureaucracy was well established and the "Party of the State" paradoxically began to impose a military discipline at the same time that the military was removed from politics. The postrevolutionary Mexican system as we know it today had taken on its definitive form.

Few armies in the continent appear to be less politically involved. It is true that until recently it was difficult to separate its leaders from the political class so that it was not necessary for them to intervene militarily in order to demonstrate their power. Since the time that officers who have been trained at the military schools have reached the highest levels, this type of "subjective control" is less and less operative. The small numbers in the armed forces and the low level of budgetary allocations are good indications that the Mexican armed forces as an institution are relatively weak.[32] Considering the importance of the country, its size, its wealth, and its regional role, there is reason to be surprised at that limitation of the military. In a way the demilitarization of politics has produced the demilitarization of the state.

Besides the antimilitary tradition already noted, we should note that the Mexican army, which has been dissolved several times in the course of its history as a result of civilian confrontations, has very little legitimacy of its own (beyond the revolutionary legitimacy that the PRI alone embodies) or ideological resources to demand lavish budgets or special institutional considerations. In addition Mexico, located between the giant of North America and the ministates of the Central American isthmus, does not need a powerful defensive apparatus. It has nothing to fear from Guatemala, which is one-twentieth the size of Mexico, and it can do nothing with respect to the United States, the most important industrial and military power in the world, except respect its security interests. There is not even a question in this situation of competition for regional leadership. It is no surprise that the second largest country in Latin America has an army hardly larger than those of Chile, Colombia, or Peru, and half as large as that of Argentina, which has a population of less than half that of Mexico.[33] Even military service is demilitarized, halfway between a census of a cohort and a fresh-air camp. This is why the colonel who was assistant chief of staff of the first military region could declare in a speech to conscripts in the *Zocalo* of Mexico City in front of President Díaz Ordaz in 1967, "In conformity with its ideological principles Mexico is a nonmilitarist state. This is why those who participate in national military service spend only a brief period in the ranks of the army, not to receive training as soldiers there, but to learn there the principles of discipline, honor, and loyalty and to return to civilian life in possession of those solid virtues."[34]

In fact, however, while the military do not intervene in politics, especially not to disturb or subvert "revolutionary" institutions, they are not absent from national life, and officers participate in important ways in the functioning of the system. One might conclude that the large number of military men who were in positions of power until recently reflected a preprofessionalized status involving a "revolutionary" confusion of roles. Thus, until 1964 a general presided over the official party, perhaps in order to discipline, by military means if necessary, the internal opposition and to assure the unity of the PRI.[35] In 1948 under Miguel Alemán fifteen of the thirty-one governors were military men—as against only one in 1972 during the presidency of Luis Echeverría. On the other hand, the number of officers in the Congress has remained nearly constant at between fifteen and thirty since 1946, with twenty-two in 1953 and seventeen in 1972.[36] It is true that these are quasi-honorific posts without power in a system in which the executive dominates everything, but nevertheless they symbolize effective political participation.

In fact, the military are in a certain way one of the pillars of the coalition along with the PRI, the presidency, and the trade unions. The authoritarian nature of the regime, as well as the intermittent outbreaks of armed struggle that have appeared since the beginning of the 1960s, have increased their repressive role. The many forms of rural agitation, ranging from uprisings involving the invasion of land to the appearance of social bandits in Guerrero, have been suppressed by military force. Force is also frequently used in industrial conflicts, to say nothing of the operation of civic action against natural calamities because of the isolation or underadministration of certain regions. Thus the military are named as zonal commanders in areas that are volatile (Guerrero, Oaxaca).

While the power of the military has disappeared, the Mexican military have still remained very close to politics. In addition to the historical processes that we have analyzed, their subordination depends on a subtle game of differentiated selective compensation. Some writers recalling the comment of Obregón regarding the generals who could not resist a salvo of 500,000 pesos have even spoken of corruption. An incident that took place in 1980 involving the award of a national literary prize to writer Juan Rulfo proves that civilian and military governmental authorities are sensitive even to references to that possibility. Rulfo's acceptance speech was refuted at the highest official levels for explaining military respect for law as resulting from "the price for peace" that was paid by the regime to its defenders.

While corruption exists the special relationship of the military to the regime uses other more readily admissible methods as well. There again the omnipotence of the president plays a central role. The monarchical character of the regime is such that the officers believe that, if not their promotions, at least their marginal personal benefits are the result of the concern of the president. It is true that among the superior officers the base salary only forms a part of one's income that varies depending on the job (one or several) and the post occupied (according to region). Variations in military salaries can be a factor

that encourages docility and dependence, especially when officers who are on active duty can receive civilian employment
without losing their military salaries, thus providing a substantial supplement to their ordinary incomes.[37] Thus one can be
both an active-duty officer and an inspector of bridges and
highways or a customs officer. As in the civilian bureaucracy,
personal relations and patronage are in full play and help to
reduce the autonomy of the military.

In Mexico a weak army, far from dominating the system, is
selectively integrated within it through a system of clientelistic
transactions. The military are not absent from the scene. There
is no doubt that they are consulted on programs relating to
public order, but their margin of maneuver is limited by the
power and cohesion of the party-state. The slow pace of the
gradual transition from warriors to military men and from politicians in arms to professional officers has permitted the maintenance of certain mechanisms of subjective control through the
fusion and confusion of origins and roles. Military men who are
so little independent of the party-political apparatus do not yet
constitute a force.

COLOMBIA: OLIGARCHIC DEMOCRACY AND
LIMITED MILITARIZATION

Judging from its principal sociocultural indicators, there are few
countries in Latin America with conditions less favorable to
democracy and political stability than Colombia. In addition to
the poverty of large sections of the society, it has a high level of
illiteracy, a lack of national integration—both geographic and
human—a powerful and theocratic Catholic church, large land
holdings that are practically untouchable, and a heritage of political violence that has been continued by Marxist guerrillas.[38]
Yet Colombia has had a two-party political system that during
the twentieth century has given it a constitutional continuity
rare in the continent. From 1910 until 1949 the political system
was an open and competitive one. Alternation in power was
not only possible but took place twice; in 1930 and in 1946 the
opposition won the elections and took power. Furthermore,

despite Castroite and pro-Soviet guerrilla activities during the 1960s, the Communist party is legal. All the varieties of the left including the extreme left run candidates freely, as could be seen in 1978. Finally, the supremacy of civilian power seems well established. If we put aside the brief period of military dictatorship in 1953–57, beginning in 1958 the presidents also appear to have made themselves respected and did not permit military encroachment. In 1969 President Carlos Lleras removed the commander of the armed forces, General Pinzón Caicedo, for opposing civilian control of military spending and protesting the inadequacy of the military budget. No garrison came to his support. In 1975 and 1977 President López Michelson had no difficulty retiring from office Generals Puyana, Valencia Tovar, and Matallana, who were leading figures in the army and were openly criticizing the conduct of the government. Finally, political life, which is very personalized and a bit provincial, does not seem to involve recourse to the barracks.

Let us see the reality and the players behind that brilliant facade. Not long ago Bogotá claimed to be the Athens of the Americas, and, in fact Athenian-style democracy functions in Colombia. The electoral abstention rate was 60 percent in 1978 and in the large cities participation does not exceed 25 percent of those registered.[39] As for the army, it is weak,[40] poor, and without prestige. Its officers generally have a low level of training. Military professionalization came late to Colombia. After the so-called Thousand Days Civil War (1899–1902) the governments made efforts to transform the rival party bands into a national army. That process of modernization was only completed in 1943, the date at which the highest positions in the hierarchy were held by graduates of the military school.[41] Military salaries still remain very moderate today. In November 1980 the retired officers, speaking in the name of those on active duty, asked for parity in their salaries with those of the public schoolteachers and university professors.[42]

The other particular characteristic of this army is that it has been in operation for more than thirty years. Its role is intimately linked to the rural phenomenon of *la violencia*, the rampant civil war between the Liberals and the Conservatives that resulted in some three hundred thousand to four hundred thousand deaths between 1948 and 1956 and only ended to be replaced by guerrillas of the left.[43] The army therefore is dispersed, atomized, and involved in controlling insecure areas and pursuing rebellious and unpacified elements. Organized for counterguerrilla operations into small detachments, although it is not an army designated for coups d'état it is not without power, if only on the local level. In the zones of violence or guerrilla activity it is not unusual for an officer or noncommissioned officer to be the mayor; the role of the local garrison is not that established in the constitution. The army therefore operates at the heart of the system of power, but militarism in the conventional form of the usurpation of government has only occurred once in the history of contemporary Colombia.

One cannot insist too much on the importance of the two-party system for better, and undoubtedly for worse—in the life of the nation. We can say that there is nothing of any importance that goes on outside that distinctly oligarchic structure, for the Colombian political class is known for its social homogeneity. It is not unusual for even the opposition that rejects the system to be led by the offspring of the great families.[44] Colombian politics is indeed, as has been written, a "conversation among gentlemen."[45] However, while the two parties meet and come to agreements at the top, their bases are mobilized against one another with an historic hatred that was insurmountable for a long time and produced the most pitiless and atrocious violence, la violencia. The force of family and hereditary party identification acts as an obstacle to class solidarity and tightens the vertical links of social domination. The two-party system that is so functional for the stability of society blocks any process of popular participation even of the populist type. The two parties as a means of control have "been in the twentieth century the most serious political obstacle to social change."[46] This bipartisan society that is not threatened by opposition mass movements functions in a relatively weak state, totally penetrated by the political system. It is not surprising that the two parties are intermediaries for everything, including the army.

The modern Colombian army was created under the aegis of the Conservative party that was in power for the first thirty years of this century. The attempts of the Liberal presidents after 1930 to favor the officers who came from Liberal families and to neutralize the army through the counterweight of the police only resulted in moving the military closer to the Conservative party.

The unsuccessful coup d'état of 1944 against President Alfonso López, who was detained by the garrrison of Pasto, and the purge of Conservative officers following the incident tended in the same direction. Today, when the majority of the officers are recruited, as everywhere else, from the middle class, it is often the sons of the Conservative oligarchy that arrive at the highest positions in the hierarchy. Nevertheless, the military leaders are careful to maintain the neutrality of the institution.

The *bogotazo* in 1948 and la violencia that followed it transformed the army and led to its direct participation in power. With the return of the Conservatives to power in 1946 the system entered into a crisis. As electoral participation reached unexpectedly high levels in Colombia,[47] a Liberal leader, Eliecer Gaitán, tried to mobilize the lower classes against the oligarchy. A Colombian type of populism was being created around a caudillo who denounced the existing separation between the *pays légal* of the programs of the politicians and the misery of the *pays réel*. The ruling elements were terrified. On 9 April 1948 Gaitán was assassinated. His supporters came out in the streets and Bogotá was filled with fire and blood. A part of the police force with Liberal sympathies joined the rioters.

La violencia was born at that time—as a result of the exclusion of the Liberals from constitutional politics and the coming to power of Ospina Pérez by means of a civilian coup d'état. The Conservative dictatorship that was imposed with the support of the army became more repressive with the election to the presidency in 1950 (thanks to the abstention of the Liberals) of an extreme rightest and admirer of Franco—Laureano Gomez. This situation left the opposition no other avenue but that of rebellion. Thus the Liberal guerrillas were produced. The civil war between the parties was grafted onto the vendettas between villages of differing party loyalties, struggles for the control of land, or personal hatreds.[48] The army that was close to power carried out a pacification program in support of the Conservative party without internal problems. It did not split as was expected, but its leaders did not appreciate the doctrinaire extremism of the "Laureanistas." It was also evident that since 1946 the military had been increasing their power substantially. In 1946 a quarter of the municipal governments were assigned military administrators; in 1948 the Ministry of War and several provincial governorships were put into the hands of the army, and in 1949 three generals entered the cabinet. Guardians of the social order and the political status quo, the military—who had not played any separate role in the violation of democratic institutions—did not intend to wage a civil war uncertain of outcome on behalf of the Conservatives.

The phenomenon of la violencia, a sociopolitical crisis that is unique in the history of contemporary Latin America, is not easy to understand, even today with the passage of time. For some it was a bloody method to "crush at the beginning any hint of a political class consciousness in the lower levels of Colombian society,"[49] as well as a way to expropriate the property of the small and medium farmers to the benefit of the large landowners (nearly four hundred thousand properties were abandoned). For others la violencia destroyed traditional social controls, but the survival of oligarchic democracy demonstrates the weakness of the threat, which had been magnified by a Conservative party with minority support among the people which had refused to accept its permanent exclusion from the benefits of the state.[50]

In any case, for many of the military and for the moderates in both parties, Laureano Gómez and the Conservatives had gone too far. The president would have to be removed and the Liberals reintegrated into public life to assure the peace. The idea of a military dictatorship began to make headway, being favorably received both by the Conservatives, who feared the decomposition of the economic and social system, and by the Liberals, who expected that it would mean an end to the ostracism that had been imposed upon them. In particular the Conservatives did not want needed reforms, while the Liberals were ready to reestablish "the party of order" along with them on condition that they were no longer treated as enemies. This is how General Rojas Pinilla was brought in as head of the state in 1953 in a "public opinion coup," as it is still referred to in

Bogotá. He came to power without great enthusiasm, according to his close associates,[51] but with the broad support of all social groups and to the relief of the principal members of the political class. By chance the price of coffee on the world market was at its peak. The economic bonanza operated in favor of the new government that represented civil peace. An amnesty was proclaimed. A majority of the Liberal guerrillas laid down their arms, and a more peaceful outlook began to prevail.

However, the policy of Rojas Pinilla was not unanimously supported by the wealthy. His economic orientation was far from the laissez-faire gospel of the Colombian elites. The state intervened, constructed large public works, and aided industry. Still worse, the social policy of the regime was based on generous subsidies to lower-class consumers. Even more, Rojas Pinilla understood that the traditional parties were against him and were opposed to any social change, and he tried to break out of the two-party framework. He even created his own party, the Alianza Nacional Popular (ANAPO) in the purest tradition of populism. But Colombia is not Argentina and his "Peronism" was nipped in the bud by the Conservatives and Liberals who soon saw the danger and became reconciled with one another in the face of the adversary.

The "New Bolívar," as he had been called by a Conservative leader in 1953, was now only an ambitious dictator whom the bourgeois aristocracy removed from government. The parties, for their part, signed a pact of nonaggression and cooperation in Spain that in view of the bloodshed would have been surprising to anyone who was not familiar with the two levels on which the system operated. According to what was called the National Front Agreement that was to be ratified by referendum, the two parties would succeed one another in the presidency from 1958 until 1978, and they would share all political and administrative positions on an equal basis. The National Front guaranteed that no party would be deprived of the spoils in a country in which the state was one of the principal industries. If party exclusivity was at the root of the violence, the National Front provided the key to peace. A new system was put into place. The dualism of war at the base and collaboration at the summit was no longer in effect. Parity permitted the Conservatives, for a long time a minority party in the country, to survive, and the fiction of a two-party system would prevent modern mass parties from being created. However, as was sometimes said, the National Front was a two-party agreement involving three partners—the third being the army that solidified the alliance. The recognition of the Conservative party by the Liberals prevented them from resorting to the power of the military, and the army in effect made up for the weakness of the Conservatives.

Colombia in recovery thus returned to oligarchic politics, but the National Front with its party system was equivalent in fact to a single party. If political demobilization was one of its goals, it succeeded perfectly. In each election abstention became a little greater. Most of the time people simply refused to vote and this reduced the legitimacy of the regime. The cooptation of the trade unions by the parties did not prevent other forms of popular participation from emerging, as was demonstrated by the general strike of September 1977.[52] The domination by the party of order represented by the Front did not continue without an increase in authoritarianism—not only because of the last outbursts of la violencia but because the official coalition did not offer any political alternative. From 1958 on, with the help and support of the army, every attempt to go beyond the system to modernize political life and to allow the masses to participate in public life was pitilessly combated. The state of siege under which democratic Colombia has been living totally or partially since 1958 under the pretext that "public order is disturbed" is the real constitution of the country. Lifted at one point by Carlos Lleras, reestablished by Miguel Pastrana after the disputed elections of 1970, rebaptized by López Michelson, it was increased in intensity again under Julio Turbay Ayala after 1978. In twenty years of the National Front, Colombia has had fifteen under "a state of exception" that increases the powers of the executive and allows him to suspend constitutional rights and freedoms in order to reestablish public order.[53]

The army plays the essential and decisive role of defender of the two-party system in that "constitutional dictatorship." The government turns to it to eliminate political alternatives when they cannot be assimilated through cooptation or "*trans-*

formismo." The system is rather simple. It consists in closing every legal avenue to the outsider, as the Conservatives tried to do to the Liberals in 1949. Against the last violent irreconcilable elements, the recourse is to the army. That was the fate that befell the sociologist-priest Camilo Torres, the creator of the popular political movement, the Frente Unido, who took to armed resistance in 1966 and was killed in the same year while fighting in the ranks of the Army of National Liberation (ELN). This was also the case with the ANAPO of General Rojas Pinilla, who according to many observers won the 1970 elections and was the victim of an electoral fraud carried out in favor of the National Front candidate—although not without producing some disturbance in the army. By 1976 the ANAPO had practically disappeared. In 1974 its last members had founded the M-19 guerrilla movement that proceeded to organize spectacular seizures, all the while being unceasingly hunted by the army.[55]

That exploitation of official violence and of the follow-up to la violencia developed by the Castroites in the 1960s was as useful to the regime as its resources were limited. The National Front, by destroying the sense of belonging and of identification with a political community, visibly reduced the traditional means of social control. Urbanization accelerated that process. The system could only survive in the absence of an alternative. In these conditions the autonomy of the military in relation to the power of the parties increased both de jure and de facto. The special legal provisions gave the military a free hand and little by little they encroached on the power of the civilians in the area of public order and of the courts, and extended their responsibilities more generally. The militarization of la Guajira to fight against the drug traffic, the occupation of the emerald mines in Boyacá to prevent smuggling, and the use of officers to run the customs did not please everyone in the ranks of the military. Some said—correctly—that this was a source of corruption, and this seems to be confirmed by various accounts carried in the press.[56] It remains to know who profited from that arrangement. The situation was a source of corruption and demoralization, perhaps, but it was also a proof that the weakened civilian power needed military support at whatever price.

For Turbay Ayala that price seems to have been the adoption of the Security Statute that had been requested in vain from his predecessor by the military.

Decree 1923 of 6 September 1978 called the Security Statute and directed at both ordinary and political crimes, makes the right to strike a criminal offense (article 4), limits freedom of the press and of organization (article 13), and gives military courts jurisdiction over disturbance of the public order. Since its adoption, arbitrary arrests of protesters and critical intellectuals have multiplied. Military courts are even used against Indians who claim their lands,[57] and many cases of the torture of prisoners have been denounced by reliable authorities.[58] The combination of the autonomy of the military and the assignment of many responsibilities to the army empties civilian power of its content. According to the former foreign minister, Vásquez Carrizosa, "The president is becoming the head of a tropical republic,"[59] and the real chief executive was the defense minister, General Luis Carlos Camacho Leyva. It seems that the time has passed when the president could remove the minister of defense or the commander-in-chief, yet despite the suspicions of a process like that in Uruguay, where President Bordaberry cooperated in a military takeover, the regime is still a civilian one.[60]

While this invading army appears to a part of public opinion as the last bastion against the "decomposition of the democratic system,"[61] the military chiefs seem in no hurry to follow the course of usurpation. Strongly supporting the elected president, the Colombian army has not taken power, perhaps because no one really desires it and also because it is not necessary. The military chiefs are sufficiently aware of the experience of neighboring countries to know the risks of direct exercise of government.[62] Besides, the state of siege and the Security Statute are the legal equivalent of a military dictatorship. One might say further that the military only respected the civilian form of government to the degree that the government respected the military elements of the regime.

In fact, the Colombian political system cannot be described in simplistic dichotomies. The army seems to have all the power that it desires. Colombian-style militarization therefore is limited to the area of public order and does not extend, for example, to the economic area as in other countries. With a free hand in the struggle against the guerrillas and an unprecedented autonomy in financial and organizational matters, the military accept the fact that other areas of the state are not under their control. Today more than ever the Colombian state appears to be made up of three parts. A weak state dominated by employers' associations to whom it delegates substantial power has given up to the private sector a good part of its economic responsibilities.[63] The military "manage" public order freely and intervene in decisions that affect national defense in the broad sense, including foreign relations. Finally, the parties divide the spoils of the state, distributing jobs and sinecures in the best clientelist tradition. This "sectorization" of power guarantees a balance that remains problematic. But what appears to be new in the present Colombian situation is not "limited democracy," since the country has known nothing else, nor a "police state,"[64] but perhaps a kind of "limited militarization" that compensates for the erosion of social control by the two parties that resulted from the National Front.

THE UNCERTAINTIES OF THE CONSTITUTIONAL ORDER

No state in Latin America or elsewhere is safe from military intervention, however little the bitterness of sociopolitical conflict threatens the rules of legal coexistence. Thus we can ask how these "model democracies" have survived in a highly militarized environment and a world crisis that has had adverse effects on the less developed countries. In reality the rule of the military in neighboring countries, perhaps because its recent accomplishments are not particularly brilliant, acts to some degree as a deterrent. This is the case in Colombia, where both civilians and the military seem to be quite aware of the weaknesses and risks of solutions that rely on force.

To continue speaking of Colombia, it is certain that the appeals to the army on the part of the civilian politicians, as well as the exaggerated praise given by the executive since 1978 to the surbordination of the military, are indications of an unhealthy institutional situation. The increase in social conflict since 1975, the enormous impact of national or local civic general strikes that raised the specter of the bogotazo,[65] revealed that the regime was defenseless. The weakening of the two trade union federations, Liberal and Conservative in tendency, has increased the importance of a left that is still atomized.[66] Its decline and indiscipline have produced a multiplicity of conflicts. The government kept denouncing "industrial guerrilla warfare," thus providing new pretexts for military encroachment.

The emergence of a class of nouveaux riches often on the basis of sources that cannot be explained but nearly always tied to the "tentacles of the underground economy,"[67] does not help to reinvigorate the moral fiber of the democracy. The "cocaine dollars" laundered in "special" departments of the banks promote frantic speculation and humiliating corruption. The traditional Colombian bourgeoisie is disturbed by these dubious activities that challenge its power and status. Drugs and drug traffickers add to the social insecurity that is becoming generalized. The destabilizing effect of that economic and social decomposition is immediately apparent. Are the frightened new and old members of the propertied class ready to throw themselves into the arms of a savior in uniform? In any case, the military are asking themselves sadly about their role. Some make it known openly that they fought against an enemy—the guerrillas—whose critical attitude toward Colombian society they share.[68] Having discovered in the field the social problems and the misery that affect the majority of their fellow citizens, they reject force alone as a way to end subversion; instead, they blame the state that has given them the thankless task of making up "with fire and sword" for the inability of the system to provide a minimum of social justice. The reformist attitude of the military also applies to the particular domain of the parties. They criticize the effects of electoral clientelism on democratic procedures and the capacities of the state. At the other extreme of the ideological spectrum an anti-Communist crusading spirit is making headway, as is proven both by recent military writings and also by the active participation of the Colombian military leaders in a continent-wide antisubversive plan. In October of 1979 these officers hosted for that purpose the Twenty-third Conference of Latin American Commanders-in-Chief in Bogotá.[69] It is an historical paradox that the Colombian army, which engaged in "regular" warfare in the East-West Korean Conflict, and which since la violencia has waged "irregular"[70] warfare, entered the cold war very late. Here the army discovered the messianic and reductionist mirage of "national security" at a time when neighboring countries were getting rid of that narrow ideological straitjacket. Caught in the crossfire, space for the civilians is in danger of being constricted. How much longer will the Colombian army remain "an example for the whole continent," as its rulers have been repeating for a number of years?

No doubt Venezuela appears as an island of serenity alongside its Andean neighbor. However, since we are to develop scenarios for the future while being aware that they are not the only possible ones, we cannot exclude developments in Venezuela that threaten the civilian order, since that happy and prosperous island (of democracy) confronts acute problems. In the area of politics a new third party has arisen, made up of ex-Communists and former guerrilla members, the Movimiento al Socialismo (MAS) that has upset the COPEI/AD arrangement to the disadvantage of the latter party. Some think that the MAS could even alter, if not overthrow, the system of relations between the politicians and the army by trying to penetrate the armed forces with a view to politicizing them in a reformist or revolutionary direction.[71] It is true that the efforts of the left to find another base in the military similar to the one it had in 1960 do not seem to have been successful. But the replacement of the generation of the founding fathers who signed the Pact of Punto Fijo could lead the civilian politicians to forget the essential rules of the game regarding relations with the military. That could produce a politically difficult situation as petroleum revenues decline, because of the pronounced drop in prices and sales. Already unplanned expenses and massive industrial projects and an excess in short-term indebtedness have led to high inflation, an end to growth,[72] and doubt on the part of the inhabitants of a country that was accustomed to constantly rising economic indicators. What would be only a temporary problem for other less well endowed countries evidently could shatter a democracy used to affluence.

It is not only the recent petroleum prosperity that threatens to destabilize the solid Mexican "democracy." The erosion of the legitimacy of the regime goes back to the massacres at Tlatelolco in 1968.[73] Since then "nonviolent" methods have not been sufficient. "Revolutionary" rhetoric and state control of the mass organizations have lost their effectiveness in a class society, and public violence has often replaced populist emphasis on unanimity. In a public opinion poll carried out among the inhabitants of Mexico City in 1977, 67 percent of those polled said that they had never participated in political life.[74] In electoral figures this was translated into an increase in the number of abstentions between 1961 and 1976 of around 40 percent.[75] Against this tendency of the political system to lose support the regime resorted to "revolutionary" ideology under the presidency of Luis Echeverría, and then to an electoral reform under his successor, López Portillo. That reform, aimed at legalizing the opposition parties and allowing them to be represented in the Congress without affecting the dominant role of the PRI, perhaps did help to weaken the left by legitimating it, but it did not diminish the indifference, indeed the rejection of the system, on the part of the citizenry. The abstention rate in the 1979 elections, the first ones to be held under the new law, was more than 50 percent; for the first time the number of voters was less than the number of those who abstained.[76]

In these conditions the petroleum wealth could have an unexpected effect on the stability of that "single-party democracy." It is certain that in a mass society that is more and more mobile and urbanized, this has raised the level of expectation of the whole forgotten population, of all those of the "revolution's poor"[77] who have not benefited from the "stabilizing development" of the last twenty years. Aroused by public and private ostentation and by the heady atmosphere of the economic boom, these social groups require a rapid response to their expectations.* The lack of any possible alternative in power

---

*This was written before the economic crisis in Mexico, which began in August 1982. (Translator's note.)

deprives the system of a resource that can be used to diminish the pressure. And the swings of the pendulum in the orientations of the presidents no longer have the moderating psychological impact that a true two-party system could offer. This is all the more true because although a well-established petroleum production that is operating at full capacity can permit a politically useful redistribution of income in a society, it is not occurring in the current phase of the Mexican extractive industry—to say nothing of the unfavorable situation in the international petroleum market since the beginning of 1981. On the contrary the burden of investment in equipment and infrastructure to develop the oil industry has created bottlenecks in manufacturing which has not been able to keep up with the dynamism of petroleum, a deepening of the agricultural crisis, and a level of inflation that had been unknown up to now. At least in the short term, there is nothing that can resolve the tensions produced by poverty and underdevelopment.

In addition, the international economic situation is no longer favorable. The ambiguous foreign policy of Mexico that maintains good relations with Washington and defends progressive causes in the name of self-determination and the liberation of peoples is, we know, an important resource for the "revolutionary" ideology. A worsening in the Central American situation, the firm opposition of Washington to the Nicaraguan Sandinista government and to the guerrillas in El Salvador or Guatemala—indeed a possible direct intervention by the United States in that part of the world in order to "contain" the presumed Soviet influence—could lead Mexico to painful choices. If, as is thought, Mexico and the United States have identical political goals in Central America and if Mexico is not indifferent to the multiplication of Marxist-Leninist regimes on its doorstep, how long can it still maintain the contradiction between an authoritarian internal development and a foreign policy that flirts with its ideological adversaries? With all that, the Mexican army, because of the situation on the southern frontiers of the country, is in the process of securing new equipment at the same time that the traditional commanders are being replaced by military men who are products of the military schools, increasing the possibilities of autonomy.

These are the dangers that Mexico must face today and tomorrow, even though it is clear that it possesses considerable resources as well.

Even in Costa Rica today there is a more or less surreptitious remilitarization as increasing numbers of Costa Ricans, frightened by the revolutionary developments taking place and the Cuban presence in Nicaragua, are thinking of reestablishing the army.[78] Those who fear the danger of Central American contagion and the operation of the domino theory are happy with the unification of the security forces and the militarization of certain police units, as well as the creation of a police academy to educate its leadership—all of which have happened recently. However, it is not just because the country finds itself near the field of battle that pacifistic rhetoric is no longer reassuring. The "welfare state" is in bankruptcy. The bad economic situation, due to the high price of petroleum and the fluctuations of the coffee market, is not the only cause. In addition, more and more frequent and bitter labor disputes have produced among the property holders a disturbing anti-Communist and anti-Nicaraguan hysteria. Groups on the extreme right are emerging and becoming vocal, while attacks from the extreme left are frightening the country. Is Costa Rica getting involved in the same entanglements as did Uruguay? Will the "Switzerland of Central America" experience the same fate as "the Switzerland of South America"?

CIVILIAN SUPREMACY, ITS WAYS AND MEANS

If we have wished to project into the future the evolution of the "model democracies," it was not for the pleasure of being correct before others—we hope to be completely wrong in that respect—or in order to avoid accusation of irreversible categorization that is soon out of date. An author's vanity has no place here. We simply wished to show that the situations remain open and are never final, and that politics is not a matter of black and white but of infinite gradations. Our discussion of the possible crises in these civilian-controlled states should not conceal from us the variety of means that have permitted the surbordination of the military to be maintained for a relatively long period in the Latin American context. It may perhaps be useful to summarize the various mechanisms that have assured that civilian supremacy.

The absence of a standing army when it is no longer necessary and even appears to be dysfunctional for the maintenance and continuation of the system is evidently the limiting case. Another would be the existence of the civilian functional equivalent of a military takeover that could take place through the establishment of a state of siege or of nonmilitary authoritarian rule. In that situation political intervention by the army is not necessary, whether because it engages in the limited repression that is adequate for a nonconsensual regime to survive, or because it is replaced in such functions by instruments that are not directly military (police, parties, state-controlled mass organizations, a single ideology, etc.). Besides these two ideal types that are not found in a pure state either in Colombia or in Mexico, nor completely in Costa Rica, there are many causes of military limitation or abstention. They are both of a military and a sociopolitical or economic character, and one must generally take into account all the factors. On the military side, contrary to general belief, weakness or late professionalization operate in favor of civilian supremacy. The fusion and confusion of political and military roles that were a source of instability in the nineteenth century appear in the mid-twentieth century to be a means of control of the armies.

The force and coherence of the party system also seems to play a decisive role, both when it is deeply rooted and identified with civil society, as in Colombia, and when it is confused with the state in a situation of historically legitimized monopoly, as in Mexico. In the latter case mass mobilization from above has permitted the regime to channel the lowest elements that could be dangerous to the status quo; in the first case a classical clientelistic mobilization has an analogous demobilizing effect.

The weakness of social involvement and the agreement not to resort to the army against the existing government relate to the very definition of democracy as compromise and—tacit or not—an agreement for social cooperation. In other words a political regime in which the opposition is incorporated into the institutional system, the forces of the political and trade union left are weak, and popular participation is mediated and channeled or kept at the margin has more of a chance to resist militarization. Having said this, there is still no simple formula against the military tide; one can simply recall in a modest way the lessons of history. All the rest is only literature.

8

FROM THE
LAW-ABIDING
MILITARY TO
THE TERRORIST
STATE

If the worst is not always sure to happen, even on the continent with "open veins," since 1973 the model democracies have entered into a period of instability. In fact a long tradition of stability and the submission of the army to civilian power did not prevent Chile and Uruguay, almost simultaneously, from experiencing fierce and lasting military interventions. Before 1973 it was often observed that Chile had a developed political system that was more stable than those of France, Italy, and Germany, while on the same continent countries with greater resources and a better distribution of income had a far less harmonious and peaceful political experience.[1] In Uruguay, a peaceful republic of European immigrants that had recently adopted a plural executive, public life was serene enough to prompt an observer to remark in 1960, that "the role of the military was so reduced that many Uruguayans had forgotten that they had an army."[2] While in Chile the subordination of the military that had been established in 1932 by a Conservative government had never been seriously questioned, in Uruguay the military had not even participated in power in the twentieth century: the two coups d'état of Terra and Baldomir in 1933 and 1942 were carried out by the police and firemen because of the lack of interest of the army.

At the beginning of the 1980s the former "Switzerland of Latin America" had a sinister world record for political prisoners: one Uruguayan in six had been in prison for the crime of opposition.[3] Torture had become an instrument of government practiced, according to some witnesses, by 90 percent of the officers,[4] who used methods that reached a terrifying degree of scientific sophistication.[5] Chile too does not take second place to the Uruguayan laboratory of repression, if only because the coup d'état of 11 September 1973 was one of the bloodiest that the continent has experienced. Thirty-five thousand died, including President Allende, who was killed, gun in hand, in the ruins of the presidential palace. The exploits of the political police of the National Intelligence Directorate (DINA), rebaptized the National Information Center (CNI) in 1977,[6] which did not hesitate to assassinate its opponents, even outside the country, hardly improved the image of General Augusto Pinochet in world public opinion. Nevertheless the Chilean military, like their Uruguayan counterparts, does not intend to give up direct power before the last decade of this century.* That durable hold has profoundly affected the societies of the two countries that since 1973 have experienced changes and structural reorganizations that are in some cases irreversible.

STATE, SOCIAL CLASS, AND POLITICAL STABILITY IN CHILE SINCE 1970

Chile after 1930 was a deviant case among the political configurations of the continent. Its political stability was based on a complex modern party system. In addition it included a significant representation of revolutionary and anticapitalist forces whose presence, even when a minority, would suffice to upset the ruling classes and the military elsewhere. It was because of an apparent resemblance to the party systems of the Mediterranean and Europe that the experience of the Popular Unity government between 1970 and 1973 so moved and divided France. Upon closer inspection we see that behind the superficial resemblances lay some significant and fascinating particular characteristics. The Radical party was social democratic in orientation. The Socialist party was not at all social democratic, but boasted

*Uruguay returned to democracy in 1985. (Translator's note.)

of its Marxism-Leninism and inclined rather to Cuba, giving only lip service to the electoral approach. In these conditions how does one explain the harmonious functioning of the democratic system and the possibilities of alternation from the Popular Front in 1938 to Popular Unity in 1970—in a dependent and underdeveloped country with extreme wealth side by side with extreme poverty, and in which immense social differences separate the grand bourgeoisie of the Club de la Union from the *rotos* in the *callampas* of Santiago or the *fundos* in the Central Valley? After September 1973 it is no longer appropriate to refer vaguely to "the Chilean spirit" or to "the tradition" unless those two loose concepts express the specific relation of the state and social classes in a dependent society with a special history.

We noted in an earlier chapter the advanced character of the establishment of a centralized state in Chile and the absence of centrifugal caudilloism at a time when neighboring countries were torn by the wars of independence. The "geographical folly" that is that ribbon of land between the Andes and the Pacific no doubt facilitated the centralization that was at the base of the state forged by Diego Portales. The War of the Pacific and the victory over Peru and Bolivia (1879–83) resulted in the annexation of the rich mining provinces of the north, consolidation of the unity of the country, and a change in its relationship to the world market. The victory in effect not only reinforced the prestige of the army but it also legitimated the power of the ruling class that the new export resources helped to unify around the state. The nitrate of the northern deserts developed by British companies became the essential source of national prosperity, but the principal basis for economic power was thus not under the direct control of the ruling classes. This is no doubt what made it possible to separate political and economic power and permitted the development of a representative system that was autonomous and the basis of its stability. A particular type of state corresponded to that particular form of dependence. The majestic structure of the Portalian state was transformed into the "enclave state" enriched by the taxes paid by the foreign companies for the nitrate industry. The ruling classes, practically exempt from taxation, divided the abundant revenues of foreign trade without conflict.[7] The absence of accumulated power facilitated internal bargaining among the elements of the bourgeoisie and removed the temptation to establish exclusive control, thus supporting the operation of an aristocratic democracy based on a limited suffrage. The wealth of the state that continued as a result of the development of copper in the twentieth century, with American capital replacing that of the British, also permitted the early recruitment and continuous growth of a large bureaucracy that is one of the particular characteristics of the system.

In fact, it was through the state that a part of the middle class was integrated into the structure of power. The expansion of public services consolidated the traditional state and "nationalized" it by disassociating it, at least in appearance, from the decisions of the ruling classes; this created an image of neutrality and judicial and political independence that would constitute one of the enduring special features of Chile.[8] The establishment of a diversified and specialized public sector and the appearance of a civil service tradition would also mean that the army did not have a monopoly on the professionalized elements of the state apparatus as one of its principal political resources. In these conditions it shared the dominant juridical ideology.

The fact that the main source of wealth was not under the direct control of the bourgeoisie and strengthened the power of the state seems to have acted to limit conflict within the propertied classes and allowed the entry of the middle classes into a system permeated with legalistic ideology and filled with administrative intermediaries. While the middle classes were incorporated electorally and socially after 1919 and especially after the depression, we should note that unlike Mexico and Venezuela they did not replace the hegemony of the oligarchy,[9] but occupied a subordinate position in the framework of traditional domination.

That incorporation went along with (and perhaps was explained by) a relatively slow political mobilization. The gradual extension of the right to vote was not accompanied by a high degree of political participation such as might frighten the propertied classes. In 1952, 54 percent of the citizens who had the right to vote were not registered on the voting lists.[10] The isolation of the peasants on their fundos, where the landowner ruled by divine right, the force of personal dependence in the campaigns, and the nonexistence of agrarian unions in practice until 1965[11] all helped to facilitate that exclusion. The absence of a break in the political development is also evidence of the strength and flexibility of the Conservative party, later the National party, which still received 20 percent of the votes in 1973 and earlier received between 25 percent and 35 percent of the votes. The negotiating capacity and the pragmatism of that political group was translated clearly into rules of the game that were not a vital danger to bourgeois domination, and a legalism and compromise that were functional for the maintenance of their control.

Another tangible consequence of the enclave economy was the structure of class relations. The organized working class was essentially located in the mining centers so that the relations of economic classes involved opposition between a Chilean proletariat and foreign employers. The parties and labor unions that arose beginning in 1920 and called for socialism were more anti-imperialist than anticapitalist or antiemployer.[12] In contrast, since the workers' organizations had antagonistic relations with the local bourgeoisie that were more political than economic, it could tolerate them more easily. This does not mean—far from it—that basic social relations were idyllic and that the condition of the worker was a happy one in Chile. The massacres of Santa María de Iquique (1907)—two thousand deaths—of Punta Arenas in 1920, and of La Coruña in 1925— three thousand dead—and the brutal repression of strikes in Valparaiso in 1903 and in Santiago in 1905 mark the bloody history of the labor movement. Nevertheless, social hostility was moderated by the altered and muted character of a skewed class struggle in which conflict was transformed into political negotiation. Social conflict was entered onto the institutional timetable. It passed from the streets to the congress, from confrontation (many times repeated but nevertheless always isolated) to compromise.

Many other forces were involved in the establishment of the "compromise state" that underlay the mechanisms of democracy. We have said that the isolation of the mining centers—the *pampa salitrera* and the large copper installations in the

Atacama desert in the north, or the coal mines in the extreme south—permitted a very radicalized worker organization that did not endanger the established order. In any case the confrontation of the nitrate and copper miners with the representatives of the foreign companies and not with the Chilean bourgeoisie reinforced the indirect and fragmented character of class relations and facilitated their resolution in a strictly political framework. Ideological legalism, transmitted especially by a middle class that acted as a buffer and identified with the state and its workings, helped to contribute to political stability. Until the Popular Unity period, the Radical party that represented the independent and salaried middle sectors was the axis around which coalitions of the left were built; no party that was associated with the Popular Front ever questioned the rules of the game.[13] The Popular Front, which came to power in 1938 and resembled its European counterpart only in name, was a developmentalist coalition that was to establish the bases for the state-promoted industrialization of the country. The participation of labor union confederations in the organizations of economic development and control increased the assimilation of the organized working class.[14] The occasional intervention of the state in labor conflicts in favor of the workers also produced the convincing image of a neutral state above class—a situation that was sufficiently rare in Latin America to justify its being noted.

The Chilean army was the army of that state. Out of the political situation from the time of its progressively oriented intervention in the years 1925–32 emerged an army that included all social classes, just as the state appeared to be one that represented the whole people. Along with the isolation of military society—whose members were cut off from civilian life and were turned in on their own special values[15]—went one political taboo: do not touch "grande muette" (the strong silent one). Legalism also affected the defense apparatus. Regis Debray could write accurately that the values of law and of parliamentarism are internalized in Chile even by the parties that represent the workers.[16] This is even more true for the military. If before 1970 there was general agreement on the legal system and if the labor movement accepted the fact that the class struggle was to be carried out on the carefully delineated symbolic terrain of the political arena, it was no different for the military. Whatever the feelings and convictions of the officers, the majority consensus in the armed forces favored supporting those who held legal power. This also meant that for the army to abandon its subordinate situation it was necessary (and sufficient) for it to prove that the executive had violated legality. That attitude therefore reinforced the autonomous character of the political sphere that underlay the voluntary limitation of the stakes and procedures, both of which are essential for the functioning of stable democracy.

Changes in the Political System and the Army

If this network of hypotheses is sound, the vulnerability of the constitutional political order appears clear. The arrangement was not capable of resisting over a long period extremist polarization, the departure from the constitutional framework, or the increase and multiplication of the matters at stake. However, when Salvador Allende and Popular Unity came to power in 1970 the political system had already been profoundly shaken. The crisis did not begin with the entry of the left into the presidential palace. Let us say rather that this crisis revealed the situation, but it went back to 1964 and to the Christian Democratic presidency of Eduardo Frei. Allende was elected by surprise, the accidental result of a three-way election that followed the split between the Christian Democrats and the conservatives of the National party who no longer trusted it. The country did not choose socialism, since Allende with only thirty-nine thousand votes more than rightist candidate Jorge Alessandri received a lower percentage of the votes than he had in the presidential election of 1964: 36.2 percent against 38.9 percent. However, Popular Unity benefited from the break between the upper bourgeoisie and the middle classes, between the traditional ruling classes and the modern bourgeoisie that was promoted by the reformist policies of Frei.

In 1964, the Christian Democrats presented an ambitious

new program in order to counteract the rise of the left. Already in 1958 with Salvador Allende as its candidate the left had come very close to defeating the classical right, which ran Alessandri. In 1964 the Christian Democrats presented an ambitious new program to bring the country out of the economic stagnation from which it had suffered since the beginning of the 1960s. Eduardo Frei, who received a massive vote thanks to the conservatives who did not present a candidate for fear of helping the Popular Action Front (FRAP) of Allende, intended to secure the support of social sectors that had been excluded from the political game and from the life of the society, while modernizing the productive apparatus. His campaign, which was characterized by a sometimes extreme anti-Communism and was partly financed by the American CIA,[17] proclaimed as a reply to the pro-Castroism of his adversary "a Revolution in Liberty"; this program was intended to place Chile securely on a "noncapitalist" road to development that was in conformity with the "social doctrine" of the church. Frei was going to try to reform the most archaic economic structures while taking from the left its main banners and its principal potential social supporters. Thus, the Christian Democrats tried to integrate under their guidance the marginal sectors of the urban population into social and political life through a network of "neighborhood committees" and "mothers' centers." The policy of "popular promotion," bearing the mark of Christian Democratic "communitarianism," was complemented by more radical measures in the countryside. The formation of peasant unions was encouraged, and an agrarian reform law was adopted in 1967. It aimed at ending the semiserfdom of the inquilinos, and at forming small family properties and integrating the landless peasants into cooperatives.

Promising social justice and a continual increase in wages, Frei raised the expectations of the working population. By altering the situation of the peasants the Christian Democrats unleashed forces that they could neither satisfy quickly nor control politically.[18] The employers were upset; the landholding upper-bourgeoisie felt that it had been despoiled by an agrarian reform that did not compensate them "sufficiently" and that liberated their *peones*. The National party felt betrayed. In 1967 a Brazilian integralist published a book that was forbidden in

Chile entitled *Frei, the Chilean Kerensky*,[19] in which the author claimed to show that Christian Democracy was opening the way to Communism. This was not far from the way that the Chilean right was thinking. While the country did not succeed in getting out of its economic morass in spite of several good years due to the high price of copper, social conflicts became more violent and the political spectrum became more radicalized, leading to a split among the Christian Democrats.

By opening a Pandora's box with the participation of those who had been excluded, Frei broke the implicit social pact that was the basis of the Chilean political model. Popular mobilization promoted by the Christian Democrats aggravated and generalized social tension without keeping it within the institutional framework in which it had traditionally been contained. The fragile equilibrium that permitted a "disjunction between the political system and the system of social inequality"[20] was broken by the entry of new actors, the emergence of sectors that had been marginalized until then, and the entrance on the scene of social issues for which compromise was not an appropriate solution.

This was when a "new" antidemocratic ideology was developed and promoted on the right, an ideology that assigned the army a role more in consonance with the "dangers" of the hour. Its authors rejected the concept of an army subordinated to civilian power and their Portalian neocorporatism assigned it an essential place in the structure of the new state. In October 1969, when the Tacna Regiment in Santiago rebelled at the command of General Roberto Viaux in protest against the reduction of the military budget, the low level of military wages, and the disdain that the Christian Democrats in power felt, in his view, for the officers, the majority of the parties minimized the affair. The *Tacnazo* was presented as a sort of incipient military strike of no political importance. The unions and the majority of the parties of the left and the right supported Frei and defended constitutional legality. But the Socialist party refused to issue an appeal in favor of bourgeois institutions[21] and made overtures to the leader of the rebellion.[22]

The Socialists, faithful to the military antecedents of their founding as well as their maximalist orientation and favoring a coup, no doubt knew that the activist Viaux was located at the other political extreme and especially that an important sector of the officers—whether because of corporate resentment or because of the influence of the new Right—was questioning its constitutional subordination and the tradition of military neutrality that had been respected since 1932. These subterranean developments, which were difficult to perceive through the public and "syndicalist" aspects of the *Tacnazo* alone, coincided with the accession to the command of the army units of a generation of officers who had been formed during the cold war and followed the antisubversive strategic reorientation inspired by the United States. The new post-Cuba orientation was particularly marked in a country that had no guerrilla movement but in which the "Communist danger" appeared to be very serious in the eyes of the Pentagon. It is true that no single counterrevolutionary ideology yet unified the leadership of the army, but the erosion of the myth of professional neutrality was a measure of the political change that had taken place in the country.[23]

URUGUAY: WELFARE STATE AND LATIFUNDIOS

Uruguay is atypical in a number of ways. Before 1973 that country differed from the majority of its neighbors in the high concentration of the population in urban areas—more than half of the population lives in Montevideo—a high level of culture, and advanced social legislation. But the party system that is a key feature of national life and goes back to the country's beginnings divides the country on a quasi-hereditary basis into two parties: the Blancos and the Colorados. As in the Colombian case, those parties are genuine communities, long at war with one another, in which party identification is very strong. One is born a Blanco or a Colorado; one does not become one, and those objects of loyalty—especially the Colorado party in the city—played an essential part in the assimilation of the European immigrants from the end of the nineteenth century until the crisis of the 1930s.

The Colorado party that governed the country without interruption for ninety-three years (1865–1958), created the army in its own image—civilian and Colorado. It reached the point that in 1917 the Blanco cadets were expelled from the military academy and that in 1958 when the National (Blanco) party won the elections the military were unhappy with the change of government and the new government had difficulty finding sympathetic generals.[24] We have described one of the reasons that the military did not intervene: the army was not autonomous. Because it was linked to a political family, it did not consider itself above the parties with the right to act as supreme authority and guarantor of the national interests.[25]

That army, controlled as it was in traditional ways, was located, however, within a society that was both modern and wealthy. A small buffer state between the colossi of Brazil and Argentina, Uruguay, with its two hundred thousand square kilometers, had certain remarkable advantages: a homogeneous and well-distributed population, essentially made up of European immigrants; exceptionally rich soil constituting 89 percent of the productive land; and a temperate climate. Thanks to its natural advantages the country became a major exporter of wheat and meat to Europe at the beginning of the century. The "differential rent" created by conditions that were particularly favorable to cattle raising allowed it to adopt advanced social legislation very early. The state thus redistributed a part of the substantial revenues from foreign trade to the urban salaried workers, whose number increased rapidly. In addition the Uruguayan state at its height took control of a number of areas of industrial production and services, and multiplied the number of bureaucrats and the like.

The urbanization (one might say the "Montevideo-ization") of the country and the expansion of the public sector contributed to the maintenance of traditional agrarian structures. Agricultural activity financed urban development in a way that acted in turn to reduce the social tensions in the productive sector and to preserve the agrarian status quo. The substantial bureaucratic elements also contributed to the astonishing stability that the country exhibited for nearly seventy years. In fact, the prosperity that Uruguay enjoyed before the Second World War produced a special socioeconomic system that combined large agrarian property holdings with a sort of urban socialism: in a way the latifundia were the basis of the welfare state. In other words, Uruguay is a European-type society that is built on an agricultural system that is typically Latin American—one in which developed consumption patterns depend on an underdeveloped productive system. Social and political stability have been achieved at the price of a low level of efficiency in the production system and a limited capacity to adapt to economic changes.[26]

In addition, since 1914 and especially since the 1930 Depression, Uruguay developed consumer industries aimed at an expanding internal market. These were hard hit beginning in 1955, following the boom produced by the Korean War, by the decline in demand for wool, the collapse of the market, and the inability to compensate for that lack of sales with new production for export since the area devoted to agriculture continued to decline. All of this resulted in the permanent stagnation of foreign trade and a progressive shrinkage in the national economy. The stagnation of exports, despite the relatively sustained character of the market for meat and cereals, was aggravated by the low productivity of the agropastoral sector.[27] The lack of dynamism in the most important sector of the nation produced a recession in the whole economy so that beginning in the 1950s the growth rate of Uruguay was at the bottom of the list for the American continent.[28]

The economic collapse was therefore not simply a cyclical recession, but rather a profound structural crisis that raised questions about the viability of the Uruguayan model in which a modern society and an archaic productive apparatus were combined to prevent change and adaptation. Confrontation between the different social sectors concerning the division of the reduced revenues henceforth replaced the permanent compromise that had characterized national life. The "pauperization" of the country produced tensions that endangered the social pact that heretofore had been respected by all. Social groups struggled more and more bitterly to obtain a larger share of a national income that was hopelessly stagnant. The galloping inflation was a manifestation of these struggles, along with the political shifts that began to take place with the 1966 elections.[29]

Those who controlled the principal means of production—

that is, the large landholders, but also the powerful financial and export sector—were forced to question the rules of the sociopolitical game. To preserve their incomes, they began to oppose the redistributionist policies of the welfare state and the transfers that favored the salaried sectors and industry. Forgetting the importance of state paternalism and involvement in the economy for the maintenance of social peace and the status quo, the dominant groups preached austerity and the reduction of public spending. The bureaucrats, around two hundred-fifty thousand people or 10 percent of the population, were the first victims of the crisis, however; in 1967 their salary level dropped much more than that of other urban workers.[30] The three hundred twenty-five thousand persons on state pensions—the number of which was an indication both of the aging of a population that followed northern European demographic patterns and the generosity of legislation adopted in times of prosperity—were also defenseless victims of the new situation. The dismantling of the "compromise state" began. It could not take place without violence. The return to economic liberalism demanded by the producing and property-owning sectors was bound to involve an attack on the very foundations of the Uruguayan system.

Direct control of political power was also indispensable in order to achieve that goal. This was why when Pacheco Areco assumed the presidency on the death of President Gestido new people in government who were businessmen, bankers, and large landholders replaced the "political class" that had come from the traditional parties. These were new men who were going to try to impose on the country a plan of stabilization and economic retrenchment, the principal feature of which was an authoritarian control over salary increases. Inflation was controlled, but the economic picture was close to bankruptcy. While the social cost of the economic plan did not seem to concern a government that was not looking for popularity, the resistance of the salaried population (more than 70 percent of the work force) was very vigorous. The government responded to the wave of strikes that shook the country with a military takeover in the case of the employees of the nationalized banks and a modified state of siege (*las medidas prontas de seguridad*) or emergency measures that substantially transformed the social climate and the nature of power.

In this tense if not desperate atmosphere dominated by a feeling of irreversible collapse, a clandestine extraparliamentary opposition of young people appeared. It used acts of "symbolic violence" to undermine the authority of the government and to try to provoke the collapse of the regime. The Tupamaro Movement of National Liberation (MLN) began by carrying out actions that did not involve bloodshed and were not without humor. Created because of exasperation with the bankruptcy of the Uruguayan dream and the collapse of the welfare state, these invisible "respectable guerrillas" defied the state and the ruling classes and established themselves as a derisive counterpower that "judged" corrupt politicians, producing a series of ministerial resignations.

Faced with this undeniably popular challenge, the police remained impotent and the political climate rapidly deteriorated. Fundamental liberties were suspended as part of the "state of urgency." Uruguay became "Latin Americanized" in a disturbing way. Nevertheless the opposition in the congress denounced several dozen cases of the torture of political prisoners, and general elections were held normally in November 1971 after a violent and feverish campaign. In addition to the two dominant parties that were divided into many different currents depending on temporary cleavages and often lacking in ideological or social content, the left established a "Broad Front" made up of Colorado and Blanco dissidents which received the support of the Tupamaros. The Front presented as its presidential candidate a prestigious and progressive military man, General Liber Seregni.

Contrary to all expectations, the candidate who favored continuity, a member of the faction of the Colorado party to which Pacheco Areco belonged, won the election because of the provisions of the electoral law. Juan Maria Bordaberry, a cattle raiser and former agriculture minister, favored strong methods and only wished to follow in the footsteps of his predecessor. The Broad Front, with only 18.28 percent of the votes, had frightened some, but did not win. For its leaders, this was a real defeat even though the Front's candidates had received 30 percent of the votes in Montevideo. In spite of the crisis the political system held good. The two traditional parties at their lowest level of support still remained above the 80 percent mark. However, the traditional voting system had begun a process of erosion and the nervousness of the conservatives, driven by a fear of change and of violence, did not allow them to wait for peaceful solutions to the problems of the country.

THE CHILEAN ARMY UNDER POPULAR UNITY: A CRUCIAL AREA OF POLITICAL CONFRONTATION

The defeat of the "Chilean way to socialism" is blamed by some on the timid legalism of the reformist leaders of Popular Unity who failed to "arm the people," and by others on the destabilizing intervention of the United States and the plotting of the CIA. These two views, which are not contradictory, should be discussed, even though they both reflect a mechanistic logic that is far from explaining the complex political and social machinations that took place during those dramatic three years.

Certainly the defenders of the "universal laws governing the transition to socialism" were not wrong to argue that a revolution cannot be carried out without a revolutionary army.[31] It is rather evident to the observer that to establish socialism against the will of 60 percent or more of the population without using coercion would be an unprecedented accomplishment. However, from the beginning the Popular Unity experiment was carried out within narrow limits, and subject to highly restrictive conditions. The first condition for its survival consisted in remaining within the framework of "bourgeois" institutions and respecting the rule of existing law. "Legality is my strength," Allende is supposed to have said.[32] It was also his weakness in the face of a hostile congress and a majority of the population that did not subscribe to his program of a transition to socialism. In these conditions the army, which was jealous of its monopoly of armed violence, was the touchstone and the guarantor of respect for institutions. How could anyone believe that the military, a significant sector of which conspired in October 1970 to prevent Allende from assuming the presidency and did not hesitate to assassinate the commander-in-chief of the army who was a strict legalist, would have benevolently permitted the distribution of arms to the workers?[33] When the military were only waiting for something like this, who can believe that all that had to be done was to choose the method of insurrection and establish a popular army parallel to the professional army, or eliminate it? The Chilean army of 1970 bore no resemblance to the demoralized legions of Batista in Cuba in 1958. Some defenders of Popular Unity still think today, as they did in 1970, that in the flush of victory everything was possible. All you had to do was name "a captain as commander-in-chief,"[34] purge the officer ranks, and play the national police against the other armed forces. It is true that they also claim that the majority of the officers belonged to the democratic sector and that it would have been useful to "make an effort to penetrate the noncommissioned officers and enlisted men." However, it is very probable that the least effort to encroach on the prerogatives of the armed forces or to take over their internal structures—certainly to modify constitutional legality—would have inevitably produced a military uprising that the "democratic" sectors of the high command would not have been able to stop or abort. To dissolve the congress, create militias, and to manipulate or subvert the military hierarchy are hardly ways to maintain the unity of any army that is unhappy with a government that is only protected by the fact that it has come to power legally.

Paradoxically, more astonishing than the coup d'état of September 1973 was the duration of Allende's government, which almost did not come to power at all. How did a "revolutionary" government with Communist ministers succeed in governing for nearly a thousand days in the face of an army whose war plans prepared it for the struggle against Communism and of a bourgeoisie knocking on the barracks doors with the agitated assistance of Uncle Sam? That feat was made possible precisely because of the fact that the government respected the autonomy and the institutional integrity of the armed forces that Allende made continual efforts to seduce, to bring along, to convince, and to reassure. To those who argued to the

"Comrade-president" that only "action by the masses will stop the coup d'état," Allende's answer was "How many of the masses are needed to stop a tank?"[35] Situated on the edge of the razor—or rather the saber—the Socialist president delayed the intervention of the military by maintaining a dialogue with the army leaders on the assumption that each day gained would reinforce his legitimacy and improve the balance of forces in his favor.

The thesis of American plotting is also based on a solid foundation. The maneuvers of ITT and Henry Kissinger, and the considerable expenditures of the CIA in Chile are known through the official publications of investigating committees in the United States.[36] The American government was behind the plot by Viaux in October 1970 to prevent Allende from taking power—which cost the life of General Schneider.[37] In 1971 it developed a plan designed to produce "economic chaos in Chile."[38] The strikes of the transport workers and shopkeepers which paralyzed the country in 1972 and 1973 were largely financed by the CIA.[39] The "invisible blockade" that consisted in cutting the loans by international agencies and American banks and limiting the sale of certain sensitive goods was designed to "make the economy scream" and therefore to weaken a government that would be held responsible for penury and economic difficulties. Nevertheless, nearly five coup attempts that were more or less advanced and possessed the not always discreet support of American specialists in "dirty tricks" and covert action were thwarted by the loyalist army leaders before September 1973. And the CIA itself had recognized since 1970 that "the military will only intervene if internal conditions demand their intervention."[40] Despite the methods put into operation the maneuvers fomented from the outside by the United States failed one after another. You do not overthrow governments with dollars, at least not in Chile. And, paradoxically, at least two of the plots supported by the CIA reinforced the Popular Unity government and even improved its relations with the army rather than destroying them.

The assassination of General Schneider by the conspirators in October 1970 convinced the congress that was supposed to ratify the election of the Popular Unity candidate to the presidency—as well as the armed forces and public opinion—that only a respect for constitutional procedures would avoid a dangerous leap into the void. The fiasco of the coup by generals Roberto Viaux and Camilo Valenzuela discouraged the parliamentary intrigues aimed at ousting the minority candidate who had come in first in the presidential election. Still more, the death of the commander in chief (a martyr to military discipline) had the effect of making loyalty to the observance of the constitution into something sacred. The casket of the dead commander, with the retiring and newly elected presidents as pallbearers, even appeared as a physical expression of the alliance between a "nondeliberating" army and democratic political forces. The "Schneider Doctrine" was no doubt a powerful instrument to neutralize the coup tendencies of an important sector of the command. Similarly, the first truck owners' strike of October 1972, following several violent demonstrations by the right against the government, brought the military closer to legal power. Disorder was on the right, and legality on the left. Three military men on active duty accepted ministerial posts at the end of October in order to put an end to the bosses' strike. The right denounced the collusion and the politicization of the generals. As minister of interior, the second most important person in the government, General Prats, the successor of General Schneider, was the principal obstacle to any coup d'état, and for the right was the man to eliminate. However, the support of the military—which some have seen as the beginning of the end of the civilian order—while it gave a respite to Popular Unity, showed clearly that the capture of the army was at the center of all the confrontations. As a French journalist noted, "From now on, power is in the barrel of the guns," but this was not true in the ways that the extreme left thought.[41]

The army therefore loyally supported Allende and guaranteed the continuation of the socialist experiment in the name of the defense of the Constitution. This was also to be the death knell of Popular Unity and the democratic regime. No one was unaware that most of the generals were not sympathetic to socialism. The leaders responsible for the political maneuvering and those, especially on the left, who understood the relation of forces and were not content to imitate the revolutions of the past and to adopt their "impatience as a theoretical argument" (Lenin) knew that the road was narrow. The army, linked to the United States, bombarded by the propaganda of the right and importuned by the siren songs of the bourgeoisie to which it felt close in every way, had to be prevented with enormous effort from sliding into disobedience and rebellion. Who would win over the military—Popular Unity, the legal government, made up of a divided coalition and badly served by its allies on the extreme left whose provocations were giving weapons to the right, or the bourgeoisie and the United States who had other powerful means besides the tenuous thread of an eroding legality?

The United States and the Pentagon in particular know well that an in-depth effort carried out with the Chilean army is more useful than the bizarre intrigues of the secret services. Since the 1960s, because the combination of a strong Communist party and the movement in favor of Cuba within the Socialist party frightened Washington, the United States had aided the Chilean army with a generosity that was both undeniable and self-interested. In fact, Chile was one of the principal beneficiaries of American aid on the continent; indeed the second ranking after Brazil, ahead of countries that faced Castroite guerrillas such as Peru, Colombia, and Bolivia. Chile, with some sixty thousand men under arms, received in military programs from the United States $169 million from 1946 to 1972 (compared with $162 million for Argentina in the same period), $122 million of which was spent between 1962 and 1972.[42] Beginning in 1965, practically all Chilean officers took training programs in American schools. From 1950 to 1970, 4,374 Chilean military men were trained in Panama or the United States (compared with 2,808 for Argentina with an equivalent level in military education).[43] The number of those enrolled in such programs approached two thousand between 1965 and 1970, attesting to the increase in intensity of American influence under Frei. Certainly the effects of those training programs were not univocal or automatic. Prats, "the Democratic general," went through Fort Leavenworth. More important, while the United States cut provisions to the Allende government, it maintained and increased military credits. Military aid, which had dropped to $800,000 in 1970, reached $5.7 million in 1971 and rose to $10.9 million in 1972, constituting the only American aid allocated to Chile in that year and one of the highest amounts of that type of aid received by that country since 1962. Furthermore, Chile under Popular Unity retained the ships lent by the United States and in 1973 participated for the first time in four years in the Unitas naval maneuvers—thus accepting, in order to please the military, something that the left opposition had always rejected under the Christian Democrats in the name of anti-imperialism.

In fact, the arms problem was very much at the heart of the concerns of the military. As General Carlos Prats recalls in his memoirs, improvement of relations with the United States was an essential condition of the government's efforts to increase the confidence of the army.[44] The military had been led to fear a change of alliances because of the pressure of Communist ministers in the cabinet and the visit of Fidel Castro in November 1971 that had been given dramatic prominence by the attacks of the conservative press. The means that Allende had to detach the army from the bourgeoisie and American control were limited, however. While he could rely on the legalism of a part of the military hierarchy and on the strict vertical discipline in effect in the Chilean army, he could not prevent the counter-guerrilla spirit and the antisubversive mentality taught by the United States in Chile itself at the Rangers school that was established in 1965 from having an impact on the lower-level officers. The links established by Freemasonry between the president and some of the ministers with the "institutional" generals, and the promilitary past history of the Socialist party which, faithful to its founder, had always voted for defense, and supported the interests of the army against the right in the congress, did not count in the face of those young officers who had been deeply influenced by anti-Communism.

Popular Unity, which controlled the government but not power, was at odds with both houses of the congress, the judiciary, and a good part of the bureaucracy; so that the party was willing to pay a price for good relations with the military. Military credits did not experience the deep cuts that were demanded by the deterioration of the economy that began in

1971. The regime gave special consideration to the army in the areas of salaries, equipment, and prestige. Allende lost no opportunity to praise the loyalty of these "different" military men, which inevitably made them a special object of attention. In a more political way, the Popular Unity president made efforts to associate the army leaders with the work of transformation by giving them positions of responsibility in the state enterprises and services, and playing on their nationalism to communicate the idea that national security also included the defense of economic sovereignty. But that approach only attracted a sector of general staff officers who knew the national situation better then the antiguerrilla captains and colonels. The "democrats," including Generals Prats, Sepulveda, Pickering, Bachelet, Poblete, and Admiral Montero, besides being strongly attached to legality, were inclined to think that the Popular Unity program would promote a process of "modernization" that deserved support in order to avoid more serious convulsions in the country.[45] These men held key positions in the military and then in the government, and they were obeyed. They broke up coups and took steps to neutralize the *golpista* majority among the officers. But neither the right and the bourgeoisie nor the extreme left (including those within the government) made their task an easy one.

Popular Unity, a coalition of parties, was divided between two lines and two strategies, as well as two economic policies and two attitudes toward the state—and therefore toward the army. For some, including a majority of the Socialist party urged on by the Guevaraites of the Movement of the Revolutionary Left (MIR), which was not part of the coalition, but had a significant influence upon it, it was necessary to move quickly in the construction of socialism. These factions wished to nationalize the economy at a rapid pace, to struggle "class against class," to advance in order to consolidate the regime. For Allende, the Communists, the Radicals, and some less important parties, it was necessary to implement the programs, to define strictly the sector that was to be nationalized and the area that should remain private and it was also important to carry out the agrarian reform without fail but without departing from the provisions of the law, if they were to win over the middle classes who had received a number of economic and social benefits.[46] Beyond that, the defenders of this political line believed that an alliance with the Christian Democrats, whose program in 1970 was very close to that of the UP, while limiting the revolutionary character of the experiment would permit it to be based on the support of a stable majority and allow it to be carried out legally—for them it was necessary to "consolidate in order to advance." The polarization into extremes of Chilean political forces decided otherwise. The Socialist party, the party of the president, and the MIR did not want an alliance with the national bourgeoisie through the Christian Democrats for any reason. Their strategy, even officially, was to go beyond the program of the UP.[47] This group was thus both in power and in the leftist opposition. Also, as J. Garcés, one of Allende's advisors, emphasizes, an alliance with the Christian Democrats would have required a break with the Socialist party, which was opposed to class collaboration, and the end of Popular Unity.[48] While the government was becoming divided, the opposition became more united. The Christian Democrats, when they failed to obtain guarantees on the limitation of the public sector and were angered by the loss of their left wing to the Popular Unity coalition,[49] fell into the arms of the right and provided a mass base for the forces of counterrevolution.

The economic approach to the problem of gaining the support of the middle classes who were frightened by the rampant nationalizations and the excesses of "popular power" did not produce the anticipated results. This was because the problem was eminently political, even though the social dimension—that is, the maintenance of the distance that separated the middle level from the workers and the middle classes' ideological identification with the bourgeoisie, was not negligible. The counterproductive effects of the actions of "dual power" carried out by the devotees of "popular dictatorship,"[50] who called for the destruction of the bourgeois state and thus undermined the very foundations of the socialist government also played a role. Those in the heart of the governmental coalition who announced that confrontation was inevitable and expressed their desire for civil war while creating so-called industrial self-defense zones (*cordones*) that collapsed without a fight on 11 September no doubt helped to present the middle classes on a silver platter to the right. This is without saying anything about the able propaganda of the "bourgeois" press that filled its daily newspapers with accounts of the "excesses" of the MIR (which were blamed on the government) and tried to create an image of "economic and social disorder."[51]

During this time the right, which was more united than the left and surer of where it was going, was not inactive. The national and foreign bourgeoisie did not intend to have its property taken away without a fight. Fortified by the support of the Christian Democrats, some of whom had welcomed their inability to come to an agreement with the UP, the parties and corporate organizations of the Chilean bourgeoisie were to launch two frontal offensives, one economic, and the other political and congressional. The first program was carried out by sabotage, and the second through obstruction and provocation. Since the 1970 elections panic had spread throughout the land. It was said that Russian tanks or cossacks were about to appear on the *Alameda*. Investment stopped, capital fled, and sometimes the employers fled as well. Bank accounts were closed and a frenzy of indiscriminate buying and consumption ensued. The politics of rumor fed the war of nerves. In the agrarian sector, when the landowners did not provoke incidents with the governmental authorities in charge of expropriations under the 1967 law, they carried out a "scorched earth" policy. Material disappeared; cattle were driven over the border to Argentina or else they were slaughtered, rather than being given to the peasants. When the drop in the price of copper and the parallel increase in imported foodstuffs in 1971 created economic difficulties, shopkeepers and individuals promoted shortages. Hoarding and willful destruction of certain consumer goods intensified a flourishing black market and obliged the state to bureaucratize distribution and politicize rationing.[52]

In the area of politics an intense parliamentary guerrilla war aggravated the situation and attempted to force the government to violate legality. In addition to the impeachment of a number of ministers,[53] there was also a systematic refusal to adopt any government proposals, however trivial, thus promoting inflation and depriving the government of the financial resources to carry out its reforms. Nevertheless, the right adopted laws that were applied against government supporters, such as that mandating arms control. While thanks to the intervention of the army the first truck owners strike failed to overthrow "the Marxist government," the action attested to the rightist radicalization of the petty bourgeoisie. It remained only to create a climate to bring over an army that had been manipulated unceasingly by the counterrevolutionaries who also offered it an ideology that would justify intervention. The mood became that of civil war. Extremist extraparliamentary groups combined the strikes by the employers with armed attacks and the sabotage of railroads and pipelines; in addition, they confronted their adversaries and the police in the streets, trying to provoke systematic chaos in order to persuade the army to intervene. In the area of ideology, integralist theory legitimized the coup d'état in advance while criticizing the apoliticism of the military. Its authors showed that the Allende government had violated "natural law" by sedition (dual power) and attacks on property. It no longer guaranteed the "common good"; therefore it was illegitimate. Also, since in the name of the general interest it was better to prefer the goals of the system (capitalism) to its forms (democracy), the executive could be considered as vacant: Allende was no more than a usurper.[54]

This was the rationale for the coup d'état that was then set in motion. Since April 1972 some of the generals had been considering it as a solution to the conflict between the executive and the legislature;[55] still, it was necessary to arouse the initiators of the movement and to break down their defenses. The attitude of the extreme left, which spoke about carrying the class struggle into the heart of the armed forces, helped to unify the military leadership, even if the incidents in the navy in Valparaiso were due to provocation by coup-oriented officers rather than to genuine infiltration by revolutionary elements in the crews. The extreme left, in its illusionary lyricism and self-aggrandizement, fell into the traps that had been set for it and proclaimed as signs of victory the violations of legality that were attributed to it, sometimes without foundation. On 22 August the majority parties in the Chamber of Deputies finally declared that the government had placed itself in an illegal situation by violating the law and the constitution through the encouragement that it had given to "parallel power" and to legally unjustified attacks on private property. The opposition parties had majority support in the country. The legalism of the army was preserved. The coup-makers had a green light. The last obstacle was removed when General Carlos Prats, discredited by rather ignoble provocations and outvoted in the Council of Generals, resigned from the cabinet and gave up his post of commander in chief a few days later. Chile held its breath and the loyalism proclaimed by the new army commander, Augusto Pinochet, who claimed to be a democrat but refused to remove the most notorious coup-plotters, only half deceived the political class. The commander in chief did not betray them, properly speaking: he followed his troops. The Djakarta Plan was thus to go into effect on the morning of 11 September. The situation was finally ripe; the coup-makers' absurd invention of a Plan Z that was supposed to have called for the physical liquidation of the civilian and military opposition by the left was a weak a posteriori explanation, which was immediately abandoned. There would be no civil war. Fascism would pass. It was time for the White Terror.

The Longest Coup d'État and the Militarization of Uruguay

The pause for elections and the truce agreed upon at that time by the Tupamaros overshadowed the important decision taken by President Pacheco Areco in September 1971. From then on the armed forces were in charge of the repression of subversive activities. Considering the anti-Communist training of all of the armies of the continent under U.S. auspices since 1962, it could be assumed that their style of activity was going to be more vigorous than that of the various police groups, especially since the Uruguayan army is without doubt one of those most influenced by the United States in South America. Not only—since there is no military industry—does it depend on American equipment, but the number of Uruguayan military men trained by the U.S. army is much higher relatively than that of its neighbors (1,723 Uruguayan military men took training in the

United States between 1950 and 1970). The Tupamaros for their part went back into action at the beginning of 1972 and began to attack the armed forces directly. That unexpected escalation testifies to the increased confidence of the movement in its capacities for mobilization due to the electoral defeat of the left. The MLN believed that the armed struggle remained the only way for popular aspirations to be realized. At the moment that the new president was calling for a vote by the congress on repressive legislation, the Tupamaros assassinated military men and policemen accused of organizing a sort of "death squad," well aware that they would unleash a response of great intensity. They chose a policy of making matters worse, hoping thus to increase the size of their movement with all the victims of mass repression.

In these circumstances the congress hastened to vote the State of Internal War and a Law of Public Order that limited civil liberties and expanded military jurisdiction. The offensive by the forces of order turned out to be extraordinarily murderous. It cost the lives of eight members of the Communist party, which had never shown great sympathy for the "adventurist" methods of the Uruguayan "Robin Hoods." However, the Tupamaros underestimated the forces of the enemy. The intensification of repressive operations, no longer restrained by constitutional and juridical limitations, took effect. The country was divided up and searched, and the capital was put on a wartime footing. The army terrorized the "terrorists," who went on the defensive. Their leaders, their hiding places, and their arsenals fell, one after another. By September 1972, the MLN was practically dismantled. The counterguerrilla strategy, based on the pursuit of information by any means, demonstrated an impressive effectiveness. National and international moral authorities denounced the cruel treatment of political prisoners without causing concern to the military, who felt that they were carrying out their profession as they had been taught.

But the agony of the Tupamaros, rather than leading the military to leave the political scene, resulted in an increase in their claims. The increasing indiscipline of the army reduced the already precarious authority of the president more each day; it seemed that the administration could not resist the vicissitudes and responsibilities of revolutionary war. By giving carte blanche to the "joint forces," Bordaberry took a political risk that was to be fatal for him. The Uruguayan military, convinced that they were defending the national interest, had great difficulty adjusting to democratic practices, even when these were limited to criticisms in congress. Official army communiques denounced parliamentary motions against the demands of the military as complicity with subversion.

The test of strength with the executive began in July 1972. The army revolted against the naming of a new defense minister, set its own conditions, and made its program known. The military communiques, which were distinguished mainly for their ambiguity, no doubt transmitted the existence of diverse feelings within the armed forces. In any case they called for the neutralization of the political and trade union opposition that, instead of supporting democratic institutions, had singled out Bordaberry as their principal enemy. There was a question as to whether a progressive "Peruvian-style" line existed within the armed forces of Uruguay, since in August 1972 the marine officers at the Naval Center attacked corruption and speculation as forms of subversion. In September, after having won the battle with the guerrillas, some military men, on the basis of information, it was said, from their Tupamaro captives,[56] attacked "economic criminals." They arrested several dozen persons from financial circles and refused to release them in spite of orders from the president: among the victims of these acts of "purification" were politicians of the government majority. In addition, army communiques 4 and 7, while emphasizing security, proposed a series of structural reforms including land redistribution and worker participation in the management of factories.

In fact, the military wished to be represented in all sectors of national life. This is why their rebellion resulted in the creation of the National Security Council (COSENA) in February 1973 that was accepted by the president and was to assist him "to carry out national objectives." This council, composed of the commanders of the three branches and four ministers, had as its secretary-general the chief of the joint chiefs of staff (ESMACO). The power of the military was thus institutionalized.

Having imposed their will on the president, the military, profiting from the disarray of the opposition, took the offensive against the congress. While the left, which overestimated the existence of progressive tendencies, sought alliances with the military, the army multiplied its antidemocratic demands against the legislature. On 27 June 1973, the interminable coup d'état finally resulted in the dissolution of the two houses of congress and the establishment of an appointed Council of State that inherited their powers. The provincial councils were also dissolved. Bordaberry declared himself responsible for that coup; the military order was to have a civilian facade.[57]

The labor unions were divided in their analysis of the orientation and role of the military. The National Workers Convention (CNT), with a majority Communist leadership, declared in March 1973 that communiques 4 and 7 corresponded in part to their program, but it called for a general strike against the coup d'état. That movement lasted two weeks and extended to practically all public and private activities. The country was paralyzed. Places of work were occupied by strikers whose combativeness surprised the government and the military. The "civilian-military" government agreed to negotiate, then signed a decree dissolving the central labor union organization that was accompanied by massive arrests of its leaders. The strike continued despite decrees ordering the firing of public sector participants. However, when the demonstrations began to taper off, the majority of the CNT decided to call a halt in the absence of political possibilities. In fact the parties of the left, especially the Communist party and the union leaders, seem to have been vainly expecting a division in the military. They hoped at least for agreement with the "progressive" officers that never materialized. Contrary to the efforts of the left, that preventive coup d'état was supported by the whole army and its unity does not seem to have been threatened at any moment. Was the "Peruvianist" tendency a myth, a smokescreen, or simply a lure to divide the opposition? Of course, there has been talk of the arrest of supposedly progressive officers, or those hostile to the coup d'état. But neither General Alvarez nor Colonel Trabal, who were considered to be the representatives of the nonexistent "Peruvian" wing, seems to have been distinguishable at that time from the entire general staff. The succession of events leads one to think that throughout the period disagreement within the armed forces remained very secondary, compared to factors of unity.

Just as Uruguay was distinctive in having "respectable guerrillas," it had patient and discreet military men who carried out their political actions against the democratic regime at a calculatedly slow speed. Was this a tactic to avoid a direct confrontation with all the adversely affected sectors in a society that is complex and has a long liberal tradition? Was it a necessity because of internal conflicts that had to be settled before acting because of tense relationships among the forces? Whatever it may have been, a mixed regime was put in place with the consent of President Bordaberry, who gave the military men who had carried out the coup the democratic legitimacy of elected officials. However, the Council of State, which was made up of twenty-five civilians and aided the regime in the legislative area, was charged with drawing up a proposal for constitutional reform. The country entered into a phase of "the institutionalization of the revolutionary process," as the official texts stated. This meant in practice that military men were massively involved in the state administration where they replaced or "duplicated" the civilian bureaucrats. Officers directed all the nationalized enterprises, and occupied the positions of secretary general in all the ministries and of assistant director or vice president in all the technical administrative councils. They were also to be found in the diplomatic and foreign service of Uruguay. Bordaberry, all of whose decisions were in fact supervised by the general staff, involved the military officials in his economic policy by appointing them as members of the Economic and Social Council that was established in June 1974.

The militarization of the state was accompanied by the destruction of representative organizations. The parties of the left that were opposed to the coup d'état were proscribed, their leaders arrested, and their press forbidden. More generally, freedom of the press was abolished and the publications that violated that prohibition were closed by decree. There, too, a slow pace was the rule. The Communist party, despite the fact that a good number of its leaders had been imprisoned since 1973, was not systematically persecuted until 1975, which would tend to prove that the Communist strategy that was based on the internal contradictions within the armed forces was perhaps not without foundation. Nevertheless, there was no doubt about the anti-Marxism of the new government. It was because of the supposed control by "Marxist leaders" over the labor unions that the right to strike was suppressed in practice and the unions were placed under the control of the labor minister, who supervised all their actions.

This bastard regime that did not dare to recognize that it was a military dictatorship but rather claimed to respect the republican constitution and its traditional components, the Blanco and Colorado parties, was faced with a decision in 1976. Should it proceed with the elections that the constitution provided were to take place every five years? When President Bordaberry was asked, his reply was in the negative. In a memorandum whose contents were later revealed, he pushed the logic of "military sovereignty" to its conclusion by proposing the abolition of the party system and the establishment of an authoritarian state with the support of the armed forces. When the general staff disagreed with the president on agricultural policy (the army favored the small producers), Bordaberry was finally removed on 12 June 1976. Was this a new military trick? The president fell for being too far to the right, in effect, because the general staff accused him of violating the constitution in opposition "to the most cherished democratic traditions of the country." This was taken to mean that there would soon be a "liberalization" that the president was supposed to have opposed. In fact it was simply a matter of getting past the date of November 1976 when general elections were supposed to take place while promising not to modify the constitution in any fundamental way and to hold an election within a short time. Some observers did not hesitate to relate those constitutional feints to the assassination in Buenos Aires of two former leaders of the hard-line sectors of the traditional parties—Z. Michelini and H. Gutiérrez Ruiz. Bordaberry had lost, if not his power, at least the presidency, but his program was not abandoned by the military. The deposed president had said in 1974,

"General elections cannot take place if Marxism and the professional politicians operate again in our country."[58]

After this new "coup d'état," the Uruguayan military still did not abandon the fiction of civilian rule. Alberto Demicheli, the eighty-year-old president of the Council of State, became provisional president, while the institutional mechanisms were established for the selection of a new president for five years. To that end the armed forces promulgated a series of Institutional Acts aimed at modifying the constitution. In a single year eight such acts were adopted. Some of these gave organizational expression to the political plans of the armed forces; others projected a new type of state based on a revised national vision that broke completely with the "Batllista" model of the welfare state.[59] The new constitutional power was essentially vested in the military.[60] According to the Act No. 3, the executive power was henceforth to be exercised by the president of the republic, "acting with the minister or ministers concerned, the National Security Council or the cabinet" (article 1). While the executive power was now shared by the military, the legislative power was given by the Act No. 2 to the armed forces.[61]

In the First and Fourth Acts the military in power ratified the anticonstitutional government created by the coup d'état. The First Act declared "the incompatibility of social peace with the free play of the political parties" and suspended elections *sine die*. The Fourth Act proceeded to purge Uruguayan politicians with a view to future elections. Most of the potential opposition was excluded from political life for a period of fifteen years.[62] These included the presidential and vice-presidential candidates in the last two elections; all who had held actual or substitute seats in the legislative bodies; all the candidates for these positions nominated by parties that had been declared illegal; and members of the directing bodies of all the parties. It was estimated that some fifteen thousand citizens were thus deprived of their rights.

The Seventh Act ended the job security and permanent tenure of government employees, which was considered as an "irritating situation of privilege." The executive was given the right to remove government employees because of length of service or for political reasons. The Eighth Act abolished the autonomy of the judiciary, which was subordinated directly to the executive. The new state was thus put into place.[63] This "pluralistic" executive was headed for five years, beginning in September 1976, by a seventy-two-year-old lawyer, Aparicio Méndez. Méndez immediately distinguished himself by making surprising statements that forced the military to limit his public declarations. In addition to antiliberal tirades borrowed from the European extreme right of the thirties, the president did not hesitate to denounce France and the Democratic party in the United States as "the allies of sedition"—which did not help to increase the credit of the regime abroad.

While the cabinet was made up of civilians with the exception of the minister of the interior, the military were everywhere. The excessive size of the military, it is true, antedated the era of military rule, but expenditure for defense more than doubled between 1968 and 1973. In 1973 the allocation for the Ministries of Interior and Defense substantially exceeded a quarter of the budget. According to some sources, the total of the forces of order reached one hundred thousand men in 1980 against twenty thousand policemen and less than twenty thousand in the military in 1970.[64] While the struggle against the guerrilla no longer required a financial effort comparable to that of the years 1972–73, the military budget did not decline. It would soon reach 50 percent of the expenses of the state.

The fiction of the "struggle against sedition" always played, it is true, a central political role in the new regime. The omnipresent military were not content to scour the whole country and to keep the citizens under surveillance. In order to dismantle the "ideological apparatus" of subversion, the continuing terror did not spare private lives. The arrests of members of the opposition knew no limit. The critics of the regime were pursued even into Argentina and Brazil by the forces of order.[65] Torture became a standard administrative procedure. While some people disappeared, the number of those killed by the military regime was somewhat less than in other countries. However, five thousand political prisoners, fifteen thousand citizens in conditional liberty under surveillance, and nearly sixty thousand persons passing through the prisons attest to the effective functioning of a terrorist machine that led one to wonder whether it had not become an end in itself.

That sinister tyranny had some bizarre aspects. Besides the disastrous speeches of the president, we might add the ransoms demanded for some of those arrested, the poisoned wine sent to a conservative member of the opposition, or the bills for room and board sent to political prisoners—without forgetting the authorized robbery of the households of "subversives." The expression, "an army of occupation," seems to be an accurate description of the regime, and its policies were carried out as if its goal was to keep the jails filled. The specialists in repression arrested citizens because there were empty places in the detention centers. The files of the interservice general staff (ESMACO), fed by fifty years of democracy and open opposition and officially encouraged denunciations, allowed the circle of suspects to be enlarged without limit. Every group or association was suspect by nature. And the repression did not hesitate to become retroactive; journalists were arrested for articles written in 1968! Generalized insecurity reigned in the name of national security. The garrison state had succeeded the welfare state.

In the workplace and in education vigilance was redoubled to prevent all meetings. The educational system of which Uruguay had been so proud became the private preserve of the military. (The public services functioned like military installations.) It is true that the university had been the bastion of the left and that the teachers' unions were strongly opposed to the new order. The Council on Scientific Research was headed by a colonel, as was that devoted to secondary education. The university was purged and its most prestigious centers dismantled. Paradoxically, after having been forced to sign a "profession of faith in democracy," more than half of those teaching on the university level were removed or exiled.[66] The new educational policy was seen as in the service of "Western civilization" or of "the natural order." Priority was given in the recruitment of teachers to the wives and relatives of the military. Thus we can better understand the words of the new dean of the faculty of agronomy, "We must abolish research since it is harmful to education."

The scorched earth cultural policy even extended to publication and artistic creation. The country of José Enrique Rodó, of José Pedro Varela, and of the weekly *Marcha* had become a cultural desert. As the exiled Blanco leader Wilson Ferreira Aldunate said to a journalist, the suppression of liberty distorts the nature of the country and even endangers its existence, for Uruguay, "squeezed between two giants, . . . was a spiritual attitude, a complex of agreed-upon values, and a political system."[67] But in destroying that subtle national essence, were not the military serving the interests of those who simply desired to transform their country into an economic space?

FROM THE STATE OF WAR TO THE MILITARY STATE IN CHILE

The violence of the coup d'état in Chile was a surprise. The equivalent of a civil war, that counterrevolutionary movement had no resemblance to the peaceful coups that punctuate the contemporary history of other countries in the continent. This was not just a matter of the lack of political experience of the Chilean military. They did not make war because they could not do anything else and because they had been trained for that purpose. The bloody character of the military operation was related to a number of goals of the seditious general staff. The class hatred stirred up by the great fear of the propertied groups and the tales of Plan Z or of a leftist coup in the navy certainly contributed to the ferocity of the "housecleaning" of the "Communists" in the shantytowns and factories. However, it is clear that the military expected a strong civilian resistance that did not materialize. After having heard the "revolutionary" left denounce "legalism" and "formal democracy" and call for an inevitable confrontation with the bourgeois state, and having seen them parade the semblance of paramilitary organizations and boast of the invincibility of the defensive power of a united people, the rebelling generals claimed to believe that the workers were armed and decided to hit them quickly and hard. Against canons, tanks, and planes what worker self-defense would have been able to resist, even if Allende had distributed arms to them? But in addition to that pretext there were other political and operational rationales.

The terror, before affecting civilians, struck the military themselves. This was done first of all to impress the enlisted men, but also because the armed forces, which for nearly three years had resisted their activist elements, included a minority of loyalist leaders who refused to follow. These were removed from any position where they might adversely affect the purposes of the leaders of the coup and with all the more brutality because dividing the army was the basis of the plan developed by Allende to prevent the coup.[68] Only military unity could guarantee the success of the rebellious generals. There was no place for those who were lukewarm. After intimidating maneuvers against the legalist noncommissioned officers and sailors before 11 September, the military opposition was neutralized. Many officers were arrested—the director general and five of the generals of the carabineros, the most civilian-oriented branch with the broadest popular base, as well as three army generals, two admirals, and about fifty junior officers. General Alfredo Bachelet was imprisoned on 11 September and died there, probably as result of bad treatment. The officer corps was thus brought into line. Doubtful elements were eliminated. According to some witnesses the Buín Regiment in Santiago refused to comply. The noncommissioned officers' school of the carabineros revolted against the coup. The fighting lasted three days, and was ended with the use of air power. When foreign radios announced the false news that General Prats had gone to Temuco at the head of legalist units, sporadic uprisings took place again in some regiments.[69] There was talk of two thousand dead among the military and national police. When the junta admitted that there were two hundred deaths among the military,[70] one might conclude that not all were victims of a quickly suppressed popular resistance. It was precisely to prevent a comeback by Popular Unity that the army hit hard and set up the system of terror. The military had a purpose. With the president dead the makers of the coup intended to neutralize the leaders of the worker parties in order to demobilize the dangerous classes for a lasting period.

Over the long term the intimidating maneuvers, the dead

stacked up in the morgue, the machine-gunned bodies left to float in the Mapocho River, the public imprisonment of suspects in the National Stadium, the hostage policy, and the raids and public executions produced a sense of something inevitable and irreversible. The military intended in that way to make any compromise impossible. The hour of the Christian Democrats had passed; the junta had not worked to bring back Frei, even though he had approved of the uprising. The bloodshed had destroyed the possibility of a restoration of the civilian right. The numerous members of the opposition who had waited for the elimination of the "Marxist" government to return to the "golden age" were wrong. The 11 September coup was a genuine break with the past sealed with the blood of the victims. To save the country from "the Marxist cancer" and to "protect democracy," the army irrevocably destroyed the "compromise state" and proclaimed a state of siege that gave them a special tutelary role. The generalized repression and the continuing state terror proved this was not a single reaction to the preceding regime and a "technical" response to the impasse in the relations of the executive and the congress, as some thought. The control by the military of the state was complete even if the organs that had not "failed" in the face of the "abuses" by Popular Unity remained formally in their previous positions. These would include the judiciary, the Contraloria General de la Republica,[71] and the constitution of 1925, which had been violated by the generals but was not formally questioned until the referendum of September 1980.

The junta composed of the commanders of the three branches and the national police gave themselves all the other powers, including that of rewriting the constitution. The definition that the military gave of their role did not set limits. Decree-Law 1 of the junta specified: "The public force which according to the constitution [sic] is made up of the army, the navy, the air force, and the national police is the organization that the state has created to safeguard and defend its physical and moral integrity and its historical and cultural identity." Henceforth, the army was no longer a branch of the administration; the state was an extension of the army. Furthermore, the barracks regime that took power established strict order.

The savage repression—roundups in the Santiago stadium and summary executions—gradually became institutionalized. The cleanup of the "red leprosy" was supposed to have resulted in thirty thousand to fifty thousand executions in the first year, according to the estimates, and ninety thousand Chileans (in a population of some nine million inhabitants) were said to have been arrested. Beginning in 1974, the DINA, a secret police force directly subject to the orders of the executive, centralized the operations that until that point had been left to the efforts of the different branches and unit chiefs. That Dirección Nacional de Inteligencia was rebaptized the National Information Center (CNI) in August 1977, following the assassination in Washington of the former Popular Unity minister, Orlando Letelier, by DINA agents. But the methods remained the same, although relegation and deportation tended to replace "disappearances" beginning in 1978. The change in the name of the DINA and a very limited amnesty law imposed by international, especially American, pressure did not change the political climate or the nature of the regime. On the contrary, at the same time in 1977 all the political parties that had escaped the prohibition affecting the political forces of the left were dissolved. That measure was intended especially to muzzle the Christian Democrats who were suspected of desiring to put some distance between themselves and the regime. Euphemisms such as "state of urgency" instead of "state of siege," "restriction of nightly movement" for "curfew," and "transfer" for "deportation" were intended to improve—especially abroad—the very bad image of a regime that had been condemned internationally.[72]

The counterrevolutionary regime that was created to protect "democracy," even "human rights," against "Marxist totalitarianism" started from the principle that the country was at war. "Foreign aggression" had been defeated in September 1973, but "latent subversion" and "foreign ideologies" were still a threat. "Western Christian civilization" must have the institutional means to defend itself. This is why the military were keeping power in Chile where minds had been profoundly perverted by collectivism. From 1973, with the exception of the economic ministries, all the cabinet posts were in the hands of the superior officers of the four branches. The prefects and regional governors, as well as the majority of the mayors, were military men. Police control of ideas and of intellectual activity was carried out by the armed forces. The purge of the professors and the elimination of critical disciplines in the universities were the responsibilities of military rectors and administrators. Even history and geography were screened by the new regime: geopolitics, in which General Pinochet was an "expert,"[73] became a separate discipline, and Chilean history ended at the beginning of the twentieth century.

The criminalization of all social criticism enabled someone to say that Chile had become "a house of correction for political delinquents." This authoritarian state with overtones of an antidemocratic crusade nevertheless lacked the ideological language to develop a consensus or to mobilize the citizens. Of course, a "doctrine of national security" had been developed after the coup d'état, and a National Security Academy was created for the officers in 1974 where civilian professors, drawn from the right wing of the Christian Democrats, from the National party, and from the quasi-fascist Patria y Libertad gave courses. However, this "doctrine" had no purpose other than to unify the military ranks, to justify a posteriori in strategic terms the political intervention of the army while avoiding any serious thought in the barracks. In order to carry out the redemption it had announced, the junta had no need to convince and arouse the citizenry. On the contrary, it aimed at depoliticizing and separating consumers and producers.

In spite of the criticisms of representative institutions formulated by its leaders, the military order had essentially one economic and social project. The reorganization of society and the restoration of capitalism was to permit the establishment of a democracy that was protected from danger and "capable of confronting the adversary who has destroyed the sovereignty of the state."[74] The anti-Marxist obsession of the military thus was joined to the ideological concerns of their civilian allies. Politics was to be eliminated in order to liberate the economy. National security coincided with the laws of capitalism and the new international division of labor. True freedom is freedom to invest. That is the way to understand the surprising declaration of General Pinochet in September 1977 that "the suspension of certain human rights in Chile protects and in fact guarantees human rights."[75] Equally clear in that respect was Arturo Fontaine, the editorialist of *El Mercurio*, when he wrote,

> Liberty and the rights of man exist in inverse ratio to the presence of the state in social life. The greater the statism in a society, the less there is effective liberty, even if the extent of the exercise of civil rights is considerable. . . . Statism injures the essential rights of the human person, especially his real liberty. More than the power to express one's choice through elections, liberty consists in the fact that one has a sure and inviolable margin to carry out one's life and work and in general to take initiatives without external interference.[76]

That classic praise for the policy of letting the fox free in the chicken coop is at the base of the project of transformation of the Chilean generals.

Capitalist Revolution and the "New Authoritarianism"

The Chilean counterrevolution in fact also had a program. The military, surprised by their own audacity and desiring to legitimate the intensity of the violence that they had employed, were not satisfied with the restoration of the capitalism that had been attacked by the participants in the socialist festival. The adoption and implementation of the superliberal approach of the school of Milton Friedman that promoted the deification of the market was in obedience to a logic that was largely military. The conspiracy theory that the Chilean army was conditioned by the United States to defend economic liberalism and multinational capitalism is not convincing. In fact the United States did not demand that much in 1973, but the rebelling generals adopted the opposite view from their adversary in economics in order to justify their power and to respond to the expectations of their civilian allies. Just as they had taken strong action in the area of political repression, they chose a shock treatment in that of economics. The Chicago boys' model, while it reestablished the "natural" laws violated by the "totalitarians," imposed redemptive mortification on the country in proportion to its past enjoyment. The high social cost of the economic program had both political and moral arguments in its favor. In addition, the general market orientation and the removal of numerous institutions and activities from state control would privatize social demands and thus signal the end of collective action and perhaps of politics. That capitalist revolution, that destructuring of the social tissue, was to assure, in General Pinochet's words, "a future without disturbance or fear." The god of the market was thus charged with the responsibility of permanently expelling the demons of collectivism. A savage liberalism would guarantee politically the freedom to invest. Military surgery would assure the continuation of the system without the necessity of resorting to force.

The freeing of market forces involved several components, some of them strictly economic. However, the removal from state control of activities that could be carried out by the private sector and the abolition of controls, subsidies, and state protection of the economy were the fundamental elements of the model. Not only were the enterprises that had become social property under Allende returned to the private sector (except for the nationalized copper mines) and the free market in agricultural land reestablished through an agrarian counterreform, but traditional areas of the state were privatized in order, it was said officially, to reduce public expenditures. The correctness and freedom of prices became a dogma. Customs barriers that had protected national industry were lowered. Duties went from 100 percent to 10 percent in order to introduce foreign competition and allow a restructuring of industry.[77] Henceforth foreign capital was to have the same advantages as domestic capital. Competition was reestablished by law in the labor market (thanks to the control of the unions, wage negotiations on the factory level, and laws permitting lockouts). Thus the invisible hand of the market could restore harmony in an economic open space in the best of all capitalist worlds.

According to the military junta, these crude orthodox measures led to a veritable "economic miracle." In fact, inflation, which had passed an annual rate of 500 percent in 1973, was reduced to 40 percent in 1978. International reserves, in constant hemorrhage since 1978, started to grow again beginning in 1978. The economic recovery that began in 1976 was undeniable. From 1976 to 1980 the Chilean economy expanded at rates of more than 7 percent per year.[78] Exports increased at a relatively sustained rate from 1974. Also, the utilization of Chile's comparative advantage as well as new uses for its raw materials allowed an increased diversification and a rise in nontraditional exports from 7.9 percent of the total in 1970 to 32 percent in 1979.[79]

The other side of the coin was less impressive. For those responsible for the Chilean economy, it was a matter of the "inevitable social cost of leading the country out of chaos." The average wage level dropped 30 percent between 1974 and 1980. Unemployment was twice that of 1970 and in 1975 and 1978 was around 13 percent to 15 percent of the population, without including the Minimum Employment Program that offered low-paid temporary work for the unemployed.[80] The contraction of the social expenditures of the state and of efforts at national solidarity produced frightening consequences. Malnutrition worsened in the cities and the countryside,[81] while the importation of luxury food and drink rose in a spectacular fashion; the importation of confectionery articles by 16 percent and that of whiskey by 116 percent.[82] The health level of the population dropped parallel to the decline in public expenditure; typhoid and veneral diseases made terrifying inroads again, testifying to the new misery.[83]

Besides the social cost to which neither the technocrats nor the masters of Santiago were very sensitive, there were weaknesses in the economic model. The trade balance was negative almost continuously following 1973. The influx of finance capital raised the burden of the external debt, the service of which represented over half of export receipts, but investment did not increase. The investment coefficient under the military (around 10 percent) was below the historical average of 16 percent. Some claimed that the country was becoming decapitalized.[84] Despite the "generous and nearly irresistible character of the guarantees offered to foreign capital" by the Chilean authorities, according to the Business International Corporation[85] Chile received less direct foreign investment per year between 1974 and 1979 than it had ten years earlier. Barely a fifth of approved investment has actually been carried out up to now, and ninety percent of it is taking place in the mining sector. We are far from confirming the relationship argued by certain authors between the "bureaucratic authoritarian" state and the "deepening" of industrialization. Not only was Chile importing fewer capital goods than consumer goods, but the country was deindustrializing in conformity with the theory of comparative advantage. The participation of industry in the national product went from 25 percent in 1972 to 21 percent in 1977, or a return to the situation of 1953.[86] The military government had emphasized the development of natural resources that accounted for much of the boom in nontraditional exports. The forests in the south were systematically cut and wood was becoming the new "wages of the country."[87] Chile was on the road to underdevelopment although not for everyone, of course. "Extreme wealth" was associated with certain great names involved with powerful financial groups (Cruzat-Larrain and Vial).[88] Concentration of wealth seemed to be a part of economic and social exclusion, just as the repression supported political exclusion. The program of economic liberalism combined well with the program of protected democracy. The weakening of industry reduced the size of the proletariat just as privatization of the state sector contracted the number of state employees: two categories in which the left opposition recruited its supporters. The "five or seven modernizations" preached by the "great helmsman," Pinochet, were to permit the privatization of health, education, and the retirement system. Also, the reformers saw two benefits from mercantilizing the public services: the retreat of the state produced the depoliticization of "sensitive" activities and the capitalization of social security encouraged support of the market system, thus increasing individualism. A change in mental attitude was the objective of that radical capitalist revolution.[89]

The same logic does not seem to have been foreign to the pseudocivilian regime in Uruguay, the economy of which, even more than that of Chile, seemed to be on the way to underdevelopment. In addition Uruguay seems to be one of the few countries in the world whose population is declining in peacetime. With a very low birthrate (1.3 percent), it lost 10 percent of its population between 1963 and 1975. Two hundred thousand Uruguayans emigrated to Argentina and others went elsewhere, even as far as Europe. The country was not only emptied of its intellectual elites but because of a drain that was without precedent, it lost a significant part of its working population. The contraction and aging of its labor force did not favor economic dynamism.

Nevertheless, the brain drain did not disturb those in power. Vegh Villegas, the economic minister, then member of the Council of State and author of the new Uruguayan economic model, is supposed to have said that the exodus would benefit the country because the funds sent back by the exiles would increase the national income.[90] In fact, the neoliberal policy practiced by the convinced monetarists put all its emphasis on foreign trade and ignored the intellectual health of the country. Inspired by the Chicago school, the Friedmanite policy of Vegh Villegas and his supporters involved, in addition to the drastic reduction in state expenditures and the opening of the borders, the concentration of wealth in the high-income sectors.[91] This program was intended to promote savings, squeeze out "inefficient industries" or those "with too high costs," and support specialization in the industries in which the country could be competitive internationally.[92] The social consequences of this kind of policy can be seen in some figures. According to the Central Bank, the index of real salaries dropped from 100 in 1968 to 69 in June 1977. Unemployment in Montevideo went from seven percent in 1972 to 13 percent in 1977. The open economic model of financial stabilization through reduced internal consumption hit in full force the nonexport industries, which only had access to expensive credit. The cattle raisers were also affected and they complained bitterly of the fiscal pressure; their production continued to decline.

The major beneficiaries were the financial export sectors. Because of the inflation and a policy of clearly positive interest rates, the profit rate of the financial lenders was high. The export industries (meat, leather and fur, textiles, shoes) received fiscal and banking assistance. These "export premiums," which were a heavy burden on the state budget, seem to have allowed a certain increase in nontraditional exports in 1974–75.

However, throughout the period Uruguay, no doubt because of the attraction of financial speculation as well as political uncertainty, remained (along with Haiti and Guatemala) below average in investment. This seemed to augur badly for the success of the new model. Despite the profound dismantling of the political and social system at the price that we have discussed, Uruguay did not become a South American Hong Kong, as some unrepentant "monetarists" desired. In spite of the new international division of production, foreign investors in Latin America were looking for expanding markets. Wages in Uruguay were not low enough to attract assembly industries which were too far from the United States to compete in that area with the *maquiladoras* on the Mexican border. But in relying more on foreign demand the new economic model increased the dependence of the country. Thus the Argentine crisis in 1976 produced a visible contraction of Uruguayan industrial exports. The Uruguayan miracle never took place. Crime does not always pay.

DID SOMEONE SAY FASCISM?

How can we define these authoritarian regimes that emerged within stable democracies, were established by violence, and dedicated themselves to reestablishing the supremacy of the market? Precedents help by allowing us to focus on what is likely to occur, at the same time that they influence the alliances that will bring it about. The question is not only one of terminology, nor is it related to the gratuitous temptation to produce typologies. Certainly the polemic on the subject that became fashionable in the intellectual circles of the Latin American left was partly a matter of the fetishism of words, but it does not stop there. At the beginning the Chilean Communist party defined the Pinochet regime as fascist. The whole culture of the party of Luis Corvalán led it to describe its adversary in this way. The classic definition by the 7th Congress of the Comintern seemed to fit the Chilean dictatorship, like a glove except for the absence of imperialism. It was only necessary to adapt the Congress' tactical formula of an "open terrorist dictatorship of the most reactionary, chauvinistic, and imperialist elements of finance capital" to a dependent country; then one knew what its character was and as in 1935 very broad alliances could be developed.

In addition, was not Pinochet's government, like the classic European experiences, a counterrevolutionary regime born out of the defeat of the working class because of the mobilization of the frightened middle classes? Did not that authoritarianism have an ideology, the doctrine of national security?[93] Furthermore did not such dictatorships always appear in late capitalist societies in which, as in Germany and Italy, the bourgeoisie had shown itself to be weak and incapable of taking over the direction of social development? All that, however, is hardly true for Chile and not true at all for Uruguay, where the slow-motion coup d'état was preventive in character. To utilize once more the classic distinction, these regimes are "executioner states" (*bourreaucraties*) that are authoritarian rather than totalitarian and lack an ideology aimed at regimenting the citizenry. The doctrine of national security only appeared for military usage, at least in Chile, after the coup d'état. The mobilization of the middle class stopped with the arrival of Pinochet to power and he never established a party. These regimes, without a single party or mobilizing apparatus, did not have a mass base and did not wish to have one. They did not mobilize the citizens, they depoliticized them; they did not indoctrinate the workers; they urged them to return to their private lives. Far from making them march together in step (*zusammenmarchieren*), they isolated them. Every dictatorship, however ferocious, and every counterrevolutionary regime, is not ipso facto fascist. In addition, there is—at least in the fascism of Hitler or Mussolini—an anticapitalist rhetoric that is lacking in the hymns of praise of the market in South America. Fascism is the "popular disguise of counterrevolution" or, to use the words of Bertolt Brecht, "it pretends to protect the proletariat in the same way that the pimp protects the prostitute." There is none of that here. The violence is undisguised. The military do not engage in tricks.

"Dependent fascism," therefore is not fascism. As to the claim that it is an "overseas fascism" exported by the United States to reduce Chile and Uruguay by force to the status of colonies,[94] the formulation is appealing but a bit brief. In order to prove this it would be necessary to demonstrate that the armies, the instruments of that domination, are strictly mercenaries in the service of a foreign state—in short, that they are nationals in name only. The diatribe departs from reality. In both cases the United States favored a "clean" solution involving "restricted democracy" and those dictatorships showed under Carter that they could ignore the American administration if they needed to do so.

In fact even in similar circumstances of social conflict different societies develop dissimilar counterrevolutionary dictatorships. Even if "the circumstances were ripe," fascism did not develop outside the context of Europe between the wars. Furthermore, the resemblances between our two fascisms are limited since the societies of Chile and Uruguay differ. In Chile the military dictatorship that appeared in a society that was "highly mobilized, polarized, and politicized"[95] evolved toward a system of personal power ratified by plebiscites that assured the preeminence of General Pinochet. A longing for order and some degree of economic success gave the regime an evident legitimacy in certain sectors. In Uruguay, where the working class was not defeated or the traditional parties dismantled, the process of militarization was carried out almost without a break. Faceless and divided generals called a referendum in November 1980 to legitimize and institutionalize their power, but they were defeated. From then on the regime drifted without a leader, without economic success, and disunited, awaiting either the imposition of a military caudillo or the final collapse.

In fact the goal of these military states is to eliminate politics, not to found a new political order. These officer-run republics enjoy a certain autonomy in their relations with the United States, as they do with the bourgeoisies who benefit from their installation in power. The spontaneous statism of these officers of state armies only accidentally coincides with the neoliberal economic policies that they support. Thus the Uruguayan officers, who are bureaucrats in uniform—especially in the ranks of the junior officers who were far removed from the lucrative businesses in which the upper grades participated[96]—were not all convinced of the necessity of privatizing the public enterprise or of "thinning out" the state. As proof, the right given to the state to remove public employees was not applied with the rigor that the Chicago school economists would have desired. A secondary contradiction, one might say. But how do you explain, then, that in Chile the copper mines that were nationalized in 1971 were not given back to the American companies? The answer is that the military were opposed to the seeming denationalization of a strategic resource of the country.

This is why, without doubt, the power of the state remained decisive in economic policy and, despite the privatization of the enterprises expropriated by Popular Unity, public expenditure represented around 30 percent of GNP in contrast to 22.5 percent in 1960.[97] Rather than define the nature of these regimes, we must speak of the function that the military assume. In the face of the crises that we have discussed, they represent a hegemony by substitution—a corset that replaces the flesh and blood of a coherent ruling class. The military prosthesis appears as a replacement for the living reality of an organized and effective consensus. A "technical" or pseudo-state replaces the state based on the relation of social forces. This does not mean that the army is above classes or that it is the instrument of the bourgeoisie, but that it can act in both ways, not alternatively but simultaneously.

9

THE EXCEPTION TO THE RULE

Praetorian Republics and Military Parties

Our discussion of a militarism that brutally breaks down an old, deeply rooted constitutional order should not conceal from us, however, the continuity of military power in other nations of the continent. Stable domination of the state by the military is more characteristic of Latin American militarism than are isolated devastating coups d'état. The lasting military hegemony that most often goes back to the thirties has frequently made "the state of exception"—involving constitutional provisions that have never been abolished—into the rule in political life. Extended over a half-century, that military tutelage has practically become institutionalized and the "military factor" has become a legitimate partner in public life while at the same time the state and the army have become transformed in different ways as a result of that permanent fact of life.* These praetorian republics possess procedures and political mechanisms that are not written down in any constitutional text. The armies that have regularized their participation in this way constitute genuine political forces whose functioning is affected by their nature and manifest purpose. This is the special characteristic of these hybrid institutions.

The chronic instability of Bolivia for half a century does not always guarantee the corporate tutelage by the armed forces of the political system. Factionalism, indeed, military anarchy

*This was written before the redemocratization of most of South America in the 1980s. For the author's later views, see the epilogue to this volume. (Translator's note)

and confrontation of caudillos in uniform, does not promote that process of hegemony. However, for institutionalization to be effective it is not necessary to borrow, as in El Salvador since 1948, the canonical model of a "party of colonels" that dominates the political game and legitimates the corporate ambitions of the military. The officers need not even exercise power directly, as in Brazil before 1964. They can also hand the government back to the civilians, as has happened several times in Argentina since 1930.

THE INSTITUTIONALIZATION OF MILITARY POWER: ARGENTINA—MILITARY TUTELAGE AND THE PERMANENT COUP D'ÉTAT

The presence of military actors is one of the recognized permanent features of Argentine political life. The savage implantation of military power in March 1976 is no more an accidental occurrence or temporary distortion than the more benign dictatorships that preceded it in 1943, 1955, 1962, or 1966. Since 1930 in this most European of the Latin American states, military hegemony has adopted a great variety of forms, including civilian legal governments. From 1930 to 1973 no president elected in a normal succession completed his constitutional term. The propensity of the military to install themselves in the Casa Rosada, the executive residence, deserves to be emphasized; of the sixteen presidents of Argentina in this period, eleven were military men. More notable still is the fact that only two elected presidents remained in power until the end of their legal terms; they were both generals and probably would never have become president except that a well-timed coup d'état gave them the necessary political resources and the support of the army to accede to the highest position in government.

This is how General Juan B. Justo was elected president by a conservative coalition in February 1932 after the coup d'état of 6 September 1930. This coup, in which Justo participated, had removed the Radical president, Hipólito Yrigoyen, and ended the broadened political participation that had been operative since 1916. Similarly General Perón, regularly elected president in February 1946 with the support of the labor unions, was already the strong man of the military regime that came to power in the "revolution" of 4 June 1943. The mixed character of those two regimes involved in the case of General Justo the recourse to a limited democracy, the first use of a procedure that became standard in Argentina during the military era. Justo was elected in 1932 because of a ban on the majority party, the Radical Union Party of President Yrigoyen, who had been overthrown. That ostracism was joined to an electoral fraud that some people at the time called "patriotic" because it permitted "reason," personified by the conservative elites that had been restored in 1930, to remain in power, thus keeping the conduct of affairs in a time of crisis from the "inexpert hands" of the Radical "plebeians."

While the Radicals were victims of proscriptions or of fraud from 1930 to 1943, Peronism, which had a majority in 1946, was also proscribed, beginning with the "liberating" coup d'état of 1955. Until 1973 the central problem of political life was the insoluble one of politically integrating the voters and masses of Peronism without endangering the system. A minority-based democracy resulted in unstable and improperly elected governments. Also, the successive coups d'état (1962 and 1966) always had among their causes the desire of the military to keep the Justicialist party "populace" from gaining power.

The proscription of those who would be the winners under a system of universal suffrage could also be associated with a "neutrality" on the part of the military that was biased in favor of those who appeared likely to lose. The de facto government supported a civilian candidate who defended its interests. However, after 1955 the disenfranchised Peronist voters kept undermining the carefully organized and executed plans of the military. In 1958, after three years of an anti-Peronist military regime, the opposition candidate was elected; this thanks to the votes of the supporters of General Perón, who, after being expelled from the country in 1955, wished to demonstrate his strength. The president elected in this way, Arturo Frondizi, was condemned from the start by an army with economically ultrafree enterprise tendencies that was determined to "dePeronize" the country.

In 1963 after the overthrow of President Frondizi as a result of a series of maneuvers punctuated by military confrontations, the army—now dominated by a *desarrollista* wing that was opposed to economic liberalism (*los azules*)—ended up allowing the candidate linked to the defeated military faction to win the elections. President Illía, who was close to the officers who overthrew Frondizi, was himself overthrown in June 1966 by "industrialist" military men who supported the economic policy that followed his predecessor.

Thus minority presidents came to power under the strict vigilance of an army that was itself divided into tendencies that had obvious civilian affinities. The dichotomy between the predominant orientation of the army and that of the civilian government produced permanent instability. The army did not intervene as a last resort or in exceptional circumstances, but as "the military party" to force the adoption of a policy that public opinion did not want. Strictly military mechanisms such as the search for compromises that would maintain institutional unity might come into operation either to moderate or aggravate, as in 1963, that destabilizing pattern. The civilian government could try to manipulate that military guidance but it was condemned from birth to be overthrown, or, in the interim, to remain impotent.

The process was not fundamentally different between 1973 and 1976 under the various Peronist governments before the March 1976 coup. The same mechanisms enabled the military, driven from power by an electoral landslide on 25 April 1973 in a situation of almost universal condemnation, to make the people forget three years later the authoritarian stagnation and unpopularity of seven years of "the government of the armed forces" (1966–73). Thus, it was possible to take power again by violence in a situation in which the public was stunned but relieved.

The return of the Peronists and of Perón himself to power in 1973 after the defeat of the "Argentine revolution" headed by General Juan Carlos Onganía seemed to mark the end of an historical cycle. When he returned from his long exile in Spain Perón offered to avoid the *Argentinazo*, a "coup by Argentines," which the rising revolutionary violence had led the disunited military to fear. The proscriptions ended. The army, after having experienced a political rout, returned to the barracks. In fact, however, despite their apparent debacle, the armed forces did not leave the political scene. One military sector intended to participate in the "Justicialist Revolution" after sanctioning Perón's removal of the transitional Peronist president, Hector Campora, whom he had had elected. At the death of the leader in July 1974 his wife and heir, who had become president, was compelled to obtain military support. The high command now played a different game, that of neutral last recourse. The patience and inaction of the general staff again legitimated the intervention of the army and justified the ferocious repression that the new regime established in March 1976.[1]

As we have seen, the relations of the civilians and the military were based on attitudes and expectations that are profoundly different from those that prevail in stable pluralist representative systems. First of all, contrary to the view of an ethnocentric liberalism, in the Argentine political system there are not two separate spheres lined up like two camps prepared for battle—the civilian on one side and the military on the other. This is for the simple reason that the intervention of the military is, if not legitimate, at least legitimated by large sectors of public opinion. Far from producing a sacred union of the political class or of the social forces organized to defend democratic institutions, every military uprising immediately secures the support—whether public or not—of the opposition to those in power. But the appeal to the military is not only a means of political revenge at the disposal of minority sectors. Militarism is present in nearly every party. In spite of their pronounced conservative tendency and traditional anti-Communism the armed forces do not appear in the discourse of the political class (even after 1976) as members, by definition or by nature, of a single defined ideological or social sector. Not only the Peronists, whether of the right or the left, reach out to the military, but even the orthodox Communist party and almost all the sectors of the nonviolent extreme left long for an alliance with "patriotic and progressive officers," or an improbable "Nasserist" revolution.[2]

Thus army intervention was never rejected by a bloc as a

danger to the free development of political life or simply as the "instrument of the ruling classes." Rather, the military were perceived as difficult—even unpredictable—partners in a complex and sometimes Byzantine game in which nothing could take place against them or without them. If antimilitarism is nonexistent on the level of representative party institutions—it was different among the ordinary citizens, especially after 1976—it was not only the civilians who knocked on the barracks doors to resolve their own conflicts; the officers themselves also sought civilian support in the internal struggles of "the military party."

Thus the opposition cultivated military action to increase their weight or even to overthrow the authorities in power, and successive governments tried to obtain from the armed forces a legitimacy that often seemed decisive. The military on their part forged alliances with the parties (or the labor unions) at times to satisfy personal ambitions, but most frequently to reinforce one tendency or group against its institutional adversaries. It was understandable that in a situation of interdependence that had produced a militarization of political life and an accepted politicization of military institutions a return to a model of liberal constitutionalism seemed unlikely. What was more difficult to understand with reference to these standardized and legitimized procedures was the unusual level of violence of the coup d'état of March 1976 that was more like a counterrevolutionary break, plunging the country into one of the darkest and most uncertain periods in its history.

The junta that deposed and arrested Isabel Perón on 24 March 1976 cited the requirements of the struggle against terrorism and the guerrilla movements, one of which claimed to be Peronist.[3] In fact the vacuum of power, the decay of official Peronism, and the economic chaos formed a pattern of political violence that could not leave the army indifferent. But the conjunction of the two threats explains the initiation of the "machine for killing" that continued its antiterrorist activities even after the guerrillas had been militarily annihilated. With the support of the government elected in 1973, the revolutionary left of the Peronist youth had infiltrated the workings of the state, from which, the military argued, they had to be extirpated. Finally, the mobilization of a working class that was highly combative and had gone beyond the bureaucratized and often corrupt official unions seemed to be a serious danger for the established order. This is why the war against the guerrillas unleashed repression against a social class (the workers) and an age group (the young) that might include "subversive delinquents." However, the astonishing element was not the counterrevolutionary antiterrorist aspect of the new version of Argentine militarism. What was especially striking was that the nonmilitary political actors behaved in their traditional way, that is, almost disregarding the demented murderousness of the repressive apparatus. Even with blood on its hands, the military party remained a legitimate partner.

THE BRAZILIAN CASE: "MODERATING POWER" AND "GUIDED DEMOCRACY"

When the armed forces in Brazil took over the government on a lasting basis in 1964 after deposing the constitutional president João Goulart, the case was different from Argentina because the military intervention was an unusual action that had never occurred since the overthrow of the empire in 1889. Nevertheless, the Brazilian army had been present at all the turning points in the history of the nation and a determining force in periods of crisis. The old army of Deodoro da Fonseca and Floriano Peixotto established the republic in 1889 before handing it over to civilians. In 1930 the army also helped to end the oligarchic republic. Likewise, in 1937 it permitted the establishment by coup of the centralizing dictatorship of the Estado Novo of Getulio Vargas. Also, the army that had supported that authoritarian experiment deposed Vargas in 1945 and established a democratic system. That nonauthoritarian period appears atypical and brief to many authors, "an experiment in democracy," to use the subtitle of the work of Skidmore,[4] that ended with the April Revolution of 1964.

The radically new institutional character of the action of the Brazilian military in 1964 was accompanied by more traditional elements in the political and economic content of the apparent rupture. In fact if we consider the purpose of the six military interventions that have taken place in Brazil since 1930 without an assumption of power, we note that the armed forces intervened four times against pluralistic democracy (in 1937, 1954, 1961, and 1964) and only twice to guarantee constitutional legality (1945 and 1955). In its program of economic development the 1964 coup was also not unique:[5] two previous interventions could also be considered to be economically liberal and anti-nationalist (1954 and 1961), to the point that authors have been able to describe those interventions that did not involve taking power as trial coups against the existing government.[6]

This series of pressures and regulating coup-like interventions in alternating directions seems to support the thesis of a "moderating power" that the army is supposed to have inherited from the emperor and exercised until 1964. This role, which is difficult to define legally, consists in avoiding crises, reestablishing political equilibrium, and "correcting" the legal authorities and national representatives when they act in opposition to the real relations of force and de facto authorities.[7] It is a "power that is not active, not creative, that preserves and reestablishes";[8] it maintains "order," and guarantees "progress" in accordance with the national motto.

In fact to reduce the action of the military to that model would be to credit the armed forces with a political coherence and a unity of views that is exactly what they lack. It has often been observed that the Brazilian armed forces do not intervene in politics because they are more united and more efficient, and better able at the same time to maintain the continuity of national policy than the civilian politicians.[9] The opposite seems to be true. If it is true that since 1930 the military, and in particular the army, have constituted a power above the government against which one cannot govern, the armed forces, which are profoundly politicized or at least "ideologized," were divided between 1930 and 1964 into two grand tendencies whose public confrontations punctuated political life. Majorities, or rather changing dominant groups, now favorable to a populist national line of Vargas and his heirs, now close to the conservative economic liberals, fixed the limits and guarantees of governmental autonomy. Not only did a hegemonic sector within the army sanction and ratify the election results to decide who should govern, but in addition every government was required to neutralize its adversaries in the armed forces before it could have a free hand. This meant placing prestigious and loyal, that is, sympathetic, officers in key positions. Without that famous *dispositivo militar*, an almost official expression to designate a quasi-institution,[10] no political stability was possible. Still, the barometer that was constituted by the elections in the Clube Militar had to be in consonance with the orientation of the government. That is, the majority in the elections for the officers of that military social center could not be hostile to the existing government. Thus, in a civilian system with a strong military component, the elections in the Clube Militar became, particularly after 1950, almost as important for the survival of the governments as national political elections.[11]

It is true that the parties and political forces extended their activities into the army in a quasi-institutionalized way. Thus the conservative party (National Democratic Union—UDN) saw itself as in the line of the Cruzada Democrática, sometimes referred to as the "military UDN," whose leaders took power in 1964. That party also played a role in the first ranks of the coup d'état and populated the civilian ministries of the first "revolutionary" president, Castello Branco. In turn the leaders of the armed forces had their clienteles or civilian alliances, and the passage from the military order to the field of politics was continuous. In the 1945 presidential elections two generals represented the two camps: the UDN was represented by Brigadier General Eduardo Gomes and the Getulists by General Gaspar Dutra for the Social Democratic party. Gomes was a candidate again in 1950 and was beaten this time by Vargas himself. In 1955 he was replaced as the candidate of the UDN by former *tenente* Juarez Tavora. In 1960 General Teixeira Lott was the candidate of the anti-UDN forces. There were military men in the leadership of the parties and in the congress. General Goes Monteiro, who was a "professionalist" and deeply involved in the national politics of the Getulist era, helped to found the PSD, one of the two parties that were heirs of the Estado Novo, and he was one of its senators as well. This is to say nothing about Luis Carlos Prestes, the "Knight of hope" who soon became a civilian and then general secretary of the Communist party.

In fact, following the logic of "praetorianism"[12] all groups tried to obtain the support of the military in order to increase their power. If an adversary gained the favor of the military, this did not diminish the "militarist" ardor of those who lost. Thus Salles Oliveira, the unsuccessful adversary of Vargas in 1937, appealed to the military at the beginning of the Estado Novo to reestablish democracy. The former candidate of the liberals for the presidency, in exile at the time, far from attacking the army that had just established the dictatorship, declared, "There is no solution outside of the army to the Brazilian crisis."[13] Thirty years later the Marxist military historian Werneck Sodrè, in his *Historia Militar do Brasil*, published immediately after the 1964 coup,[14] revealed a touching blind faith in the democratic and popular character of his country's army and refuted those who at that time were denouncing the collusion of the Brazilian military with social reactionaries and the interests of grand foreign capital.

While between 1930 and 1964 all the political actors sought to coopt the officers, the interventions of the army were often not strictly military. This was also true of the seizure of power by the army in 1964. We can ask, however, why it was that the military took power at that time directly and for a lasting period, contrary to their earlier practice. In other words, why did the army not limit itself to a corrective intervention? There was no lack of civilian or military justification, which should not be confused with the contemporary or profound causes of the change of regime. In the cold war climate produced by the Cuban crisis it was possible to believe or to pretend to believe in Rio de Janeiro as well as in Brasilia or Washington that the situation was a revolutionary one and that the Communist danger was urgent.[15] The military were seizing power in an extreme situation to save "democracy"—defined, according to the military and their allies, as "a form of development in which a substantial part of the decisions are made as a result of the free play of market forces"[16]—in short, capitalism. Given the intensity of the threat regulatory pressure was not enough.

However, the events of 1964 were responses to more complex determinants, some of them immediate, and some more general. It is true, as Peter Flynn emphasizes, that in 1963–64 under the presidency of Goulart everybody in the government and in the opposition was trying "to destroy the formal political system,"[17] to distort it, or to short-circuit it. In addition, the military leaders were disturbed to see that with Goulart the populist nationalism that they had removed in 1954 had returned to power. The leaders of the right wing of the military, when they could not prevent him from occupying the presidency in September 1961, prepared his overthrow from that time on, and retained the power to prevent a return of the "old demons." Thus Goulart in 1961 was in the situation of Allende in Chile in 1970.[18] The economic crisis—especially the inflation to which the military bureaucracy is so sensitive—as well as a revolt of the sergeants in Brasilia in September 1963 that was perceived as a revolutionary threat to the hierarchy,[19] helped to bring about the unity of the military leadership against the constitutional regime and the acceptance within the army of a military tutelage over the state. However, another reading is also possible.

The program of national development that was initiated in the 1930s and that supported the populist political regimes entered into a crisis around 1953–54. This was concealed by creation of the national petroleum company, Petrobras in 1953, but was expressed symbolically by the suicide of Getulio Vargas in the following year.[20] In the presidency of Juscelino Kubitschek (1956–61), who built Brasilia, the *desenvolvimentista* policy opened the country to grand international capital and Brazil experienced a new phase of industrialization. In that phase, during which strongly capital-intensive industries were established to produce durable consumer goods with a complex technology, the model of income distribution was changed. The relative expansion of the market among the urban lower classes that was characteristic of the "populist" period ended. Also, social tensions increased at the same time that the "integrating" resources of the state established by Getulio Vargas became more limited and ceased to absorb social conflicts.

Thus, state control over labor based on paternalistic labor legislation was transformed into pressure from a radicalized labor force upon the machinery of the state. The specter of a "syndicalist republic" along the lines of the Peronist model appeared to be an "inversion" of the populist system that no longer served as a guarantee against the social threat. Evidently this phenomenon was perceived as distinctly subversive by the military. A revolutionary general in 1964 saw it in this way when at the same time he condemned both the creator of Brasilia and the former labor minister of Vargas: "An inflationary and pharaonic development . . . was aggravated by the demagogic doctrines of Communism and both of them produced a disastrous wage policy in which the labor unions were manipulated by leaders who were known Communists and wage claims were transformed into demands placed on the government."[21]

In addition nationalism no longer acted as a restraint on social struggles. The national solidarity of the populist period could not resist the denationalization of large sections of the economy. Also one could see that certain sectors of the internal bourgeoisie that had been sheltered until then by the state now rejected it and embraced the old liberal ideology and/or sought association with foreign firms. The crisis of the populist state was indeed a general crisis of the state. Also, 1964 was a sort of *coup pour l'état*, that is, an institutional break that was aimed at reconstituting and reinforcing the structure of the state on different bases.

It is not surprising that along parallel lines within the military the nationalist tendency lost ground in the face of the ideological offensive posed by the so-called democratic current that was closely tied to the American army. The cold war and the exhaustion of the program of nationalist development in effect operated in favor of the "Atlanticist" liberals, dominated by the former members of the Brazilian expeditionary force (FEB) during the Second World War. In effect the Brazilian officers of the FEB, which was part of the Fourth Corps of the American army that fought in Italy, formed a nucleus of prestigious officers, a veritable military pressure group devoted to the defense of American-Brazilian friendship as well as that of "the American way of life." This same group of pro-American officers, anti-Vargas and attached to free enterprise, took an important part in the development in the *Escola Superior da Guerra* (ESG) of the doctrine of *segurança nacional*. Although an American mission helped to reorganize the ESG in 1949, this was not in any way a foreign transplant but responded to an intellectual tradition within the army that goes back to tenentismo.[22] That doctrine, based on the internalization of the values of the cold war of the 1950s, links development and security and gives the army the function of defining "permanent national objectives" while also justifying its usurpation of power. The overall concept of a "dominant antagonism" and of the insurmountable nature of the East-West confrontation that forms its central theme appeared well before the Pentagon in the 1960s invited the armies of the continent to prepare for antisubversive struggle and counterrevolutionary war. However, it is obvious that the strategic reorientation of the Kennedy period reinforced the group of "democratic" officers of the Brasilian *Sorbona* in opposition to the nationalists who were weakened by the Castroite threat. When the cold war took over the Americas the ESG group was ready to translate that situation in politicocorporate terms and to achieve hegemony within the armed forces.

Furthermore, in 1964, General Castello Branco, head of the revolution, did not claim to be establishing a genuine military dictatorship. The mobilization against Goulart was carried out in the name of a constitutional order that was felt to be threatened by the Communism and demagogy of the populist state. The victors in 1964 were liberals who wished to strengthen and protect the state by purifying the democratic system then in force without abolishing it. For them it was a matter of defending the institutions of the 1946 constitution by forbidding the participation of its presumed "adversaries," the leaders of the left and the populist politicians. That "moderate" program of a protected democracy turned out to be inoperative very quickly in the face of the strength of the traditional parties, the pressures of the more hard-line sectors of the military, and general dissatisfaction with the economic model that was chosen.[23] After electoral defeats that were unacceptable to the new regime in 1965, who perceived the results as a dangerous popular mobilization against the limitations on democracy and the social cost of the economic model, the president assumed dictatorial powers with the Institutional Act No. 5 of December 1968, thus formalizing a movement toward authoritarianism that had been going on since 1966.

THE CAUSE OF THE STATE

The praetorian reversal that in different ways characterizes the Argentine and Brazilian political systems is only explained tautologically by civilian attempts to coopt the military. To try to understand what has taken place over a period of fifty years in terms of the danger of revolution or control by the Pentagon is both anachronistic and irrelevant. The propensity to intervene and the search for military alliances by the civilian political forces are clear indications of the low level of coherence of the ruling class. In this connection the concept of crisis of hegemony is often used to signify that the dominant group or sector no longer has the legitimacy to direct the society; indeed that no group within the ruling classes is recognized as able to direct development. The alienation of the middle classes that are becoming radicalized and the seizure of the mechanisms of control by the lower classes manifests in a dramatic way the incapacity of the bourgeoisie to "organize the consent" of the lower elements. In these conditions the thesis of a "Bonapartist exchange" between the bourgeoisies and the armed forces seems to have some foundation. In exchange for its economic security the bourgeoisie in crisis cedes to the military the direct control of the state and the political system. As a defensive apparatus, by its nature the military defends what exists and thus in the face of social disintegration, it constitutes a last recourse for the continuation of the system. Nevertheless, these explanations, however attractive they may be, also seem to be inadequate.

Why indeed the military? Would not civilian dictatorships be more reliable, with a lower political cost and greater predictability? The "Bonapartist exchange" with a tractable Napoleon III rather than a state institution could be a better way to overcome the crisis of hegemony. An explanation that concentrates solely on the "inputs" of the crisis does not explain an inevitable resort to the military "output." We must therefore return to the armies themselves to discern the basic reasons for their control. Usurpation or hegemony of the military takes us back to the nature of the military apparatus and of the state. The transformation of a body within the state into the state itself does not involve only the actions of society.

The Brazilian case illustrates rather well the importance of the relation between the army and the state. Historically the state in Brazil dominated and directed the centrifugal forces that pulled apart the continental immensity that is Brazil. Under the empire and under the new republic after 1930 the state bureaucracy possessed a high level of autonomy. The size of the state machinery can be explained by referring to external dependency and the need for the political center to intervene to counterbalance the instability of world economic fluctuations;[24] the financial history of the coffee trade testifies to that role. Reference has also been made to the slave trade, the lateness of abolition, and the necessity of state protection of slave masters both abroad and also within the country. The state thus regulated the participation of social actors and served as an intermediary. As Luciano Martins observes correctly, it is difficult to determine the line between the state and the political system,[25] and parties and pressure groups are directed toward the centralized state—indeed are almost a part of the state. And since the state easily replaces the nation and absorbs and stifles civil society, it is not surprising that its central element should take over the state.

Also the army, the guarantor of that preeminent role, easily becomes the manager of the state machine. It acts to reject social groups and political forces that are obstacles to its functioning and expansion. The military are not "the watchdogs of the oligarchy" or big capital, but the guardians of the state who keep it free from the action of those that they believe may be dangerous or useless. As the gatekeepers of participation in the 1960s, they justified their "statolatry," which was both voracious and rational, in economic terms. Certainly the grandeur of the country and the strategic capabilities of its industry are major concerns of the military. However, growth is also in a way another name for the state. Also, the doctrine of national security that tightly links security and development has no other goal than to remove economic expansion from the vagaries of political life[26]—which also means eliminating the uncertainty that democracy produces in the state.

The definitions of "national power" developed by the Superior War School are clear in that respect. "National power is the integrated expression of all the means at the disposal of the nation in a given period for the promotion and maintenance by the state, both internally and in the international domain, of the objectives of the nation in spite of all existing opposition."[27] And the policy of national security is "all the measures, plans, and norms that are directed at removing, reducing, neutralizing, or eliminating the present obstacles to the realization or maintenance of the objectives of the nation." There is a continuity from General Goes Monteiro in 1937 calling for a "progressive augmentation of the power of the state . . . to regulate all collective life"[28] to General Emilio Garrastazú Médici in 1970, after he became president, defending the suppression of liberal democracy by referring to the "violent mutations of the socioeconomic structure" in one phase of planned industrialization.[29] The dream of the tenentes of a conserving modernization carried out by a "depoliticized" state was finally realized after 1964. The only large bureaucratic corporate group within the state created "the administrative state." If that technocratic authoritarianism remains today to guarantee the system of domination against those who wish to change it, that fact is not merely a translation into military terms of a conservative orientation. The military are not defending the cause of the people, it is true, but they are defending, above all, that of the state. Their ideology is neither fascism nor liberalism, but an "ideology of the state," or as F. H. Cardoso correctly emphasizes, a "nationalistic statism that has replaced the anti-imperialist national populism that preceded it."[30] This does not mean that the military are endowed with an objectivity that transcends society or that the policies that they support do not favor one or another propertied sector. The ultraliberal model of an economic opening that they imposed in 1964 is a completion of the political counterrevolution. It was intended to liberate the state from the influence of the labor unions and the burden of the nationalist and populist parties. It punished "bad producers and bad consumers"[31] and produced a regressive redistribution of income.

While doing so, the military maintained their political autonomy, although they did not increase it, and in general they did not act as simple courtiers of the bourgeoisie.

THE STATE AND NONHEGEMONIC DOMINATION

The mechanisms of military domination in Argentina do not differ fundamentally, at least in their apparent goals, from those of Brazil. Through periodic intervention that produced political discontinuities, the Argentine army successively removed from power the middle classes and their representatives (1930), the export agriculture oligarchy (1943), the labor unions and populist parties (1955), the industrial sectors (1962), the traditional political parties (1963), and again the unions and populism in 1976. These measures were preliminary steps to breaking up the combination of the working class and the radicalized middle classes. These interventions, which might seem to be removing the state from the control of the industrialists, the agriculturalists or cattle-raisers, or the organized workers, are most often favorable to the wealthy classes—although not always, as the "1943 revolution" that produced Peronism demonstrates. While the coups d'état of 1955, 1962, 1966, and 1976 took place in periods of high wages that the new regimes ended, in 1943 the wages of labor were low when the conservative president, Ramon B. Castillo, was overthrown and salaries rose sharply under the military government from 1943 to 1946.

Also, in Argentina, the army is neither the party of the middle classes nor the protector of the industrial bourgeoisie, nor the spearhead of the large agrarian bourgeoisie or of the multinational companies. Its interventions change the meaning of the transfers between sectors, and play the role of alternator of social currents. The alternations of coups d'état and military pressures of different content has no other explanation in a society marked since 1930 by recurrent sectoral disequilibria combined with cyclical stagnation.[32] The external constriction of the Argentine economy that imposes an uneven and unpredictable pace upon it, is the result of a major distortion that can be summarized in general terms as follows: industry, which is the dynamic and preponderant sector today, depends on the income from agriculture and cattle raising—sectors that are not very dynamic but are central to the economy because they provide foreign exchange. There are no spillover effects. Rather the growth of one sector is at the expense of another. However the interventions of the military shift the respective positions of the various sectors in different directions. In particular they produce transfers to or from agriculture and cattle raising.[33] This is why, to take a recent example, the replacement of General Rafael Videla by the ephemeral General Roberto Viola in 1981 at the head of the Process of National Reorganization that was established in 1976 was temporarily beneficial to the agro-export sectors, while with José Martinez de Hoz as economic czar during the five preceding years the overvaluation of the peso essentially benefited the financial and speculative sectors. Even with a programmed political succession the fragility of the system was revealed in the rapidity of the oscillations among the sectors.

How does one explain this situation of permanent crisis in a rich country with a highly skilled labor force with almost none of the sociocultural characteristics of underdevelopment? One can single out some special characteristics of that social structure to try to determine the origin of the blockages that paralyze it and then formulate some hypotheses. The specific character of Argentine society is above all the existence of a relatively homogeneous dominant national group that has prestige and dominates the central sector of the economic machine. As distinct from enclave economies (Chile or Venezuela), more diversified export systems (Peru, Mexico), and in contrast with countries that have experienced different cycles of economic prosperity resulting in a temporary period of regional domination (Brazil), modern Argentina has in a way only had a single historical "natural" elite that goes back to— or at times descends directly from—the dominant group that led the country to prosperity at the beginning of the century and revealed it to the world. That group, which has become larger and more diversified, descends partly from those who built the agro-export economy that brought the country into the world market as the provider of wheat and meat.

An initial striking characteristic of Argentina is the small size and social exclusiveness of that minority as opposed to the modern mass character of the society. In a country that is made up of European immigrants working in the tertiary sector and was highly urbanized even before the beginning of industrialization, the expansion of consumption at the beginning of the century was far in excess of the development of productive forces. However, because the agro-export system is worshipped even by those who are its less favored beneficiaries to the point that no political force or social group can put forward an alternative model of development, the geographical expansion of the country that would have assured a dynamic equilibrium and the stability of the whole was ended in 1930. The areas of cultivation have not grown since then, nor has intensive production on the land. The increase in demand for exportable products at the same time as the production remained static created certain significant and unsurmountable confrontations. In 1900 Argentina consumed 46 percent of its agricultural production; in 1958 it consumed 89 percent.[34] The figures are even more striking for cattle raising alone.

A second relevant characteristic derives from the model of traditional accumulation that gives special consideration to the mobility of investment and consequently permits the grand bourgeoisie to be present in many sectors. This is evidently only possible because of its exclusive access to the state. Before 1930 the low level of economic diversification and the optimal utilization of its comparative advantage lent itself to this strategy and legitimated the role of those who applied. After 1930 with the changes in the structure of the economy and especially after 1950, eclecticism and speculative activities in the economy, rather than leading to the development of the country, produced cyclical stagnation and increased political instability. It is not a matter of holding a dominant multisectorial group responsible for the political constraints, but of describing a socioeconomic mechanism that is based on a financial fluidity that is only made possible because of the permeability of the state.

Without indulging in conspiracy theories, if we consider that the continuity of landed property in Argentina is linked at the highest levels with mobility of resources and diversification, we may conclude that the upper bourgeois groups, instead of orienting and promoting development, play a destabilizing role. Time after time, ranchers, farmers, and always financiers and traders, make efforts to protect themselves against "rigid investment schemes"[35] in order, as good speculators, to be able to take advantage of favorable economic situations and to spread the productive risks. However, the very existence of an influential multisector bourgeois minority prevents the social hegemony of any dominant sector. The confrontations and economic oppositions take place in the different strata within each productive sector, between nondiversified and diversified groups. In addition, the economic diversification of the upper part of the grand bourgeoisie extends to the political scene. Sectoral mobility is reproduced in the area of alliances that allow its permanent domination but prevent its hegemony. Thus, the elite group can ally itself with the lower agrarian elements to form a rural common front (as was the case in 1970); it can team up with certain industrial groups against the nondiversified ranchers as in 1935–40, but these alliances are always precarious and transitory. The objective of the elite and of those who share its socioeconomic and political behavior is to be free of any longer-term commitment and to preserve immediate access to the decisions of the state. In spite of its antistatism and its extreme economic liberalism, this dominant group in fact owes everything to the state, which distributed landed properties in the last century, continues to concede the most lucrative commercial operations, and can favor this or that social group through revenue transfers. Because of its dearly defended vital position, this group possesses a veritable economic veto power that it can transform rapidly into a power of political "delegitimation."

It is easy to understand how these activities—which are imbedded in the underlying fabric of a political system that has little autonomy—and this central position of a versatile dominant group constituted the underlying bases for a praetorian system. The war of all against all is precisely the destiny of that watchful "oligarchy." This is true because the aristocracy is involved in structural opposition to all economic and social groups: to the agricultural producers because it is more closely tied to international trade and the places where prices are determined, and to the nondiversified industrialists because of monetary policy, the assignment of financial resources, and the character of industrialization. It is no accident that of the three largest countries in Latin America, Argentina is the most backward in heavy industry and capital equipment. In addition, as a minority "alternative" group in conflict with nearly all domestic social sectors, the bourgeoisie cannot adopt compromises or forge the stable and permanent alliances necessary to establish hegemony because it would lose its power and domination. For that structural reason it is opposed in principle to a government that is responsive to public opinion and the "blind law of numbers." Argentina thus has domination without hegemony, which is indicated, for example, by the lack of a modern conservative party that can win elections.

As for the armed forces, apart from the fact that they constitute the terrain and the objective in the struggles among the wealthy groups, their relation to the system lies in their identification with the state. This army-state that has a margin of autonomy in relation to the upper classes—specifically the dominant section—is marginally linked to all the organized groups. This permits it to "aggregate" divergent sectoral interests from an institutional perspective—that is, in pursuit of professional objectives. Thus at times the army can impose on the system, in order better to defend it, the changes that appear to be necessary in the economic, political and social areas. The social policy of Peronism—neutrality in the Second World War and the development of heavy industry—are all striking examples of actions in defense of the status quo that went beyond the wishes of their own beneficiaries.

Thus the actions of the military, which seem to be opposed to the lasting supremacy of any sector, reinforce, in most cases involuntarily, but sometimes voluntarily, the multisector oligarchy linked to the state. When it reestablishes the social equilibrium and prevents any one sector from dominating the others, the army aims at the preservation of the system. In fact it imposes a social deadlock that does not allow it to overcome the hegemonic crisis, but rather perpetuates it. By blocking social disequilibria that are the motors of evolution and progress, stabilizing interventions congeal Argentine society and prolong its overall crisis. They reproduce the political instability from which the "activist businessmen" of the grand bourgeoisie draw their profit. The "institutionalization of illegitimacy,"[36] rather than creating the bases for a "strong and solid democracy" that will no longer require the recourse to the military (as the "revolutionary" texts of the military proclaim), each time further weakens the chances of a representative system.

MILITARY INVASION, OR WAR BY OTHER MEANS

There is no doubt that once in power the army, as a usurping body of the state, tends to take over the government, whatever deference its chiefs may pay to representative institutions. Thus in Brazil the system of military domination went from the "manipulated democracy" of General Humberto Castello Branco to a form of modernizing authoritarian state with a constitutional and pluralist facade, beginning in 1968. The "compulsory two-party system" and a tolerated peripheral competitiveness gave a popular appearance to the emergency regime. Nevertheless, the military guardians seem to have made it a rule between 1968 and 1976 to violate their own laws. The militarization of the state appeared to be the natural inclination of the regime.

Not only did the armed forces control the presidential succession without paying attention to constitutional provisions, as could be seen at the time of the illness of President Costa e Silva in 1969,[37] but until 1978 the naming of the official candidate for president was the private preserve of an assembly of generals, with the dominant party and the legislature being content to ratify their choice. In 1978, in place of a meeting of the "little senate" of generals, the Planalto Group around President Ernesto Geisel imposed a crown prince, General João Batista Figueiredo, without the endorsement of the grand electors in uniform—which produced a serious crisis in the army and initiated a certain "deinstitutionalization" of the military regime.[38]

In addition, that regime, which was quick to modify the rules of the game whenever they were unfavorable to it,[39] began to concentrate the powers of the other branches in the executive. Furthermore, in a parallel way bureaucratic military organs or those with a military preponderance began to develop as centers of executive decision making. Among them we should note the army high command, the National Information Service (SNI), and the National Security Council, the last two created by the regime after 1964. The SNI, the command of which seemed to constitute an inside track to the highest political responsibilities, began to appear as an "invisible ministry."[40] Its representatives were present in all the ministerial departments, and it covered the country with a dense network of informers. One can understand the political resources of the head of the SNI within the military apparatus.[41] The National Security Council, only created by decree in 1969, was in a way the theoretical center of power. The constitutional reform of 1969 assigned it the task of "establishing the permanent objectives and bases of national policy"—no less. Its twenty-one members included, besides the president, the vice president, the head of the SNI, and the heads of the civilian and military staffs of the president. It was the holy of holies in a regime that by definition put questions of national security in first place. From 1964 until 1974, the date when General Geisel became president, the hardening of the armed forces in the face of the progress and radicalization of the opposition resulted in an expansion of the jurisdiction of the military, as well as the militarization of the institutions of government. We can even ask if attempts were not made, with little success it is true, to militarize society as well. Along with the ideology of "Brazil, as a great power," the Rondon Project to mobilize the students, the work camps in the northeast, and the TransAmazonian effort seemed to reveal such a perspective. From 1969 until 1974 in particular the important decisions of the regime were based on essentially military criteria. We might even say that what was happening at that time was a process of "decivilianization" of Brazilian society. The spread of concepts of national security to the center of the productive apparatus because of the presence of officers of high rank in the directorships of large companies and of the civilian trainees at the Superior War School would seem to be examples of that phenomenon.[42]

During that period decisions in the areas of energy and natural resources seem to have depended more on strategic concerns than simple economic rationality. The historical confrontation with Argentina, the rival power for continental leadership, and geopolitical considerations were the reasons for the "hard-line" conflictual positions concerning the development of the Mutún iron mines in Bolivia, the construction of the Itaipú dam on the Paraná River, and the signing of the 1975 nuclear agreement with the Federal Republic of Germany. The recent rapprochement with Argentina that ended the "war of the dams" and amounted to Argentine acceptance of Brazilian supremacy seems to confirm this interpretation. In any case, the Brazilian veto on the use by Argentina of Bolivian iron, the intransigence of Itamaraty with regard to the states that border on the Paraná, and the German-Brazilian nuclear development plan were not decided only on the basis of the country's energy needs, still less because of its needs for iron ore of which Brazil is a major exporter, but totally for military reasons.[43]

In Argentina, where military intervention totally suspended all the procedures of representative government, militarization was still more obvious. However, it adopted different forms depending on the regime. The bureaucratic-political institutions were not the same in 1966 and in 1976; the military presence was at different levels. In 1966 the sine qua non condition that General Onganía posed in order to assume the presidency was that the military chiefs would be kept out of power. The junta of commanders in chief only governed the country on the day of the coup—just long enough to name the president. Onganía acquired total power in the country. The military chiefs who put him in office owed him obedience. Right there, no doubt, there was a source of conflict, since the inspired autocrat who overthrew President Arturo Illía set no limit on his term of office.

The monarchic character of the executive did not prevent military concerns from permeating the orientation of the regime and its political organism. As in Brazil, national defense legiti-

mized the "state of exception." "No security without development, no development without security," said the secretary of
the National Security Council. The regime's legislation therefore was directed toward the possibility of war and the needs
determined by the general staff. The laws on national defense
and on the civil service thus demonstrated, according to a
Catholic magazine, "an over-development of the concept of
security and the militarization of civilian life."[44] This excessive
character of the power of the military is also evident in the
considerable prerogatives given to the National Security Council (CONASE) and the State Information Service (SIDE). Nevertheless the army was not in power and the number of executive
functions taken over by officers remained rather limited.

In 1976 it was entirely different. The Onganía precedent,
and the requirements and effects of the "dirty war" against
subversion, reversed the relationships between the junta of
commanders in chief and the president. After a few attempts at
independence by General Videla, the president was reduced by
the junta that appointed him to the position of an executive to
carry out the directions given by the armed forces. Collegiality
replaced military monarchy. The desire to remain in power, to
keep the initiative against the civilians and to maintain a harmonious institutional continuity, was the justification for that new
organization of power. Development was no longer the order
of the day as in 1966, and because the Argentine military
thought of themselves as at war, bureaucratic machinations
were more limited and the administration was colonized by
officers. The planning councils that were the instruments of
military participation under Onganía no longer had a reason for
existence.

The important thing was to avoid internal military conflicts
or to institutionalize them. The Military Legislative Council
(CAS) and the secretariat of the presidency played a certain role
in this regard.[45] For the rest, officers were everywhere in the
central administration, the provinces, the decentralized organ-
isms (including even the organization of the world soccer foot-
ball championship in 1978—*Ente autárquico Mundial 1978*—and
the Industrial Pension Fund). Never in any preceding regime
had there been such an invasion—yet another distinguishing

feature of the bloodiest military dictatorship in the history of Argentina.

The Expansion of the State and the Logic of Corporatism

Authoritarianism never functions without an increase in the political bureaucracy that is responsible for the control and repression of dissidents and opponents. A strong state does not necessarily require the development of the economic responsibilities of the government. However, political systems of military domination, even those that subscribe to an ultraliberal creed in economics and open the country to international capital, generally also produce an increase in the size of the nationalized sector. We can assume that the natural inclination of the technocrats in uniform is toward statism; nevertheless, their statist behavior and natural institutional tendency to extend the area of state control is no doubt reinforced by more individual considerations. The military in power, by creating, multiplying, and colonizing public enterprises and services, thus join the bourgeoisie through the state. This can lead to an "attachment" to state capitalism or it can stimulate fruitful movements of privatization. It all depends on the strength and power of the local bourgeoisie.

In Salvador between 1972 and 1978 the military were at the head of twenty-five of the most important autonomous state institutions—as different as the Institute of Rural Colonization, the port of Acajutla, the Salvadoran Coffee Company, the administration of the dam on the Lempa River, telecommunications, the central bank, and social security.[46] However, faced with the oligarchy of the "fourteen" or so families, the majority of the military defended the state, which explains the fits of reformism and autonomy of the army—a recent instance of which took place on 15 October 1979. Such reforms as have occurred have generally been overcome by the intransigence of a grand bourgeoisie that has forgotten nothing and learned nothing since the peasant massacres of 1932.

In Guatemala things have gone differently. In that militarized state in which the army owns a very successful commercial bank, the officers buy land or expropriate it from the Indians and engage in business, while the Guatemalan bourgeoisie of large landowners has ceased to be a dominant class. The "tranversal fringe" in the north of Guatemala that produces lumber and has good land for agriculture and cattle and where some petroleum deposits have been found is a kind of Wild West or El Dorado for the speculators of the "rising class," including the military. General Lucas García, president from 1978 until 1982, is reported to be an important property holder in that region. The left and the extreme left use the term "bureaucratic bourgeoisie" for the superior officers and their civilian partners who have become rich over the last fifteen years because of their control of the state through means that are not always licit. The opposition attacks the greed of those bureaucratic *camarillas*. One of the guerrilla movements operating in the country characterized the "class enemy" and the situation in which the guerrilla war is being carried out as follows: "The army, until recently the exclusive servant of the oligarchy is now directly involved in the establishment of the *bureaucratic bourgeoisie* . . . and has become the exclusive instrument of its political and military power."[47]

Bolivia, with its cocaine-trafficking colonels, would seem to be similar to Guatemala in this regard. It may be thought that the succession of coups d'état that have been carried out since 1978 was the result of the greed of a military without masters, with each faction or even each graduating class of officers wanting its part of the booty. Nevertheless the conflicts of interest within military society, the involvement of business, and even the gangsterism of certain "pure hard-line" officers is not enough to explain the whole reality. The creation during the 1970s of the Armed Forces Corporation for National Development (COFADENA) also indicates the desire of certain of the military to replace indirectly the languishing bourgeoisie and to turn the army into an entrepreneur. The COFADENA establishes not only industries with military purposes but also agro-industrial enterprises. Furthermore, the army, for reasons related to the economy as an extended element of frontier security, has become a land developer in Bolivia.[48] If we add to that some 150 enterprises that depend more or less directly on the state and that are directly run by military men at the same time, we will understand that here as well the officers form a ruling bureaucratic caste whose known excesses do not make it easy for them to give up power.

In this respect, Argentina has been an institutionally militarized state for a long time. Concerned about the "critical strategic dependency" of an agricultural country without industry the Argentine military has demonstrated an interest in industrialization since the beginning of the century and acted as a pressure group in favor of industry in the face of a bourgeoisie that was convinced of the virtues of laissez-faire and the permanence of comparative advantage. Military nationalism that was demonstrated in the area of petroleum by generals Mosconi and Baldrich,[49] also worked with General Savio in favor of an Argentine steel industry that was to take many years to be developed. Nevertheless in 1927, General Justo, minister of war under President Alvear, dedicated an airplane factory in Cordoba that in the following year began to produce a small series of models under European license.

However, the important date is October 1941, when in the middle of World War II and at the urging of the army, a law established the General Directorate of Military Manufactures (DGFM) as an autonomous agency under the Ministry of War. The articles of incorporation of the DGFM expressed in clear terms the deliberate intention of the state to establish a national industry. In fact, the declaration went well beyond the simple production of arms and munitions. The law gave the DGFM extensive powers to study the industrial capacity of the country, the responsibility to explore for and develop minerals, and to produce the industrial elements needed for "civilian consumption when they were not being produced by private industry."[50] Thus, we can understand why from that time on the military controlled either implicitly or explicitly the bulk of the public sector of the Argentine economy. The military led the way in steel with the Altos Hornos de Zapla; they were never totally absent from the railroads, which appealed to them in periods of crisis; and they were involved in the national oil company that from the time of General Mosconi under President Hipólito Yrigoyen formed part of their natural zone of influence.

The participation of the DGFM in the creation of joint ventures in accordance with the 1941 law further increased the industrial responsibilities of the military. This kind of company was established in most of the steel industry and many kinds of chemicals from phenyl alcohol and fertilizer to plastics. If we add that the factories of *Fabricaciones Militares* produced the cars for the Buenos Aires metro and plow wheels and bottles of butane, we can understand the way in which the military began to be linked to the public enterprises and that at the same time these industrialists in uniform could easily "move over" into private industry.

If we now examine the policy that was followed beginning in 1976 with General Videla, which was characterized by a savage economic liberalism, we can ask whether the orientations of the army were not contradictory. In fact the program of Martinez de Hoz, his finance minister, which was supported by the army, reduced internal consumption and opened the country to foreign competition. This policy produced a deep industrial recession, the elimination of many national enterprises, and even the closing of industries that produced durable consumer goods and of branches of the multinationals (automobiles, electronics, etc.). The "deindustrialization," which was in a way planned, did not however produce a notable tapering off of public expenditures. In addition, the general philosophy favoring the "subsidiary" character of the role of the state in the economy did not result in a notable wave of privatization. The economic crisis produced by the monetarist policy was no doubt partially responsible, but the size of the military apparatus was also important. The opening of the economy not only went against the statist behavior of the army leadership but also their vested interests, which had been increased because of the expansion of the state. In the administration itself the game of clientelism and fiefdoms did not allow the rationalization so often proclaimed and sanctioned by law. For the military, no doubt as a result of their training, the number of men is more important than the values of a balanced budget or profit. We should also not forget that a program of arms production requires the development of heavy industry.

In Brazil the 1964 coup d'état established an authoritarian regime that was ultraliberal in the area of economics. A good number of observers believed at the time that the liquidation of the public sector, or at least of a part of it, figured among the most important objectives of the new government. In fact, the Castellista or Febista group that took over the state seemed to have an unlimited enthusiasm for the values of free enterprise. That orientation was also written into the constitution that described the role of the state as "complementary" to that of private enterprise.[51] Successive presidents, even those who did not identify with the ESG group, seemed to share those same concerns. Thus the Plan of Government of General Médici in 1970 called among other things for "the consolidation of an economic system based on national and foreign private enterprise" and "the rationalization of the public sector" in order to "reverse the pre-1964 tendency to nationalization."[52] Nevertheless, the expansion of the public sector and of state capitalism seems to have been one of the distinguishing features of the Brazilian regime.

This phenomenon had several aspects. First of all, the Brazilian federal state, no longer burdened with the pressures of the politicians and electoral constraints, improved its administration and made it more technical. Its ability to tax became very much improved. In addition, thanks to a program of forced savings imposed on the workers, the state in the larger sense accounted for 64 percent of national savings.[53] Between 1970 and 1973 50 percent of gross national investment came from the government or from the public enterprises.[54] Some writers claim that that figure reached 70 percent in 1980. Since 1964 the Brazilian state has had the means to direct the whole of economic life. Not only has it until recently strictly determined the annual wage increases but it controlled national savings since it was the principal banker; it also had new instruments for regulating the economy, such as the National Monetary Council and the Interministerial Price Council,[55] two high-level instrumentalities that developed the financial policy of the country in a bureaucratic manner.

The increase in state responsibility in the area of industry is not the least parodoxical element of Brazil under the military. While the state's control over savings and investment gave it enormous economic power, its role in production, which began before 1964, apparently allowed it overwhelming power in that sphere as well. In 1974, out of the 5,113 largest companies 39 percent of the assets belonged to public enterprises, 18 percent to foreign firms, and 43 percent to private national capital. But only one private enterprise (a foreign one) ranked in the 25 largest. Among the 100 companies in the country with the largest liquid capital, 41 were public enterprises in 1970, and 46, in 1972. And out of 550 or 580 companies that belonged to the state in 1980, around 200 did not exist before the April Revolution.[56]

While the share of national private capital seems to have steadily declined since 1964, the public enterprises have expanded more rapidly than the foreign private sector. Certainly, the state has invested in particular in infrastructure, energy, and intermediate goods, but it controls some dynamic sectors and the integrated structure of giants such as Petrobras and Vale do Rio Doce (steel) sometimes makes it compete with the private sector, especially in the area of banking and finance.

It is certainly not correct to argue that the Brazilian state is content to invest in areas of low return that do not interest private capital. The thesis that public enterprise and the economic policy of the military state were at the service of the interests of national, and especially of foreign, industrialists has to be seriously qualified. Proof of this is the *antiestatização* campaign against the "tentacles of the state" carried out by the large industrialists and defenders of private enterprise in 1975–76. That sector seemed so little ready to admit that it was the principal beneficiary of the expansion of the public sector that General Figueiredo,[57] to calm the capitalists and to reestablish their confidence, promised to limit the increase of the state as entrepreneur and to privatize a certain number of nationalized companies as part of his campaign of "debureaucratization."[58]

The debate on estatização and the "state bourgeoisie" showed how the regime was perceived by certain economic circles. The disenchanted polemics of the large liberal press and of certain officers of the multinational enterprises who viewed present day Brazil as "a socializing regime," or even a socialist one,[59] indicated their surprise and disappointment at an apparently unresolvable contradiction. Why did Brazil after 1964 become, to use the words of Fernando Henrique Cardoso, a "hybrid system" that aspired at the same time "to respond to the interest of oligopolistic capitalism and to strengthen public enterprise, while enlarging the area of decision of the government and its ability to control civil society"?[60]

We can assume, of course, that the choice of a type of accelerated growth implies today a strengthening of the control capacity and the intervention of the state—that is, "a growth state is a growing state," in the words of Henry Lefebvre. But one should be especially careful to relate that view to the behavior of the actors. A continuing effort to expand and centralize the state by the armed forces in Brazil is a reality that goes back, as we have seen, to the first military presidents of the Old Republic. However, besides that national characteristic we cannot neglect the many similar examples of statist behavior in other militarized states. It is significant to read in the June 1981 issue of *Búsqueda*, the organ of the Uruguayan "Chicago boys," a violent attack on the dangerous "socialist" tendencies of the Montevideo regime.[61] The argument juxtaposes the ideal of economic freedom to the national security concerns put forward by the military to preserve the public enterprises.

DIVISIONS AND DECISIONS WITHIN THE "MILITARY PARTIES"

The general tendency of the military state that we have just described does not mean either that characteristics common to the military will orient all praetorian systems in the same way or that the armed forces of Latin America are monolithic organizations with ways of acting that are mechanically predictable. Since they are political forces, they are affected by different currents, and they experience internal disagreements and deep divisions that are not concealed by the obligatory rhetoric concerning institutional unity. While armies, by definition, are not political parties, neither are they islands cut off from civil society. Their involvement in the body of society is all the greater when they have significant power. This does not mean that politically they simply reflect the struggles among the civilians. They are a mirror and a player in praetorianized public life, of course, but with specific internal processes that result from a special institutional mould. It would be difficult to believe that the distortion of the institution that military usurpation produces would destroy the particular nature of the strongly statist Latin American armies. Their extramilitary role transforms these armies into ambiguous political forces. Except when they break up or decompose and thus lose their politically distinguishing features, the "military parties" resemble party organizations very little, even though they may carry out the same functions that the parties do. Two of the principal differences— besides the essential and obvious purpose of providing the defensive structure of the state through a monopoly of arms and preparation for combat—are the authoritarian process of socialization and the marginal character of the ideological beliefs of the army.

The internal groups and political tendencies are organized around specific cleavages. These often appear to follow organizational lines. While in France the air force as a quasi-civilian branch is traditionally considered to be rather republican in its orientation, the Argentine air force appears to be fascist in its leanings, the navy is supposed to be ultraliberal economically, and the tank corps—that is, the cavalry—is supposed to be typically aristocratic, the last refuge of the "great names" of the oligarchy of the pampas. In Cuba under Batista the navy was considered unreliable and sympathetic to the opposition, as Fidel Castro recalled publicly after the attack on the Moncada barracks.[62] Only historians can keep track of the particular views of the services or branches. More frequently, hierarchic divisions within a group of officers in the same branch give rise to conflict because they reflect differences in generations or in education or experience. In Guatemala after 1944 the career officers who graduated from the military school were opposed to the officers promoted from the ranks, who considered them as too intellectual and liberal.[63] In Brazil, as we have seen, the military rebellion of the "lieutenants" in the

1920s figured as a sort of "generational insurrection," the cohesion of which affected in a decisive fashion the evolution of the army and the country until 1964. More recently in Bolivia, the coup d'état of General Padilla in November 1978 marked the emergence of a new generation of officers (the *grupo generacional* in the politico-military jargon of La Paz) that graduated from the military school after the 1952 army purge and the reform that the new revolutionary power carried out at that time.[64]

A change in the content of the training produces ideological shifts. Foreign military influences affect these reorientations whether they modify or transform the concept of the threat perception or the war theories, or they produce hierarchical distortions that very soon acquire political significance. In Chile, as we have seen, an army that was supposed to be democratic and apolitical "tilted" toward the opposition to Allende partly under the pressure of the commanders of the units formed after 1965 to fight the guerrillas and against the internal enemy. In Brazil from 1919 to 1925, the French mission strengthened the current of renewal among the young officers who supported military reform against their superiors who were members of the establishment.

The cleavages that are related to the experiences of a group or unit are particularly decisive when it has participated in an internal or external conflict. Most of the officers who took power in Brazil in 1964 had been members of the Brazilian expeditionary corps in Italy (the FEB), as had General Castello Branco. General Costa e Silva, who succeeded him as president, represented a group that was not as close to the GI's and had no contact with the ESG created by the FEBistas. He represented the group of "troopers" that was separated by more than slight differences from the intellectuals of the *Sorbona*. This reached the point that General Hugo Abreu, in speaking of him later, made the naive observation, "At that time I did not really understand why the departure of President Castello Branco and the succession to the presidency of General Costa e Silva was viewed as the coming to power of an opposition party."[65]

It is evident that the special characteristics of these politico-institutional cleavages do not always derive from a clearly identifiable ideology. In fact, armies, even when they act as political forces, are not structures that "function on the basis of ideology." The political inconsistency of the military—which only is asserted as a result of a partisan version of what it means to be faithful to a political creed—is a general characteristic of the most "militarized" armies of Latin America. Thus in Argentina the labor-oriented and antioligarchical colonels of 1943 were the same persons who were the fascist-oriented and antipopular captains of 1930. In the case of the Dominican Republic, it has been demonstrated how little ideological motivations had to do with the participation of the military in the overthrow of the progressive government of Juan Bosch in September 1963 and of that of his rightist successor. In general it was the same officers who carried out the coup against Bosch and then, seventeen months later, revolted in order to bring him back, producing the intervention of the American marines.[66] It is true that the Dominican army is not a model of a professionalized institution. But how to explain the recent about-face of the famous Brazilian parachute brigade? This elite corps that spearheaded the repression of the guerrilla movements of the left and that on several occasions publicly manifested extreme positions against an authoritarian regime that it judged to be too liberal for its taste found itself in the avant garde of the "dissidents" of the military in 1978, opposing Geisel and Figueiredo by raising the unexpected standard of democratization.[67] This phenomenon which surprised the political analysts and the Brazilian "barracks experts," can be explained in good part by the personal evolution of General Hugo Abreu, who successfully commanded the parachute troops for more than four years. Formerly chief of the military staff of Geisel, president of the National Security Council, and member of the FEB, after breaking with the Planalto Group (the presidential circle of General Geisel), Abreu brought his military base with him.[68] One can never underestimate the effect of personal loyalty on the mechanisms of political alignment.

Just as spectacular and as difficult to explain for the political class is the politico-military evolution of Honduras in the 1960s and 70s. The same general who established a repressive cold war dictatorship in 1963 took power again in 1972 in order to impose reforms that had an undeniable popular support. Was it opportunism, a change of heart, a shift in the international situation? The Communist party of Honduras was upset. A member of the party leadership wrote in 1974: "How can we explain what is happening today in Honduras? How can we explain that General López Arellano, the same person who carried out the bloody coup d'état in 1963 and fiercely persecuted the Communist and popular leadership, now heads a progressive government which respects democratic and labor union freedoms, and, what is more important, is carrying out programs of social change that undoubtedly affect the very bases of oligarchic power?"[69]

These clear movements from extreme right to the left, to use the cardinal points of the classical political landscape, are nevertheless not insignificant. They result from internal struggles and oppositions, and at times an intense political life in which the whole ideological spectrum is represented. In Brazil in the 1950s the debates and the publication of the Military Club indicate that even the pro-Communist left was represented in the army. Certainly, the scandal produced by an article favorable to North Korea in the July 1950 number of the club's magazine does not mean,[70] as was said at the time, that the club was about to turn into a "Soviet island,"[71] but rather that these opinions were in a minority. However, they were present. We can better understand the clearly political functioning of the military structure as it appears in the testimony of Marshal Odilio Denys, one of the initiators of the conspiracy of the military against Goulart. He declared, "In 1960 in the army and the other branches there were leftist elements who clearly argued for a program of the left. This has been the case since 1930. When I was Minister of War in 1960 and foresaw that the danger was becoming greater, to defend ourselves I made an alliance between the center and the right within the army. In that way I obtained the harmonious front needed to struggle against Communism which was emerging among the officers of the left."[72] Who would believe that these subtle parliamentary maneuvers were carried out within a highly professional military structure?

If the internal conflicts are evident and the cleavages authenticated and explicable, we can ask how the cohesion and consensus necessary for extramilitary action was arrived at. It would evidently be wrong to believe that the political decisions of the armed forces are entirely disciplined and impeccably hierarchic. Indiscipline does not exercise command. Political action by the army requires political resources. The most institutionalized and apparently unanimous interventions only take place without problems if there has been a long preparation of public, and especially of military, opinion. The most spectacular case of this kind of programmed intervention was the 1966 coup d'état in Argentina, the date of which was announced by the press one year in advance, with an error of only a few days. On the other hand, a certain amount of violence is necessary to maintain operational unity. If the Chilean army did not split in September 1973 as expected, it was because the senior and junior officers who supported Popular Unity were quickly removed by force for refusing to obey. In Brazil in 1964 the leaders of the "revolution" were content to retire several hundred officers. It is true that the opposition is not always in a minority and there are occasionally violent confrontations between military tendencies which do not split the army as an institution. The limited internal war between the Azules and Colorados in 1962–63 in Argentina passed the stage of symbolic violence but observed certain rules to safeguard the institution.

Most often a subgroup, a faction, or simply a tendency imposes its intellectual leadership and ideology. Thus, a kernel of activists succeeds in polarizing the whole leadership structure and imposes its hegemony by restructuring the ideological-strategic field to its benefit. The development of an articulated overall "doctrine" such as took place in the Superior War School in Brazil facilitates that control and leadership. The perception of a threat to the group allows the ranks to be closed and makes the moderates and legalists "tilt." In Brazil the maladroit support given by Goulart to the rebellions of the noncommissioned officers dug the grave of the democratic regime. The attacks by the guerrillas against officers created a corporate reaction that led to a coup in both Uruguay in 1973 and Argentina in 1976. In addition, the effort to consolidate military unity often dampens conflicts or challenges. It leads to a restructuring of alliances in pursuit of a unifying objective. This can be the struggle against an exaggerated enemy—Communism, subversion, or imperialism—or a movement to take direct action to facilitate coincidental agreements among ideologically opposing sectors. In Argentina in June 1943, the proaxis neutralists and the proallied liberals joined together to overthrow the government as each group deceived the other. In the same country the confrontations between the military factions in 1962–63 produced a rapprochement of points of view between the victors and the vanquished in the name of institutional unity.

The fluidity of ideological tendencies allows for political shifts that respond to the relations of forces and in particular to the external situation. Since by nature armies are situated where national and international interests meet, the changes in power within the military society are often linked to changes in the global context. However, corporate political codes, indeed veritable tribal rites, act to limit confrontation and to reestablish consensus within the officer corps in regimes that are profoundly praetorianized. Assemblies of generals electing a military president have been standard practice in militarized states for a long time. That system worked well in Brazil for fourteen years. It seems to have been established with more difficulty in Argentina in 1976. Stricter "rules" governing such elections have been progressively imposed in the "Colonels' Republic" of El Salvador. In the oldest military state in the continent each class graduating from the military school (*tanda*) had the "right" to one president.[73] The tandas formed alliances to be sure, but in this way each of some 500 officers had some chance of approaching the joys of power and the system avoided caudilloism and a monopoly by one clique. This system guaranteed the maintenance of military power until 1979. In Guatemala the conflicts between classes of the military school are attenuated by an internal institution of the officer corps that assures a certain intergenerational cohesion: the practice of the *centenario*. In the polytechnic school those who have the same last two registration numbers have a relationship of aid and support. Thus, number 421 has special responsibilities for cadet number 521 when he enters the school.[74] This military compadrazgo tells us a great deal about the importance of personal loyalty in the operation of "complex differentiated organizations," the political character of which should not make us forget their functional specificity and institutional nature.

10

REVOLUTION
BY THE
GENERAL
STAFF

The majority of the military interventions in Latin America today are carried out to reestablish order—indeed, to put forward a "new order." Most of the coups d'état in the 1960s and 1970s have produced de facto governments that, by linking political regression and social counterrevolution, resulted in guaranteeing the status quo and limiting popular participation in power. The world image of the Latin American military man who carries out a coup is correctly that of a "gorilla" who is willing to identify the struggle against subversion with a rejection of change and support for a continental anti-Communist crusade under the aegis of the United States.

This is why coups d'état that proclaim themselves nonconservative and say they intend to place themselves on the side of the people produce considerable incredulity. Observers are at least surprised,[1] or they attribute the new military policy to a trick by "imperialism" or to the opportunism of the military. Domestic political forces are equally perplexed when faced with these apparently new militarisms, to say nothing of the members of the international social science community who rack their brains to define and classify these reformist authoritarian regimes.

Nevertheless, it would be wrong to identify the Peruvian coup d'état purely and simply with the so-called "revolutions" that took place in Brazil in 1964 or in Argentina in 1966—which is not to say, however, that its "revolutionary nationalism" was unique and unprecedented because of some nontransferable particular national characteristic. There is no need to appeal to an improbable "Inca utopia" or to the domination of the "Asiatic mode of production" in the Peruvian highlands in order to comprehend the meaning of the regime of General Velasco Alvarado. The coming to power of General Alfredo Ovando in Bolivia on 26 September 1969 and that of General Juan José Torres a few months later seemed to confirm the Peruvian experiment by indicating that it was not unique, while in a very different geopolitical context the style of behavior adopted by the government of the national guard in Panama beginning in October 1968 had a sufficient number of affinities with the two Andean regimes to prevent one from believing that this kind of neomilitarism is limited geographically. Furthermore, the military who took power in Ecuador in February 1972 also appealed to revolutionary nationalism while promulgating reforms that were a silent echo of the ones carried out by the "nationalist revolutionary government of the left" in Lima. Even Honduras, still in the shadow of Don Tiburcio, the prototype of the patriarch, did not escape this tendency. The officers who overthrew its fragile constitutional government on 4 December 1972 intended to carry out structural reforms "to modernize the economy and national society." Furthermore, what shall we say about the military participation in the coup d'état that ended the conservative military dictatorship of General Romero in El Salvador? The defeat of Colonel Carlos Majano and his supporters in a situation of violent social polarization should not conceal from us the existence of reformist sectors within a military "establishment" historically linked to the fierce defense of the status quo.

In fact, the novel character of these military orientations is entirely relative. From a historical viewpoint reformism has numerous precedents in the region. As we have seen, it even appears in several countries as the first manifestation of a modernized military.[2] Also, it was for a long period a constitutive element of political militarization in Latin America, to the point that some authors have correctly emphasized "the movement of the pendulum in contemporary military interventions."[3] Nevertheless, far from being unique to the Latin American continent these "military utopias" are represented in a more prudent and pragmatic form than in other continents where progressive military are not rare. Europe had the "red" praetorians of "the revolution of the carnations" in Portugal. Today in Africa we see officers imposing a socialist orientation on their countries and sometimes boasting openly of their Marxist-Leninism, as in the Congo-Brazzaville, Benin, or Ethiopia.[4] Certainly, Africa is a geopolitically divided area and the weak link in the Western armor, while the locking-up of the American "backyard" after 1960 seemed more propitious for a conservative retrenchment than a wave of reform. This diversity is what makes these experiments in a "revolution from above" interesting, and their accomplishments and limitations are related both to the particular military of each country and to changes in the situation in the continent.

HUMANIST MODERNIZATION AND THE "NONCAPITALIST" PATH IN PERU

The coup d'état of October 1968, the eighth in this century, took place after nearly five years of civilian constitutional rule and produced nearly unanimous protests from the parties and labor unions.[5] Nevertheless, neither the statute of the revolution or the manifesto of the revolutionary government repeated the old military phraseology. It was not a question of the threat of international communism, or of preserving order or defending patriotism, but of putting an end to the "abandonment of the natural sources of wealth,"[6] of condemning "an unjust social order," and of "transforming social, economic, and cultural structures."[7] The first important decision of the junta that deposed President Fernando Belaunde was not to arrest the heads of the labor unions or dissolve the parties of the left, but to seize the refinery of Talara and the oil wells that belonged to the International Petroleum Company, an affiliate of Standard Oil of New Jersey, and then to nationalize the holdings of that American company without compensation. The government also proclaimed the date that Talara was seized as "The Day of National Dignity."

The new government, which did not claim to follow any model and rejected capitalism as well as communism and anti-communism, as a way to conceal a refusal to change,[8] sought to achieve a "humanist revolution" that would result in the establishment of a "social democracy with full participation."[9] In fact the "process" of "the Peruvian experiment," as those who carried it out called it, was inspired, President Velasco Alvarado himself said,[10] by "revolutionary socialism." And as Velasco Alvarado said in a speech in July 1969,

> Almost ten months ago . . . the armed forces in the first revolutionary movement in their history took over the government of Peru. It was not just one more military coup d'état but the beginning of a nationalist revolution. . . . The whole nation and the armed forces took up the march towards their definitive liberation, and established the bases for their genuine development by breaking the power of an egoistic and colonialist oligarchy, recovering their sovereignty despite foreign pressures.

It is not surprising also that the military in Peru, unlike the others, received revolutionary endorsement from Fidel Castro beginning in 1969.[11]

The orientation, however, was not only explained in "revolutionary" declarations, but also expressed in action. The junta that replaced President Belaunde was determined to use its position to force the reforms that the weak constitutional government had been incapable of carrying out. To that end it was going to struggle on two fronts—to modernize the very archaic Peruvian society and to lessen the external dependence of the country while taking account of geopolitical constraints. The objective consisted in removing the internal and external obstacles to a harmonious development in solidarity. Observers of different persuasions generally agree on that point.[12]

The measures adopted formed a system in which basic reforms continued to be carried out with a view to the necessity of increasing the political "capital" of the military government. The expropriation of IPC was both a quasi-symbolic act and the beginning of a program. Just as the denunciation of Belaunde's Act of Talara, which gave huge advantages to the IPC in return for the recovery by Peru of a declining oil well, had set off the coup, the expropriation asserted the authority of the Peruvian state over foreign economic interests. At the same time, the reinforcement of the state through the resolution of an old conflict legitimized the actions of the military in the eyes of the public. While it was easy to obtain the unity of the army on that theme, the "patriotic" decision by the junta also disarmed any "democratic" or legalist opposition.

Although the government had announced that the nationalization of the IPC was a special case, the possibility of a conflict with the United States was not removed. However, the specific threat by the government in Washington to apply the Hickenlooper Amendment—which provided for the suspension of economic aid in cases of the expropriation of American goods without adequate compensation—and the possibility of economic pressure (suspension of the sugar quota, reduction of international loans) were viewed with calm by Lima. The Peruvian government also adopted a tough position regarding the extent of its territorial waters. The announcement of the suspension of military aid by the United States in response to interference with American fishing boats produced Peruvian action that made the Nixon government think twice,[13] since it seems that it did not wish to radicalize the military, with whom Washington counted on being able to cooperate.

The major action of the new regime was the preparation and implementation of the agrarian reform law. The crisis in the countryside that had fed the guerrillas in 1965, the massive exodus from the sierra highlands to Lima, as well as the deficit in food production and the increase in imports fixed the overall direction of a reform that constituted the key element of social change. In Peru the unequal distribution of land and the concentration of landed property, which are not unique to that country,[14] also became an ethnic question that paralyzed development because of the size of the Indian population. Large masses of peasants who produced and consumed little were left at the margin of the national community. The moderate reformist government of "the architect" Belaunde had not been able to impose an overall land reform program on a conservative congress. The weak "technical" law adopted in 1964 that placed the burden of a limited (and rarely applied) reform on the most archaic sector of the country (the highlands) was satisfactory for the large land-holders, especially those who had modern industrialized planta-tions on the coast that were exempted. The law had as its pur-pose the reduction of peasant pressure, but not the modification of the precarious equilibrium of Peruvian society.

The principal characteristic of the agrarian reform adopted by the military government was its universal application. In fact, it affected the large cotton and sugar plantations, which were left intact but transformed into cooperatives that also in-cluded related industries. Still, it was not a revolutionary re-form. Related to the programs of "American presidents and specialized organizations of the United Nations,"[15] it provided, in line with the recommendations of the Alliance for Progress and the Economic Commission for Latin America of the United Nations (ECLA), for compensation to the former owners. The program had as its limited objectives: (1) to defend the small and medium-sized property holders; (2) to develop coopera-tives; and (3) to increase production.[16] Nevertheless, it had con-siderable economic and social consequences.

It seemed at first that the aim was to reduce the dualism of Peruvian society, which the military felt was excessive, and to make it more fluid by destroying the property bases of the great families of the oligarchy. Certainly, that essentially coastal oli-garchy had all the elements of a modern capitalist elite, and its interests were not limited to agriculture, or export, but included large areas of finance, commerce, and industry. The extraordi-nary concentration in landholding and the congenital interpene-tration of foreign interests and the holdings of the oligarchy appeared to the military in power as an obstacle to a program of national development. Thus the expropriation of the coastal plantations was a first step in weakening and "nationalizing" a dominant economic group that controlled public affairs and the development of the society.

An increase in production through the elimination of ar-chaic social relationships in the highlands and the reinvestment of the profits of agricultural enterprises was one of the main thrusts of that voluntarist reform that left no room for spontane-ous peasant demands. Thus, in order to overcome the social and cultural heterogeneity of the Andean Indian sectors, Agricultural Societies of Social Interest (SAIS) were created in the highlands that allowed the indigenous communities to partici- pate in structural transformations, while maintaining the pro- ductivity of the large holdings that most often were based on lands from which the *comuneros* had been expelled. These groups that linked the expropriated haciendas and the commu- nities cleverly allowed the former workers and sharecroppers, aided by technicians, to be grouped with the Indians, who received incomes from the SAIS but did not recover their lands. Similarly, in the large cooperatives on the coast, "cooperativi- zation" did not mean absolute self-management. The important role of the state representatives, the attempts to weaken the former unions,[17] and the underrepresentation of the largest and less well off categories were measures designed to prevent an exclusive concern with immediate social satisfaction.

The text of the law specifically emphasized in the case of the coastal plantations the "inalterability of the structures of production" and "administrative continuity."[18] While social jus- tice was listed first in the introduction to the reform law, and the official slogan, "Peasant, the boss will no longer live from your poverty," recalled the Tupac Amaru Indian revolt of the eighteenth century, the transformation of agriculture was actu- ally directed at "forming a large internal market."[19] That is why very few of the holdings were divided: the individual beneficia- ries of the reform were only a tiny minority (around 10 per- cent). Furthermore, the desire not to destroy the agrarian econ- omy while giving special attention to social considerations and responding to the land hunger of the most backward peasants led to the creation of a large bureaucracy in the cooperative sector which, certain studies claim, was the principal benefi- ciary of the reform.[20] In any case some 10 million hectares and more than 350,000 families, or 2 million persons out of the 6 million in the rural population, were affected by the reform.

Above all, however, that reform was an effort at "economic rationalization" that was to provide, among other things, "the necessary capital for the rapid industrialization of the coun- try."[21] The expropriated landowners could, under certain condi- tions that were rather advantageous, convert the bonds given in compensation into shares in industry.[22] Perhaps there was a desire here to convert an agriculturally based oligarchy that was oriented toward the exterior and hesitant to invest, into a genuine industrial bourgeoisie. In any case the financial transfer was organized, as noted above, in such a way that in the last analysis the agricultural workers who were the "beneficiaries" of the agrarian reform were supposed to finance new industries with the payment on the compensation bonds, and the Indians of the highlands were to support the dynamism of the coast.

A whole series of measures by the military government involving the extension of the public sector was aimed in the same direction. The nationalization of the export trade in certain products that were principal sources of foreign exchange such as iron ore and fishmeal,[23] as well as the banking reform that limited the share of foreign capital after the state bought out the large commercial banks, were aimed at channeling national savings into productive investment while avoiding the temptations of overseas tax havens. We can ask if the creation through the General Industrial Law of a mechanism of association of capital and labor—which was applauded by the Peruvian Communist party as a "limitation on capitalist property"[24] and violently denounced by all the employer confederations as collectivist—did not tend to link to the goal of "social harmony" through worker involvement a continuing requirement of self-financing that would act as an additional guarantee against "denationalization." That clause mandating worker participation called in effect for the employer to turn over 15 percent of annual profits to the "industrial community" to which the wage earners belonged, and these funds were to be reinvested in the enterprise up to a limit of 50 percent of its capital.

The extension of the public sector, the increased role of the state in promoting development by (among other things) the creation of a national development bank,[25] the preference given to collective forms of agrarian organization, the creation (late and after much controversy, it is true) of a sector of self-managed "social property,"[26] did not mean, however, that the strategy of the Peruvian military regime was anticapitalist. Thus the Industrial Law, while providing for state control of basic industries, heavy chemicals, and steel, left a large area to the private sector, while foreign capital, although subject to strict regulation in industry notwithstanding certain advantages, was invited to invest preferentially in the mining sector.[27]

The ambiguity of the revolutionary government which, while proclaiming its intention to limit foreign economic dependence invited foreign capital to develop the natural resources of the country, has been pointed out. In fact, in 1969 the junta imposed a strict development calendar and a list of specific obligations that the foreign companies were required to honor under penalty of losing their rights. Many large companies returned their undeveloped concessions to the state at that time. In 1973 Peru nationalized the powerful copper company, Cerro de Pasco, a symbol of neocolonialism that engaged in practices that were not compatible with the economic and social concerns of the government, and had ceased to invest in 1968. Nevertheless, the rich copper mine of Cuajone was developed by an affiliate of American Smelting that planned a considerable investment ($620 million). Also, departing from the example of Talara and the IPC, the military government, while it gave the national oil company a legal monopoly on production, signed a number of contracts with foreign companies, especially in Amazonia. These arrangements, however, involved very strict risk and deadline conditions. There is no doubt that the military government, despite strong criticism from its "anti-imperialist" supporters on the left, believed that it was possible to make good use of foreign capital provided that it was subject to conditions imposed by a strong state determined to defend the national interest. From their productionist point of view, the main consideration was strengthening the country's economic potential and the state, which for the "revolutionaries" in uniform were the sole guarantees of national independence.

The Peruvian model, which only lasted until the fall of General Velasco Alvarado at the end of 1975,[28] was very difficult for observers to understand. This was especially true since, while the national business groups and the bourgeoisie were fiercely opposed to a strategy of development that spoke in deprecating terms of the "relative importance" of the private sector[29] and imposed an unacceptable system of worker co-management on it, the international financiers were rather favorable to the model. Its prudent fiscal policy and restraint of wages in order to fight inflation seemed to them a good sign, as did the absence of a collectivist ideology and the pragmatism of the military.[30]

While Marxists refused to use the term "socialist" and preferred to speak of "corporatism of the left" or "Neo-Bismarckism," the more serious studies seemed to lack a way to classify this attempt at a third economic approach and its experiments at "self-management in uniform."[31] The search for causes and origins of that "revolution," which was not "foreseen in any text,"[32] led to much writing and created a considerable mythology that the civilian ideologues of the regime were happy to spread. If we limit ourselves to the explanations that concentrate on the emergence of a "new military mentality in Peru,"[33] leaving aside imaginary instrumentalist approaches, the large number of factors discussed is surprising. In fact none is persuasive and all present a part of the truth. The following have been proposed: the lower-class origins of the Peruvian officers and their social isolation from the upper classes;[34] the military's more profound understanding of the reality of the nation; the impact of the guerrilla movement that they had to repress in 1965 and the awakening of a new social sensitivity;[35] the movement to the right of their hereditary enemy, the APRA populist party, which ended the alliance of the military with the oligarchy;[36] and finally, the influence of the Center for Advanced Military Studies (CAEM), in which the officers since 1951 had studied the nation and in which economics and sociology were taught, have often been presented as decisive.[37]

However, each of these explanations taken by itself is ambiguous since it could also just as well have made the leaders of the Peruvian army incline in the direction of a vigilant defense of the status quo. The social origins of the Peruvian military had not changed for the half century before 1968 during which the military appeared to act as "the watch dogs of the oligarchy" and the Chilean officers were no less cut off from the civilian elites than their neighbors to the north. The assignment of garrisons throughout the whole of the territory and the direct contact as a result of conscription with the lower-class elements were also characteristics that were common to the armies of Argentina, Brazil, and Chile. The "traumatism resulting from

guerrilla warfare" generally orients military attitudes in a counterrevolutionary and antireformist direction. The traces of an
Aprista influence on the ideology of the military and the good
relations of certain leaders of the process with the leaders of the
APRA refute an interpretation based on a dialectical evolution
between related enemies.[38]

As for the CAEM, it is a good idea to minimize its role. First
of all, none of the leaders of the revolution—Colonels Leonidas
Rodríguez, Jorge Fernández Maldonado, Enrique Gallegos, and
Rafael Hoyos Rubio—went to the CAEM, but all went to the
School of Information and Intelligence Services.[39] General Velasco Alvarado was not an alumnus of the School of Advanced
Military Studies, and none of the members of the initial revolutionary group had participated actively in the struggle against
the guerrillas. Finally, we should understand that the study of
the national policy is not carried out only in Lima. Similar institutions exist in Rio de Janeiro and Buenos Aires, and their
progressive influence seems rather slight. It was only because
of the presence among the civilian professors and collaborators
of certain radical intellectuals that that institution was able to
play a decisive role in the opening of the military to the problems of dependence and social development. The content of the
education is not the key. It is necessary to explain why the
experts of the Economic Commission for Latin America, Father
Lebret of *Économie et Humanisme*, and leftist sociologists and
technocrats returning from Israel and Yugoslavia were invited
to teach at the CAEM. Thus, we have the eternal problem of the
chicken and the egg.

On the other hand, that bundle of apparently disparate
factors cannot be isolated from the specific functions of the
military and internal political mechanisms related to the work
of the armed forces. The military role is the result of a special
international and domestic combination of forces. The doctrine
of "internal security" arose out of the concern of the CAEM
with the preparation of national defense of the nation that
placed the struggle against underdevelopment and poverty and
the "attainment of optimal social well-being" in the first rank of
the objectives of the military. As General Marin, creator of the
CAEM, put it very clearly, "It is necessary to give Peruvians

something worth defending."[40] The activist officers who took power in 1968 because of the political deadlock were convinced of that. However, they were only a minority. By erecting an institutional facade over their action, they succeeded for a time in involving the whole of the armed forces behind them.

BOLIVIA—FROM NATIONALIST OPPORTUNISM TO LYRICAL ILLUSION

The Peruvian model seems to have influenced the neighboring "tin republic" of Bolivia. The reorganized army taught by an American mission to fight against guerrilla threats after its quasi-dissolution in 1952 had been in power since 1964. General René Barrientos, who was president, opened the country to foreign penetration and in the name of the struggle against communism violently repressed the demands of the workers. This army was especially noted for wiping out, with the aid of "American advisers," the guerrilla center of Ñancahuazú where Ernesto Guevara died. After the accidental death of Barrientos, General Ovando, the commander in chief and patient supporter of the general-president, took power in a coup d'état. On his arrival in the Palacio Quemado, he adopted a Revolutionary Mandate of the Armed Forces, signed by the chiefs of the three branches. Its eighteen points formed a whole that was clearly nationalist in inspiration although there were certain concessions to the armed forces' antisubversive and repressive concerns that were not present in the Peruvian revolutionary texts.

Ovando, the official candidate to succeed Barrientos, let it be known that he wished to avoid the inconveniences of a genuine electoral competition. Nevertheless, he had already campaigned before the coup d'état on a program of "national economic liberation" and "accelerated industrialization." He denounced the betrayal of the 1952 revolution (but what military man had not?) and the surrender of the riches of the nation to foreign interests[41]—which was more interesting. Was he trying to separate himself from his predecessor so as to make people forget his recent past? For Domitila and the miners of the Siglo XX mine, which was occupied by the military on the orders of the Barrientos-Ovando tandem, he had put on a disguise as "a man of the left," which fooled no one.[42]

However, the ambitions of the indecisive General Ovando were not the only factors. The army was exceedingly unpopular. "We did not dare to take the bus," General Torres, the successor to Ovando, is supposed to have told his peers to justify his reform. Faced with the possibility of another 9 April, that is, a civilian explosion that would destroy the army as in 1952, the strategy of seduction replaced strongarm methods. The movement to the left was accepted by the officers in order to defend an institution that was divided between a "nationalist" wing around General Torres and a sector that was more concerned with order and the struggle against subversion, which was headed by General R. Miranda.

In practice, the accomplishments of the "nationalist revolutionary" government of Ovando were slight. Caught in a paralyzing set of contradictions, he was only to last until the right-wing coup d'état of 4 October 1970, and could not fulfill the promises of the "mandate of the armed forces." This program called for the recovery of natural resources, the establishment of refineries for the iron ore of the nation, the creation of heavy industry, an independent foreign policy, and the participation of workers in the profits of private enterprises. Nevertheless, the two first actions taken by the government were impressive, both of them modeled on the initial decisions of the Peruvian junta. The abrogation of the petroleum code—written in 1955 by American experts Davenport and Evans—that repealed the nationalist laws of 1937 and encouraged foreign investment, was a response to the expectations of an important group of civilian and military men. Surrounded by anti-Barrientos ministers who were intransigent nationalists such as Marcel Quiroga Santa Cruz, Alberto Bailey, and José Ortiz Mercado, General Ovando decreed the nationalization of Bolivian Gulf Oil Company on 17 October 1969; this action gave him the unexpected support of the Bolivian Workers Central Federation (COB), the bête noire of the military during the Barrientos years. In the social arena, the Ovando government ended the military occupation of the mining areas and reestablished trade union freedom.

Four days after the fall of Ovando, on 4 October 1970 a

countercoup d'état took place, led by General Torres with the support of the civilians in the Union of Popular Forces made up of unions, the leftist parties, and the students. That civilian support was an indication of the weakness of the left wing of the army. However, in contrast to Ovando, Torres, isolated and deprived of military support, was able to become very popular with the miners and the urban lower classes thanks to a series of long-awaited measures. He expelled the Peace Corps, nationalized the Mathilde zinc mines that had been privatized to the disadvantage of the country, and above all satisfied the main demand of the miners—the raising of salaries that had been cut by 40 percent under Barrientos. Although Torres was a "fortunate accident" for the Bolivian left, in the process of working with these "allies" he signed a suicide pact that precipitated his fall that was already predictable in January 1970.[43] The Marxist parties and the unions decided to create a Popular Assembly that Torres, with some reluctance, recognized. While the president with some difficulty restrained his adversaries within the army, the Popular Assembly established a system of "dual power" and made a chamber revolution in an orgy of neo-Leninist lyricism. Those "fireworks of the infantile left,"[44] to use the words of Augusto Cespedes, sacrificed Torres, without whom nothing could have been possible, on the altar of revolutionary orthodoxy. The coup de grace awaited by the right wing of the military was a manifesto of the noncommissioned officers, which some considered to be a provocation or a gross mistake, demanding the "immediate democratization of the military hierarchy." On 21 August 1971 Colonel Hugo Banzer, who had made an earlier attempt on 10 January that had been defeated, overthrew Torres and took power.

PANAMA AND THE RECONQUEST OF SOVEREIGNTY

In Panama, whose relatively recent political emancipation from Colombia had left it with a colonial enclave of an interoceanic canal wholly controlled by the United States, the nationalist orientation of the national guard government that emerged from the coup d'état of 8 October 1968 was another "happy surprise." In fact, in addition to the strategic position of Panama in the defense plans of Washington, the Panamanian national guard seemed less likely to defend national independence than any other military force in Latin America. That police force, most of whose members had been trained by American instructors in the Canal Zone, seemed to have very little authority in relation to the desires of the Southern Command.

In addition, at first glance the October coup d'état that overthrew President-elect Arnulfo Arias a few days before his inauguration was only one more episode in the struggle of the family clans that, in the absence of strong middle-class groups or of an organized public opinion, took the place of an official political life before 1968. Arias, who had been president twice before (1940 and 1949) had already been overthrown twice by the national police, who accused him of gaining his support from the poorest classes by promising demagogic reforms and preaching an aggressively xenophobic *Panameñista* nationalism.[45] In addition, while the United States maintained an attitude of prudent neutrality, the meaning of the 1968 coup d'état did not seem to be in doubt. Nevertheless, everyone expected a government that would cooperate in a friendly way with the "protecting" power as had the government of Colonel Remón in 1950s. However, after many reversals, internal crises, and a period of repression of the unions and parties of the left, the junta, under the strong influence of General Omar Torrijos, the commander of the Guard, adopted an instransigent attitude toward the United States beginning in February 1969. Thus the new government rejected the American request for an extension of the lease on the air base of Rio Hato, and denounced three projected treaties relating to a future sea-level canal, the management of the present canal, and military cooperation. Finally, once the predominance of General Torrijos was assured, the new government demonstrated a very pronounced nationalism.

This policy took several forms. Some of them were symbolic, such as the expulsion of the Peace Corps in 1971, or social, such as the recognition of the labor unions in the banana plantations that belonged to American companies and the support given to them in their conflicts with the foreign employers.

Others were economic, as in the case of the nationalization of the principal gas and electric company in 1972. Social justice was also one of the objectives of the government that proclaimed that the revolution was "for the dispossessed, not for the propertied."[46] New labor legislation protected the unions, established a minimum wage, provided for collective bargaining, and fixed the severance pay and working conditions of workers and domestics.[47] A social housing program financed by local savings was designed to improve the living conditions of the people.

In the countryside, Torres promulgated a gradual agrarian reform that provided for the progressive and nonradical takeover of unproductive latifundia and of a great part of foreign landholdings. A cooperative sector was created alongside the state enterprises operating in the area of agricultural products for export (bananas, sugar).[48] The government-controlled National Peasant Confederation (CNC) established under the aegis of the new regime received the political benefits of these changes.

As in the case of other military revolutions, the Torrijos regime sought neither coherence nor purity in its ideology. It flirted with Cuba and renewed diplomatic relations with Castro and a number of socialist countries. Panama supported Salvador Allende and the Peruvian military "revolution," with which the members of the national guard in power maintained close relations. General Torrijos became involved very early in direct aid to the Sandinista guerrillas with a view to overthrowing the dictatorship of Somoza. The government of the National Guard was always on the side of the anti-imperialist forces in Latin America.

However, at the same time profiting from the free market in dollars in Panama, the military regime transformed the country into a banking haven, thanks to an ultraliberal law on the deposit and circulation of funds. By guaranteeing the secrecy of these operations, exempting the movement of capital to and from foreign countries from taxation, and freeing transfers from regulation, Panama attracted banks and deposits. The number of banks tripled between 1962 and 1967, and Panama became ranked in first place in Latin America,[49] replacing Nassau and the Bahamas. In return for this liberal legislation, the foreign banks made low-interest long-term loans to the government. While the bourgeoisie engaged in plotting and sought a confrontation with the government—such as the case in the province of Chiriquí in 1973 where the pressure of the large landholders resulted in the resignation of a Communist governor[50]—the international financial community supported General Torrijos. The United States tried to weaken him by making accusations of drug trafficking against his brother when it was not able to overthrow him through his colonels in December 1969,[51] but it remained very cautious in the face of a regime and a man who had retained many bargaining chips.

In fact, the principal objective of the Panamanian government, which was seen as essential and justified its existence, was the recovery of the canal and the reassertion of sovereignty over the zone occupied by the United States. For that purpose Torrijos established a national front involving all social classes. That is why the strongman of Panama did not want to be identified with the left or the right and claimed that in the interests of the country he was "working with both hands," involving employers and workers, large landholders and peasants, in the struggle for the canal. An agreement among the classes was a consequence of the effort to achieve the national cooperation necessary to the great patriotic design. The canal was the key to the foreign policy of the regime. In 1977 at the end of long and difficult negotiations an agreement was reached with Washington for a new treaty that provided for the complete recovery of the canal in the year 2000 and the evacuation of the Canal Zone. Both sides made concessions, but the sovereignty of Panama was recognized and its material interests consolidated. Did this agreement mark the end of the Torrijos era and his program of nationalist mobilization? In any case, he gave up power in 1978 to a civilian president chosen at his direction and supported by a party that claimed to be carrying out his program, and he kept the post of commander of the Guard.

We may ask whether with Torrijos from 1969 until 1978, or even until 1981, the date of his accidental death, we still had a militarily dominated regime. Torrijos had many of the traits of a more enlightened traditional caudillo—the desire for unanimity and for personal contact, appearances in various parts of the country, physical courage, prudence, and audacity combined with a good-natured *machismo* that completes the picture. He was not simply the most senior person in the highest rank or the officer who happened to be at the top of the organizational chart. Both head of the Guard and head of government, Torrijos popularized that confusion of powers and the constitution recognized it when it stipulated, "Brigadier General Omar Torrijos Herrera, commander in chief of the National Guard, is recognized as the principal leader of the revolution."[52] Nevertheless, it was from the Guard that the *lider maximo* drew his power. With a disparate official party made up of businessmen and Marxist intellectuals that was only unified by Torrijos, all observers agree that after the death of the founding hero the future of the regime was once again in the hands of the officers.[53]

AUTHORITARIAN REFORMISM AND PETROLEUM IN ECUADOR

Without attempting to cover all the more or less abortive attempts at "radical praetorianism" our panorama would be incomplete without studying Ecuador, the only petroleum-exporting state in which, between 1972 and 1976, an experiment in military reformism appeared that seemed to be a somewhat pale reflection of the Peruvian "process."

The coup d'état of February 1972 that appeared very institutional in character coincided with the petroleum boom. The commanders in chief of the three branches deposed the aging and picturesque President Velasco Ibarra, who was serving his fifth term, having taken over full power in 1970 in opposition to the pressures of the businessmen of Guayaquil. When the petroleum bonanza opened a period of prosperity, the military did not want just anyone to profit from the windfall. Specifically, they wished to prevent the likely victory in the June 1972 elections of the mayor of Guayaquil, who was a demagogue close to the export sector.

The new government under the presidency of General Rodríguez Lara proclaimed itself "revolutionary, nationalist, social-humanist, and in favor of autonomous development."[54] It subscribed to a number of objectives: a better distribution of income, the fight against unemployment, an agrarian reform, and a fiscal reform. It published an Integral Plan for transformation and development for 1973–77 that called for an acceleration of development and the strengthening of the public sector. The nationalist character of the new government was not in doubt: it was demonstrated by the intransigent defense of the maritime sovereignty of the country over a 200-mile zone against the California tuna fishers—as well as by its international policy, especially with reference to Cuba. The military were most active and decisive in the domain of petroleum. In 1972 General Rodríguez Lara created the Corporación Estatal Petrolera Ecuadoriana (CEPE) to control the development of the recently discovered petroleum. The CEPE owned 25 percent of the shares of a consortium that also included Gulf and Texaco. It bought all of Gulf's shares and a part of those of Texaco.[55] The state thus controlled about 80 percent of the shares in the petroleum industry. Then the government decided to revise all the contracts and concessions belonging to foreign companies—which was not likely to take place without problems, especially when Ecuador, having become the fourth largest petroleum exporter in the continent, entered OPEC against the wishes of the United States, resulting in the suspension of U.S. military aid. A new refinery was created at Esmeraldas, as well as a network of pipelines that made up for the inadequacy of the highway network. Petrochemical projects were created. Thanks to the intervention of the state, Ecuador under the military intended to make the best possible use of its petroleum.

In 1974 hydrocarbons comprised 60 percent of the total exports and for the first time in Ecuadorian history the most important natural resource was essentially controlled by the state. The economic growth that resulted from the stimulus of petroleum reached impressive rates (13 percent in 1974) and the transfer of the profits to the private sector permitted strong industrial growth. A restructuring of the agrarian sector was also made possible by the new revenues and the military's desire for change. The transformation and development plan called for "an acceleration in the elimination of poverty by breaking with the traditional agrarian structure, the increase in the domestic supply of food products, and the stimulation of the expansion of agro-pastoral exports."[56] The implementation of the agrarian reform law of October 1973 produced significant results. Wage labor became generalized while the unpaid or forced labor that was traditional in the Andes disappeared. Sharecropping was practically abolished. The number of large landholdings and their size declined, and medium and small property holdings increased. That cautious reform failed, however, to accelerate the establishment of cooperatives, while the lack of change in the availability of land and in social domination limited the expansion of the market.

In fact, the accomplishments of the regime were very far from its change-oriented rhetoric. Also, while the petroleum wealth made it possible to improve somewhat the inadequate highway system and thus to unify a national territory that had been fragmented because of the Andean mountain chain, it did not transform the country.

Ecuador adopted a stockholder mentality. Beginning in 1972 imports of luxury products increased at an annual rate of 60 percent.[57] The bureaucracy grew. Speculation enriched a "new class," of which the military were a significant part. But proven reserves were limited and it seemed possible that Ecuadorian petroleum would be exhausted by 1990. The internal consumption of petroleum products that was subsidized by the government because of pressure from the road transport lobby (high-test gasoline at 20 cents a gallon in 1979!) increased at a wild rate. Furthermore, Ecuador was in danger of becoming the first OPEC country to become a net importer of petroleum. Boycotted by the oil cartel, hampered by technical problems, production and exports dropped beginning in 1975. General Rodríguez Lara tried to limit imports in order to improve the financial situation: the importers in Guayaquil who protested against the revaluation of the sucre (the Ecuadorian currency) initiated major maneuvers against the "progressive" military, accusing them of communism. While the unions initiated very bitter strikes in order to secure wage increases, the business interests and the parties of the right attempted to involve a part of the army in a coup d'état at the time of the "uprising" of 1

September 1975. On 11 January 1976, General Rodríguez was removed by the three commanders in chief, who announced their intention to return power to the civilians. The "nationalist revolution" was over.

REFORMS FROM ABOVE

The different experiments in military reformism that we have just described have the same political style in common. These regimes are not very repressive; they do not persecute the parties and the labor unions. Most of the time they do not prohibit them. They often have the support of some of the parties of the left, but they remain authoritarian. The regimes began with a coup d'état. This "original sin" of the military affects everything that they do, for conspiracy and surprise are at the opposite end of the spectrum from social progress. Plotters, far from mobilizing politically the social forces interested in change, exclude or ignore them. From the outset radical praetorianism appears like enlightened despotism: everything for the people, nothing by the people. By giving power to a bureaucratic elite, military intervention helps to isolate the state. The popular support that is indispensable for social change and the carrying out of a radical experiment remain to be secured.

The leaders of the progressive military regimes in Latin America have an ambiguous and hesitant attitude toward popular participation. With the exception of Panama, which succeeded in demilitarizing itself, they refused to make use of the support developed as a result of the reforms that they promoted by giving it ways to express itself. On the contrary, they had a tendency to keep the dominated groups that benefited from the regime demobilized. The introduction of the people into the political sphere was not appreciated at the upper levels of the state. Military men in power distrust the spontaneity of the masses and sometimes express their hostility to the autonomy of popular organizations through strong measures. At best because they are conscious of the danger of a social vacuum the revolutionary soldiers of Latin America reluctantly admit a certain kind of conformist mobilization that is strictly controlled, if not manipulated, by the state, and is specifically oriented rather than institutionalized.

In Peru, the regime of General Velasco Alvarado was marked by its paternalism. The people were asked to remain as spectators of reforms that would benefit them. It was a matter of "humanizing society by decree."[58] A strange combination of self-management and authoritarianism emerged as a result of an "antipolitical" concept of participation that was exemplified by General Alvarado's continual rejection of the possibility of creating a party of the Peruvian revolution. "There is nothing inevitable about forming a party. It is not imperative," he said in an interview.

> The essential meaning of participation is incompatible with that of an institutionalized party. A political party is an instrument for the manipulation and concentration of power, and not a mechanism directed at transferring power. Since our revolution aims at initiating a process of the transfer of political power and economic power to social organizations at the base—as the supporters of a new conception of the state and the foundation of fully participatory social democracy which we are going to construct in Peru—our essential goal is in fundamental contradiction with the meaning and purpose of political parties which is by definition to monopolize power and to exercise it through their bureaucracy in the name of the people. . . . In addition a political party would inevitably lead to the fragmentation and division of the popular sectors to which our revolution is addressed.[59]

Having said this, we should add that when we examine the implementation of that program of liberation we perceive that the participation in question is limited at best to the immediate environment of the citizen, to his workplace or residential area, but excludes the system of national decision making that remains the monopoly of the military.[60] In addition, in order to protect the people against "imported ideologies," the military government offers "to orient the development of the associations while preventing them from being manipulated by minorities or groups whose interests would be foreign to theirs."[61] In practice, the distrustful and even hostile attitude of the government toward the Committees for the Defense of the Revolution that were created quasi-spontaneously in 1969 after the adoption of the agrarian reform, confirms that the military government would only allow a mobilization that it stimulated and controlled. The creation of a bureaucratic agency for that purpose in 1971 reinforces this. Named The National System of Support for Social Mobilization (SINAMOS), it never passed the stage of an office of social manipulation aimed at weakening the Marxist-controlled unions, and its history is marked by more failures than successes.

Furthermore, the technical approach to participation that is expressed by the term, "system," was aimed more at demobilizing than at mobilizing. This "indigenous Peace Corps," with its seven thousand preacher-bureaucrats was not a party even though it was the only political arm of the revolution. According to those who established it, it was supposed to wither away as power was transferred to the social organizations.[62] However, rather than acting in accordance with the play on words implicit in its title (*sin amos* in Spanish means "without masters") the SINAMOS was under the tight control of the military, and this disturbed the leftist intellectuals who were promoting it. All its regional directorates were led by the local military unit heads. As one of the (civilian) creators of the "system" remarked, the logic of the military and participation do not get along well together. The contradiction between the model of society that was proposed and the desire for control by the state is obvious. One of the military heads of SINAMOS declared that it was a "school for participation."[63] From there to treating the citizens as pupils or conscripts is only a small step.

Not all bureaucratic authoritarian regimes are conservative. But the exclusiveness of the military also affects reformers in uniform. A culture of nonparticipation dominates military society, the norms of which are based on perception and command. The professionals in a "wholly simple art of execution," attempting to govern a country in the same way that they command a regiment, continue to exhibit a voluntaristic attitude. Also, the more the army is state oriented and professionalized, the more these traits are reinforced, as is evident in a comparison of Peru and Panama, or Ecuador and Bolivia. Mistrust of a populace divided by conflicting interests leads to an overestima-

tion of the institution to which the officers belong. Organization men before becoming politicians, for them institutional
values come first. In addition social change can only be related
to defense in a very indirect way. While the conservative military unhesitatingly eliminate their internal adversaries, radical
praetorians are concerned about the defense of corporate unity.
Perhaps this is also because they are generally in the minority.

Thus Torres in Bolivia did not give in to the urgings of his
civilian allies to arm them and to purge the officer corps. The
army is not a party. Esprit de corps overcomes ideological
choices. In El Salvador one of the explanations of the defeat of
the "young Turks" who overthrew General Carlos Romero in
1979 with the specific purpose of preventing the Salvadoran
military institution from meeting the same fate as the Nicaraguan national guard, was their refusal to touch the army. While
the junta adopted reforms and reached out to the guerrillas in
order to pacify the country, the officers who belonged to the
extreme right unleashed the terror against the civilian left and
buried the hopes for an agreement. The unit chiefs undid at
night what the junta decided by day, thus pushing the country
into civil war. The young reformist captains and colonels would
soon be removed from the army, indeed in some cases assassinated. In Peru the institutional element in the October coup
concealed the internal struggles and the minority character of
the intervention against President Belaunde. The progressive
colonels who brought along with them the chief of the interservice general staff, General Velasco Alvarado, could make
use of the resources of hierarchical obedience in order to coopt
the mass of indifferent officers. However, few of the officers of
the three branches agreed with the change and the revolutionary nationalists in Lima governed through generals who were
hostile to the process, conservative ministers, and an active
military extreme right. In addition, very soon the promotion
pattern turned against them. Ideological unity is not the main
force in armies.

In the list of abortive revolutions there is no doubt that
those led by the military would rank at the top, as we have just
seen. The progressive experiments carried out by the army turn
out to be short-lived when they are not transformed into ex-

plicit counterrevolutions. Sudden reversals, unexpected swings of the pendulum, and 180 degree turns seem to be characteristic of the military in power. Bolivia, Ecuador, and Peru demonstrate that. However, perhaps we have taken the "verbal socialism" of the radical praetorians too literally. Does not military reformism such as that in Peru and Panama attempt to use the state apparatus and nationalist dynamic nationalism to achieve a cohesion and a synthesis of contradictory interests? And does not the military and authoritarian style prevail over their progressive goals? Those "revolutionaries" really only seek to recentralize the state and to centralize decision making by strengthening the state in order to assure that it can act as arbiter. It is tempting to eliminate the main emphasis of those "centralizing revolutions" and to group them with the military counterrevolutions since their motives and causes are the same. But how could it be otherwise?

MILITARY MECHANISMS AND INTERNATIONAL ECONOMICS

Nevertheless, it is undeniable that there exist or have existed in nearly all state armies of the subcontinent currents and tendencies that are anti-imperialist and reformist. It is not surprising that among patriots by profession in countries that are dependent or semicolonial all the varieties of nationalism would be represented. Nor is it surprising that in an appropriate situation preparation for war should turn into a concern for the welfare of the populace and the morale of the troops, and for national unity and social cohesion as well as the autonomy of the defensive apparatus. However, whatever the words of these officers, they remain professional military men and it would be wrong to believe, except in a specific case, that a leftist officer is really completely a man of the left. The workers' parties in Bolivia found this out at their own expense during the brief presidency of Torres.

The changes in political attitude of the Latin American military, however, are not the result of cynical opportunism or of an adjustment everywhere and always to the "needs" of large capital. National military traditions have an effect on the original character of radical praetorianism and perhaps facilitate its recurrence. In Bolivia the political tradition of the Chaco War, which is reformist and antioligarchic and has elements of xenophobia, is piously preserved within the army. It limits antimilitarist reflexes on the part of the civilian population and awakens among certain officers a nostalgia for a reliable alliance between the army and the miners and peasants. The Chaco War (1932–35), in which the Bolivian army was beaten by Paraguay, still affects the fraternal and heroic aspirations of nationalist officers. Equality and the discovery of one another by the social classes, and social mingling on the field of battle, have had much to do with the formation of national consciousness.[64] It was the veterans and the reserve officers of the Chaco who founded the National Revolutionary Movement that ended the oligarchic regime in 1952, with the humiliation of the defeat even affecting officers who had not personally experienced it.[65] In May 1936 it was also junior officers who were unhappy with the conditions of the armistice that had ended that bloody and useless war who seized power from the traditional politicians, whom they considered incompetent and corrupt, with the intention of carrying out reforms and fighting against the control by foreign interests, especially those in petroleum, whom they felt had decisive responsibility for the 1932 conflict. Colonels David Toro and Germán Busch were successive leaders of a nationalist authoritarian regime from 1936 to 1939. In addition, from 1943 to 1946 Commander Gualberto Villaroel in quasi-fascist style tried to mobilize the masses with a program of basic social reforms that directly threatened the large mining companies and the landholder interests. A "popular" insurrection in La Paz ended the military-nationalistic regime by assassinating the president, to the considerable satisfaction of the democratic "tin barons." Villaroel joined Busch who had tragically disappeared in 1939 in the pantheon of martyrs of national independence.

Certainly the tradition of the Chaco and of the three nationalist military heros became an obligatory reference for all generals who wished to carry out a coup. General Barrientos mentioned them, as did the Machiavellian Banzer in 1971, or the generals of the "cocainocracy" who were associated with General Garcia Meza after 1978. In the name of the same spirit more conservative generals since Barrientos have signed strange and solemn "pacts" with the peasants who are concerned to preserve the plots of land given to them as a result of the agrarian reform and are upset by the propaganda of the left parties and the radicalism of the miners. It is also true that the gap between the actual role played by the Bolivian army and that cult of "patriotism" has created a malaise in the ranks of the military. In 1969 many officers had difficulty in choosing between the army of the Chaco and the army of Ñancahuazú and were not happy to see their unpopularity increase. When General Ovando announced the nationalization of Bolivian Gulf Oil, he recalled that as a result of that revolutionary decision, "The blood poured out on the sands of the Chaco had not been shed in vain."[66]

In El Salvador the reformist activism of the young military ending a long series of counterrevolutionary dictatorships that had been unable to control institutionalized terrorism, was not without precedent. In 1948 a group of young officers revolted against the successor of the sorcerer-president Hernández Martínez, established a junta, and had a constitutional assembly adopt a progressive constitution. The 1950 elections brought Oscar Osorio, "the people's colonel," to the presidency and his government cautiously put into effect certain reforms announced earlier: social security was created and the unionization of labor promoted. However, partly because of the crisis in coffee prices, the six-year term of Osorio was transformed into a regime that was concerned with order.[67] The reforms that were promised in the "glorious action of December 14, 1948" seem only to have served to reduce social agitation.[68] In 1956, through the use of fraud, Colonel José Maria Lemus was elected unopposed as successor to Osorio. In 1959 the drop in the price of coffee and the Cuban revolution led to social agitation that was strongly repressed. On 26 October 1960 Lemus was removed by a coup d'état. A military junta announced bold reforms and the reestablishment of political and union freedom. According to some the new program was simply a move to the left within the framework of the system in order to retain control and to calm agitation. Others said it was Castroism. In January 1961 a civilian-military directorate overthrew the junta because it felt it was too radical, while insisting that it would continue to carry out the program of the deposed government. The directorate, which was closer to Kennedy than to Castro, wished to modernize the country, increasing the involvement of the state and developing industry within the framework of the Latin American Common Market that had been created by the Treaty of Managua in December 1960. However, the enthusiasm for modernization was soon dampened by the pressure of the agrarian oligarchy, the consequences of the war with Honduras in 1969, and especially by the desire of the military to cling to power by any means.

The cyclical character of these changes appears to be a corporate reversal with the whole hierarchy turning as a bloc, as in a parade. This is not the case. There are always decisive activist minorities that, occasionally at a risk to their careers, succeed in imposing a change of course on the whole military structure. This does not mean that there is unanimity or that the conservative military have become progressives. The image that the Peruvian military government of 1968 succeeded in giving to this process has added to the confusion. The coup d'état appeared to be impeccably institutional. Did not the commanders in chief of the three branches together depose President Belaunde and jointly issue the first revolutionary declarations? In fact, the intervention succeeded because the socialist-oriented colonels were able to win over General Velasco Alvarado, head of the interservice general staff, who was believed to be a conservative but had retained some Gaullist inclinations following his stay in Paris as military attaché. Before the fait accompli, the navy was reticent and the air force uninvolved. The opposing officers were outmaneuvered by the patriotic occupation of the IPC because the nationalist actions of Velasco Alvarado often resulted from purely internal considerations and operated to close the ranks and to neutralize the conservative and liberal military. The rule of hierarchy prevailed. While the radical colonels formed the Advisory Council to the Presidency (COAP) before being appointed to key ministries, General Velasco Alvarado also governed through conservative officers, even those of the extreme right. For eight years, until the victory of the moderates, the internal struggle of the radicals to overcome or convince their companions in arms was unceasing. This is the reason for the hesitations and the compromises in the reform legislation, and for the confrontations around General Velasco when he became ill beginning in 1973. It was in this way that the "revolutionary" military made an alliance with the "institutionalists" whose leader, General Francisco Morales Bermudez, was to become president in 1975 against the fascist-oriented extreme right represented by the powerful minister of fisheries, General Javier Tantaleán, who had become close to General Velasco. These Byzantine maneuvers were to be fatal to the process and to its "socializing" leaders.

We may ask how a determined minority, even an able one which is able to command the resources of the hierarchy, can coopt or neutralize officers who are not convinced of the benefits of socialism, even of humanist socialism. It is clear that the application of a coherent set of ideas helped to convince them. While the CAEM provided a common language, a flattering and well-wrought military rhetoric was also to result in the adhesion of the more reluctant officers. Is the army the only organization able to carry out the reforms that are necessary for modernization and still the subversive destabilization that takes place in the case of progressive civilian governments? It may be that officers subjected to psychological warfare and patriotic rhetoric are more likely to accede to the idea that it is possible to make use of the dynamic of nationalism to direct and control the masses while at the same time attacking both the causes and the effects of subversion. Does not "Nationalism . . . one of the most powerful propellants for the transition from traditional to modern societies"[69] allow the nation to avoid the fatal slippage into civil war, while a "revolution from above" effectively replaces counterguerrilla activities?

We must still explain why and when those radical minorities were able to take over. One might suppose that a successful and admired experiment might tempt chronic coup-makers seeking to find new programs. But the domino theory does not apply to Bolivia in 1969, or clearly to General Lopez Arellano in Honduras, or to Ecuador in 1972. Again, it is easy to talk about the specific characteristics of individual nations. The circumstances of the period 1968–72 also seem significant to us. The parallel developments that we have described took place in a favorable economic environment. There is no doubt that they would have been impossible without an international climate of détente. The new configuration of forces working in the Western hemisphere permitted the undeniable nationalist thrust that swept the continent and freed the progressive sectors within the national armies.

That hemispheric thaw reflected changes in the local strategy of the two great powers, and more specifically a change of attitude by the two poles in tension, Cuba and the United States. Beginning in 1968 in Cuba there was a period of flexibility. Castro abandoned—temporarily perhaps—his hope of creating "many Vietnams" or establishing a "second Cuba" in Latin America. Under the pressure of serious economic difficulties and on the advice of the USSR he adopted a policy of building "socialism in one country" and "tacit coexistence" with the United States. In addition, the defeat of the bold attempt in Bolivia to build a continental Sierra Maestra that resulted in the death of the best-known guerrilla fighter in October 1967 marked the beginning of Cuban disengagement and symbolized the end of an era. In the United States the election of Richard Nixon to the presidency coincided with the Peruvian coup, and while the U.S. did not forget the existence of a Communist state in the Caribbean, the Vietnamese quagmire and the Middle Eastern crisis overshadowed the less pressing Castroite threat. The "low profile" policy produced an attitude of caution and circumspection with regard to Latin America. The State Department demonstrated a clearly conciliatory attitude to avoid confrontations with the countries to the south, even at times when American economic interests were involved.

Thus, the United States made a prudent adjustment to the nationalist wave sweeping over the South American capitals. Secretary of State William Rogers even declared in January 1970 that "nationalism is a good thing in Latin America" and added, "The fact that the Latin Americans feel responsible for their future and are proud of their countries is a good thing. It is natural that the national pride might express itself at times in the form of anti-Americanism."[70] The attempts at destabilization of the socialist government of Chile remained, even in their discreet character, isolated from the context of the continent and did not compromise an overall policy. It was not until 1973 that Washington policy toward the Latin American nations began to harden. Up to that time there was a weakening of the tensions produced by Cuba's support for armed revolutionary movements and the counterrevolutionary obsession of the United States.

A relaxation was even perceptible on the level of the armies, which were no longer as obviously mobilized for the struggle against the internal enemy. The main theme of the Eighth Conference of Chiefs of General Staffs of the American armies that was held at Rio de Janeiro in September 1968 was "development." General Westmoreland, who represented the United States and was former commander in chief in Vietnam, made an important speech emphasizing the economic and social aspects of the phenomenon of revolution, and asserting that "action on the social and political front aimed at removing the causes of frustration [is] . . . more decisive than military action properly speaking."[71]

We should not conclude too rapidly, as extremist guerrilla groups and certain leftist intellectuals did in Peru, Bolivia, and elsewhere, that the "military revolutions" constituted the "new strategy of imperialism." They considered these events as a very clever maneuver of the United States to guarantee at a low price its control of the Latin American countries and as programs of civic action promoted by the Pentagon in order to gain popular support and sympathy for the armies of the continent. It would be an exaggeration to believe that the conflicts that took place between the military revolutions and the United States were fictitious, and that the endorsements of Fidel Castro had the approval of the State Department. However, we can believe that there was a coincidence between the internal desires of some armed forces and what one might call the militarization by the United States of the reform program of the Alliance for Progress and of the recommendations of Punta del Este.

We can apply the same type of analysis to the fragile reformist impulse of the "nonconservative" militarism in El Salvador in 1979 under Jimmy Carter, or earlier in Bolivia in 1978. The human rights policy had replaced the "benign neglect" of Nixon by that time. Thus the desire of the United States to get rid of embarrassing allies allowed the Sandinistas to drive the Somoza dynasty out of Nicaragua. In the same way in El Salvador the corporate interest of the army coincided with the policy of the White House. The same coincidence of interest occurred again under Ronald Reagan a few months later, but in the diametrically opposite direction with the militaries choosing another strategy. From then on the international situation was no longer favorable to progressive adventures.

Neither a historical exception nor a clever ruse by reaction, radical neomilitarism is therefore a phenomenon that is symptomatic of the politicization of the armies. It illustrates the specific mechanisms of praetorianism. In effect, political action can have no other legitimacy within the army and among its leadership than a military one. The army reacts more than it acts. The perception of threats determines its decisions and dictates its strategies, even those that are extramilitary. Nevertheless, the defense of the nation can lead in different directions. The survival and maintenance of the nation as an entity consists above all in increasing the defensive capacity of the country and strengthening its military potential. This can explain everything, from concern with the physical condition of conscripts to the demand for an independent industrial base and the interest demonstrated in the morale of the civilians. This is why these "revolutions" are not the local version of the managerial revolution, as has been said,[72] but rather flow from a classic conception of "the nation in arms." The officers are not managers or technocrats in uniform, even if their function of controlling territory locates them within a type of state that we must still define. In those "general staff revolutions" their military characters always conditions their revolutionary content.

11

THE MILITARY
STATE AND ITS
FUTURE

---

*Adventures and Misadventures of
Demilitarization*

A judgment on the possible future evolution of
military-dominated regimes depends on the theories adopted
to explain their unprecedented emergence in Latin America. If
we view contemporary militarism as a type of culturally produced anachronism that provides temporary resistance to the
supreme political good—representative democracy—this will result in a theory of a predictable and practically inevitable
unilinear evolution. Structural interpretations of the appearance of modern authoritarian regimes also emphasize their transitory character. Functionalist determinism, by establishing a
more or less instrumental correspondence between the dominant economic actors and the type of regime, predicts an end to
the authoritarian systems when their supposed "objectives"
have been fulfilled. Because of the "inevitable" or indispensable
character of the authoritarianisms for peripheral capitalism in
the present period, their disappearance is also historically determined. These two contradictory views have in common a fixed
dogmatic attitude concerning the "exceptional" character of authoritarian regimes. In effect both those who interpret Latin
American history in terms of the "struggle for democracy" and
those who view the field of politics as directly subordinated to
the needs of capital assume the inevitability of liberalization.

We should note that the supporters of these two theses
generally pay little attention to the fact that the great majority of

the Latin American authoritarian regimes are military. The first group does so because they have decided once and for all that armies in politics are a thing of the past. Since the mark of modernization is representative democracy and functional specialization, the obstacles to popular sovereignty are the result of the weight of the traditional past. On these premises there is no attention given to the bureaucratic modernity of professionalized military institutions and the need to discover its relevant effects on politics. "Economistic" views also ignore the military component. Their approach neglects an institution that is at the center of power because it is assumed to be nothing more than the expression or instrument of other socioeconomic forces. In short, its special characteristics and particular processes form a sort of epiphenomenon.

A nonreductionist approach that focuses on the real holders of power in the political systems under military domination while taking into account group differences, alliances, and civilian support, as well as extrainstitutional political resources within a framework of the structural constraints experienced by national societies, cannot accept as predetermined the types of political organizations that will succeed authoritarian regimes. This does not mean that military power will last forever, but that it has a logic of its own. The successive waves of militarization and demilitarization that the continent has experienced since 1945 argue for caution.

In fact, while in 1954 twelve of the twenty republics were governed by military men who had taken power by force, only one remained by the middle of 1961, Stroessner in Paraguay. In seven years, revolution or assassination had ended the rule of ten military presidents, while another in Peru had "retired."[1] It is true that those generals headed very different regimes, including democracies, and the removal of the leader did not always change the system, as the situation in Nicaragua after the assassination of the rather unmilitary dictator, Somoza, in 1956 demonstrates. Often these systems are only military in terms of the original profession of their president; however, they have evolved in contrasting ways. Should one attribute to an antimilitary movement the deposition of Perón, who had been legally reelected constitutional president in 1951, or those of the Venezuelan tyrant, Pérez Jiménez, General Magloire in Haiti, or Colonel J. M. Lemus in Salvador, even though it is true that all those military men along with Batista in Cuba and Rojas Pinilla in Colombia were, for the time being at least, indeed the candidates of the military for the presidency? What are we then to say after those changes concerning the military tidal wave that ended civilian regimes in nine countries of the continent between March 1962 (Argentina), November 1964 (Bolivia), and June 1966 (Argentina again)? Furthermore, how are we to situate—as a continuity or a new phenomenon—the series of coups d'état at the beginning of the 1970s that struck countries with solid traditions of civilian government such as Chile and Uruguay, while in Argentina a new military intervention exhibited a violent character that was unheard of in the history of the nation?

Nevertheless, beginning in 1976–77, democracy seems to have been gaining ground. It appears to be time for a liberalization of regimes based on force and a return to civilian government. If we judge only by the figures, in 1978 twelve popular elections took place on the continent. That intense electoral activity seems to indicate that there will be a return of representative procedures. In fact, that figure covers both authoritarian votes and competitive elections or ambiguous maneuvers. The referendum in Chile and the reelection of Stroessner for the sixth time do not seem to indicate—far from it—the end of despotic systems. In Venezuela and Colombia elections that are customary in those model democracies do not constitute anything special. In Brazil the legislative elections took place within the framework of the military system under restrictions and manipulations that were aimed at guaranteeing its continuation in power, but nevertheless they had unfavorable results for the government. However, in Peru, Ecuador, and Bolivia those consultations were aimed at preparing for the return of the civilians to power, the free play of democratic institutions, and an orderly withdrawal of the military to their barracks.

This historical survey does not argue for a single simultaneous interpretation of military rule, as we have explained above. Nor do we believe that these continental movements condemn the states of the subcontinent to an indefinite alternation between civilian and military regimes. Rather they indicate that the forms of demilitarization are complex and diversified and that they may have their limits. Recurrences and retreats, rather than confirming a priori generalizations, invite us to examine the realities of demilitarization and therefore the real impact of the militarization of the state. Does it consist in a simple interlude with no institutional consequences after which there is a return to the previous regime once the army is back in the barracks? Or, on the contrary, do the military withdraw only when they believe that they have eliminated the political obstacles to a civilian regime and created the socioeconomic conditions favorable to the normal functioning of democratic institutions? These are questions that we can answer only by looking at what happens after military rule.

Controlled Usurpation

The instability of governments based on force has often been noted. Institutionalized military regimes, even when they appear to be the rule in a country, still remain exceptions, as paradoxical as that may seem. In fact, the dominant official ideology throughout the continent is liberal and pluralistic. The constant changes in military systems and the short duration of noncivilian governments are partly related to their lack of legitimacy, as perceived by those involved. In the cultural and normative context of Latin America those who hold military-based power always know, whatever they may say, that above them there is a higher legitimacy, that of constitutional legality that they may claim to possess, but to which they must finally appeal.[2] Military regimes are only really legitimized by the future. While elected governments are legitimate because of the way they originate, de facto governments only acquire a legitimacy in exercise, from their performance, so to speak. The past can justify the arrival in power of the military; the customary references to social and political chaos, to the vacuum of power, to threats of all kinds, nevertheless become transformed into objectives to be achieved. Military regimes thus look to the future. They are essentially transitory. Also, a permanent military system is a contradiction in terms.[3] An army can govern directly for an extended period of time only by ceasing to be an army. Also, it is precisely the following government, the successor regime, that is the basis for the legitimacy of the military usurpation of power.

Even if we work with the relatively arbitrary distinction between *provisional* (or *caretaker*) and *constituent* military governments, in neither case there is an avowed and declared intention to create a new type of state, a definitive and lasting power. A democratic regime is always more legitimate in Latin America than the omnipresent "state of exception." Contemporary military regimes in Latin America differ in this respect from the modern dictatorships that Europe and other continents have known precisely because of their constitutive weakness. They do not claim to create a new legitimacy or to put forward a new system of political values among the ruins of the old. The authoritarian regimes of Europe between 1920 and 1945 aimed at the creation of a "new order," even a "thousand year Reich," as opposed to liberalism and democracy. The military dictatorships of Latin America today are first of all regimes without an ideology. The "national security doctrine" that those institutionalized military governments share to a lesser or greater degree furnishes a rhetoric that conceals their illegitimacy, rather than providing a new source of legitimacy. That doctrine was above all a way to forge a mobilizing consensus within the military institution around an image that was related to their professional alarmism. Their theories of war, by enlarging the spectrum of threats and locating them within the nation itself, gave a corporate basis for the army's intervention in politics, but they did not explain it. They could justify a lasting presence in positions of command in the state, but they did not establish a new power. In a word, the theory of national security in no way takes the place of an ideology, not in its consistency, or its diffusion, or its constitutive function.

This is why representative democracy is always on the horizon of these regimes. They appeal to it both in their legitimation and in their objectives, proposing to improve it, to strengthen it, to amend it, even to protect it, but never to abolish or destroy it, as was the case in other areas. This tells us something about the

Brazilian "system" that has always retained (with proper safe-guards) parties, elections, and a congress—and even about the archaic militarism of Stroessner who, like all the classic dictators of the continent, keeps having himself reelected to the presidency and tolerates under strict surveillance a decorative but genuine multiparty system. The proclamations, declarations, programs, and maneuvers of the military in power in Uruguay or in Argentina refer to no other political system, to no other legitimacy than the traditional one of liberalism. Perhaps this is only a facade, but it operates against military messianism and prevents any program of remaining permanently in power. The military in power, however central their position in the political system and however great their autonomy, are participants in a political culture of the dominant internal and external classes who share a self-interested liberalism that acts as a check on the organic ambitions of the men of the barracks. Everything happens as if the dominant classes believed that the reestablishment of the market in economic affairs could only truly be legitimized in the name of a certain reestablishment of the political market.

Thus in Argentina every corporatist and antiliberal intention on the part of the military in power, from Uriburu in 1930 to Onganía in 1966–70, produced a reaction in the economic and social establishment and the replacement of the "anticonstitutionalist" generals by liberal military men.[4] In Uruguay, Bordaberry, the civilian president of a military dictatorship imposed by the gradual coup d'état of 1973, was removed by the general staff in June 1976 for having been accused of favoring "new institutions" that were opposed to democracy.[5] In fact, he had proposed the elimination of the party system and the establishment of an authoritarian "new state," the legitimacy of which would be guaranteed by the armed forces alone. However much they militarized the real exercise of power and however strongly the overpowering presence of military institutions and its representatives marked the whole life of the society, the Uruguayan generals found it difficult to give up the fiction of a civilian president: the garrison-state of Uruguay had a nonmilitary president until 1 September 1981 as well as a government from which the officers were practically absent. The parties were only "suspended" and the text submitted in the constitutional referendum of 30 November 1980, while it formalized the participation of the armed forces in the executive, provided for the legalization of the two traditional parties and the return of a restricted and purified version of representative procedures. The rejection by the electorate of that proposal after the semblance of a campaign was able to demonstrate that the military had been correct not to underestimate, even after seven years of prohibition and hostile propaganda, the strength of the support for the party system. This was also demonstrated in other countries such as in the Peruvian elections of May 1980 and the Argentine elections in 1973 after, respectively, twelve and seven years of the suspension of institutionalized political life.

The government in Chile, of which General Pinochet has been president since 1973, figures among the most antiliberal military regimes in the continent and is among those that concede the least to democratic rhetoric. On the contrary the authoritarian language of the Chilean military, with its insistence on the need for new institutions, has Francoist accents. Corporatist tendencies are expressed without concealment by the advisers and leaders of the "hard" line of the regime—the "renovators," to use their expression—who absolutely reject the institutional system that was in force until 1973. After the coup d'état General Pinochet himself announced a new constitution that was supposed to "banish forever the politicians, sectarianism, and demagogy."[6] The minister of the interior declared in September 1975, "All the political parties only divide the citizenry, favor their supporters in a demagogic way, and undermine the soul of the nation." The influential *El Mercurio*, spokesman for the moderates (blandos) and supporter of a moderate opening, commented on his statement as follows: "The government desires the destruction or the progressive disappearance of the parties."[7] In the constitutional debate, while the goals and time periods announced in the plan of Chacarillas (July 1977) reflected the desires of the "hardliners" for the establishment of an "authoritarian democracy," the constitution submitted to the plebiscite of 11 September 1980, apart from its gradualism and the restrictions on freedom that it contained, called for the establishment in the relatively distant future of a representative system that would include parties, a congress, and a president elected by universal suffrage. It is obvious that that juridical apparatus is aimed above all at justifying Pinochet's remaining in power. However, the utilization of a constitutional text that is not corporatist in inspiration and the fixing of a time limit to the state of exception is sufficient proof that even in the Chilean case the antiliberal temptation, the desire to exclude the "vanquished" forever, has given way to accommodation with the dominant democratic ideology.

The attempt to place representative practices under strict surveillance differs fundamentally from the ways and means adopted by dictators in other continents who had the same objectives. If we compare the regime of General Franco with that of General Pinochet the similarities are obvious, but the differences are no less clear. The two counterrevolutionary systems intended to break with the previous political situations, to refuse civil rights to political dissidents,[8] to keep the "vanquished" definitively out of power by prolonging the victorious (by coup d'état or civil war) coalition through the unlimited personal authority of the military leader of the counterrevolution. However, in Franco's case there was no concession to pluralism for forty years except at the summit of the state in his bourgeois-technocratic coalition. Liberal democracy was rejected forever regardless of internal changes and the international context. Franco, caudillo of Spain *por la gracia de Dios* never put into question even incidentally his remaining in power permanently. Neither the referendum of 1947 nor that of 1966 posed the question of the choice of the chief of state nor the length of his mandate. The opposition also finally adopted the idea that the dictatorship was for life and that a change of regime could only take place after the death of the caudillo.[9] General Pinochet, however, specified the time period of his provisional regime (it is true, after only four years), whatever may have been his real intentions for the future, and he did not exclude the possibility of the return of the parties and of competitive elections, modified of course by various prohibitions aimed at "protecting democracy." Thus, Pinochet proved that however much one might desire it one cannot create a new form of legitimacy in an environment that is hostile to such ideological adventures. Having made these remarks describing the limits of the militarization of the state in Latin America, let us see in what way demilitarization has been carried out—as well as on what level, to what degree, and with what kinds of regimes.

THE POSTMILITARY STATE AND THE FORMS OF INSTITUTIONALIZATION

The withdrawal of the army from power involves very diverse phenomena. The "civilianization" of the military state, however complete it may be, does not necessarily mean a return to "normal democracy." In order to analyze comparable situations we will only examine genuine systems of military domination, that is, regimes established by a coup in which the sovereignty of the armed institutions is exercised collectively over the selection of the chief executive and over all the major decisions of national importance, apart from the extent and content of civilian alliances or the background of the members of the government. We will therefore leave aside authoritarian regimes of other kinds, whether patrimonial or party, even when coercion and the participation of the officers play a major role.

We can dismiss at the outset a first type of demilitarization, the one secured by force through a civilian pronunciamiento. In fact, it is generally the military who overthrow the regimes of their peers by violence (more often, through the threat of the use of violence). Certainly many personal dictatorships, patrimonial autocracies, and postmilitary tyrannies have been removed through civilian uprisings allied at times to groups within the armed forces. Without going back to nineteenth-century Peru or to the civilian montoneras of Nicolás Pierola, a civilian-military revolution in Guatemala in 1944 overthrew General Jorge Ubico and his short-lived heir. In the same year in El Salvador students and soldiers ended the dictatorship of Hernández Martínez, whom his army no longer supported. Guerrillas, that is, civilians, defeated the National Guard of Somoza in 1979, and ended the dynasty in Nicaragua, repeating thus in different circumstances the Cuban precedent. However, among institutional military governments, only that of

Bolivia in 1952 was overthrown by civilians. The military junta that annulled the electoral victory of the Movimiento Nacionalista Revolucionario (MNR) was in fact driven out in the streets of La Paz. The militarization of power that in time, at least, had been relatively limited, was followed by a drastic demilitarization with the Bolivian army being largely demobilized and its leadership violently purged so as to remove any possibility of its being a threat to the new revolutionary government.

The most frequent forms of demilitarization consist in leaving the military system in place but removing the army from power. Since for reasons that are both internal and external to the armed forces direct military government cannot be permanent, a number of methods are employed to maintain the continuity of martial power. They can be classified into two main tendencies—that of personalization, and of legalization—with the two models linked or not to a real or only apparent opening toward democracy.

The transfer of power to a military leader who takes control over those who put him in power constitutes one way of subordinating the armed forces to the executive and returning the army to its professional tasks. The transfer of power from impersonal institutions to the person of one man never takes place very easily. That process is evidently less difficult when the army is less statist and bureaucratic. Somoza, jefe director of the National Guard in Nicaragua, and Trujillo, generalisimo of the Dominican army, "personalized" the neocolonial military institutions that were entrusted to them before seizing power in their own names, and not as representatives of the army. It was different in Bolivia where Barrientos could overcome his rivals while having his power as first among equals ratified through an election and also drawing on an historical-military legitimacy (the tradition of the Chaco war) and a quasi-personal popular support (the military-peasant pact). The installation of Barrientos as constitutional president prolonged both the military junta and at the same time the preceding legal regime of which Barrientos was vice president. General Banzer had less luck in this area, it seems, than his predecessor. Having come to power through a coup d'état in 1971, he governed until 1974 at the head of a conservative coalition that was made up of part of the political class. In 1974, when he reorganized his government and replaced the politicians of the MNR and the Falange with generals, he seemed to emerge with increased personal power, but in fact the army took over the state once again.[10] General Banzer, after having announced on several occasions beginning in 1974 that there would be presidential elections, in 1978 had to resign himself to not being a candidate as a result of pressure from the army. He supported Juan Pareda, his former interior minister, while the armed forces, which were divided, announced that they would remain neutral. The elections of July 1979 were followed by a coup d'état by the "official" winner, who remained in office after being improperly elected and clumsily institutionalized by the military.

Democratic endorsement can also make it possible for there to be a legal resolution of a deadlock in a regime of the military that allows them to survive. In Argentina in 1945 the regime that emerged from the 1943 coup d'état was caught in the cross fire of internal and external opposition that was intensified by the defeat of the Axis powers, but the "workers' colonel" was at the height of his popularity. Critically regarded by a part of the army that was opposed to his proworker behavior and his political ambitions, Perón provided by his candidacy in free presidential elections an honorable way out for the institution that had brought him to power and which he claimed to represent. The "revolutionary" officers, even those hostile to the *lider*, had a choice between allowing the return of the traditional parties and a continuity represented by the former vice president of the military government. During his first presidency General Perón was careful to recall his military origins and to appear as the inheritor of the "revolution of June 4, 1943." Thus, by electoral endorsement of a candidate of the army, or what could be described as such, the military institution found coherence again and in theory ceased to make decisions. The vertical hierarchy of discipline was established once more, recreating the internal unity that had been disrupted. The process of demilitarization can stop there or it can go further and be extended using the alternative political resources available to the military leader to the point that he can sometimes cut himself off to a large—and dangerous—degree from his bases within the armed forces. This is what happened to Perón beginning in 1951.

The transfer of power to a military head of state can allow demilitarization without immediate recourse to dangerous electoral procedures. The military takeover thus ends up with a one-man dictatorship. This seems to be the pattern today in Chile. From 1977 the prolongation of the role of the military in response to the tutelary role that the armed forces had assumed strengthened the absolute power of General Pinochet. His irresistible rise, which relegated the junta simply to a legislative and constitutive role, was cleverly ratified by the success of the unexpected referendum of January 1978; the text of this document, which was imposed on the other members of the junta, stated, "I support General Pinochet."

In the Chilean case we may conclude that the high level of professionalization and the lack of political experience of the armed forces were factors that had much to do with that process of personalization-cum-institutionalization of the military regime. Hierarchic discipline took the place of political consensus, and fear of the return of the "vanquished" cemented cohesion around the leader who was a symbol of a counterrevolutionary policy that no one in the army questioned. This is why we can understand the lack of response within the institution to the criticisms of the political proposals of General Pinochet by General Gustavo Leigh, the air force representative in the junta, and to Leigh's subsequent removal and early retirement, as well as to the resignation of eighteen of the twenty-one air force generals. The slow pace of the "constitutional timetable" and Chile's international isolation operated in the direction of reinforcing military support for an institutionalization without an opening that gave the army a guarantee of what was essential to them. While the army no longer governed it was never far from power, and, more important, it felt that its needs were understood.

In most cases what is called the institutionalization of military regimes amounts to their legalization in conformity with the prevailing constitution. That change, which has some elements in common with a return to democracy and produces a certain liberalization, means that military power is exercised purely and simply within the institutional framework that is considered to be legitimate and makes use of it. At the same time, of course, the major sources of uncertainty that are inherent in the democratic process are removed. These procedures can produce "military governments that are both elected, constitutional, and anti-democratic"[11] as in Guatemala. This process of legalization is carried out generally in one of two ways: the formation of *a controlled and coercive multiparty system,* or the creation of a *dominant military party.*

An example of the latter is the system in force in El Salvador from 1950 until October 1979, the date of the overthrow of General Carlos Humberto Romero by a civilian-military junta. The military in power in 1948 tried to create an official party, the Revolutionary Party of National Unification (PRUD),[12] a veritable party of colonels modeled on the Institutional Revolutionary Party of Mexico but without its popular bases. The Party of National Conciliation (PCN) that succeeded it was the party expression of the military institution as well as its electoral extension.[13] However, it was also the state party in which under the aegis of the army, arrangements were made between the civilian or military bureaucracies and the dominant class. Alternately allowing or forbidding political competition (when the PCN lost ground) the "military party" controlled political life, obtained a majority in the Congress, and had a colonel or general elected to the presidency—although not without a certain amount of fraud in 1972 and 1977. The defeat of the PCN by the opposition in 1972 produced the disintegration of the semiopen electoral system. The fraud, repression, and the limitation of electoral competition that followed demonstrated the impotence and decomposition of the machinery that had been created to provide a legal guarantee of the continuismo of the military state.

The institutionalization of the nationalist military regime of General Torrijos in Panama seems to have followed a course parallel to that of the Salvadoran colonels, apart from their differences in political orientation. The Democratic Revolutionary Party (PRD) established by his supporters nearly ten years after the coup d'état carried out in 1968 by the national guard against the traditional oligarchic parties also seemed to aim at becoming a Mexican-style institutional party. Its success in the congressional elections of 1978 enabled the new civilian president who was elected by the assembly to democratize the regime without taking great risks.[14] Would the revival of political life take place at the expense of the PRD and would the process of democratization go as far as the acceptance of a possible defeat of the official party? By keeping the command of the National Guard, General Omar Torrijos, the strongman of Panama, had reestablished the classic pattern on the continent of a military caudillismo that does not allow such a possibility to be predicted. Also, it was whispered in Panama that Aristides Royo had only a six-year lease on power, granted by Torrijos.[15] However, Torrijos's accidental death in August 1981 opened a political vacuum that the National Guard could be tempted to fill.

The very fluid political-military situation in Honduras offers a special example of institutionalization through a traditional two-party system. Although, as in Peru, after the military reformers came to power in December 1972, they faced conservative forces who called for a return to institutional normality. Only following the removal of General Lopez Arellano, and then of his successor, Melgar Castro in August 1978, did the government of the armed forces begin a third period in which it ended the cycle of reform. The National party (conservative) that supported the new government offered to play the role of "military party, that is, of a civilian organization through which the military could continue to exercise power."[16] For that purpose elections were necessary. They took place on 20 April 1980, but unexpectedly the Liberals, the traditional adversaries of the National party, were victorious. That vote of protest against the military—thanks to the goodwill of the Liberals and to international circumstances—did not result in a coup d'état to annul the unforeseen electoral results: liberal and conservative members of the Congress joined in voting to elect as provisional president of the republic until the next elections (after the adoption of a new constitution) General Paz García, the head of the military junta,[17] and the party that won the elections found itself in a minority in the government! Finally, after many uncertainties the candidate of the Liberal party was elected president with a comfortable majority in the general elections of November 1981. But President Roberto Suazo Cordova had given so many guarantees to the *ultras* in the army that the new civilian regime could not upset the military.

In Guatemala the state was profoundly militarized. The army not only exercised power but also many civilian functions, constituting a veritable bureaucratic bourgeoisie,[18] while the chiefs of the general staff supervised the nominations to all posts of responsibility. Despite the use of more or less regular competitive elections, there was no military party. However, in 1978 all three candidates for the presidency were generals, and since the overthrow of the progressive civilian president, Jacobo Arbenz, in 1954 by Castillo Armas, "anti-Communist" governments supported by the army have been in power with or without popular ratification. Beginning in 1970—in a climate of increasing violence—generals regularly succeeded one another in the presidency as a result of elections that the army always won. The same scenario was repeated with some variations: the armed forces chose a candidate who was necessarily to become the chief executive and then they negotiated with one or two parties of the right or the extreme right that could provide the electoral bases. Pluralism was limited by a "constitutional range" from which the left parties were banned by definition.[19]

In 1970 Colonel Carlos Arana Osorio was elected president with the support of the Movement of National Liberation, "the party of organized violence" and of counterterrorism. In 1974 General Kjell Laugerud was the candidate of a coalition of the MLN and of the Institutional Democratic Party (PID); in 1978, the so-called Revolutionary party allied with the PID to elect General Romeo Lucas García. It seems that only Arana Osorio actually won the elections and his successors gained power by fraud or the use of force by the preceding government. Thus General Laugerud definitely obtained fewer votes than General Rios Montt, but the government had his election ratified by the congress.[20] Rios Montt, not having enough support in the army, had to leave the country. These constitutional governments are therefore the expression of a military state that is legalized along the lines of "controlled coercive multipartyism." However, they also represent forms of demilitarization that can alternately close and open toward the establishment of less exclusionary pluralist systems.

The evolution of Brazil shows both the ambiguity and the ease with which a controlled redemocratization can be carried out by the military when it has not eliminated democratic procedures, even if it has emptied them of their content. The policy of "decompression" and of opening initiated in 1974 by General Geisel and pursued by his heir, General Figueiredo, clearly produced a liberalization. The elimination of the dictatorial powers given to the president by Institutional Act No. 5, the ending of censorship, an amnesty, the return of the political exiles, the reestablishment of direct election of governors and of most of the senators, were so many steps in a "gradual" redemocratization carried out by the government at a speed of its own choosing. The reactivation of civil society and the enlargement of the recognized political arena (as demonstrated by the multiplication of publications of the extreme left that circulate legally) can still be viewed as involving a new strategy of institutionalization following the failure of the coercive two-party strategy adopted in 1965.

The continuing electoral advance of the tolerated opposition front (the Movimento Democratico Brasileiro) beginning with the legislative elections of 1974 and the weak hold of the official ARENA party, put the government in a delicate and possibly unstable situation. A well-ordered opening, on the other hand, could assure continuity while ending the situation of a "plebiscitary impasse"[21] into which the system had been driven through its identification with the government party and the dual choice offered to the electorate. Some observers believed that the return of the pre-1964 leaders to political activity and the reestablishment of a multiparty system were measures that would lead to a split in the MDB and would therefore weaken the opposition by freeing it.[22] While for the time being the new party law certainly did not succeed in isolating the left by producing basic political realignments, it resulted at least in the formation of two conservative parties: the Partido Democratico Social, the president's party, and a progovernment opposition Partido Popular Brasileiro (PPB), incorporating the moderates. That new political spectrum was to make it possible to have an alternation without risk that was acceptable to the military provided that the opposition was divided and, better still, atomized. However, the prohibition of "electoral alliances" aimed at preventing the establishment of a united opposition front forced the PPB to combine with the PMDB, the new version of the MDB, while the unexpected rise of the "Workers party" (PT) further complicated the programmed opening.

We may therefore conclude that that opening constituted a new effort at legitimation of an isolated regime in crisis that was seeking to enlarge its base. The "slow and gradual" democratization was not supposed to be a prelude to the transformation of the "system," but a continuation of its long-term practice of changing the rules of the game when they were unfavorable to it. This new manifestation of *casuismo* and of the flexibility of a regime that was a past master at elections in which the loser won had an effect on the nature of the system itself,[23] despite all its built-in safeguards. As F. H. Cardoso correctly points out, up to this point "the system legitimated the parties,"[24] but now the parties had become essential elements for the regime to function, so that the head of the state was presented as the leader of a party. In this setting liberalization develops its own dynamic. The utilization of authoritarian measures to channel a democracy that has been conceded in this way is no longer possible. It is only by playing the political game that the program can succeed and provide the regime with what it expects. A return to authoritarianism, which is always a possibility, would result in the loss of the political dividends of the whole strategy. However, political liberalization is not supposed to produce a social opening, as long-repressed and restricted demands emerge almost spontaneously. The repression of the large-scale strikes of April and May 1980 and of free trade unions seemed to indicate that the regime did not intend to give up its powers of control over "the dangerous classes" that were a legacy of the Vargas era and that, it is true, the "democratic experiment" of 1946 to 1964 had not changed. Will that authoritarian restriction remain and does it indicate the limits beyond which liberalization cannot go—even the price that must be paid for it to be permanent? Whatever the case, the regime does not intend, it seems, to surrender power or to lose the initiative. It has taken every step to ensure that democracy will operate in its favor. Rather than a relative democracy, therefore, it is a democracy in which those in power cannot lose control of what comes after them.[25] The test that remains is evidently the presidential succession and the way that it is carried out.* The revival of civil society, and the reactivation of the parties and of congressional life by narrowing the scope of authoritarianism, have reduced the space for the exercise of military sovereignty. The regime has changed its nature, but to whom does power belong?

CIVILIAN GOVERNMENT AND MILITARY POWER

We have seen the ambiguous character of a liberalization that is carried out without a break, but we have also seen that the means that are provided in order to maintain a facade of democracy already imply a certain form of demilitarization. In the recent history of Latin America noninstitutionalized military governments have generally agreed to withdraw from power only in exchange for certain guarantees. They make efforts to fix the rules of the game. Better still, when the situation permits it, they do not hesitate to demand a place for the military institutions in a democratic constitutional order that enables them to exercise a permanent right of supervision over political decisions. The draft constitution submitted by the Uruguayan military to a referendum in November 1980 in order to provide a juridical basis for their de facto power stipulated that the National Security Council (COSENA) made up of superior officers would have the right to make accusations against the members of the executive and the legislature without being responsible themselves to any other body, that it could intervene in "activities relating to national security," and could even (with the president) declare a "state of urgency" without referring to the congress, except after the fact.[26] That tutelary democracy, as we know, was rejected by the voters after being condemned by all the parties from the Frente Amplio on the left to the traditional Colorados and Blancos.[27]

---

* For the events that led to the election of a civilian president in Brazil in 1985, see the Epilogue. (Translator's note).

In Argentina in 1972, the military, who had been in power since 1966, decided, in order to avoid a social explosion, that elections would be held from which, for the first time since 1955, no group would be excluded. However, they wanted to avoid a "leap into the void" that might permit, in their words, a return to the "fatal errors of the past." To that end, General Lanusse, president of "the government of the armed forces," wished to conclude an agreement with the political forces on guarantees that were to be implemented by the army. Looking for an honorable way out, the army even made the holding of elections conditional on the conclusion of a "Grand National Accord" by all the political groups under its aegis. A military transitional candidate of national unity would not have displeased the general staff. After the political forces rejected any institutionalization of the participation of the military in a reestablished democracy and the attempts at an official candidate failed, the military put in place *in extremis* a double insurance policy by amending the electoral law to prescribe a two-round balloting system for the election of the president and a residence requirement that would prevent Perón, who had been forbidden to participate in political life since 1955, from becoming a candidate. The accumulation of protections and stratagems imposed by the de facto regime did not secure the support of the political forces. Finally, the junta of commanders in chief, in the absence of an agreement, issued a declaration that listed the principles that the military wished to have respected. Its text provided that the armed forces would be opposed, among other things, to an "indiscriminate amnesty" for crimes of subversion, and stipulated that they ought to "share in the responsibilities of government."[28]

In reality the regime had lost the initiative. The electoral victory of the Peronist candidate swept away the checks put in place by the outgoing government. The slogan "Campora in government, Perón in power" was a direct challenge to the proscription imposed by the generals. In addition, despite the provisions of the electoral law, the military declared Perón's candidate, Hector Campora, elected with only 49.5 percent of the vote in order to avoid a second defeat in a presidential electoral round that would be more agitated and more massively hostile to the government. The two political groups against which the 1966 coup d'état was carried out, the Peronists and the Radicals, received 70 percent of the votes. A semiofficial candidate did not even get 3 percent of the votes. All the candidates who represented continuity with the military hardly received 18 percent of the votes.[29] What is more, the new government promulgated an immediate general amnesty, and the president-elect rejected all the institutional suggestions as to who was to represent the armed forces. The leadership of the army was even decapitated by the nomination of a commander in chief who did not belong to the cavalry, which had dominated the army since 1960.

Similarly, in Ecuador the army that had seized power in 1972, when it withdrew tried to secure the acceptance of demands analogous to those of the Argentines. When the Ecuadorians decided to hand over power to the civilians after a palace revolution in 1976 had removed General Rodríguez Lara, they announced their wish to give the country a truly representative democracy. Nevertheless, the junta took some precautions, or rather tried to institute a democratic system that conformed to the image of the military. The process of democratization therefore was characterized by a prudently slow pace. It took no less than three years and began with the prohibition of the candidacies of the three most representative candidates who were considered to be dangerous demagogues by the army. A made-to-measure electoral law adopted in February 1978 provided that the future president was forbidden to have occupied that post in the past—which blocked the way to Velasco Ibarra, the eternal caudillo who had already been president five times, as well as to Carlos Julio Arosemena. Another ad hoc provision provided that the future president must be an Ecuadorian and the son of an Ecuadorian. The requirement was directed against Assad Bucaram, head of the Concentration of Popular Forces, one of the largest parties in the country, who was the son of a Lebanese. That populist leader and moving speaker, who enjoyed a large support in the subproletariat of Guayaquil, was the main favorite in the electoral race, as he had been in 1972 at the time of the coup d'état.

The use of the veto on the selection of candidacies, which

was contrary to democratic principles, augured badly for the reestablishment of a constitutional regime. The utilization of the French-style two-round election system, which only allowed the two front-running candidates to remain in the second round, seemed to be aimed at the establishment of a right wing front in the second round. The separation of the two rounds by nearly ten months and the numerous incidents during the campaign did not lead one to expect that the military would respect the results if they did not correspond to their wishes. They supported the conservative candidate, Sixto Duran, in an almost open way, while Bucaram, who had been excluded, was represented by his nephew by marriage, Jaime Roldos. However, Roldos won the elections and became constitutional president of Ecuador in August 1979 without any attempt by the military to question the election results that emerged at the end of a difficult and uncertain process.

It does not always happen in this way. The military seem to agree to retire only if the civilian government is very similar to their own or their candidate wins the elections. In all other cases the election may be invalidated, either immediately or after a period of observation that is more or less long, and when the circumstances are appropriate. The increase in the number of "contentious elections," to use the term of F. Bourricaud, is a result of that continuista behavior. The agitated political life of Bolivia from 1978 until 1980 is a good example of that tendency. General Juan Pereda, the official candidate of General Banzer, "unelected" in the July 1978 election, was the originator of a coup d'état on 21 July in order to guarantee a "victory" that was very much disputed, especially by the candidate of the moderate left, Hernán Siles Suazo. In November 1978, the legalist sector of the army led by General David Padilla overthrew General Pereda and called new elections for June 1979. When those elections did not produce a clear majority, the president of the senate was put at the head of the state. The process of constitutionalization was continuing when Colonel Natusch Busch seized power on 1 November 1979, but he was forced to resign two weeks later. He was replaced by the president of the Chamber of Deputies, Lydia Gueiler. New elections took place on 29

June 1980 which demonstrated a clear movement to the left. Siles Suazo, who came in first with a center-left coalition, was supposed to be named president by the congress on 4 August. General Banzer, who was a candidate in the elections, only received 15 percent of the votes. On 17 July 1980, a victorious and bloody coup d'état installed General García Meza in the presidency. Those who carried out the coup no longer spoke of elections. Their primary objective, "the extirpation of the Marxist cancer," postponed any form of institutionalization for the indefinite future, while military instability continued.*

Lacking the power to impose a government to their liking that would keep them in power, the armed forces can make use of measures of corporate defense that are far from promoting the reestablishment of civilian supremacy in all areas. Also, the "postmilitary" civilian regime does not completely resemble those that have preceded it if the elected authorities lose the upper hand in the nomination of those responsible for the army. In fact, the affirmation of military autonomy is often the legacy of the militarization of power or the price to pay for the return of the military to their barracks. In Peru President Belaúnde, who had been elected after a military interlude in 1962—and who was to be deposed in October 1968, and then reelected in 1979 following the return to democracy—was forced in 1963 to designate as head of each branch the officer who was at the top of the promotion list and to choose his military ministers in conformity with the wishes of the High Command. In Ecuador, shortly before the first round of the presidential elections in July 1978, the military amended the organic law of the armed forces and declared that the future president would be required to name as minister of defense the officer who was highest in the hierarchy.[30]

A military defeat at the ballot box that is accompanied by a complete rejection by an exasperated public opinion, such as happened in March through May of 1973 in Argentina, does not guarantee a return to full representative democracy, even

---

*In 1982 Siles Suazo reassumed the presidency for the remainder of his term. See the Epilogue (Translator's note).

when the army respects the results of the elections. The fact that the government has been demilitarized does not mean that the military have given up power in cases in which they have become quasi-legitimate players in the political game. Thus, from 1973 to 1976 the military, who had apparently been removed by the electoral tidal wave of Peronism, followed the development of the political situation step by step. Perón removed his lieutenant, President Campora, only after the general staff had returned to him his rank of general and had signaled approval. The army was not absent from the public stage under a series of commanders in chief, who, whatever their inclination to neutrality, were faced with a regime that was rapidly coming apart after the death of the leader. The desire on the part of the government of Isabel Perón for the participation and, at the outset, legitimation of the military was to produce a very serious crisis in August 1975 that was a prelude to the fall of the civilian government. The ostentatious apoliticism of the Argentine general staff turned out in March 1976 to be one of the more subtle forms of military intervention. The theory of the "ripening of the fruit" and the willingness of the military to let the situation deteriorate argue that the 1976 uprising was neither spontaneous nor accidental.

The fact that the Argentine army never left power completely does not mean that if a country has experienced military intervention even once in the modern period it is condemned to its continuing recurrence.[31] There is no doubt that with a half-century of military domination Argentina is an extreme case of a military-dominated political system. Yet, who would deny that the withdrawal of the armies is never definitive and that the postmilitary state, however democratic, always lives in the shadow of the barracks? The burden of that shadow affects the conduct of the actors, whether they wish to avoid a coup or to produce one. However, there is nothing inevitable about it. The longer military intervention does not take place, the more civilian power is reinforced, military usurpation made more difficult, and the political system demilitarized. On the other hand, the threat or continuing fear of a coup already amounts to actual intervention, as we see in Spain, where, since the death of Franco, for good reasons references to the "tolerance" of the military are common in political life, while the ghost of General Pavia's horse haunts the parliament.[32]*

Demilitarization therefore is a matter of degree. The return of the civilians to government is not automatically equivalent to the "civilianization" of power, even after free and representative elections. We must ask why and under what influences and circumstances the military hand over power to the civilians; but also it is necessary to understand the limitations on the process of "extraction" of the military.

THE HOUR OF THE CIVILIANS

The many theories that can be suggested concerning the causes of the transition from military authoritarianism to representative government in Latin America do not clarify the problem. The political, social, and economic factors that are generally cited actually apply to all kinds of authoritarianism, not just to the military version. Furthermore a number of them seem to be of little explanatory value because they can be turned in the opposite direction and thus seem to possess a "mythological" character. This is the term that is used by Wanderley Guilherme dos Santos when he criticizes the contradictory "economistic" explanations of authoritarian intervention. As he writes:

> Thus economic recessions are cited both as an explanation of the erosion of authoritarianism, since they make it impossible according to these theories for these regimes to coopt the masses and/or the elites by the distribution of benefits, and yet the same recessions are presented as an explanation for the survival of authoritarianism because only the conditions of authoritarianism will permit those regimes to suppress demand in conditions of extreme penury.
> Conversely high rates of economic accumulation and growth are used to explain the maintenance of authoritarianism because thus the governments can anesthetize the population, especially the masses, by

*In 1874 General Pavía organized a coup against King Alfonso in Spain (Translator's note).

distributing new gains to them, as well as to explain the
erosion of authoritarian systems, since the social groups
that benefit selectively from economic growth begin to
demand greater political participation. Both the erosion and
the continuation of authoritarianism as political phenomena
are thus "deduced" as easily from economic growth as from
economic decline. When opposing processes are used at the
same time to explain opposite results, they can be
characterized as "mythological."[33]

Infrastructural theories of more direct application are no
more convincing or operative. This is true of the interpretation
of the recent wavering of the military regimes of Latin America
and their tendency to move toward opening and institutionalization as the result of the completion of the process of "authoritarian restructuring of capitalism" that produced them.[34] If we
consider that General Pinochet's Chile is the most thoroughgo-
ing example of such a transformation, to the point that we can
speak of it as a veritable "capitalist revolution," the recent evolution of the Chilean situation amounts rather to a disproof of
that thesis. That regime, like a certain number of its fellow
regimes that were endowed with "constitutive" powers, declared that it had "objectives" (metas) to complete rather than
deadlines (plazos) to meet. However, the initiation of the "seven
modernizations" aimed at privatizing and "modernizing" by
removing essential sectors of national life from state control[35]
(in order to establish the domination of the market and to
change mental attitudes) has not prevented the regime from
fixing a calendar for the progressive establishment of an institutionalized juridical system.

While it is evident that the actions and expectations of the
different actors, the range of resources at the disposal of the
military, their duration in power, and the initial justification of
their emergence are factors to be taken into consideration, the
continent-wide situation and the internal processes within the
military institutions seem to be the most important elements in
determining the political changes within military-dominated
systems. Two mechanisms that are not exclusive but are rather
often complementary or alternative can give the most complete
explanation of those transformations. The first, involving the

will and intention of the constituent military actor, goes back to the overall legitimacy of which we have spoken and to the need to avoid or prevent the risks of democracy. The second, which includes many social factors and the particular functioning of the "military parties," emphasizes the *problematical* and non-programmed or indeterminate character of demilitarization that is the result of a whole series of "unintended effects," of chance, or of the mistakes or errors of those involved.

The effect of the hemispheric situation on the expansion and the involvement, as well as the orientation, of the military does not need any lengthy demonstration.[36] The hemispheric policy of the United States, which has alternated between anti-Communist vigilance and a concern with democratization has produced an almost clockwork rhythm in the phases of autocracy and the waves of demilitarization. This does not affect the particular dynamics of the most autonomous Latin American states, but in their case produces adaptations that are formal and "cosmetic." If the overthrow of President Frondizi in March 1962 was a response to strictly national conflicts that went back at least to 1955, the military who carried out the coup borrowed their justification from the defense perspectives developed by the Pentagon in the framework of the post-Cuban strategic changes. They dressed up their illegitimacy in a legal cloak—putting Vice-President Guido in the presidency—in order to satisfy the need for democratic respectability required by the Alliance for Progress. In this case the contradiction between the Kennedyite civilian reformism and the counterrevolutionary antireformism of hemispheric defense of the Pentagon permitted a dualistic reading of political-military events on the basis of two levels of interpretation.

More recently, the defeat in Bolivia of the coup d'état of 1 November 1979 and the success of the coup of 17 July 1980 were not unrelated to the continental situation and the policy of the United States. Colonel Natusch Busch was compelled to resign after two weeks under pressure from the Carter administration, which was promoting the process of democratization. The other member countries of the Andean Pact, acting as a veritable democratic bloc,[37] supported Washington in not recognizing the usurping government. In July 1980 President Carter, at the end of his term and in the midst of an electoral campaign, could do no more than issue a moral condemnation of a determined and brutal military intervention that was counting on his defeat. Indeed, observers have noted that the coup by General García Meza took place immediately after the presidential nomination by the Republican convention of Ronald Reagan—the hope of all the conservative forces in the continent.

In addition, the proper thing for a military regime to do is to demilitarize and legalize its situation—both because of the overall ideology that we have described and also because of the specific characteristics of the military apparatus in relation to power. The internal tensions produced by military participation in government weaken corporate cohesion and thus the defensive capabilities that are precisely the basis for the (temporary) legitimacy of the military takeover; in addition, participation reduces the political resources of the institution that then becomes dangerously "desacralized." Also for the military in power and those who support them, direct and nonlegal military government is neither a necessity nor a good solution. It corresponds rather to a stage, to a moment of political domination. Legalization is the next step. According to a cost-benefit analysis, the military in power act as if they are trying to find a balance between the social cost of the risk of democracy, and the institutional cost of military authoritarianism. This is why institutionalization is only rarely the same thing as the withdrawal of the military from power, and why legalization often does not have full and complete democracy as its goal. The withdrawal of the military is rather a mark of continuity and of the accomplishment of the mission announced at the time of the intervention. The calling of elections, even when they are not limited in an authoritarian manner, does not ipso facto involve the restoration of the establishment of authentic democracy. If we adopt the definition of procedural democracy of Joseph Schumpeter according to which "the people are able to accept or reject the men who are to govern them,"[38] the postmilitary state is more likely to organize elections that are without surprises or without results. The true holders of power are not affected.

Furthermore, the leaders of conservative military systems and their ideologues and allies openly reject the uncertainties of the democratic game. Their avowed ideal, "protected democracy," involves a search for an absolute guarantee against the risk of the arrival of adversaries of the status quo by legal means to power. One of the ideologues with the most influence over successive military regimes in Argentina wrote after the overthrow of the civilian government in 1976 that the new governments in the Southern Cone were in the process of founding "future democracies on the solid base of order and development" so as to make them more stable.[39] For their part the hardliners of the Chilean regime aim at the establishment of permanent safeguards against democratic subversion, since, to quote one of them, "One cannot live always on one's guard."[40] However, the best "protection" for democracy is in fact the utilization—devious, distorted, or directed?—of the procedures of democracy to legitate authoritarianism. The postmilitary state that is truly established and stable, like all lasting authoritarian governments in Latin America, involves a semicompetitive system. This is a system in which political competition, whether open or controlled, remains contained on the periphery of power while those who hold power keep electoral competition far away.[41] This system gives those who utilize it the advantages of the legitimacy of a representative regime without the risks of "alternation." It is evident that systems of military domination tend to move in the direction of formulas of this kind when they can, and if they have not lost the initiative. The conservatives among the military have no monopoly on it, if we are to believe the experience of Panama under Torrijos, which gradually became an exemplary semicompetitive system.

Brazil under General Figueiredo seems to be moving toward this formula through alternating relaxation and opening. Certainly the convergence of forces favorable to liberalization—from the tolerated political opposition to the industrial bourgeoisie, from the new middle class to the old political class—has played a role, but the system had a choice of methods and timing. The institutionalization program of President Geisel not only tried to break the opposition front by ending the system of two parties but also aimed at making the system independent of the army. General Figueiredo was chosen by Geisel as his successor in opposition to the military apparatus. The army lost its role as the great elector. Since, as the election results showed, the legitimacy of the military presence was questioned by civil society,[42] it was no doubt appropriate to provide a legal basis for the system without appealing to the army. Demilitarization without taking risks was also evident in the care taken by General Geisel, Figueiredo's successor, and the "palace group" that surrounded him to separate those in the army who were responsible for government from the military leaders (*chefia* contra *liderança*)—to use the distinction of Rizzo de Oliveira)[43]—in order to establish the hegemony of the bureaucracy over the armed forces and especially to prevent the emergence of political-military leaders with a legitimacy of their own.[44] This nondemocratic program may get out of the control of the sorcerer's apprentice who establishes it. The "perfect political crime," as an opposition deputy put it, may not be committed. There is a close relationship between risk and legitimacy. The more uncertainty—and therefore electoral fair play—there is, the more legitimacy. Thus in Brazil the game is not over despite the precautions that have been taken (election law, division of electoral districts, weakening of the opposition). If the opposition parties could unite to defeat the official candidates in the future direct elections of the governors (if they take place), the "system" would have some difficulty in designating a president without taking account of that situation, and in any case the semicompetitive system would be destroyed.[45] This is all the more true from now on because the tensions within the military structure created by the awakening of civil society may produce some sudden shifts. However, it is unlikely that those in power will take that risk. The well-timed prohibition of electoral coalitions will no doubt be sufficient to prevent this and to assure the "legal" survival of an exhausted regime.*

Most of the time the internal processes in the military apparatus determine the timing of the phases of demilitarization and open the way to democratic alternation. Weakness in the military apparatus or a serious corporate conflict discredits the in-

---

*For an analysis of the subsequent transition to civilian rule in Brazil, see the epilogue. (Translator's note.)

stitutionalization program. Then an appeal can be made to the
civilians and to democratic approval to resolve the deadlock
and to overcome the destabilizing cleavages. We do not want to
say that the behavior of other actors does not have a role, or
that the completion of the process of demilitarization and institutionalization does not depend on other factors, such as the
length of time in power of the noncivilian government, the
circumstances in which it was established, and the level of violence that it has applied to the society. However, the return of
the military to the barracks is first of all a military problem and
it would be paradoxical not to view it from that decisive angle.
It is evident that since the exercise of power is more demoraliz-
ing for a state institution such as the army than for a party,[46]
economic and social schisms increase the conflicts that divide
the institution on nonmilitary questions.

A civilian restoration through elections without conditions
or prohibitions is frequently the consequence of a palace revolution that results from a political change within the armed
forces. The program that justified the military exercise of power
is thus abandoned after a period of uncertainty that can last
several years (three years in Argentina after 1970, three years as
well in Ecuador after 1976, but five years in Peru from 1975 to
1980) and the military then have only to prepare an orderly and
"honorable" withdrawal. The rejection of a single political orientation or of a caudillist attempt was at the origin of such shifts.
Thus in Peru and Honduras in 1975 and in Ecuador in 1976, the
conservative sector of the army was opposed to the reformist
military men in power, resulting respectively in the fall of
Velasco Alvarado, of López Arellano, and of Rodríguez Lara.
However, a refusal in the name of the corporate functioning of
the military in power to give a blank check to the man whom
the army has put in the government results in the same consequences. The two causes may sometimes reinforce one another
as in Peru. In the name of institutional rotation of those who
hold the title of chief executive—similar to that applied in Brazil
since 1964 and Argentina after 1976—the Peruvian general staff
deposed Velasco Alvarado, who wished to maintain his power
beyond the time prescribed by military regulations and tried to
acquire personal support. The change of policy of the military

party, which could be explained according to some observers by the economic crisis and the urgent need to negotiate with social forces,[47] led to the restoration of democracy. In the absence of the resources of a charismatic leader and because it refuses to mobilize the support of a party, a bureaucratic system that lacks support and lacks a program can only retire or collapse. The regime of General Morales Bermudez, which lacked party support or the will to acquire it, still lasted five years—providing an unprecedented example of political levitation, of course, but also illustrating the difficulties of organizing an orderly transfer of power in an internally nonconsensual corporate situation.

In Argentina, after the overthrow of General Onganía who had placed no time limit on his power and claimed to be leaving the army out of government, General Alejandro Lanusse, commander in chief and king maker, for a short period enthroned General Roberto Levingston. Levingston then broke with the policy of economic liberalism of his predecessor without having the means to do so or specifying the aims of his government. The only thing that was left for the general staff to do was to recognize the defeat of the "Argentine Revolution" and to prepare the army's withdrawal. Acute internal divisions and intense social tension did not allow any solution other than the transfer of power to the civilians and the termination of the proscriptions that had both undermined the authority of elected presidents since 1955 and encouraged the development of political violence—or to engage in increased repression that the divisions among the military did not permit.

In such cases everything happens as if the recourse to the civilians, the opening of the democratic game without any guarantees for those who are in power, appears to be the only solution that would make it possible to reestablish the internal front of the armed forces. Faced with the danger of a breakdown and decomposition of the institution, the elections relieve the tensions, and reunify a military apparatus that has been torn by contradictory tendencies. It is not a taste for paradox that leads us to say, parodying the rhetoric of the military, that in such a case civilian intervention puts an end to military dissension. In the absence of a minimal consensus, if not of a program of the armed forces, the solution is formal demilitarization by means of democracy. However, in order for the tactical retreat to be effective there still must be a minimum agreement on the maintenance of neutrality or else the politicization of the military will produce a Bolivian-style cascade of coups and countercoups. In addition, since the divisions among the military are linked to differences among the civilians, demilitarization can only result if a majority of the political forces are convinced that it is a necessity and the military do not see in the return of the civilians any direct danger or possibility of revenge.

Tomorrow the Military? How to Get Rid of Them?

There are many obstacles to the departure of the military from the public scene, that is from the government, that impede or make impossible the return of freely elected civilians to their business. These derive mostly from a corporate logic. The continuation of the threat that justified the coming of the army to power obviously represents the most frequently occurring reason. An outburst of urban terrorism or an unsubdued center of rural guerrilla activity produces military reactions that are not propitious for a democratic relaxation. The overall invocation of the "danger of Communism" or of "the Marxist cancer" that must be rooted out before returning to the normal functioning of institutions is only viable as long as the specter of subversion has a concrete character for a part of public opinion. The logic of counterrevolution can only be fed by the memory of the revolutionary threat. The memory of the three years of Popular Unity is still the surest foundation of the dictatorship in Chile. However, in Brazil, sixteen years after the overthrow of the populist regime and the establishment of control over the popular forces, the leaders of the "system" that created the Manichean doctrine of "ideological frontiers" have muted that worn-out source of legitimation so that it now has little effectiveness. In Argentina, on the other hand, the chaotic conditions of the government of "Isabelita" and the "subversive aggression" that undermined the values of democratic coexistence gave the counterterrorist regime that was installed in 1976 a considerable capital of acceptance.

The level of official violence is a decisive factor. A military regime that employs little violence enjoys a great degree of freedom of maneuver. A terrorist government, on the other hand, will see a demand for an accounting on the part of the nation. The violations of human rights and the problem of those who have "disappeared" in the course of the struggle against subversion call for explanations, if not punishment, of those who were responsible when the situation returns to normal. In Argentina the specter of Nuremberg haunts the barracks and explains its present immobility. "Argentina only confesses to God,"[48] declared the minister of interior of General Videla. The demoralization and defense reflexes of an army involved in the "dirty job" of revolutionary war can lead to the indefinite prolongation of the military in power. It is therefore unlikely that the Argentine military can abandon the game as they did in 1973. This time the stakes are too high for them to leave the initiative to the civilians.* It is a question of the future and of the honor of the institution. In Brazil, despite an adroit amnesty that whitened the "stains" of repression, public revelations and denunciations of the responsibility of the officers for the assassination of members of the opposition produced a very strong reaction on the part of the military ministers in February 1981, who warned against any "revanchist" attempt that might impede the process of opening. "The honor of the military is more important than human rights," said the headline of an opposition weekly.[49] At the very least, liberalization must deal with this demand.

On this question the strategies of the civilians come into play, but their margin of maneuver is narrow. The search for a compromise, the acceptance of the "law of silence"[50] imposed by the military, can give the party forces and those of democracy the opportunity to gain ground. Avoiding direct confrontation and dissipating any personal or corporate concerns among the officers most involved in the repression can in a curious

*For the transition to civilian rule in Argentina, see the Epilogue. (Translator's note.)

way facilitate a gradual movement toward the rule of law and representative procedures. However, this also means restoring legitimacy through an act of weakness, guaranteeing that there will be no punishment for usurpation—in a word, placing the military apparatus in the role of irresponsible arbiter, therefore demilitarizing the government while maintaining the militarization of the political system. It is the eternal dilemma of the capable and principled—accommodation or intransigence. But there is also a fundamental difference between a transition as a result of concessions and a democratic rupture, and it perhaps has to do in fact with the evolution of the relation of forces.

In combination with the preceding characteristic, the nature and duration of the military government also affect the process of demilitarization. While democracy involves both competitive procedures for the choice of those who will govern and a substratum of freedoms that make that possible on a regular basis, some Latin American military systems eliminate the first, but only place limitations on the second. The restriction of party and trade union freedom, and to some degree of freedom of expression, was not in fact a major characteristic of the Peruvian and Panamanian regimes after 1968, or that of Ecuador between 1972 and 1979. Argentina under Onganía, Levingston, and Lanusse (1966–73) in comparison with other earlier or later regimes experienced a remarkable level of tolerance of the opposition. The continued vitality of civil society no doubt encouraged the different forms of demilitarization of the government undertaken by those regimes.

The duration of noninstitutionalized military power and the corruption that results from absolute power is likely to make political alternatives more improbable. The Bolivian case of an army that is divided into clans in which promotion to the rank of officer is a means of social mobility perhaps explains this phenomenon. It has even been hypothesized that their repeated refusal in 1979–80 to recognize the results of elections that did not guarantee the continuity of the military was based both on the fears of many officers that they would have to explain the origin of their increased wealth to public opinion or to the courts, and on the desire of those in the secondary levels of the army to have a share in the corruption. However, beyond these psychological and anecdotal explanations,[51] it is true that in the Bolivian case there are more profound elements relating to the militarization of the whole political system.

In Bolivia, while the defense of an institution that believed that it would be threatened by the return of the civilians and especially by a victory of even the moderate left blocked a transition, this also took place because the army is the area where political struggles are carried out. In that "praetorianized" system civilian political sectors are always involved in military interventions. It is rare that a military group launches a coup without party backing or an alliance with civilian groups. The overlapping of civilians and the military, the permanent interrelation of the two spheres, make the "extrication" of the military and the "civilianization" of the government difficult. In such a militarized system every military uprising has or does not have the public support of civilians who are involved. It seems in Bolivia that "praetorianization" is related to the absence of a political majority in the recent elections. In Argentina, where the army has dominated political life for the last fifty years, the demilitarization of governments still does not change the system or end "praetorian regression." The disengagement of the military and a lasting return to a liberal constitutional model in civil-military relations seems unlikely in the short or medium term.* This situation, which is an expression of a structural crisis and especially of a social blockage, cannot be overcome in Argentina without a profound transformation of national society.[52] This does not mean that the conduct of the actors is insignificant or inconsequential, but that behavior and tactics are not programmed and are themselves conditioned by social reality that recurrent military interventions both affects and distorts.

A FAREWELL TO ARMS?

There is no doubt that it is easier to demilitarize the government than to remove the military from power. The various openings and institutionalizations often represent tactical re-

---

*To understand why this prediction turned out to be false, see Epilogue. (Translator's note.)

treats that permit new interventions after the military apparatus has reconstituted its political instruments. It may also provide a way to guarantee a juridical basis for the continuation of
a regime that was established by force. An objection can be
made citing examples of successful demilitarizations. Without
referring to the examples of Chile and Uruguay, let us examine
the model democracies of today that for twenty years have been
spared the military storms that have shaken their neighbors. If
we examine the relations between the civilians and the military
in Mexico, Costa Rica, Venezuela, or Colombia, without thinking of what might happen tomorrow in one or another country,
we can still inquire about the methods and stages of civilian
preponderance. We should ask ourselves first if these countries
have experienced phases of militarization in the past and how
they have overcome them.

In fact, only Venezuela and Colombia ended a military dictatorship with the restoration of civilian rule. However, in the
Colombian case the brief interlude of General Rojas Pinilla in
1953 had the support of the majority political groups who had
called him to power in order to put an end to the violence that
was destroying the country.[53] The rapprochement between the
two traditional parties that took place in 1957 sounded the death
knell for the military government, just as the disagreement between them had enabled it to be born. In Venezuela, which in
1948 had barely emerged from decades of dictatorship by
caudillos, the army removed from the government the civilian
reformists that it had put there at the outset; however, the rise to
supreme and absolute power of General Pérez Jiménez brought
the officers who had lost power close to the democratic opposition. The coup attempts from both extremes that punctuated the
presidency of Romulo Betancourt after 1958 underlined the difficulties of civilian supremacy. Nevertheless, the military base of
the Acción Democrática party helped to strengthen the democratic regime that was all the more sure because Pérez Jiménez
had discredited the intervention of the army in political life.

In Mexico the generals of the revolutionary army were part
of the power elite and then of the dominant party. Also, the
stabilization of the revolutionary order that was in their collective interest facilitated the absorption of a spontaneous and

predatory military caudillismo. In a way the "generals" had to recognize the civilian power in which they participated in order to assure their political preeminence. Finally, in Costa Rica, which has not had a real military intervention since 1917, the army was abolished in 1948, but even before its legal abolition, the permanent military apparatus was already on the way to disappearing.[54] Therefore, in that case as well, there was no transition from military domination to civilian preponderance.

Are we saying that the uprooting of militarism only takes place as a result of a miracle and in exceptional historical circumstances? Or, as some observers of the Cuban and Sandinista revolutions think, only "total politicization of the military . . . will exclude any militarization of politics in the future"?[55] Certainly an army that is the guarantor of the revolutionary process that has created it and is led by political commissars and selects its officers on the basis of nonmilitary qualifications presents little danger for those in power.[56] The maximization of the power of civilians produces a sort of "subjective control"—to use the phrase of Samuel Huntington—that is very reliable. However, besides the fact that we should not mix governmental types and that we are now no longer in the context of a liberal democracy that is characterized by pluralism and alternation, the elimination of the distinction between the civilians and the military often amounts to the militarization of all of the life of the society. Among the Cuban ruling elite that fusion has taken place, it seems, to the advantage of military concerns. Also, the model of the *civic soldier* that results from that fusion, according to Jorge Dominguez,[57] does not avoid a conflict of roles.

If we remain with the capitalist societies of the continent and the solutions arrived at within the framework of pluralism and constitutionalism, it is evident that there is no preestablished scenario for the reconstruction of democracy. Apart from the revolutionary schema that we have just described that is based on the liquidation of the army of the state, there are only limited precedents that can give us the first approaches of a model of demilitarization. Let us note, however, that the armed route to "civilianization" does not always involve systems that reject capitalism over the short or medium term. Civilian supremacy in Mexico originated in the dissolution of the army of Porfirio Díaz and its replacement by revolutionary armies that were closely linked to the future of the new regime. However, the same scheme, when it was applied in Bolivia in a different international context, led to a defeat. The 1952 revolution purged the army to the point of practically annihilating it, but instead of creating a political and lower-class-based army the MNR governments, which were frightened by social agitation and worker militias that they did not control, hastened to reconstitute the classic army with the aid of a United States military mission.[58] In Bolivia, rather than favoring demilitarization, the fear of the dissolution of the military as an institution became one of the resources of militarism.

The liberalization of military regimes often gives the impression that it is a stratagem. Some sacrifice is made in order to survive. The temporary character of military power is emphasized in order to disarm the opposition. This gives the opposition a difficult choice—whether to accept the loaded dice of the regime, thus assisting it in acquiring legitimacy, or to pull out and paralyze its institutional program. In fact the distinction between a sham election and an opening that is acceptable to the civilian forces is not measured by the degree of competitiveness of the elections. Elections without surprises and won in advance by the government can advance demilitarization, first, by endorsing the system apart from the action of the military, and second, in giving civil rights to the forces of the opposition. The decisive criterion is not the level of competition, but rather that of civil rights and freedoms. The holding of elections that appear to be pluralistic establishes a facade of legality that the authoritarian nature of the government does not change. Acceptance of the game of politics requires a space of freedom that can bring about a "qualitative change." The logic of the two actions is different and the risks are not the same. In the last case if the opening has any content and even if it does not result immediately in a "democratic breakthrough," it seems that the "low profile" tactic of political forces that are moderate—but not moderately democratic—and capable of temporary compromises can be effective. It allows an improvement in the correlation of forces.

In that case the precarious character of the civilian regime that is under intense military surveillance means that the construction of democracy must come before a change in society and that political maneuvering must be limited to allow a political agreement that the politicians will not resort to the military to resolve political conflicts.[59] This was what was agreed to by the Venezuelan and Colombian parties in the 1950s and it is also what has emerged from the behavior of the parliamentary political forces of the right and the left in Spain since 1976.[60] On this basis several steps can be envisaged, without prejudging the order. One of them consists in the democratization of the institutions of the state (army, police, courts) and the other, which is almost contradictory to the first, is the creation in a undramatic way of the conditions for the alternation in power. This latter condition is the very expression of true pluralism and constitutes at that time the real "democratic breakthrough."[61] That long and uncertain road to democracy is based on a wager: one accepts the game proposed by those in power in order to beat them at their own game. To do that it is helpful if the entire political class and the majority of the participating social sectors give a special position to democratic values and procedures and accept the uncertainty of the ballot, while the political and social forces bid a definitive farewell to arms.

We have tried to give a comparative presentation of the many diverse manifestations of military power in what is called Latin America. It seemed to us that to clarify the various methods of militaristic usurpation and the individual kinds of military domination would enrich reflection and give it order. You may reproach the author for his pessimism and even accuse him— why not?—of a shameful inclination in favor of the military. There is no doubt that it is more comfortable to study the positive heroes of history than the villains, and easier to denounce than to understand. But who knows in advance the cunning of history? Nevertheless, while we have shown that exceptional conditions are necessary for democracy to resist the tensions of development or the crisis of capitalism in the Latin American context, we have also recalled rather forcefully that there is no inevitability, whether geopolitical or historical, about the militarization of the state in the subcontinent. To explain reality by means other than prefabricated schemes does not mean that you consider it to be rational—and still less desirable.

This book has devoted all its attention to the mechanisms of militarization and the process of military hegemony precisely because they are usually passed over in silence, no doubt to avoid giving too much respect to regimes that should be condemned. Similarly, we have concentrated our attention, to the degree that the documentation permitted, on the principal protagonists, the army and the military, who are misunderstood and ignored by those who oppose them.[62] In lectures and seminars to informed audiences even in Latin America we have been impressed by the fact that all the questions concentrate on knowing the *why* of militaristic usurpation. The impatience to know the immediate causes of praetorianism seems all the greater because its manifestations have been insufficiently examined and the empirical knowledge of the subject is relatively limited. On the other hand, it is paradoxical to state that in Western Europe, and especially in France, where political science possesses a formidable arsenal of analyses and data on the functioning of the political system and where electoral studies have reached an impressive level of sophistication, no one ever asks why we enjoy a stable pluralist representative system. Nevertheless, the problem of the "invention of democracy," never directly addressed, should merit some consideration, and no doubt would be easier to analyze in France than that of the emergence of military power in the republics which are our concern.

We have also left aside sweeping generalizations to look more closely at the actors, their environment, and their behavior. We have not asked whether the militarization of the state in Latin America is a response to the need for capitalist accumulation in a context of underdevelopment, or whether we are confronted with a universal march toward authoritarianism that would affect our "industrial democracies" in a different way. It is indeed possible to ask if the Latin American military are the local agents of a transnational authoritarianism that, in the view of some, will establish in our countries a "new internal order," or a "soft fascism"[63] that will place our freedoms in peril. Are they rather the representatives of a "Neo-Bismarckian" model in which the state will authoritatively allocate resources with a view to accelerating development?[64] Are the authoritarian systems that we have examined peripheral and local manifestations of the antilibertarian declarations of the Trilateral Commission[65] or the antiegalitarian lucubrations of the Club de l'Horloge that proclaim the agony of the welfare state and the destruction of political democracy in the countries of the center? Or, on the other hand, do they correspond to a temporary situation of industrial catching-up and accelerated modernization that is preparing the terrain for the future emergence of the "hundred flowers" of a delayed but still promised democracy? This impassioned and passionate debate has not yet begun. In fact whatever paradigm is chosen, the same question remains. Why in either theory in Latin America are the armies the specific institutions that direct development and put it in operation, since neither in yesterday's conservative modernization nor in the planetary neoauthoritarianism of today do the military play a preponderant role?

The reader who is attracted to unity and coherence will no doubt have also noticed that in accounting for change we have emphasized the conditioning structures and the conduct of the actors—the role of organizations and that of their leaders. We know that there is a raging debate between those who hold the two approaches, and our culpable eclecticism demands an explanation that will only underline the importance that we attach to the specificity and the rich diversity of national situations. When the conditions for a democratic "takeoff" are met over a long period in a society, it is evident that the role of the actors in the preservation of stability or the return of a pluralist system is decisive. On the other hand in countries in which structural blockages exist the virtues and abilities of political men are not a factor. What would Romulo Betancourt have done in Argentina, and what would Ricardo Balbín have not done if he had been a Venezuelan? Besides knowing something about what appears to be an exotic phenomenon, there is still therefore the central question of the conditions for democracy. Is it a privilege that belongs to the Atlantic area or to the northern hemisphere, or is it a form of public life that can be universalized? Neither political philosophy nor history has a satisfactory answer to that question. However, that is no reason to ignore it. The answers, if there are any, must involve the dynamic relationship and dialectic interaction between national and international socioeconomic conditions and the capabilities of the actors. May this book be useful in advancing in that direction since, in politics at least, knowledge of oneself comes from the knowledge of others.

October 1981

EPILOGUE (1986)

The Twilight of the Legions: Demilitarization Revisited

Following the publication of the original French edition of this book, Latin America ceased to be dominated by the military. The tendency toward demilitarization that was already evident in 1979 continued and became more accentuated. By 1986 throughout the South American continent there remained only the unshakeable General Stroessner in Paraguay and General Pinochet in Chile as representatives of what appeared to be an endangered species.[1] This is not the only wave of democracy in the history of the continent. In 1961 Paraguay was the only country in which civilians had not reestablished themselves in power. We know what took place in the years that followed. The basic question that this rapid and wholesale withdrawal of the military from government poses is how lasting and profound it is. To use military terms, is it more likely that this is a tactical retreat in order to realign the ranks in preparation for new assaults on the power of the civilians, or is it a strategic withdrawal? To put it another way, are we witnessing one of those swings of the pendulum that seem to have characterized military-civilian relations in Latin America since 1930,[2] or is democracy indeed on the way to establishing itself permanently in power after a prolonged and painful period of adolescence?

To clarify this central question and to provide some elements of an answer it is useful to examine the different experiences of demilitarization, beginning at the still uncertain point at which we left it, it order to identify the conditions that led the military to give up power to the civilians. While elections are not the same thing as democracy, postmilitary regimes have certain distinctive features. Indeed, we can inquire as to the degree and causes of the failure to institutionalize the power of the military through the manipulation of democratic procedures. An overall evaluation of the functioning of the pluralistic representative systems of the continent will permit us to draw lessons from that historical phenomenon, and to distinguish the respective roles of political culture and of strategic and diplomatic circumstances in explaining its emergence and survival. A further question still remains after the restoration of the civilian authorities—what will be the future role of these armies that usually do not have an enemy on their borders, and no other doctrine than that of "national security" that has been so little supportive of democracy?

CONTROLLED TRANSITIONS AND ELECTORAL SURPRISES

The military who were in power in Brazil, Argentina, and Uruguay attempted to negotiate their departure; the arrangements they sought included the establishment of protective devices and buffers that would guarantee them either, in the best case, a right of review of the programs of the constitutional regimes, or, through the use of legal clauses or unacknowledged political alliances, an honorable and assured outcome that would protect them from reprisals. Even in the Argentine case where the military debacle of the Falkland Islands and the seriousness of their violations of human rights made it impossible to have a permitted and controlled opening, the military who had lost the political initiative tried discreetly to influence the results of the elections of 30 October 1983. A hastily adopted self-amnesty law, an excessively long ninety-day period between the election and the inauguration of the new authorities, numerous basic appeals to the right-wing Peronists (amnesty for their leaders, return of trade union assets) that demonstrated the existence of an agreement between the army and the old guard of the Peronist unions—were all attempts to prevent the victory of a

Radical party candidate who was committed to raising the moral standards of public life and restoring democracy. the army general staff thought that a Peronist victory would guarantee that the military would not be prosecuted for the excesses of their antisubversive struggle. Thus it was possible to ask whether the election of October 1983 was only a short detour, as in 1976, or the end of a cycle in Argentine political life.[3]

In Brazil the "slow and gradual détente" initiated by General Geisel in 1974 did not, as in Argentina, turn into a humiliating rout. However, as in the case of its southern neighbor, the awakening of civilian society undermined all the protections that the casuistry of the system had been so adept at creating up to that time in order to conceal its rejection by public opinion. The opening was well controlled in the sense that the gigantic "*direitas ja*" mobilization in favor of the election of the president of the republic by universal suffrage did not succeed and the chief of state was elected by a restricted electoral college. While the transition was negotiated step by step with the military, the manipulation of the rules of the game was turned against its authors, ending the series of elections with variable rules that had allowed the loser to win that had characterized the period between 1968 and 1980. A split in the Democratic Social Party (PDS), the official party, as a result of maladroit government support for a candidate who was unpopular and unacceptable even to those in the corridors of power, allowed the opposition to secure a majority in the electoral college. In a way it was the lack of appeal of Paulo Maluf that allowed for the success of Tancredo Neves on January 15, 1985. However, everything took place Brazilian-style by means of procedures that involved conciliation and informal arrangements—without strident sudden changes, to the point that one could ask whether the split in the PDS had not allowed the regime (at least its civilian section) to "save the furniture" and to participate in the victory of the Liberal Alliance that brought Tancredo Neves, the leader of the PMDB, the principal opposition party, to the presidency. The vice president, Aureliano Chaves, was one of the principal opponents of the official candidate and the creator of the alliance formula that was victorious. Finally, in a tragic and surprising trick of history, the illness and then the death of Tancredo Neves brought José Sarney, the former president of the PDS, official party of the military government, who was on the ticket with Tancredo, to the presidency of the republic. Thus a feeling of the breakdown and defeat of the military regime gave way to a genuine sense of continuity, owing to the last minute conversion of the conservative political elites to the program of the opposition—perhaps because the demilitarization of the regime was carried out by its own civilian supporters.

In Uruguay, the electoral results were no less surprising. However, they were more extended over time, as was appropriate for a country that in 1973 experienced a slow-motion coup d'état that was certainly the longest in the history of the continent. One might have expected more, however, from the military than an orderly retreat. The anonymous dictators of Uruguay had not been defeated militarily as in Argentina, or worn down by twenty years of quasi-absolute power as in Brazil. In 1980 when the regime decided to institutionalize itself by establishing a system of restricted democracy under military control, it was defeated in its first move—the referendum of November 30. Fifty-six percent of the voters said "no" to military sovereignty; "no" to the constitutional supremacy of the National Security Council; "no" to the absolute right of the general staff to name civil servants and the holders of elective offices; "no," in short, to the creation of institutions that were opposed to democracy. This was the first surprise. The second was the primary elections within the two traditional parties that were authorized again in 1982. This was a second defeat; the candidates opposed to the military received nearly 80 percent of the votes and the Blanco party, which was more clearly antimilitary than the Colorados, led in electoral preferences. In 1984 the military, faced with a widespread popular mobilization (banging of pots at preappointed times as well as general strikes) opened negotiations with the political parties that were aimed at preparing for elections. The parties were divided on this subject. The "negotiators" and the realists, including the Frente Amplio on the left whose leader, General Liber Seregni, had spent the whole period of dictatorship in jail, signed an agreement with the commanders in chief on 3 August. The Blanco party, whose leader had been imprisoned when he returned from exile in Europe, refused to sign but decided to participate in the elections, which were marred by the proscription of Wilson Ferreira Aldunate of the Blanco party and of General Seregni of the Frente Amplio. Another surprise—intransigence did not pay. The "realists" won. Julio Sanguinetti from the Colorado party who had favored dialogue—a moderate except in his devotion to democracy—was elected president. Seventy percent of the voters voted for the parties that had signed the so-called Naval Club Accords of 3 August. Democracy was reestablished. The military went back to their barracks.[4]

In differing degrees in all three cases the military participated to a greater or lesser extent in the establishment of the conditions for their own departure from power. This was true even in Argentina, and the Peronists will not deny it. Nowhere do we see the expulsion of the military after the collapse of the authoritarian regime—such as occurred in the case of the fall of Pérez Jiménez in January 1958 in Venezuela. Sharp breaks were not the order of the day. Were they negotiated transitions that produced democracies that were a gift of the military? The smoothness of the demilitarization this time did not, however, mean that everything would remain the same. The situation throughout the continent no longer favored the arrogance of the legions. After remaining uncertain until the end, a transition was carried out that was uncontroversial but effective. While the twilight of the legions did not resemble the (Wagnerian) twilight of the gods in either Brazil or even in Argentina, it may be that the method of small steps and dialogue was better than any other in avoiding a democratic restoration that would only be a brief interlude. The moderation that was exhibited in the change was an indication, perhaps, not of weakness of the civilians, but of the maturity of the democratic forces.

MILITARY IMPOTENCE AND THE CONTAGION OF DEMOCRACY

Since 1970 the military had staged successive retreats in Ecuador, Peru, and Honduras. However, one swallow does not make a summer, and one election does not make a democracy.

The establishment or the reestablishment of a representative pluralist regime is a long-term effort. Its first test is whether it completes its constitutionally mandated term of office. The transfer of power from one elected president to another, especially if his successor is not of the same party or the official candidate, constitutes genuine proof. We looked for this in the countries that were the first to return the military to their barracks. Despite the fragility of those newborn democracies, the test turned out positive in Peru, in its neighboring country, Ecuador, and in Honduras, thus giving the lie to the pessimistic predictions that cited both past history and present difficulties.

In Ecuador, the accidental death of a center-left president who had promoted reforms and defended human rights did not prevent the vice president, who was his constitutional successor, from serving out his term of office. The election employing the French system of a two-round vote, of a new president, León Febres Cordero of the center-right, finally demonstrated that democratic institutions were well established. It is true that in 1978 a group of low-profile military men who were more reformist than repressive had handed over power without much resistance.

In Peru, the stakes seemed to be much higher. This was not because the military, torn between their desire for order and their hope to change the structures of a chaotic society, had actually opposed the weak and conservative civilian president, but because this time the two most popular candidates were both situated clearly on the left—one an adherent of Marxism who had the support of the Communist parties, and the other representing the APRA, which had been the bête noire of the military since the 1930s. The movement to the left was related to a social and economic crisis and to the rise of a messianic and nihilist guerrilla movement that was centered in the poorest regions of the Andes and was leading Peru into a fatal involvement in violence and massive repression. Despite all these problems, the brilliant young candidate of the APRA, Alan Garcia, won by a comfortable margin over the mayor of Lima, the candidate of the left. On 28 July 1985, for the first time in forty years, a transfer of power took place between two presidents who had both been elected in free elections.

In a very different context electoral legalism also triumphed in Honduras where there was uncertainty concerning both the evident desire of the president who had been elected in 1982, Suazo Cordoba, not to surrender power, and his capacity to rule in the face of the army chiefs. Whether it is viewed as an advance post in the struggle of the United States against Sandinismo or the unfortunate victim of Communist expansionism by Nicaragua, Honduras, the poorest country of the Central American isthmus, has never been a model of democratic stability. The victory of the Liberal candidate in 1982 had raised great hopes— all the more because the army had been traditionally linked to the National party. Very quickly the new president, who seemed to sacrifice all the ideals of his party to anti-Communism and an extravagant clan spirit, allowed the commander in chief of the army, General Gustavo Alvarez, to assume more and more power. Alvarez, who headed the Association for the Progress of Honduras that was made up of prosperous factory presidents and was supported by the "Moonie" sect and its local branch, CAUSA, appeared to have relegated Suazo to the post of a constitutional monarch. However, the excessive power of the general and the unrestrained corruption of which he was guilty, especially in the utilization of American aid, led to his removal in disgrace. His companions in arms arrested him and forced him to resign and leave the country on 1 April 1984. Without his powerful support President Suazo Cordova engaged in a number of maneuvers that were aimed at retaining power in 1985. That desire for "continuismo," very much a part of the Honduran political tradition, manifested itself step by step in attempts at constitutional reform and a veritable internal coup to impose his candidate within the Liberal party. All of this led to a conflict with the congress as well as with the judiciary. On the eve of the 24 November elections no one knew what election law would be in force or which candidates would be valid. To avoid a split within the Liberal party and the paralysis of government institutions it was decided that the primary elections of the two large parties (the National and Liberal parties) would be held at the same time as the general elections. As in the case of the "ley de lemas" in Uruguay the winning candidate would be the one who had the most votes within the party that had received the most votes. Since the total vote for Liberal candidates was 51 percent the anti-Suazo Liberal, José Azcona Hoyo, won the election with 27.5 percent of the votes against 42.4 percent for his rival, Leonardo Callejas of the National party. The official candidate supported by Suazo Córdona received half the votes of his elected adversary. Not only did democracy triumph but—a little point of history—for the first time an elected Liberal turned over power to another elected Liberal president.[5]

The consolidation of democracy in these three countries is undeniable. This is less surprising, however, than the experience of democratization in the countries that have had long-standing military dictatorships. The return of Bolivia to democracy in 1982 seemed to have an element of the miraculous, unless it was simply a demonstration of the disasters that the Andean nation faced: drought, a drop in the price of tin, an increase in narcotics traffic, inflation of Weimar proportions, and a debt that could not be repaid. However, what are we to say of the election of 14 July 1985 of Victor Paz Estenssoro to the presidency, and of the harmonious transfer of power—the first in a quarter of a century—from an elected president, Herman Siles Suazo, to his constitutional successor in the warmly supportive presence of presidents Raúl Alfonsín, Belisario Betancur, and Julio Sanguinetti? Bolivia had still more surprises for us. Not only did General Hugo Banzer, an unsuccessful candidate for the presidency after having been military dictator for a decade, recognize his defeat, but he hastened to sign a democratic pact with Paz Estenssoro forbidding resort to the military.

Democracy has never been very strong in Guatemala, since it has been in effect for an absurdly short period—only ten years from 1944 to 1954 in the last three-quarters of a century. The military system seemed very well institutionalized with its general-presidents and its rump parties. However, after having brutally crushed a guerrilla movement that had arisen in the sixties, the army decided to hand over power, and to call elections while the disappearances and assassination of opponents were still going on. General Mejía Victores kept his promise. In December 1985 the candidate who was most opposed by the military, Vinicio Cerezo of the Christian Democratic party, won with an overwhelming majority of 68 percent of the votes, relegating the extreme right that had been dominant since 1⁹ the rubbish heap of history. Thirty-one years later demo____, arose from the ashes in Guatemala, permitted by military forces that had acquired a reputation for brutality and ignorance and had brought the economy to the edge of collapse. However, at what price, or rather in what conditions—and for how much time?

In the face of this continent-wide panorama, the contagiousness of democracy cannot explain everything—nor can the possibility of a conversion of the Latin American officers to the discreet charms of pluralism. In Bolivia as in Guatemala, in Uruguay and in Honduras, one can only be struck by the fragility of the democracies that have been reestablished facing armed forces that are intact and have lost none of their arrogance (even in Argentina), or their independence, or their interventionist ideology. And yet, one figure is more telling than any other in suggesting a special combination of forces that marks a break with all historic precedents: there has not been a single coup d'état or forceful takeover of power by the armed forces since 1976. Ten years, a century in the history of the continent! Better still, everywhere the uniformed caudillos have been reduced to impotence and putsches crushed by the legal authorities. General Alvarez, the strongman of Honduras, did not take power, but a plane into exile. In Ecuador, an insubordinate general, Frank Vargas Pazzos, who revolted in March 1986, was not supported by the military and his uprising was throttled by military action.

There is no doubt that the historical outcome that most characterizes the period is the fact that henceforth the military will not be able to govern with impunity. For the first time in Argentina the dictators in uniform who were guilty of violations of human rights have had to answer for their actions and their misdeeds before a human tribunal. Admiral Massera and General Videla were condemned to life imprisonment in December 1985. No doubt it is easy to agree with the activists from humanitarian organizations who found the sentences of the other guilty parties too mild in relation to the overwhelming weight of the evidence. Yet what an exemplary precedent it was! How could one establish a worthwhile and respected democracy while shamefully forgetting the thousands of people who had disappeared and had been killed? It is true that neither Uruguay nor Brazil followed the Argentine example. Guatemala had issued an amnesty in advance for all political acts since 1982. Only Alan García as he took office retired the leading generals, and removed several hundred police officers for corruption or the massacre of civilians. Vacillating democracies took in hand the sword of justice. The military snorted and reared in the traces, but the law prevailed. Even in the most "praetorianized" systems, it seems, there is no longer room for the "military juntas." Put in another way, there are no longer civilians who are willing to support them. The obstacles in the way of stable restoration of democracy are so numerous and the terrain so full of potential explosions in most countries that, short of a "cultural revolution," it is difficult to see how the current experiments can establish permanent roots. Only the demilitarization of the civilians can paralyze the political inclinations of the military.

The Demand for Democracy and Cultural Revolution

While it is easy to call elections, it is more difficult to govern after many years of destructive military rule and sometimes twenty, thirty, or fifty years of the hegemony of the military. The economic disaster alone cannot explain the return of the military to their barracks. Nevertheless, their legacy everywhere was uniformly catastrophic. Still more negative, however, than the latest military adventure was its impact on the political forces and the behavior of authoritarianism. The "praetorianization" of attitudes is more difficult to exorcise than incompetent conduct of government.

Take the example of Argentina. Everyone knew that in spite of the fact that he was the first civilian president elected by universal suffrage in regular free elections since 1928, and in spite of the size of his victory and his personal prestige, Raúl Alfonsín had only a narrow margin of maneuver in his effort to reestablish democracy. It was evident that the civilians had returned to power because of the nature of the former regime, which was in a more precarious and uncomfortable situation than the military regimes of 1958, 1963, and 1973. It is true that never before had an Argentine government confronted so many dramatic and potentially explosive problems. But the well-known time bombs left by the dictatorship (the "disappeared," an external debt of $50 billion, galloping inflation, conflicts over the Falkland Islands and the Beagle Channel) were only the visible part of a generally dark picture that was not favorable to the development of an harmonious and stable political life.

The effects of "state terrorism" and of an economy oriented toward speculation are not easy to eliminate. If it is true that absolute power corrupts absolutely—and not only those who hold it—then it is also certain that Argentina in December 1983 faced more serious problems than in the past, while possessing fewer means to resolve them. It was in this context that the new occupant of the Casa Rosada undertook to govern with the consolidation of democracy as his principal goal. His first objective was to remove the obstacles from the terrain. Thus he took steps to defuse nationalist pressures and the costly demands of the military concerning the two territorial disputes. The Beagle Channel affair was completely resolved. Because he wished to avoid both forgetfulness and vengeance concerning the demands of the "dirty war," he attempted to neutralize any corporate reaction within the armed forces by handing over to the courts only the highest responsible officers, the members of the three juntas that had succeeded one another since 1976.

In the area of economics, after a period of indecision and direct negotiation with the banks and the International Monetary Fund in June 1985, Alfonsín changed course. The struggle against inflation became his number one priority. For that purpose the Plan Austral called for a reduction in public expenditures, a freeze on prices and salaries, and a currency reform. The "economy of war" produced results and it is popular. Volunteer brigades denounced shopkeepers who were guilty of violating government regulations. The monthly inflation rate fell to 2 percent in September; it had surpassed 1 percent *per day* four months earlier. The miracle was not an economic one.

Despite a surge in unemployment, difficulties in everyday life, and the complaints of the Peronist trade unions, the president's party won the legislative elections of November 1985, and Raúl Alfonsín enjoyed an enviable popularity after nearly three years in power.

What was it that allowed him to eliminate "the unemployed work force" of the paramilitary, to immobilize attempts at destabilization, to halt the inflation, to fire the generals, and to carry out a judicial procedure that was both exemplary and risky? A rupture had taken place with the general elections of 30 October 1983 that were won by a candidate who had not been expected to win. We can ask if the surprising defeat of the party that appealed to the memory of General Perón was not a veritable turning point in history—the end of a cycle dominated by the destabilizing confrontation between the Peronists and the military. The arrival to power through free elections of a party that for thirty years had not passed the barrier of 25 percent of the vote demonstrated the intention of the electorate to break with the past. Is he Alfonsín or the exorcist? He was the only one to denounce the practices of a "praetorianized" political life in which alliances with the military did not disgrace those who formed them, and the preservation of democratic institutions was evidence of anachronistic naiveté. It was his denunciation, that some called "suicidal," of certain corrupting practices of the "politics of sedition" that permitted Alfonsín to win the last-chance election.

Paradoxically, the catastrophic results of the military regime provided an unexpected opportunity to reconstruct democracy and to establish durable roots for it. The isolation of the armed forces, discredited politically, economically, morally, and even professionally, created the minimal conditions for a transformation of the system. The new suspicion of the military on the part of the upper bourgeoisie after the Falkland War, which was seen as a dangerous anti-Western adventure, may act as a deterrent to their traditional tendencies toward coups, while the defeat of the Peronists proved for once that crime does not pay and that an "invincible" pact between the army and the unions could be the prelude to defeat. Is it still necessary for there to be a complete reorganization within the "first political party of the West" to allow the removal of the most anti-democratic elements? The margin of maneuver of the civilian government is weak. Nevertheless, we can assume that the Argentines no longer expect miracles and that, having demonstrated in the elections of 1983 their desire to survive and to expel the old demons, they can work together to assure the triumph of the rules of social coexistence over corporate egoism. The survival and identity of a society that came very close to collapse are at stake.

Argentina is certainly a limiting case. The debacle of the Falklands and the horrors of the "dirty war" have contributed decisively to discrediting the appeal to the military and to rehabilitating the "dull gray old system" that is called democracy. But the cultural shifts and political changes that have taken place elsewhere in different ways have been no less significant.

In Brazil business circles and the conservative politicians have each in turn experienced a conversion on "the road to Damascus." The businessmen rose up against the expanding statism of the military regime, and perceived in a confused way that only a representative pluralist regime free from military tutelage would give them back the right to participate in major economic and social decisions. The politicians who abandoned the official party in 1984 were overwhelmed by the popular mobilization that emerged in the campaign for direct elections. The "Nova Republica," despite the death of Neves and the heterogeneity of its cabinet ministers, is very popular—so popular that Brazilians gave massive support in the streets to a plan for economic recovery that was very similar in its effects and objectives to the Argentine Plan Austral. While the "martyrdom" of Tancredo Neves, "symbol of national unity and the struggle for redemocratization,"[6] in a certain way gave the regime a sacred quality, the military moved discreetly into the background. We do not know the agreements that were made with the civilians concerning overall directions, political and social rights, or the constitutional framework. The election of a Constituent Assembly scheduled for 1986 should resolve that mystery.[7] One thing is certain. The military apparatus has not been breached; in contrast to Argentina, until now no member of the military has had to answer to a court for his political or repressive actions. However, the legalization of the parties of the left, including the Communist party, the recognition of the trade unions, and even the lifting of the ostracism that was directed at the presidential ambitions of Leonel Brizola, the governor of Rio de Janeiro, indicate either a deal, or an evolution in conduct. There is no evidence, however, that the dreaded intelligence community, the "monster" SNI, has been weakened, dismantled, or turned over to civilian control. Gradual and prudent demilitarization, Brazilian-style, has not been translated into an overall change concerning democratic values. However the resurgence in the recent municipal elections of a populist and authoritarian right around former president Janio Quadros who was elected mayor of São Paolo with the support of the conservative establishment proves that the game has not yet been won.

In Uruguay less time was needed than in other countries for the middle and upper classes, who in 1970–73 had been frightened by the Tupamaro guerrillas and the strikes, to demonstrate their rejection of authoritarianism and military tutelage. Beginning with the constitutional referendum of 1980, the first defeat of the regime, it was clear that the country did not support it. Certainly there were economic reasons for that rejection—the discontent of the large agricultural sector that felt that it was paying the cost of the economic policy of a regime that wished to promote nontraditional exports. However, the attachment to democracy was based on broader and deeper motives. Historically democracy had been part of the culture, indeed of the self-definition of the country.[8] The military also accepted these values so that the leaders of the Uruguayan army believed that there was no other source of legitimacy but free elections. Military men who respected the rules of democracy organized their own defeat in electoral consultations that were supposed to legitimize their power.[9] The opposition was able to express itself, there was no resort to fraud, and basic liberties were reestablished for the occasion. The Uruguayan army was trapped in its own legalism at the moment that it tried to institutionalize its participation in power. While the military leaders in their negotiations with the parties did not obtain the recognition of the special political rights that the 1980 referendum had refused them, they nevertheless imposed a certain number of limitations on the new president—in the areas of nominations for the upper ranks in the army, that of the proclamation of the state of siege (urgency), and in the matter of the repression during the period of military rule. This did not prevent the legalization of the trade unions and the parties of the left, or the removal of three extreme-right generals who had not observed their obligation to maintain the reserve that is appropriate for the military in a system of representative institutions.

In the same area one wonders what will become of the relations between the army and the recently democratized government of Guatemala. Before they left power, the military put in place arrangements for the antisubversive struggle that gave them exorbitant civilian and political prerogatives and established a veritable dualism of power, so to speak. The maintenance of the civilian self-defense patrols in the villages, the creation of "poles of development" under military tutelage (a type of strategic hamlet in which the rural population is regrouped in the guerrilla zones) and, at the regional level, the organs of interinstitutional coordination headed by the local commander, all reduced the powers of the legal authorities. Prudently, President Cerezo did not seek a confrontation with the power of the military, either in this area or in that of human rights, although he ran the risk of appearing to be a president without power like his predecessor, Julio Mendez Montenegro elected in 1966, who was content to cover the absolutism of the military with a fig leaf of representative government.[10] Nevertheless, despite the seriousness of the economic crisis inherited from the preceding regime, there are indications here and there that prove that demilitarization is in progress. The new government is adapting the institutions inherited from the authoritarian government by civilianizing them. The political police have been dissolved. The organs of "interinstitutional coordination" have been placed under the governors. Will what seemed impossible at the end of the 1960s become a reality today? Certainly history does not repeat itself, but why should Cerezo succeed where Mendez Montenegro failed? To answer that question—which extends far beyond Guatemala—means to draw lessons from the wave of democracy that is now sweeping over the continent and to understand the special characteristics of a regional situation that goes beyond the particular elements of each nation and the strategies of their internal political forces.

WHY THE CIVILIANS?

The contagiousness of democracy, the solidarity among regimes of the same type facing the same dangers, should certainly not be underestimated. However, we must look elsewhere for the genuine lessons to be drawn from a phenomenon of a duration that seems unprecedented since World War II. It has often been said that the military was not unhappy to no longer be obliged to direct countries that they had led to bankruptcy. The extent of the economic disaster is supposed to have been the essential element that dictated their actions. In the past, economic crises were fatal to democracy and favored dictatorship. The extent of the challenges that the countries in which democracy has been reestablished must face (external debt, a drop in prices of raw materials among others) does not seem to argue for the longevity or the stability of those regimes. We have shown that those deterministic explanations are debatable because they are so unpredictably reversible.

If we look more closely at the political processes involved in the transitions to democracy now under way, we can only note, first of all, the defeat of the attempts at institutionalization of military power, whatever their form. Panama remains an exception that should be discussed separately, for the simple reason that in the present situation liberalization cannot be carried out only halfway. You cannot stop democracy in its tracks in a continent in which the liberal ideology is, and remains, dominant. The transition appears to possess an internal dynamic that is self-sustained, if not irresistible, except at an excessive social cost. That dynamic means discord and division in the ranks of the military, but it can only arise in specific conditions. In fact its emergence presupposes a rather large consensus in favor of democratic values among the dominant sectors and organized forces. If a decisive social sector refuses to accept pluralism, the fragile balance of the edifice of representative government will be shattered to the benefit of civilians and military men who prefer to fish in troubled waters.

But what are we seeing in a great number of the recently "democratized" countries? First of all, the discovery by the immense majority of the dominant classes, and very often by the middle classes as well, that the worst democracy is less damaging to their interests, properly understood, than the best dictatorship. Whether it is in Argentina, Brazil, or Uruguay, those who yesterday flattered the military and saw salvation for the country and for themselves in the abolition of the "anarchy" of representative government and the establishment of a strong and undiluted authoritarianism have abandoned those views or have become converted to the openness and liberty of a democratic order. However, they are not alone. On the left a parallel process of conversion has often taken place. The defeat of the strategy of armed struggle, and the responsibility of the guerrillas for the emergence of the terrorist state, have produced a change in their partisan outlook. The contempt for "formal" liberties and the confusion between a metaphorical "dictatorship of the bourgeoisie" and the realities of military dictatorship have been abandoned. Unions and parties of the left have understood that they cannot develop outside the liberal system, and that the politics of negation is the most negative of policies. It is true that there are hard cores here and there of those who have not given up their old belief systems, but they no longer produce a response among the young and the intellectuals, much less among the workers. Also, as in Venezuela in the past, former guerrillas are preparing to enter into the legislatures that they had once spurned. Thus it may be that the implacable ferocity of the recent periods of the military rule has increased the chances of democracy. The demand for democracy extends to all social classes.[11]

The argument to the contrary in these developments is the difficult situation in certain countries in Central America where a conversion to democracy has not taken place. This is the case in El Salvador where after fifty years of military rule a process of democratization is being carried out in the context of a civil war. It is a democratization that is both suspect and unfortunate. In effect, it is supported by all those who have never believed in the virtues of democracy, and combated, even with arms, by those who should have an interest in supporting it. The right supports it for tactical reasons—to win the war and regain its privileges—and the left combats it in the name of its Leninist ideology without taking into account the changes that it has already brought about in national life. Of course it is a transitional phase, but it situates the country apart in the community of nations moving toward demilitarization. We can ask if Guatemala is not in a middle position between the restored democracies of the Southern Cone, and its southern neighbor. At least the democratic left is not totally behind the guerrillas, and they themselves, it is true, no longer appear to be a credible alternative.

If it is true that the dictatorships are dying, it is no less true that their parallel final agonies and deaths are not unrelated to the economic situation. The effects of the economic crisis and foreign debt on their social bases certainly should not be neglected. The erosion of support is also reflected in the sudden increase in the "demand for democracy" that affects all sectors, even those that are not demanding in the area of civic participation. However, the policy of the United States with regard to authoritarian governments no doubt also plays a determining role, less because certain sectors of the apparatus of the American government have ceased to favor antidemocratic intrigues than because the official policy of Washington seems to consist in resolute support for democracy while cutting the ground from under the feet of would-be dictators—as long as American interests are not at stake.

The human rights policy of President Carter, despite its maladroit moralism and interventionism, helped to launch the movement. It even succeeded in aborting successful coups d'état, as in the case of Bolivia: where Colonel Natusch Busch seized power in October 1979 but could only retain control for seventeen days because of the ostracism of Washington, which was reinforced by its regional allies. However, one of the characteristics of this wave of demilitarization is that the arrival in the White House of a Republican administration that was determined to reinforce American power did not produce a turnabout in this area. The hardline policy of President Reagan in Central America and the Caribbean in order to "contain" Communism was not translated elsewhere in the continent into support for counterrevolution on the part of a usurping military. Ten years of recent Latin American history without a successful coup d'état, as well as a number of timely and efficient actions by Washington, are sufficient to discourage military adventurism.

Different reasons could be given for this apparent paradox. The first is the democratic excuse sought by the Reagan administration to gain acceptance by its allies to the south for the military policy that it is pursuing against Sandinista Nicaragua. A more profound and lasting reason could be that the American "decision makers" have understood after Cuba and Nicaragua that support for unpopular dictators (even if they are the moderate autocracies that are dear to Jeane Kirkpatrick), merely because they are strongly pro-American, is the best way to promote Communism. Finally, the democratic crusade of President Reagan does not seem to be simply a tactic or to be limited to the problems of the American Central American "backyard." The role of the United States in the eviction of Baby Doc, president-for-life of Haiti, and in the fall of the dictator Ferdinand Marcos in the Philippines at the beginning of 1986, attests to the global and worldwide character of the antiauthoritarian policy of Washington. However, that new and subtle form of "containment" will not succeed unless it takes into account the economic impotence of the civilian and military dictators, and the mortal danger to the West that their unpopularity represents. The recent hardening of U.S. policy toward General Pinochet is part of that overall context. As is evident, the phenomenon is related to a complex and unique alliance of internal factors and international variables.

Never Again?

"Never Again" was the title of the report of the National Commission on Disappeared Persons that met in Argentina under the chairmanship of Ernesto Sabato. The title of that vision of hell echoed the slogans chanted by the Peronist youth in 1973, that served as an inscription for that book. Does the extent of the horror and disaster constitute a guarantee against the return of the military state, or indeed is it true that "the belly is still fertile that produced the monster"?

There is no doubt that there is not today, nor has there been for several years, the political space either internally or internationally for a military offensive against the new democracies. However, the military are still there. They have repudiated none of their past actions and have in no way modified their values or their conduct. The democracies ask about their purpose. Should they transfer the responsibility for the struggle against subversion to the police as Raúl Alfonsín tried to do? If they settle frontier disputes by negotiation in order to limit arms purchases, what will the armies do? Disarming the paramilitary, returning the intelligence services of the state to civilian control is a priority task for demilitarization, but is institutional legitimacy sufficient in the face of force? Who will bear the arms of legality against plotters clinging to their political capital? The old Latin adage *Quis custodiet ipsos custodes* (Who will guard the guards?) has never been more true. It is not easy to reestablish the majesty and mystery of civilian power. As we said in the introduction to this book, how is it that armed men obey an unarmed sovereign?

If it is accepted that coups are not made only by the military and that the present situation is not very encouraging for military intervention, it is still true that they are awaiting the appropriate moment and do not seem to believe that a corner has been definitively turned regarding the military in government. The Argentine military celebrate their victory over subversion and publicly justify the "dirty war." The Uruguayan military leaders do not hesitate to recall that if the situation of 1970 were to be repeated, it would be their duty to intervene again. In Brazil, the civilian and military right raises its head to condemn the agrarian reform that is being carried out, as well as the legalization of the Communist parties, and it even criticizes the presence of a "leftist" minister in the Sarney government.[12] More disturbing still, perhaps, is the advance of the military in one of the oldest democracies of the continent. In Colombia President Betancourt, who was elected in 1982, ended martial law and the application of the security law and the militarist policies of his predecessor. He opened negotiations with the guerrillas with the purpose of reintegrating them into the constitutional life of the polity by way of an amnesty. The foreign policy of the new president broke with the pro-American attitude of President Julio Turbay. The active role of Colombia within the Contadora group and its cooperation with the "progressive" countries in the region also disturbed the military who had been conditioned by thirty years of struggle against Communist guerrillas. In January 1984 the minister of war, who was very critical of the policies of the president, was forced to resign. In November 1985 it was the army that made the decision to attack the Palace of Justice in Bogotá, which had been occupied by the M-19 guerrillas. The refusal to negotiate led to ninety-five deaths, including eleven justices of the supreme court, and to a considerable weakening of the Colombian president's support.

Nothing is ever permanent in the area of civilian supremacy. Democracy can only be a collective goal that implies a permanent state of tension. It does not follow as an automatic consequence of given objectives. Nevertheless, a coup d'état produces military interventions and a lasting period of civilian rule has a multiplier effect. We may even consider that the bitter memory of past dictatorships and the desire to live together will be the hidden sources of the "virtue" that, since Montesquieu, has been recognized as the basic principle of democracy.

San Salvador
April 1986

NOTES

INTRODUCTION

1. Cecil Jane, *Liberty and Despotism in Spanish America* (preface by Salvador de Madariaga) (New York, 1966), p. 173 (1st ed., Oxford, 1929).
2. Edwin Lieuwen, "The Changing Role of the Military in Latin America," *Journal of Latin American Studies* (October 1961): 559–569.
3. See especially the discussion of these ideas in Richard W. Morse, "Toward a Theory of Spanish American Government," in Hugh M. Hamill, ed., *Dictatorship in Spanish America* (New York, 1965), and Howard Wiarda, "Toward a Framework for the Study of Political Change in the Iberic-Latin Tradition: The Corporative-Model," *World Politics* (January 1973): 205–235.
4. Susanne Jonas and David Tobias, *Guatemala. Una historia inmediata* (México, 1976), p. 210.
5. See chapter 1 of Alain Rouquié, *La Politique de Mars. Les processus politiques dans les partis militaires* (Paris, 1981).

1. IN SEARCH OF THE AMERICAS: SOCIETIES AND POWERS

1. An exception would be the marginal zones that lacked precious metals and an Indian working force, such as the plains of the La Plata River.
2. M. Le Lannou, *Le Brésil* (Paris, 1961), p. 44.
3. Claude Lévi-Strauss, *Tristes Tropiques* (Paris, 1965), p. 89.
4. According to the study of the Interamerican Committee on Agri-

cultural Development (CIDA) described by Solon Barraclough and Arthur Domke, "Agrarian Structure in Seven Latin American Countries," in Rodolfo Stavenhagen, ed., *Agrarian Problems and Peasant Movements in Latin America* (New York, 1970), p. 48.

5. República argentina, Congreso de la nación-Cámara de Diputados, *Diario de sesiones* (1932), I:914, "Familias dueñas de más de 30,000 has . . ."

6. See Edelberto Torres Rivas, *Centroamérica hoy* (México, 1975), pp. 31–33.

7. See Albert Meister, *Le Système mexicain. Les avatars d'une participation populaire au développement* (Paris, 1971), pp. 61–65.

8. Michel Gutelman, *Réforme et Mystification agraire en Amérique latine. Le cas du Mexique* (Paris, 1969), p. 101.

9. For examples of this process, see the cases described in Germán Caycedo Castro, *Colombia amarga* (Bogotá, 1976), pp. 4–8. For a careful and in-depth study of the relations between *la violencia* and the capitalist modernization of the agrarian sector in Colombia, see Pierre Gilhods, *La Question agraire en Colombie* (Paris, 1974).

10. See especially Jaime Sautchuk, Horacio Martins de Carvalho, and Sergio Buarque de Gusmão, *Projeto Jari, a invasão americana* (São Paulo, 1979), and "Ludwig sem misterios," *Movimento* (São Paulo) (19 November 1979). This giant project seems to have suffered financial reverses, causing Ludwig to sell his empire in the Amazon to Brazilian businessmen in January 1982.

11. These systems of quasi-serfdom that have now been outlawed nearly everywhere established a common model for the provision of nonsalaried services. They are called by different names depending on the country: *concertaje, colonato, huasipungo, yanaconaje,* or *pongaje.* For an example of the type of limits placed on peasants employed under this system, one can read the study by Julio Cotler on a hacienda in the Peruvian highlands: "Traditional Haciendas and Communities in a Context of Political Mobilization in Peru," in Rodolfo Stavenhagen, ed., *Agrarian Problems and Peasant Movements,* p. 545.

12. Manuel Scorza, *Redoble por Rancas* (Barcelona, 1970), pp. 113–121.

13. This was the case in the large sugar plantations of northern Argentina at the end of the thirties. See Ian Rutledge, "Plantations and Peasants in Northern Argentina: The Sugar Cane Industry of Salta and Jujuy," in David Rock, ed., *Argentina in the Twentieth Century* (London, 1975), pp. 89–113.

14. According to H. Favre, *Changement et Continuité chez les Mayas du Mexique (Contribution à l'étude de la situation coloniale en Amérique latine)* (Paris, 1971), p. 73.

15. See the excellent Brazilian film *Iracema* directed by J. Bodansky. The investigative reporting by Robert Linhart in the sugar-producing areas of the Brazilian Northeast, *Le Sucre et la Faim* (Paris, 1980), emphasizes this transformation of labor relations.

16. At least this was what is claimed in the dominant ideology. The representatives of the Movement for the Defense of Brazilian Blacks cites numerous cases of discrimination and selective violence toward blacks. See "Movimento negro," *Movimento* (São Paulo), 19 May 1980.

17. In 1979 this was denounced for a full week by the official newspaper, *Granma*, through prescribed slogans (*bandas*).

18. Milton Senna, *Como não se faz un presidente* (Rio de Janeiro, 1968), p. 22.

19. For Haiti see Kern Delince, *Armée et Politique en Haiti* (Paris, 1979), pp. 26–30, and Micheline Labelle, *Idéologie de couleur et Classes sociales en Haiti* (Montreal, 1978).

20. We base this definition rather freely on the one given by Charles Tilly in *The Formation of National States in Western Europe* (Princeton, N.J., 1975), chap. 1, pp. 70–71.

21. Fernando Henrique Cardoso distinguishes between societies that have national control over their production, and societies that are dominated by enclave economies. See F. H. Cardoso and E. Faletto, *Dépendance et développement en Amérique latine* (Paris, 1978), pp. 94–125. (*Dependency and Development in Latin America*, Berkeley, Los Angeles, London, 1979).

22. Mario Benedetti, *El País de la cola de paja* (Montevideo, 1966), p. 56.

23. This is the thesis that is argued by Merle Kling in his article "Toward a Theory of Power and Political Instability in Latin America," in James Petras and Maurice Zeitlin, *Latin America: Reform or Revolution. A Reader* (Greenwich, Conn., 1968), pp. 76–93.

2. The Establishment of the Military and the Birth of the State

1. Gabriel García Márquez, *El Otoño de Patriarca* (Bogotá, 1978), p. 14, English version, *The Autumn of the Patriarch* (New York, 1979).

2. Miguel Cané, "Mi estreno diplomático," in *Prosa Ligera* (Buenos Aires, 1919), p. 163.

3. This is the term used by the Uruguayan historian, Carlos Real de Azúa in "Ejército y política en Uruguay," *Cuadernos de Marcha*, (Montevideo) (March 1969):7.

4. Samuel Huntington, *The Soldier and the State* (Cambridge, Mass., 1957), p. 8.

5. On armies as complex and specific organizations, see chap. 1 of Rouquié, ed., *La Politique de Mars*.

6. On the military fueros and the colonial armies, see Lyle N. McAllister, *The "Fuero Militar" in New Spain: 1764–1800* (Gainesville, Fla., 1957); Leon G. Campbell, *The Military and Society in Colonial Peru: 1750–1810* (Philadelphia, 1978); J. Kuethe, *Military reform and Society in New Granada: 1773–1808* (Gainesville, Fla., 1978).

7. See John Schulz, "O exército e o Imperio," in *O Brasil monárquico*, vol. 3: *Historia geral da civilizacão brasileira*, ed. Sergio Buarque de Holanda (São Paulo, 1974), pp. 235 ff.

8. This was the case in Mexico where the war was ended with the adoption of the Plan of Iguala, and the establishment of the empire of Iturbide.

9. This is the Leninist formulation that is utilized by Agustín Cueva in his book, *El Desarrollo del capitalismo en América latina* (México, 1977).

10. Georg Lukács, *Histoire et Conscience de classe* (Paris, 1960), pp. 78–79.

11. Guillermo Bedregal, *Los Militares en Bolivia. Ensayo de interpretación sociológica* (La Paz, 1971), p. 23.

12. Tulio Halperín Donghi, *Historia contemporánea de América latina*, (Madrid, 1969), chap. 3.

13. See Alain Joxe, *Las Fuerzas Armadas en el sistema político de Chile* (Santiago, 1970), pp. 44–45.

14. This is the thesis of the Ecuadorean historian, Enrique Ayala, especially in his article "Gabriel García Moreno y la gestación del Estado nacional en el Ecuador," *Crítica y Utopía* (September 1981):126–163.

15. F. García Calderón, *Les Démocraties de l'Amérique latine* (Paris, 1912), p. 199.

16. John Reed, *Le Mexique insurgé* (Paris, 1975), p. 302 (*Insurgent Mexico*, New York, 1969).

17. Ibid., p. 93.

18. *Tata* means "papa" in Quechua, an affectionate term that is given to a protector.

19. Samuel Finer, "State and Nation-Building in Europe: The Role of the Military," in Charles Tilly, ed., *The Formation of the National State in Western Europe* (Princeton, N.J., 1975), pp. 96–100.

20. These involved the agrarian guerrilla war of Canudos and the peasant movement of the *Contestado*. These two social and religious uprisings that were linked to problems of land tenure also demonstrated the lack of material and technical preparation of the Brazilian army.

21. Quoted in Eduardo Acevedo, *Manual de historia uruguaya* (Montevideo, 1936), p. 141.

22. We can point to a popular insurrection in the northeast of Brazil in 1838–1840, *A Balaiada*, that originated as a protest against forced recruitment.

23. José Murilho de Carvalho, "As forcas armadas na primeira República. O poder desestabilizador," *Cadernos do Departamento de ciência politica*, no. 1 (March 1974): 132.

24. Although it was weak internally, the state, whether imperial or republican, was strong externally because of the support that it received from the classes that benefited from its actions; thus Brazil successfully opposed the prohibition of the slave trade by England for a period of several decades.

25. On the different interpretations of the role of the national guard, in addition to Schulz, *Historia geral*, see the article of Maria Auxiliadora Faria, "A guardia nacional en Mina Gerais," *Revista brasileira de estudios politicos* (July 1979).

3. Modernization by the Army

1. See Etienne Schweisguth, "L'institution militaire et son système de valeurs," *Revue française de sociologie* 19 (1978):385–390.

2. See especially the secret reports of Captain Salats to the Navy Ministry of France, série BB7 136, Archives SHM, Paris, cited by Manuel Domingos Neto, "L'Influence étrangère sur la modernisation de l'armée brésilienne, 1889–1930" (Master's thesis, University of Paris-III, 1979), pp. 140–150.

3. Ibid., p. 199.

4. Joxe, *Las Fuerzas armadas*, p. 50.

5. This is the thesis of Frederick Nunn in "An Overview of the European Military Missions in Latin America," in Brian Loveman and Thomas M. Davis, eds., *The Politics of Antipolitics in Latin America*, (Lincoln, Neb., 1978).

6. Major Armando Duval, *A Argentina, potencia militar* (Rio de Janeiro, 1922), vol. 2, p. 368.

7. A. Maligne, "El ejército en octubre 1910," *Revista de derecho, historia y letras* (Buenos Aires), (March 1911):271.

8. *A Defesa nacional* (Rio de Janeiro), no. 154 (10 October 1926), quoted by Manuel Domingos Neto in Alain Rouquié ed., *Les Partis militaires au Brésil* (Paris, 1980), p. 60.

9. *Revista do Club militar* (Rio de Janeiro), no. 53 (April 1940):35.

10. Jorge Amado, *Fardo, fardão, camisola de dormir* (Rio de Janiero, 1978), p. 66.

11. General Gamelin, *Notes sur l'action de la mission militaire française au Brésil*, Rio de Janeiro, April 1925, Archives SHA, Paris, quoted by Eliezer Rizzo de Oliveira, "La Participation politique des militaires au Brésil, 1945–1964" (Ph.D. diss., Institute of Political Studies, Paris, 1980), p. 80.

12. Argentina, Cámara de diputados, *Diario de sesiones* (Buenos Aires, 1901), 1: 620.

13. Bertoldo Klinger, "Apontamentos sobre a organisação militar do Peru," Fundação Getulio Vargas, CPDOC, 22.02.07 GER, B. Klinger Archives, p. 6.

14. See for Guatemala, Jerry L. Weaver, "La élite política de un régimen dominado por militares: el ejemplo de Guatemala," *Revista latinoamericana de sociología* (Buenos Aires), 1 (1969):21–37.

15. R. S. Adams, "El problema del desarrollo político a la luz de la reciente historia sociopolítica de Guatemala," *Revista latinoamericana de sociología* (Buenos Aires), no. 2 (1968):183.

16. Initially this simply meant legitimate birth. Cf. Guillermo Bedregal, *Los Militares en Bolivia. Ensayo de interpretación sociológica* (La Paz), 1971, p. 40.

17. *Boletim do exército*, no. 40 (1942), and no. 18 (1943), quoted by Carvalho in "Forças armadas e Política, 1930–1945," (Rio de Janiero, FGV-CPDOC, 1980, Mimeographed, p. 25. See also Werneck Sodrè, *Memorias de um soldado* (Rio de Janeiro, 1967), pp. 185–186.

18. Steve C. Ropp, "The Military and Urbanization in Latin America: Some Implications of Trends in Recruitment," *Inter-American Affairs* 24, no. 2 (Fall 1970):27–35.

19. See Carlos A. Astiz and José García, "El ejército peruano en el poder," *Aportes* 26 (October 1972), and Luigi Einaudi and Alfred Stepan, *Latin American Institutional Development: Changing Military Perspectives* (Santa Monica, Calif., 1971), p. 56.

20. Luigi Einaudi, ibid., and Victor Villanueva, ¿*Nueva Mentalidad militar en el Perú?* (Buenos Aires, 1969), pp. 232 ff.

21. According to Joseph Love, *Rio Grande do Sul and Brazilian Regional-*

ism, 1882–1930 (Stanford, Calif., 1971), p. 117, cited by Carvalho, *As Forças armadas*, p. 147.

22. José Ibaré Costa Dantas, *O Tenentismo en Sergipe* (Petropolis, 1974), p. 71, following Dermeval Peixoto, *Memorias de um velho soldado* (Rio de Janeiro, 1960), p. 180.

23. Jacques Dumaine, *Quai d'Orsay, 1945–1951* (Paris, 1955), p. 19.

24. Rouquié, *Pouvoir militaire et Société politique en République argentine* (Paris, 1978), p. 647.

25. Stepan, *The Military in Politics: Changing Patterns in Brasil* (Princeton, 1971), pp. 32, 33.

26. According to a study of R. A. Hansen, *Military Culture and Organizational Decline: A Study of the Chilean Army* (Ann Arbor, Mich., 1967). Microfilm. See Hansen, "Career Motivation and Military Ideology: The Case of Chile," in Morris Janowitz and Jacques Van Doorn, eds., *On Military Ideology* (Rotterdam, 1971), pp. 119–136. The results of Hansen's survey are commented upon by Liisa North, *The Military in Chilean Politics* (York University, Toronto, 1974), pp. 11 ff.

27. Einaudi and Stepan, *Latin American*, p. 14.

28. According to Daniel Van Eeuwen, *Pouvoir militaire et Mutation de la société péruvienne* (Ph.D. thesis, Aix-Marseille, 1979), p. 50.

29. See James Petras, "Los militares y la modernización del Perú," *Estudios Internacionales* (Santiago de Chile), no. 13 (June 1970):122–123.

30. Stepan, *The Military in Politics*, pp. 32, 33.

31. Rouquié, *Pouvoir militaire*, p. 641.

32. Hansen, "Career Motivation," p. 135.

33. Lourival Coutinho, *O General Goes Depõe* (Rio de Janeiro, 1955), p. xii.

34. According to Neil Macaulay, *A Coluna Prestes* (Rio de Janeiro, 1977), p. 43.

35. Florencia Varas, *Conversaciones con Viaux (Primeras exclusivas revelaciones del general Roberto Viaux desde la prisión)* (Santiago, 1972).

36. Perón disclosed this during a personal interview that he granted us in Madrid in 1969.

37. Carvalho, *Forças armadas e Política* p. 24.

38. Olavio Bilac, *A Defesa nacional (Discursos)* (Rio de Janeiro, 1965, 1st ed. 1917), pp. 107, 70.

39. Bilac, *A Defesa nacional* pp. 26–27, 108–109, quoted by Frank McCann, "Origins of the 'New Professionalism' of the Brazilian

Military," *Journal of Inter-American Studies and World Affairs* (November 1979):513.

40. Manuel Carlés, "Diplomacia y estrategia (Conferencia dada en el Colegio militar)," Supplement to no. 270 of *Revista Militar* (June 1915):13.

41. According to Joxe, *Las Fuerzas armadas*, p. 53.

42. XX, *El Ejército argentino por dentro. Estudio para contribuir al restablecimiento de nuestras instituciones militares arruinadas* (Buenos Aires, 1904), p. 9.

43. R. N. Adams, "The Development of the Guatemalan Military," [Offprint Series, no. 90] (Austin: University of Texas, n.d.), p. 100.

44. Bedregal, *Los Militares en Bolivia*, pp. 42–45.

45. Mario Monteforte Toledo, *Guatemala. Monografía sociológica* (México, 1965), p. 360.

4. The Rise of the Power of the
   Military

1. This is the argument of Victor Villanueva in his book *100 Años del ejército peruano. Frustraciones y cambios* (Lima, 1971), p. 64.

2. See Captain Severino Sombra, "Lyautey e o Brasil," *Revista do Clube militar* (Rio de Janeiro), no. 48 (26 June 1937), 241–244.

3. This is proven by numerous publications. See for example, for Guatemala the book of Benjamín Paniagua Santizo, published for the centenary of the foundation of the Escuela politécnica: *Vida y obra de militares ilustres, primer centenario de la fundación de la Escuela politécnica, 1873–1973* (Guatemala, 1973), 273 pp.

4. Speech of Juan D. Perón, 1 May 1944, in J. D. Perón, *El Pueblo quiere saber de que se trata* (Buenos Aires, 1944).

5. Speech, 25 June 1944, ibid.

6. Hipólito Yrigoyen, *Pueblo y Gobierno*, vol. 4: *Mensajes* (Buenos Aires, 1953), p. 322.

7. Francisco Reynolds, *La Revolución del 6 septembre de 1930. Acción Militar* (Buenos Aires, 1969), p. 11.

8. Ernesto Corvalán, "Pensamientos radicales," *Revista argentina de ciencias políticas* (12 July 1915), p. 412.

9. Vicente C. Gallo, "Aspectos y enseñanzas de una obra," *Revista argentina de ciencias políticas* (12 July 1915), p. 334.

10. See Maria Cecilia Spina Forjaz, *Tenentismo e Politica* (Rio de Janeiro, 1977), pp. 31–68.

11. See Neil Macaulay, *A Coluna Prestes,* and Peter Flynn, *Brazil: A Political Analysis* (London, 1978), pp. 47–50.

12. See Francisco Frias, *Manual de historia de Chile* (Santiago, 1969), pp. 485–493.

13. According to Paul W. Drake, *Socialism and Populism in Chile, 1932– 52* (Urbana, Ill., 1978), p. 74.

14. Drake, *ibid.,* p. 76.

15. The candidate of the opposition lost the elections because he was "too popular." See Frederick B. Pike, *The United States and the Andean Republics, Peru, Bolivia, and Ecuador* (Cambridge, Mass., 1977), p. 190.

16. According to the revolutionary proclamation of July 9. See Agustín Cueva, *El Proceso de dominación política en Ecuador* (Quito, 1974), p. 19.

17. This is a theory that has been widely held in Brazil since the pioneering work of Virgilio Santa Rosa, *O que foi o tenentismo* (Rio de Janeiro, 1936, reissued 1963). See the discussion of the question in the book of Forjaz, *Tenentismo e Política,* especially the introduction by Francisco Weffort.

18. This is the thesis of Stepan, *The Military in Politics,* p. 269.

19. See for Brazil the arguments in Decio Saes, *Classes medias e politica na primeira Republica brasileira, 1889–1930* (Petropolis, 1975), pp. 15 ff. and in the classic work of Boris Fausto, *A Revolução de 1930. Historiografia et história* (São Paulo, 1979, 1st. ed. 1970), 118 pp.

20. Maligne, "El ejército en octubre 1910," p. 397.

21. Juan Ramón Beltrán, "Misión del oficial frente a los problemas sociales contemporáneos," *Revista militar* (September 1936):508.

22. *A Defesa Nacional* (Rio de Janeiro) 1, no. 1 (1913).

23. Irving Louis Horowitz and Ellen Kay Trimberger, "State Power and Military Nationalism in Latin America," *Comparative Politics* 8, no. 2 (January 1976):223–243.

24. The Alianza Popular Revolucionaria Americana was created and led by Haya de la Torre. It was a party with continental aspirations, oriented toward the Indians, and very strong in the north of Peru. See Peter F. Klaren, *Modernization, Dislocation, and Aprismo (Origins of the Peruvian Aprista Party, 1870–1932)* (Austin, Tex., 1967), chap. 7.

25. See François Bourricaud, *Pouvoir et Société dans le Pérou contemporain* (Paris, 1967), pp. 280–287.

26. According to Flynn, *Brazil,* p. 61.

27. Pedro Goes Monteiro, *A Revolução de 30 e a Finalidade política do exército (esboço histórico)* (Rio de Janeiro, n.d.), p. 183.

28. Monteiro, ibid., p. 163.

5. THE SIXTH SIDE OF THE PENTAGON?

1. As McCann shows with respect to Brazil where the representatives of the United States were favorable to the French military mission. See Frank McCann, "Foreign Influence and the Brazilian Army," (Rio de Janeiro, 1980, pp. 5–6, mimeographed).
2. According to Pablo González Casanova, *Imperialismo y Liberación en América latina* (México, 1978), pp. 15–16.
3. See Leslie Manigat, *Évolutions et Révolutions: l'Amérique latine au XXe siècle, 1889–1939* (Paris, 1973), p. 334, and Hans Joachim Leu et al., *Las Relaciones interamericanas. Una antología de documentos* (Caracas, 1975), p. 20.
4. See Allan Reed Millet, *The Politics of Intervention. The Military Occupation of Cuba, 1906–09* (Columbus, Ohio, 1968), pp. 40–41.
5. Undersecretary of State Robert Olds, in a confidential memorandum quoted by Richard Millett in his book *Guardians of the Dynasty: A History of the US-Created Guardia Nacional de Nicaragua and the Somoza Family* (New York, 1977), p. 52.
6. According to American political circles in the period. See Dana G. Munro, former chargé d'affaires of the United States in Nicaragua and minister to Haiti, reply to Richard Millett, ibid., p. 41.
7. Luis A. Pérez, Jr., *Army Politics in Cuba, 1898–1958* (Pittsburgh, Pa., 1976), p. xv.
8. Ibid., p. 45.
9. Millett, *Guardians of the Dynasty*, p. 21.
10. Ibid., p. 22.
11. According to Jaime Wheelock, *Imperialismo y Dictadura, Crisis de una formación social* (México, 1975), pp. 104–107, and Edelberto Torres Rivas, *Centroamérica hoy* (México, 1977), pp. 98–100.
12. According to John Parke Young, *Central American Currency and Finance* (New York, 1925), quoted by Wheelock, *Imperialismo y Dictadura*, p. 109.
13. See Virgilio Godoy, "El ejército de Nicaragua," in *La Crónica*, 8 December 1970.
14. Millett, *Guardians of the Dynasty*, p. 125.
15. U.S. Congress, House Committee on Foreign Affairs, *Foreign Assistance Act of 1966: Hearings*, 89th Cong., 2d sess., 16 April 1966, p. 239, quoted by Don L. Etchison, *The United States and Militarism in Central America* (New York, 1975), p. 106.

16. Delince, *Armée et Politique,* p. 18.

17. Manigat, *Évolutions et Révolutions,* p. 363.

18. Delince, *Armée et Politique,* p. 19.

19. Paul Laraque, preface to Delince, *Armée et Politique,* p. 10. For an American and self-styled technical point of view, consult James H. McCrocklin, *Garde d'Haïti, 1915–1934 (Twenty Years of Organization and Training by the United States Marine Corps)* (New York, 1956).

20. According to the phrase of Pedro F. Bono, quoted by Manigat, *Évolutions et Révolutions,* p. 348.

21. Marvin Goldwert, *The Constabulary in the Dominican Republic and Nicaragua* (Gainesville, Fla., 1962), p. 21.

22. This is the title of a well-documented book by Germán Ornes, *Trujillo, Little Caesar of the Caribbean* (New York, 1958).

23. See F. Benham and H. A. Holley, *A Short Introduction to the Economy of Latin America* (London, 1960), p. 73.

24. According to the Organization of American States, Inter-American Economic and Social Council, *Foreign Investment in Latin America* (Washington, D.C.), p. 17, and United Nations, *External Financing of Latin America* (New York, 1965), pp. 15–32.

25. Joseph S. Tulchin, "Latin America: Focus for U.S. Aid," *Current History* (July 1966):28.

26. See David Green, "The Cold War comes to Latin America," in B. J. Bernstein, ed., *Politics and Policies of the Truman Administration* (Chicago, 1970), p. 165.

27. Ibid., p. 167.

28. In March 1954 at Caracas the United States had an Inter-American conference vote a resolution condemning Communism and asserting that the establishment of a Communist regime in the continent was a danger to peace. That resolution preceded by several months the overthrow by U.S.-trained mercenaries of the democratic reformist regime of President Jacobo Arbenz, a government that was supported by the Communist party of Guatemala. This intervention was denounced by Guillermo Torriello, the Guatemalan foreign minister, as "international McCarthyism."

29. According to the official figures: U.S. Agency for International Development, Statistics and Reports Division, *US Overseas Loans and Grants and Assistance from International Organizations. Obligations and Loan Authorizations, July 1, 1945–June 30, 1972* (Washington, D.C., 1973).

30. We only count these three programs and not, as do certain authors, the economic assistance of the Agency for International Development that was used to equip the police, and the Food for

Peace Program that included the "food weapon," to say nothing of the Peace Corps. If everything is military, then nothing is. By proving too much, you prove nothing.

31. According to the U.S. Department of Defense, 1967, 1971, 1975, quoted in *Aportes* (October 1967):55; *Marcha* (14 July 1972); *NACLA Report*, (January 1976).

32. According to Fernando Rivas Sánchez and Elisabeth Reimann Weigert, *Las Fuerzas Armadas de Chile. Un caso de penetración imperialista* (México, 1976), p. 50.

33. Ibid., pp. 44–50 and Etchison, *The United States and Militarism*, appendix B.

34. U.S., House, Committee on Foreign Affairs [*Report of the Special Study Mission to Latin America on Military Assistance Training*], Subcommittee on National Security Policy and Scientific Development, 91st Cong., 2d sess., 1970, H. Res. 143, p. 29.

35. This term comes from H. F. Walterhouse, "Good Neighbors in Uniform," *Military Review* 45, no. 2 (February 1965): 10–18.

36. Gordon to Rusk, attn. Mann, 4 March 1964, CFB vol. 1 NSF, L. B. Johnson Presidential Library, Austin, Texas, quoted by Phyllis Parker, *Brazil and the Quiet Intervention, 1964* (Austin, Tex., 1979).

37. U.S. Department of Defense, *Military Assistance and Foreign Sales Facts* (Washington, D.C., 1973), p. 2.

38. Nelson Rockefeller, "La Calidad de la vida en las Américas (Informe presentado por una misión presidencial de los Estados Unidos al hemisferio occidental)," 30 August 1969 (Washington, D.C.), Mimeographed, pp. 18–22.

39. See for example. U.S., Congress, Senate Committee on Foreign Relations, *United States Military Policies and Programs in Latin America,* Hearings before the Subcommittee on Western Hemisphere Affairs, 91st Cong., 1969.

40. The following is the eloquent chronology:

Date	Country	President Overthrown
March 1962	Argentina	Arturo Frondizi
July 1962	Peru	Manuel Prado
March 1963	Guatemala	Ydígoras Fuentes
July 1963	Ecuador	C. Julio Arosemena Monroy
September 1963	Dominican Republic	Juan Bosch
October 1963	Honduras	R. Villeda Morales
April 1964	Brazil	J. Goulart
November 1964	Bolivia	V. Paz Estenssoro
June 1966	Argentina	Arturo Illía

41. B. H. Liddell-Hart, *L'Alternative militaire. Deterrent ou défense* (Paris, 1960), p. 279.

42. See "Chili: encore une preuve du role des USA dans le coup d'état. Un avion a coordonné toutes les opérations militaires du putsch," *Libération* (Paris), 16 November 1973.

43. The question has been discussed in the United States in a number of articles. For the figures in the debate, see John Duncan Powell, "Military Assistance and Militarism in Latin America," *The Western Political Quarterly* (June 1965):382–392, as well as John Samuel Fitch, "The Political Impact of U.S. Military Aid to Latin America," *Armed Forces and Society* 5, no. 3 (Spring 1979):360–386.

    James Kurth has shown that the six countries that received the most military aid in the years 1962–70 range from conservative military (Brazil) to moderate civilian (Venezuela) to progressive civilian (Chile). See James Kurth, "United States Foreign Policy and Latin American Military Rule," in Philippe Schmitter, ed., *Military Rule in Latin America: Function, Consequences and Perspectives* (Beverly Hills, Calif., 1973), p. 303.

44. According to Schmitter, "Foreign Military Assistance, National Military Spending and Military Rule in Latin America," in Schmitter, ed., *Military Rule*, p. 148.

45. Calculations made by Joxe, *Las Fuerzas armadas*, pp. 103–104.

46. Gilhodes, *Paysans de Panama*, chap. 17, "La garde nationale."

47. On the massacres of 1932 under the presidency of General Hernández Martínez, we follow the interpretation of Alejandro Marroquín in his article "El Salvador en los años treinta," in Casanova, ed., *América latina en los años treinta* (México, 1977), pp. 145–159.

    On the participation and responsibility of the Communist party (whose general secretary was Farabundo Martí), and the uprising of 1932, see Roque Dalton and Miguel Mármol, *Los Sucesos de 1932 en El Salvador* (San José, Costa Rica, 1979).

48. "Turcios Lima. La révolution, sa raison d'être jusqu'à la mort," *Granma* (Havana), international ed., 11 October 1970.

49. According to Fitch, *The Military Coup d'Etat as a Political Process: Ecuador, 1948–1966* (Baltimore, Md., 1977), p. 118, quoted in J. S. Fitch, p. 366.

50. Stepan, *The Military in Politics*, pp. 236–247.

51. Project Camelot of SORO (Special Operations Research Office) at the American University in Washington, D.C., was denounced in the press and the Chilean Congress. It produced an abundant literature. The affair is discussed in the collective book, edited by

Horowitz, *The Rise and Fall of Project Camelot* (Cambridge, Mass., 1967). The project created an uproar in the Latin American scientific community which thereafter was ready to see a spy behind every foreign sociologist.

52. R. N. Adams, "The Guatemalan Military," *Studies in Comparative International Development* 4, no. 5 (May 1968):91–109.

53. In October 1967 Peru decided to buy fifteen Mirage planes from France. For a general view at the beginning of the 1970s, see Alain Rouquié, "Les ventes d'armes françaises en Amérique latine," *Politique aujourd'hui* (January-February 1974):139–142.

54. See Rouquié, *Pouvoir militaire*, pp. 595–597.

55. Brazil equipped the Iraqi army selling it 200 Cascavel armored cars and 200 Urutu amphibian vehicles. It is not known how they performed at the Iranian front but the press has widely reported their presence. See "Para frente Cascavel," *Isto É*, 1 October 1980.

56. Fifteen to twenty percent of the total, but since the whole budget depended on direct American aid at that time, that figure is not very useful.

57. Juan Bosch, *El Pentagonismo: sustituto del imperialismo* (México, 1968).

58. In Chile the publicity given to the prohibition on the export to that country of successful Hollywood films seems to have been part of the psychological warfare against Allende; the frustration of the viewers was directed at the government.

59. Nearly $3 million went from the CIA to the Frei campaign without, it is reported, the candidate knowing the source of his financing. See U.S. Congress, Senate, Select Committee on Intelligence Activities, *Covert Action in Chile, 1963–1973*, Staff Rept., 94th Cong., 1st sess., 1975, pp. 9–15.

60. Philip Agee, *Inside the Company, CIA Diary* (New York, 1975), pp. 130–145.

61. We are referring to Antonio Arguedas, interior minister and "double agent" involved in 1969 in the incredible story of the diary of Che Guevara. See his confession to Carlos Cocciolo in *L'Express* (Paris), 29 June 1970. The *Los Angeles Times* reported in November 1978 that M. Hernán Cubillos, Foreign minister of Chile at the time, "is supposed to have belonged to the CIA" (*Le Monde*, 16 November 1978).

6. PRAETORIAN GUARDS AND THE PATRIMONIAL STATE

1. This is the description of Domingo Alberto Rangel, *Los Andinos en el poder. Balance de una hegemonía, 1899–1945* (Caracas, 1964), p. 59.

2. Sergio Ramírez, "Balcanes y volcanes (Aproximación al proceso cultural contemporáneo de Centroamérica)," in Edelberto Torres Rivas, ed., *Centroamérica hoy* (México, 1973), pp. 336–337.

3. Millett, *Guardians of the Dynasty*, p. 55.

4. P. J. Chamorro, *Estirpe sangrienta: los Somoza* (México, 1978), p. 67.

5. Millett, Guardians of the Dynasty, p. 177.

6. Ibid., p. 184.

7. According to William Krehm, *Democracia y Tiranía en el Caribe* (Havana, 1960), pp. 13–15, and Emiliano Chamorro, "Autobiografía," *Revista conservadora* (Managua), nos. 1–18, quoted by Wheelock, *Imperialismo y Dictadura*, p. 150.

8. According to Alejandro Bendana, "Crisis in Nicaragua," *NACLA Report* 12, no. 6 (November-December 1978):6–8, and Wheelock, *Imperialismo y Dictadura*, pp. 159–170.

9. "Nicaragua, la voie 'socialiste' de Tachito Somoza," *Le Monde*, 4 September 1971.

10. There were essentially two groups, corresponding in their regional base and activities to the two traditional dominant groups—the Conservatives and the Liberals. The ranchers and the sugar producers created the Banamerica (Banco de América) group, the coffee producers and the cotton growers of the northwest plus the businessmen in Managua supported the Banic (Banco de Nicaragua) group.

11. J. A. Robleto Siles, *Yo deserté de la guardia nacional de Nicaragua* (San José, Costa Rica, 1979), pp. 189–191.

12. "A Loyalty Test for the Guard," *Newsweek*, 16 July 1979.

13. Siles, *Yo deserté*, p. 52.

14. Pedro Joaquín Chamorro speaks of this from first hand knowledge. The editor of *La Prensa* whose assassination in 1978 set off the final offensive against the dynasty was tortured in the "sewing room" of the palace by Tachito himself after the assassination of Tacho in 1956. P. J. Chamorro, *Estirpe sangrienta*, p. 67.

15. Chamorro tells of some of the gross "jokes" played by the first Somoza on the opposition members of the upper bourgeoisie. Ibid., p. 142.

16. This procedure was carried out either at the level of the voting booths or later in the Electoral Tribunal. See P. J. Chamorro, ibid, p. 59.

17. According to A. Klement, "Feds Target Foreign Agents," *The National Law Journal* (25 August 1980):10, quoted by Marie-France Toinet, "Le lobby latino-américain à Washington," *Problèmes d'Amérique latine*, no. 60 (2d trimester, 1981):77. That official figure seems rather modest. No doubt it is only the tip of the iceberg.

18. Richard Millett, *Guardians of the Dynasty*, pp. 235–237 and 241.

19. According to Howard J. Wiarda, *Dictatorship and Development: The Methods of Control in Trujillo's Dominican Republic* (Gainesville, Fla., 1968), p. 50.

20. See Juan Bosch, *Trujillo. Causas de una tiranía sin ejemplo* (Caracas, 1961), pp. 147–148.

21. With evocative names: The Kikuyus of the Andes, The Foreign Legion, and The Riders of the East. They totaled 5,000 men according to the *Hispanic American Report* 14:161.

22. This is the thesis of Abraham Lowenthal, "The Political Role of the Dominican Armed Forces: a note on the 1963 Overthrow of Juan Bosch and the 1965 Dominican Revolution," in Lowenthal, ed., *Armies and Politics in Latin America* (New York, 1976), pp. 314–316.

23. Hugh Thomas, *Cuba or the Pursuit of Freedom* (London, 1971), p. 568.

24. Quoted in Louis A. Pérez, Jr., *Army and Politics in Cuba, 1898–1958* (Pittsburgh, 1976), pp. 56–57.

25. Casanova, *Imperialismo y Liberación*, p. 183.

26. Pérez, *Army and Politics*, p. 84.

27. Thomas, *Cuba*, p. 580.

28. See Dennis B. Wood, "Las relaciones revolucionarias de clase y los conflictos políticos en Cuba, 1868–1968," *Revista latinoamericana de sociología* (Buenos Aires), no. 1 (1969):48–60.

29. According to Ramón de Armas, "Fulgencio Batista, principales circunstancias condicionantes de la instauración de sus dos períodos dictatoriales," (Havana and Mexico City, Latin American Social Science Council [CLACSO], June 1980, mimeographed), pp. 14–18.

30. Thomas, *Cuba*, see chapter 60: "Batista and the Communists," and pp. 724–725.

31. Blas Roca (Francisco Calderío) and Carlos Rafael Rodríguez, *En defensa del pueblo* (Havana, 1945), quoted by Thomas, *Cuba.*, p. 736.

32. This is emphasized by Mario Llerena who sees the university as

the laboratory in which the Castro movement was born. See *The Unsuspected Revolution: The Birth and Rise of Castroism* (Ithaca N.Y., 1978), p. 41.

33. At least this is what is said by General Espaillat, his minister of the police in Arturo Espaillat, *Les Dessous d'une dictature: Trujillo* (Paris, 1966), p. 208. He himself considered Batista "a maladroit common type without class."

34. See American University-Foreign Area Studies, *Area Handbook for Paraguay* (Washington, D.C., 1972), p. 139.

35. Ibid., p. 274.

36. According to the majority of witnesses, especially the members of the Febrerista opposition. See "Partido febrerista. Sinopsis de la situación política paraguaya, 1972" in *Nueva Sociedad* (Caracas) (September-October 1972):49–71.

37. An opinion that is less frequently held. See Omar Díaz de Arce, *Paraguay* (Havana, 1967), p. 50.

38. See François Chartrain, *La République du Paraguay* (Paris, 1973), p. 35.

39. Since the 1967 constitution, the Liberal Radical party, the Liberal party, and the Febrerista party are tolerated. The Colorado party has two-thirds of the congressional seats. President Stroessner received 89.62 percent of the votes in the 1978 election.

40. See "Paraguay, la dictadura olvidada," in *Alternativa* (Bogotá), no. 226 (August 1979):31.

41. See Hector Borrat, "Contacto en el Paraguay," *Marcha* (Montevideo), 16 June 1972, as well as "Joseph Ricord, un parrain déchu," *Le Monde*, 13 December 1972.

42. "Paraguay. The Price of Paz," *Newsweek*, 12 February 1973.

43. "Paraguay. Des prêtres dénoncent la terreur policière dans le pays," *Le Monde*, 5 December 1974.

44. Frederic Hicks, "International Relations and Caudillismo in Paraguay," *Journal of Inter-American Studies and World Affairs* (January 1971):89–111.

45. See Hicks, "Política, poder y el papel del cura de pueblo en el Paraguay," *Suplemento Antropológico de la Revista del Ateneo Paraguayo* (June 1969):35–44.

46. According to Hicks, "International Relations." In 1963 at the beginning of the school year the Colorado party distributed 20,000 school blouses, 40,000 notebooks, 100,000 pencils, and 66,500 readers.

7. MODEL DEMOCRACIES AND CIVILIAN SUPREMACY

1. That of General Federico Tinoco from 1917 to 1919. See Orlando Salazar Mora, "Le Système politique au Costa Rica, 1889–1919" (Ph.D. diss., Paris-III, Mimeographed), pp. 298–301.

    For the problem of the army in Costa Rica we rely on the work of Constantino Urcuyo Fournier, especially his Ph.D. diss., "Les Forces de sécurité publique et la Politique au Costa Rica, 1960–1978," (Paris-V, mimeographed), 432 pp.

2. See José Luis Vega Carballo, *Costa Rica: Una interpretación sociopolítica de su desarrollo reciente* (San José, 1977), p. 10, and the interview with José Figueres in Alfredo Peña, *Democracia y Golpe militar. Entrevista a Juan Bosch* (Caracas, 1979), p. 43.

3. José Figueres had a personal and paternalistic relationship to the members of the guard. He went to the funerals of those who had died, and assisted their families. See Constantino Urcuyo Fournier, "Les Raisons, les Fonctions et les Limites de l'abolition de l'armée au Costa Rica" (San José, 1979, Manuscript), p. 5.

4. Interview with Alain Rouquié, San José, Costa Rica, 29 April 1981.

5. According to the analysis of Rodolfo Cerdas, *La Crisis de la democracia liberal en Costa Rica* (San José, Costa Rica, 1976), p. 76.

6. Carballo, *Costa Rica*, p. 16.

7. A Costa Rican deputy said recently to the author: "The Costa Rican people are very attached to democratic institutions. When two peasants have a conflict about their boundaries, they do not shoot each other as in our neighboring countries, they go to court."

8. On the rotation of members of the police force and their professional instability, see Fournier, *Les Raisons*, p. 9.

9. See Samuel Stone, "Las convulsiones del istmo centroamericano: raices de un conflicto entre elites," *Estudios CIAPA* (San José, Costa Rica), no. 1 (1979):23–24.

10. According to William Cline and Enrique Delgado, eds., *Economic Integration in Central America* (Washington, D.C., 1978), p. 68.

11. Carballo, *Costa Rica.*, pp. 12 ff.

12. According to Winfield J. Burggraaff, *The Venezuelan Armed Forces in Politics, 1935–1959* (Columbia, Mo., 1972), p. 13.

13. Silvio Villegas, "La Politique extérieure de Juan Vicente Gómez," vol. 1 (Ph.D. thesis, Paris-III, 1980), pp. 277 ff. Domingo Alberto Rangel, *Los Andinos en el poder. Balance de una hegemonía, 1899–1945* (Caracas, 1964), p. 169. See also Robert L. Gilmore,

Caudillism and Militarism in Venezuela, 1810–1910 (Athens, Ohio, 1964).

14. See Daniel H. Levine, "Venezuela since 1958: The consolidation of Democratic Politics," in Juan Linz and Alfred Stepan, *The Breakdown of Democratic Regimes* (Baltimore, Md., 1978), p. 96, and Burggraaff, *The Venezuelan Armed Forces*, p. 84.

15. Burggraaff, *The Venezuelan Armed Forces*, p. 113.

16. Humberto Njaim et al., *El Sistema político venezolano* (Caracas, 1975), p. 12.

17. On the coalition AD, COPEI, URD (Democratic Republican Union) see Gene E. Bigler, "The Armed Forces and Patterns of Civil-Military Relations," in John Martz and D. Myers, eds., *Venezuela: The Democratic Experience* (New York, 1977), pp. 119–127.

18. We simply note that the income from petroleum helped to weaken if not to eliminate the large agrarian bourgeoisie as a social force and to retard the industrialization that no doubt facilitated the entrenchment of a stable representative system.

19. Njaim et al., *El Sistema*, pp. 41–56.

20. On 24 June 1960 Betancourt was the victim of an attack that cost the life of the head of his military staff. After they were arrested the organizers of the attack revealed that Rafael Leónidas Trujillo, the dictator of the Dominican Republic, had been directly involved. See Rómulo Betancourt, *Tres Años de gobierno democrático*, vol. 2 (Caracas, 1962), p. 318.

21. See *U.S. Army Area Handbook for Venezuela* (Washington, D.C., 1965), chapter 18, pp. 545–547.

22. See Betancourt, "Palabras de optimismo y conciliación al comenzar 1961," in *Tres Años*, vol. 1, p. 413, as well as "Quatrième message présidentiel," ibid., vol. 2, pp. 320–321.

23. Ibid., vol. 1, pp. 390, 414.

24. Peña, *Conversaciones con Carlos Andrés Pérez*, vol. 2 (Caracas, 1979), p. 122.

25. Ibid.

26. Ibid., p. 123.

27. This is the term used by Casanova in "El partido del Estado, cincuenta años del PRI," *Nexos* (México) (April and May 1979).

28. See Franklin D. Margiotta, "Civilian Control and the Mexican Military: Changing Patterns of Political Influence," in C. Welsh, ed., *Civilian Control of the Military: Theory and Cases from Developing Countries* (Albany, N.Y., 1976), p. 233.

29. See Guillermo Boils, *Los Militares y la Política en México, 1915–1974* (México, 1975), p. 54.

30. This is the thesis of, among others, Jean Mayer, in *La Révolution mexicaine, 1910–1940* (Paris, 1973), passim and pp. 305–307.

31. Jorge Alberto Lozoya, *El Ejército mexicano, 1911–1965* (México, 1971), p. 65.

32. With around seventy thousand men in the armed forces, Mexico has spent less than 10 percent of the national budget since 1950 on defense. See Joseph Loftus, *Latin American Defense Expenditures, 1938–1965* (Santa Monica, Calif., 1968), pp. 11–36.

33. Mexico, which has the second-largest population in the continent, is only in fourth place in numbers in the military, far behind Brazil (200,000 men), Cuba (120,000), and Argentina (150,000).

34. *Novedades* (Mexico City), 6 May 1967.

35. See Margiotta, *Civilian Control*, p. 234.

36. Ibid., pp. 236 and 237.

37. See Boils, *Los Militares*, pp. 112–113, and Margiotta, ibid., pp. 225–226.

38. Alexander W. Wilde, "Conversation among Gentlemen: Oligarchical Democracy in Colombia," in Linz and Stepan, eds., *The Breakdown of Democracy* (Baltimore, Md., 1979), p. 28.

39. Gilhodes, "Les élections colombiennes de 1978," *Problèmes d'Amérique latine* (Paris), no. 3 (July 1979):63–88.

40. In 1922, the Colombian infantry only had 1,500 men and 139 officers. See J. León Helguera, "The Changing Role of the Military in Colombia," *Journal of Inter-American Studies* (July 1961): 351–357, and Richard Maullin, *Soldiers, Guerillas and Politics in Colombia* (Lexington, Mass., 1973), pp. 6–56.

41. Francisco Leal Buitrago, "Política e intervención militar en Colombia," *Revista mexicana de sociología* 33, no. 3 (May-June 1970):501–502.

42. See "Los sueldos militares," *La República* (Bogotá), 19 November 1980.

43. There are many works on *la violencia*. The classic work is that of Germán Guzmán et al., *La Violencia en Colombia*, 2 vols. (Bogotá, 1962, 1964). For an interpretative synthesis see Gilhodes, "La violence en Colombie, banditisme et guerre sociale," *Cahiers du monde hispanique et luso-brésilien-Caravelle* (Toulouse), no. 26 (1976): 69–81.

44. Thus the Firmes movement in which Gabriel García Márquez participated was led by Enrique Santos Calderón and Daniel Semper Pizano, both journalists and sons of the Liberal oligarchy linked to the large daily newspaper, *El Tiempo*.

45. This is the title of the penetrating article by Alexander Wilde cited in note 38, this chapter.

46. Gilhodes, *Politique et Violence. La question agraire en Colombie* (Paris, 1974), p. 503.

47. According to Wilde a veritable "explosion of participation" took place in 1946 with a 60 to 70 percent voting turnout ("Conversation," p. 41.)

48. See Gilhodes, *Politique et Violence,* and Paul Oquist, *Violencia, Conflicto y Política en Colombia* (Bogotá, 1978), pp. 277–290.

49. According to the interpretation of L. A. Costa Pinto, "Clase, partido, poder: el caso colombiano," *Aportes* (Paris) (October 1971):100.

50. See Wilde, *Conversations,* pp. 62 ff. and Oquist, *Violencia,* pp. 327–332.

51. "Hablan los generales Gabriel París y Deogracias Fonseca," *El Espectador* (Bogotá), 18 December 1979.

52. See Jaime Carrillo Bedoya, *Los Paros cívicos en Colombia* (Bogotá, 1981), pp. 144 ff.

53. Gustave Gallón Girardo, *Quince Años de estado de sitio en Colombia, 1958–1978* (Bogotá, 1979).

54. The news of the electoral fraud on April 1970 produced the rebellion of two battalions near Bogotá but the army did not follow them, and Rojas allowed the plotters to be arrested. See Gérard Fenoy, "L'armée en Colombie," *Cahiers du monde hispanique et luso-brésilien-Caravelle* (Toulouse) 26 (1979):102.

55. The *Movimiento 19 de abril,* because it is not Marxist and still less Leninist but rather is anchored in a national political tradition supposedly "based on the frustration of the Anapista masses after the electoral fraud carried out by the oligarchy in 1970" (pamphlet, May 1981) is more dangerous to the system. We recall that it was the seizure of the Dominican embassy where a number of diplomats were kept hostage by a commando group of M-19 in February 1980 that made that organization known to the world.

56. Some headlines in the major newspapers: "New Military Court for Cocaine in the Gloria" (the navy training ship), *El Tiempo,* 7 March 1978; "Four Sergeants to Military Court for Drugs," *El Tiempo,* 8 April 1978; "Eight Military Men Arrested for Marijuana," *El Colombiano* (Medellín), 21 September 1980; "Military Court for Military Men Linked to Drug Traffic," *El Tiempo,* 21 September 1980; "No Members of the Military Involved in Drug Traffic: Minister of Defense," *El Espectador,* 1 November 1980.

57. "Convening of Military Court to Judge Indians of the Cauca," *El Espectador,* 17 January 1980.

58. Not only Amnesty International or the International Association

for Human Rights, but a forum on human rights in which members of the Conservative and Liberal establishments participated, such as Vásquez Carrisoza and Díaz Callejas.

59. "La República tropical," *El Espectador*, 16 December 1979.

60. That is, following the Uruguayan model of a prolonged coup d'état during which the military kept the elected civilian president, Bordaberry, as head of state but took away his real power (see chap. 8).

61. After the Dominican embassy affair, *El Espectador* received (and published) numerous letters from readers who called for military rule to save the country's institutions (*El Espectador*, 29 March 1980). *El Siglo* (Conservative) has specialized in exaggerated praise for the virtues of the military. The following appeared in its number of 1 June 1979: "In an indolent and decadent country in which the modes of behavior are insipid, the stern confident and lofty presence of the military is an unusual phenomenon which provokes both admiration and hatred."

62. See on this point the view of the general who was head of the army in 1979, Fernando Landazábal Reyes, in his book *La Subversión y el Conflicto social* (Bogotá, 1980), pp. 112–113.

63. As is demonstrated by the operation of the Coffee Producers Federation, an autonomous but quasi-governmental agency.

64. This is the view of Fernando Rojas H., *El Estado en los ochenta, un régimen policivo?* (Bogotá, 1978).

65. See Daniel Pecaut, "La Colombie de 1974 à 1979, du 'mandat clair' à la 'crise morale,' " *Problèmes d'Amérique latine* 52, pp. 46–47, and Bedoya, *Los Paros cívicos*, passim.

66. The Confederation of Colombian workers (CTC) is Liberal, the Union of Colombian workers (UTC) Conservative. The extreme left is strong in the independent unions (teachers, petroleum workers) and the Communist Confederation of Colombian Workers Unions (CSTC) has become stronger at the expense of the traditional parties. See Pecaut, ibid., pp. 42–45.

67. Pierre de Charentenay, "Bourgeoisie nouvelle en Colombie," *Amérique latine* (Paris), no. 5 (Spring 1981):50.

68. At least this seems to be indicated by the interviews with generals Matallana and Puyana that appeared in *Alternativa* (December 1979) (see *El Espectador*, 18 February 1979). General Valencia Tovar seems to share their point of view in "El pensamiento militar," *El Tiempo*, 22 February 1979. See also "La desilusión de los generales" by Fernando Cepeda Ulloa in *El Tiempo*, 23 March 1979.

69. " 'Communist subversion is spreading' says General Forero in

Conference of American Commanders," *El Espectador*, 31 October 1979. The appointment of General Landazábal Reyes as chief of the general staff follows the same lines. General Landazábal Reyes is the author of many works on subversion: *Estrategia de la subversión y su desarrollo en América latina, Política y táctica de la guerra revolucionaria, Guía de asuntos civiles para el mantenimiento del orden público*, etc.

70. See Leal Buitrago, "Política e intervención," pp. 509–510.

71. Bigler, "The Armed Forces," p. 128.

72. See "Doubts Plague Big Oil Producer," *Financial Times Survey*, 8 June 1981, and "Venezuela Growing Pains," *Newsweek*, 22 June 1981.

73. Hundreds of students demonstrating peacefully in the Plaza of the Three Cultures in the Tlatelolco section on the eve of the Olympic Games were dispersed by the army using its weapons. The exact number killed is not known but the figure involves several dozen. See Jorge Carrión et al., *Tres Culturas en agonía. Tlatelolco* (México, 1968), 1971.

74. Rafael Segovia in *Vuelta* (Mexico City), August 1977, reprinted in Comisión Federal Electoral, *Reforma política*, vol. 2. (Mexico City, 1977): p. 506.

75. Javier López Moreno, *La Reforma política en México* (Mexico City, 1979).

76. In evaluating that figure it should be noted that participation in legislative elections is always lower than in those for the presidency. In addition, as Rafael Segovia notes in a study of the federal elections of 1979 in *Foro Internacional* (Mexico City) 20, no. 3, p. 398, the drop in participation may be due to increased reliability of voting lists because of the presence of representatives of the opposition parties.

77. To use the expression of Susan Eckstein, *The Poverty of Revolution: The State and the Urban Poor in Mexico* (Princeton, N.J., 1977).

78. See Fournier, "Les Forces de sécurité," p. 290 ff.

8. From the Law-Abiding Military to the Terrorist State

1. See Ernst Halperin, *Nationalism and Communism in Chile* (Cambridge, Mass., 1965), pp. 27–28.

2. Theodor Wyckoff, "Tres modalidades del militarismo latinoamericano," *Combate* (San José, Costa Rica) (September-October 1960):15.

3. Figures presented to the United Nations Subcommittee for the Prevention of Discrimination and the Protection of Minorities. See *Le Monde*, 21–22 August 1977. See also the reports of Amnesty International.

4. According to an officer, Julio César Cooper, in a press conference organized by Amnesty International. See "Uruguay: Filling Gaps," in *Latin American Political Report* (London) 9 March 1979. See also the revelations of a military man, H. W. García Rivas, in *Proceso* (México), 16 June 1980.

5. See "Répression en Uruguay. A côté des méthodes de torture 'classique,' des techniques pharmacologiques sont de plus en plus souvent employées," *Le Monde*, 20 June 1978, and "Le laboratoire uruguayen," *Le Monde*, 14 June 1979.

6. The Dirección Nacional de Inteligencia, directly attached to the head of state was replaced in August 1977 by the National Center of Information, which had the same functions.

7. Except during the crisis of 1891 in which President Balmaceda opposed the Congress, ending in the suicide of the president after a brief civil war. Balmaceda favored a more active role for the state in the national economy. On the "enclave state" see among others Aníbal Pinto, "Desarrollo económico y relaciones sociales en Chile," *Trimestre económico* (Mexico City) (October–December 1963):641–658.

8. See Antonio García, "Reflexiones sobre los cambios políticos en América latina. Las clases medias y el sistema de poder," *Revista mexicana de sociología* (July-September 1968):593–602.

9. See Fernando Henrique Cardoso and E. Faletto, *Dépendance et développement en Amérique latine* pp. 118–135.

10. Atilio Borón, "El estudio de la movilización política en América latina: la movilización electoral en la Argentina y Chile," *Desarrollo económico* (Buenos Aires) (July-September 1972):211–243. See also Ricardo Cruz Coke, *Geografía electoral de Chile* (Santiago, 1952), pp. 13–50.

11. Until 1937 peasant unions were illegal. Then they were tolerated but it was difficult to establish them legally. The exclusion of illiterates from voting also reduced the participation of the peasants.

12. See Maurice Zeitlin, "The Social Determinants of Political Democracy in Chile," in James Petras et al., *Latin America. Reform or Revolution?* (Greenwich, Conn., 1968), pp. 220–234.

13. Ibid., p. 232; García, "Reflexiones sobre," p. 548.

14. See Liliana de Riz, *Sociedad y Política en Chile* (*de Portales a Pinochet*) (México, 1979), pp. 60–63.

15. See Hansen, "Career Motivation," pp. 119–136, and Antonio Cavalla Rojas, "Organización y Estructura de las fuerzas armadas chilenas" (México, 1978, mimeographed), pp. 60–65.

16. Régis Debray, *Entretiens avec Allende sur la situation au Chili* (Paris, 1971), pp. 34–41 (*The Chilean Revolution, Conversations with Allende*, New York, 1971).

17. The CIA was authorized to spend $3 million to assure the election of Frei. At least half of that sum was used. See U.S. Congress, Senate, Select Committee on Intelligence Activities, *Covert Action in Chile, 1963–1973*, Staff Rept., 94th Cong., 1st sess., 1975, pp. 9–15. Frei is supposed to have received this aid without his knowledge.

18. The slow pace of the reform was made still worse by the exclusion of the temporary workers on the fundos from its benefits. In his first year and making use of the same law, Allende expropriated as many holdings as Frei had done between 1965 and 1970. He too had a problem with the temporary agricultural workers.

19. Fabio Vidigal Xavier de Silveira, *Frei, el Kerensky chileno* (Buenos Aires, 1968), 173 pp.

20. de Riz, *Sociedad y Política*, p. 199.

21. See the declarations of the different parties, "Declaraciones para la historia," *Punto Final* (Santiago) 28 October 1969. See also the debates in the senate with the speech by A. M. Carrera in favor of the army, República de Chile, *Diario de sesiones del Senado*, 29 October 1969, pp. 130–134. Senator Aniceto Rodríguez was forced to answer accusations of *golpismo* in later statements while declaring that his party could not defend "a decadent (*trasnochado*) civilianism." See *Ultima Hora* (Santiago), 11 November 1969.

22. This is the claim at least of General Viaux. See Florencia Varas *Conversaciones con Viaux* (Santiago, 1972), p. 120. Allende is supposed to have offered him an ambassadorship.

23. See Augusto Varas, Felipe Aguero and Felipe Bustamente, *Chile. Democracia, fuerzas armadas* (Santiago, 1980), chap. 11, pp. 170–177.

24. Federico Fasano Mertens, *Después de la derrota, un eslabón débil llamado Uruguay* (México, 1980), p. 139.

25. Wyckoff, "Tres modalidades," pp. 13–14.

26. Uruguayan productivity is strikingly low compared to that of other specialized economies of the same type. For example, the productivity of milk production is one fourth that of New Zealand. Sheep produce 2.9 kilos of wool per head against 4.5 kilos for New Zealand. To produce a ton of meat it is necessary to have

twenty-seven cows in Uruguay; seventeen are sufficient in Argentina and thirteen in Holland. A lack of investment is one of the causes of that situation.

27. The rate of increase in production fluctuated around 0 percent between 1951 and 1968.

28. The annual rate of increase in per capita GNP was .7 percent between 1950 and 1960, and −.1 percent from 1960 until 1978. ONU-CEPAL (Economic Commission for Latin America), *Estudio económico de América latina* (New York, 1970).

29. The rise in the cost of living reached 136 percent in 1967.

30. On a scale in which 1957 represented 100, it was at a level of 60.2 compared with 91.4 for industry. Universidad de la República, Instituto de Economía, *El Proceso económico en el Uruguay* (Montevideo, 1969), pp. 274–330.

31. See, among others, the book by Gabriel Smirnow, *La Revolución desarmada. Chile 1970–1973* (Mexico City, 1977), 278 pp.

32. According to Joán Garcés, one of the Allende's advisors. See especially "Allende, les militaires et la voie socialiste au Chili," *Le Monde*, 18 and 19 December 1973.

33. The incident of the "Cuban crates" addressed to the president's office that were unloaded at the international airport of Santiago suffices to prove the vigilance of the military. At the beginning of 1972 it was learned that mysterious crates coming from Cuba had arrived at Pudahuel. The opposition spoke of the importation of arms. The government responded that they contained works of art. The tension that followed led to the adoption of the Law on the Control of Arms that permitted the armed forces to carry out raids anywhere that they suspected that their monopoly was being violated. The law was used against the left by seditious sectors of the military. See Paul E. Sigmund, *The Overthrow of Allende and the Politics of Chile, 1964–1976* (Pittsburgh, Pa., 1977), p. 183.

34. Carlos Altamirano, *Chili, les raisons d'une défaite* (Paris, 1979), p. 130. Altamirano attributes that suggestion to General Prats, the night before his resignation.

35. According to Régis Debray, "Il est mort dans sa loi," *Le Nouvel Observateur*, 17 September 1973.

36. *Covert Action in Chile*, pp. 9–15, U.S. Congress, Senate, Committee on Foreign Relations, *Multinational Corporations and United States Foreign Policy*, Hearings, 93d Cong., 1st sess., 1973, Part 1, "The International Telephone and Telegraph Co. and Chile, 1970–1971." See also the Committee on Foreign Relations, *Alleged Assassination Plots Involving Foreign Leaders*, Interim Report, 1975.

37. *Alleged Assassination*, pp. 240–248, and P. García, ed., *El Caso Schneider* (Santiago, 1972).

38. See *Covert Action in Chile*, p. 25, and "The International Telephone," pp. 626–720.

39. Thirteen million dollars were spent for that purpose. See Joán Garcés, *Allende et l'Expérience chilienne* (Paris, 1976), p. 62.

40. "The International Telephone," pp. 623–624.

41. Marcel Niedergang, "Le pouvoir derrière les fusils," *Le Monde* 2 November 1972.

42. U.S. Agency for International Development, Statistics and Report Division, *U.S. Overseas Loans and Grants and Assistance from International Organizations: Obligation and Loan Authorizations, 1945–1972* (Washington D.C., 1973). See also U.S. House, *United States-Chilean Relations, Hearings before the Subcommittee on Inter-American Affairs of the Committee on Foreign Affairs*, 93d Cong., 1st sess., 6 May 1973, pp. 13–14.

43. According to the U.S. Defense Department, *Military Assistance and Military Sales* (Washington, D.C., 1967, 1971, 1975), reproduced in *Aportes* (Paris) (October 1967):55; *Marcha* (Montevideo), 14 July 1972; *NACLA Report* (New York) (January 1976).

44. Carlos Prats, *Una vida por la legalidad* (México, 1976), p. 44. The memorandum presented by the generals to Allende in April 1973 insisted on two points—the delimitation of the sectors of the economy, and relations with the United States.

45. Ibid., p. 34.

46. The policy of economic expansion and the increase in the buying power of the workers raised the profits of the small- and medium-sized enterprises; the extension of social security to independent workers helped the middle classes. See the debate on the middle classes and a possible "historical compromise" in *Punto Final*, a publication close to the MIR, "En pos de las clases medias," 15 February 1972; "La clases medias y el poder de los trabajadores," 25 March 1972. Also Antonio Bandeira, *Ideological Struggle in Chile: The Middle Class and the Military* (Toronto, 1974).

47. The Twenty-Second Congress of the Chilean Socialist party in Chillán in 1967 supported "revolutionary violence (as) the only way that will lead to the taking of political and economic power," legal forms of actions being considered as leading to armed struggle. See Joxe, *Le Chili sous Allende* (Paris, 1974), pp. 38–39.

48. Garcés, *Allende et l'Expérience chilienne*, (Paris, 1976) p. 177, and Joxe, ibid.

49. The split of the left of the Christian Democrats began in 1969 with

the creation of the MAPU (Movement for United Popular Action) by founders of the Christian Democratic party such as Rafael Gumucio and important personalities such as Jacques Chonchol. The MAPU was part of Popular Unity. In July 1971 another left group that supported Allende broke with the Christian Democrats to form the Izquierda Cristiana.

50. See Manuel Cabieses Donoso, "Una dictadura popular necesaria," *Punto Final*, 3 July 1973 for the point of view of the MIR. On popular power see the article of A. Silva and P. Santa Lucía, "Los cordones industriales," *Les Temps modernes* (January 1975): 707–743.

51. From October to March 1971, 177 articles on page 1 of *El Mercurio* gave examples of that "disorder." See Garcés, *Allende*, p. 191.

52. In fact food supplies were taken over by popular councils, the JAP Provisioning and Price Committees, established in July 1971, which became transformed into a partisan political army. Food supplies were also handled by a secretariat for distribution and marketing that was headed from 1973 by General Alberto Bachelet.

53. See Garcés, "L'affaire Toha," in *Le Problème chilien. Démocratie et contre-révolution* (Verviers, Belgium, 1975), pp. 139–182.

54. Ricardo Cox, "Defensa social interna," in Instituto de Estudios Generales, *Fuerzas armadas y Seguridad nacional* (Santiago, 1973), pp. 91–117.

55. This was revealed by General Pinochet in 1974. *Le Monde*, 15 March 1974.

56. See among others Federico Fasano Mertens, *Después de la derrota*, pp. 150–151.

57. See the detailed analysis of the events and resolutions in the article by François Lerrin and Cristina Torres, "Les transformations institutionelles de l'Uruguay, 1973–1978," *Problèmes d'Amérique latine*, no. 49 (November 1978):9–57.

58. In an interview with the Brazilian weekly, *Veja*, 30 December 1974.

59. From the name of the reformist Colorado president, Batlle y Ordoñez, founder of modern Uruguay.

60. As Act II, article 7, specifies, "The preservation of national security is the area of direct responsibility of the armed forces through the organs established by law." *Diario oficial de la República oriental del Uruguay. Documentos*, 28 June 1978, p. 3.

61. That act created a national council made up of the twenty-five members of the Council of State and the junta of generals that included twenty-one officers. That new council legislated by a

two-thirds majority, giving military a veto power. Its function was to name the president of the republic.

62. *Actos institucionales*, suplemento especial de *El Soldado* (n.d.), p. 31.

63. As stated in the introductory clauses of the Second Act: thanks to the "coherent and systematic action of the armed forces" the executive is the "backbone of the political organization of the nation," *Diario oficial*, p. 2.

64. See the anonymous report apparently of military origin published by the Mexican magazine, "Uruguay la vida cotidiana," *Cuadernos del Tercer Mundo* (January 1978):95. The official figures that appear in the *Military Balance* of London are much lower.

65. Thanks to the newly permitted press freedom in Brazil, the kidnapping of two refugees in Porto Alegre (Rio Grande do Sul) by the Uruguayan police revealed what had been standard practice in earlier years. Since the political climate had changed in Brazil, the incident caused a certain amount of diplomatic tension between the two countries. See *Veja*, 29 November 1978, and *Isto é*, 29 November 1978.

66. There is a very complete report on the changes that took place and the policies followed in the dossier prepared by the International Organization of Professors (OIP) and the International Federation of Teachers Unions (FISE). This was submitted to the UNESCO General Assembly in Paris in October 1978, "Uruguay (1973–1978). Notes on Education, Science, Culture, Communication," mimeographed, 62 pp.

67. See the interview with Wilson Ferreira Aldunate by J. P. Clerc, *Le Monde*, 7 September 1978.

68. Interview with Garcés, 13 November 1973. See also Paul W. Drake, *Socialism and Populism in Chile, 1932–1952* (Urbana, Ill., 1978), pp. 333–335, and Joxe, "L'armée chilienne et les avatars de la transition," *Les temps modernes* (June 1973):2006–2036.

69. See *New York Times*, 27 September 1973; *Latin American Political Report* (London), 9 November 1973; *Le Monde*, 15 September 1973; *Le Nouvel Observateur*, 1 and 8 October 1973; also, interview with J. Garcés, 13 November 1973.

70. See interview with General Pinochet published in *Le Monde*, 15 March 1974.

71. The Contraloría, an institution halfway between the French Council of State and the Court of Accounts, made life difficult for Salvador Allende.

72. In December 1977, The General Assembly of the United Nations condemned Chile for its violations of human rights. In January

1978 General Pinochet organized a plebiscite asking the voters to choose, either supporting him or approving the UN resolution.

73. Augusto Pinochet, *Geopolítica* (Santiago, 1968).

74. Speech of Augusto Pinochet, *El Mercurio* (Santiago), international edition, 11 June 1977.

75. Quoted by Philippe Grenier, "Le Chile du général Pinochet," *Problèmes d'Amérique latine*, no. 58 (December 1980):46.

76. *El Mercurio*, international edition, 11 August 1975.

77. Sergio Bitar, "Libertad económica y dictadura política. La junta militar chilena, 1973–1978," *Comercio exterior* (México) 29 October 1979, p. 1070.

78. See the writings of Mario Lanzarotti and Carlos Ominami, especially "Vers une nouvelle régulation économique," *Amérique latine* (Paris), no. 6 (Summer 1981):42.

79. Ibid., p. 43. Banque Sudaméris, *Études économiques. La situation économique du Chili* (Paris, October 1980).

80. Bitar, "Libertad económica," p. 1074.

81. The protein consumption per person per day went from 53.2 grams in 1974 to 43.1 grams in 1978. See H. Vega, "Políticas económicas y desmultiplicación de los panes," *Análisis* (Santiago), no. 6 (1979). See also "¿Cómo vive nuestro trabajador? Los salarios reales," *Mensaje* (Santiago) (September 1977), and BID, *Progreso económico y social en América latina* (Washington, D.C., 1978).

82. Sergio Spoerer, *Los Desafíos del tiempo fecundo* (Mexico City, 1980), p. 43.

83. R. Urzúa, "Salud: impacto de la recesión y deterioro de sus niveles," *Mensaje* (July 1977), and Bitar, "Libertad económica," p. 1076.

84. Ibid., p. 1073.

85. *Business Latin America*, 30 March 1977, quoted by Carlos Ominami, "Libéralisation au Chili," *Le Monde diplomatique* (January 1981).

86. According to Bitar, "Libertad económica," p. 1073, and from 27.2 percent in 1970 to 24 percent in 1979 according to Ominami and Lanzarotti, "Vers une nouvelle," p. 42.

87. "Chile-ficción. La política en 1982," *¿Qué pasa?* (Santiago) 26 April 1979.

88. See the classic *Mapa de la extrema riqueza* of F. Dahse (Santiago, 1979).

89. See "Chile's Radical Experiment," *Newsweek* 25 May 1981, and the dossier published by *Amérique latine:* "Chili, un projet de révo-

lution capitaliste." On the changes in mental attitudes see the economic supplement to *Ercilla* (Santiago), no. 6 (1981), explaining the advantages of the market system. On the capitalization system of retirement funds as opposed to that based on social solidarity, see "Reforma provisional: compare su futuro," *Ercilla* 26 November 1980, and the pertinent comments by Javier Martínez, "Chile Nuevo: une fois encore," *Amérique latine* (Summer 1981):27–29.

90. *El Día* (Montevideo), 27 May 1977.

91. For a study of the theoretical foundations of the new economic policy see José Manuel Quijano, "Uruguay: balance de un modelo friedmaniano," *Comercio exterior* (Mexico City) (February 1978):173–211. For a more political interpretation of the relations between the military regime and the overall economic program, see Nelson Minello, *La Militarización del Estado en América latina. Un análisis de Uruguay* (México, 1976), 42 pp.

92. According to the neoliberal publication that speaks for Vegh Villegas, *Búsqueda* (Montevideo) (May 1975).

93. Theotonio Dos Santos, "Socialismo y fascismo en América latina," *Revista mexicana de sociología* (January-March 1977):186–187.

94. This is the thesis of colonial fascism advanced not long ago by Helio Jaguaribe for Brazil (see *Le Temps modernes* [October 1967]: 602), and often repeated today. See "Fascismo y colonialismo en el caso chileno," *Chile-América* (Rome) (July-August 1977):70–80. For a criticism of these views see Atilio Borón, "El fascismo como categoría histórica: en torno al problema de las dictaduras en América latina," *Revista mexicana de sociología* (April-June 1977): 481–530.

95. Manuel Antonio Garretón, "Procesos políticos en un régimen autoritario. Dinámicas de institucionalización y oposición en Chile, 1973–1980" (Santiago, 1980, mimeographed), p. 9.

96. According to Federico Fasola Mertens, *Después de la derrota*, p. 148.

97. Sudaméris, *Etudes économiques. La situation chilienne.*

9. THE EXCEPTION TO THE RULE: PRAETORIAN REPUBLICS AND MILITARY PARTIES

1. See Rouquié, "Argentine 1977: anarchie militaire ou Etat terroriste?" *Etudes* (October 1977):325–339.

2. Thus the Communist party, which was legal at the time, commenting a year before the coup d'état on a speech of President

Isabel Perón already called for the "formation of a democratic coalition government made up of civilians and patriotic military men," (*Nuestra palabra*, organ of the Argentine Communist party, 26 February 1976).

3. The movement of the Montoneros. The Marxist-Leninist Revolutionary Army of the People (ERP) emerged out of Trotskyism.

4. Thomas E. Skidmore, *Politics in Brazil, 1930–1964. An Experiment in Democracy* (New York, 1967).

5. See Stepan, *The Military in Politics* pp. 85–88, and Luciano Martins, "Notes sur le rôle et le comportement des militaires au Brésil," in Anouar Abdel-Malek, *L'Armée dans la nation* (*Alger, 1975*), pp. 241–254.

6. See Lewis A. Tambs, "Five Times against the System: Brazilian Foreign Military Expeditions and their Effect on National Politics," in Henry H. Keith et al., eds., *Perspectives on Armed Politics in Brazil* (Tempe, Ariz., 1976), pp. 179–206.

7. According to the interpretation of Charles Morazé in his classic book *Les Trois Ages du Brésil* (Paris, 1954), pp. 80–88.

8. João Camilo Oliveira Torres, "As fôrças armadas como fôrça política," *Revista brasileira de estudios políticos* (Belo Horizonte) (January 1966):39–41.

9. See Flynn, *Brazil*. p. 518.

10. See especially María Victoria Mesquita Benavides, *O Governo de Kubitschek: Desenvolvimento economico e estabilidade política, 1956–1961* (Rio de Janeiro, 1976), pp. 158–165.

11. On the political role of the Clube Militar see Robert A. Hayes, "The Military Club and National Politics in Brazil," in Keith, et al., eds., *Perspectives on Armed Politics*, pp. 139–171 as well as Paul Manor, "Factions et idéologies dans l'armée brésilienne; nationalistes et liberaux, 1946–1951," *Revue d'histoire moderne et contemporaine* (Paris) (October-December 1978):556–586, and Antonio Carlos Peixoto, "Le Clube militar et les affrontements au sein des forces armées, 1945–1964," in Rouquié, ed., *Les Partis militaires au Brésil* (Paris, 1980), pp. 65–104.

12. We are borrowing the concept of Huntington without agreeing with his neoinstitutionalism. The "general politicization of all social forces and institutions" that characterizes "praetorian societies" is not explained by a tautological reference to the weakness of political institutions. See Huntington, *Political Order in Changing Societies* (New Haven, Conn., 1967).

13. Quoted by Skidmore, *Politics in Brazil*, pp. 57–60.

14. Werneck Sodrè, *Historia militar do Brasil* (Rio de Janeiro, 1965), especially pp. 405–408.

15. The U.S. ambassador, Lincoln Gordon, did not hesitate to hail the fall of Goulart as "a great victory for the free world . . . in which the West could have lost all the South American republics." Message from Gordon to Dean Rusk, 2 April 1964, quoted by Phyllis R. Parker, *Brazil and the Quiet Intervention, 1964* (Austin, 1979), pp. 82–83.

16. Clearly expressed by the Foreign Minister of General Medici, Gibson Barbosa, to the representatives of Business International in 1970, *Jornal do Brasil* (Rio de Janeiro) (29 October 1970).

17. Flynn, *Brazil*, p. 274.

18. As a result of the sudden resignation of President Quadros who had been elected with the support of the UDN.

19. Several authors claim, even today, that the sergeants' revolt, as well as the later navy mutinies, were prepared and initiated by anti-Communist *agents provocateurs.*

20. As L. Martins correctly observes, *Notes,* p. 252.

21. General José Campos Aragão, "A revolução en marcha," *A defesa nacional* (Rio de Janeiro), (May–June 1965):14.

22. See Flynn, *Brazil,* p. 321.

23. See Ronald M. Schneider, *The Political System of Brazil: The Emergence of a Modernizing Authoritarian Regime, 1964–1970* (New York, 1971).

24. According to the thesis by Raymundo Faoro, *Os Donos do poder (Formação de patronato político brasileiro)* (Rio de Janeiro, 1958), pp. 226–270.

25. L. Martins, *Pouvoir et Développement économique. Formation et évolution des structures politiques au Brésil* (Paris, 1976), p. 28.

26. See Wanderley Guilherme Dos Santos, "Uma revisão da crise brasileira," *Cadernos braileiros* (São Paulo) (November-December 1966):51–57.

27. See *Revista brasileira de estudios políticos* (Belo Horizonte), special issue on national security (July 1966):136.

28. Monteiro, *A Revolução,* p. 181.

29. Lecture of General Garrastazú Medici at the Superior War School, 12 March 1970, reproduced in *Estrategia* (Buenos Aires), no. 5 (1970):59–60.

30. Cardoso, *Autoritarismo e Democratização* (Rio de Janeiro, 1975), p. 48.

31. Michel de Certeau, "Les chrétiens et la dictature au Brésil," *Politique aujourd'hui* (November 1969):45.

32. See Carlos F. Díaz Alejandro, *Essays on the Economic History of the Argentine Republic* (New Haven, Conn., 1970), pp. 370–400, and

Aldo Ferrer, *La Economía argentina* (*Las etapas de su desarrollo y problemas actuales*) (México, 1963), p. 250.

33. See UN-CEPAL (Economic Commission for Latin America), *El Desarrollo económico y la Distribución del ingreso en la Argentina* (New York, 1968), pp. 217 ff.

34. UN-CEPAL, *El Desarrollo económico de la Argentina* (New York, 1959), p. 23.

35. This has been well demonstrated for the beginning of the century by Jorge F. Sábato in his very suggestive, "Notas sobre la formación de la clase dominante en la Argentina moderna, 1880–1914" (Buenos Aires, CISEA, 1979, mimeographed). This was also noticed at the time by perceptive foreign observers such as Jules Huret, *En Argentine: de Buenos Aires au grand Chaco* (Paris, 1911), especially p. 36.

36. This is the expression of Horowitz, "The Norm of Illegitimacy: The Political Sociology of Latin America," in Irving Horowitz et al., *Latin American Radicalism* (London, 1969), p. 5.

37. During which a junta of ministers from the three services temporarily seized power removing the vice president, Pedro Aleixo, who was the constitutional successor.

38. See Cardoso, "Les impasses du régime autoritaire: les cas brésilien," *Problèmes d'Amérique latine*, no. 54 (December 1979):89–108.

39. On the "elections with variable rules" see Rouquié, "Le modèle brésilien à l'épreuve," *Etudes* (May, 1977), pp. 625–640.

40. According to *Veja* (Rio de Janeiro), 15 October 1969.

41. We know that two of its former heads became president. General Médici declared just before he took power: "The exercise of the direction of the organization of national information has enabled me to know the inside and outside of men and things." *Industria e Produtividade* (Rio de Janeiro) (November 1969).

42. There were 646 civilians among the 1,276 graduates of the ESG between 1950 and 1967, according to Barry Ames, *Rhetoric and Reality in a Military Regime: Brazil since 1964* (Beverly Hills, Calif., 1975), pp. 8–9.

43. See J. E. Greño Velasco, "La controversia argentina-brasileña en el Alto Paraná," *Revista de política internacional* (Madrid), no. 133 (May–June 1974):94–109, and Osny Duarte Pereira, *Itaipú: pros e contras: breve analise da historia das relações entre Argentine, Uruguai e Brasil e ensaio político-juridico sobre o aproveitamento hidrelétrico do Rio Paraná* (Rio de Janeiro, 1974), 667 pp.

44. *Criterio* (Buenos Aires), 23 March 1967.

45. This emerges from the first conclusions of the unpublished field-

work carried out in 1981 by the team of Dr. Roca of the *Communitá di ricerca* of Milan.

46. According to C. Andino Martínez, "El estamento militar en El Salvador," *Estudios centro-americanos* (San Salvador, July–August 1979):625.

47. "Ejército guerrillero del pueblo. Manifiesto internacional," communique published in *El País* (Madrid), 26 October 1979.

48. Hélène Rivière d'Arc, "L'armée aménageur et entrepreneur en Bolivie," *L'Espace géographique* (Paris), no. 2 (1979):93–103.

49. General Mosconi, the dynamic director of the national petroleum company, persuaded the state to decree a single price for petroleum products, to the considerable damage of the foreign companies.

50. Law No. 12,709, "Dirección general de fabricaciones militares," *Boletín oficial* (Buenos Aires), 9 October 1941.

51. Article 170 of the federal constitution of 1967.

52. *Jornal do Brasil* (Rio de Janeiro), 2 October 1970.

53. Werner Baer, Richard Newfarmer, and Thomas Trebat, "On State Capitalism in Brazil: Some New Issues and Questions," in *Interamerican Economic Affairs* (Washington, D.C.) (Winter 1976):81.

54. Because of the Employment Guarantee Funds (FGTS) and the Program of Social Integration (PIS) to which the workers are obliged to contribute.

55. See Celso Lafer, *O Sistema político brasileiro* (Rio de Janeiro, 1975), p. 79.

56. See Riordan Roett, "The Brazilian Military and the Expansion of State Power: Implications for Social Change" (Washington, D.C., 1976, mimeographed), pp. 10–11; " 'Quem é quem' as grandes empresas no Brasil," *A opinião* (São Paulo), 8 October 1973; "A Monopoly Game," *Newsweek,* 18 June 1979; *Veja* (Rio de Janeiro), 22 July 1981.

57. See *Movimento* (São Paulo) (February 1977) "Os empresarios brasileiros e a democracia," and Peter Evans, "Multinationals, State-Owned Corporations and the Transformation of Imperialism: A Brazilian Case Study," *Economic Development and Cultural Change* (Chicago) (October 1977):56–60.

58. "O Estado abre espaço," *Veja,* 22 July 1981.

59. Editorial in *O Estado de São Paulo,* 16 January 1977, and "Brazil tolhe multinational, diz *Wall Street Journal," Jornal do Brasil,* 9 October 1976.

60. Cardoso, *Autoritarismo e Democratização,* p. 198.

61. Quoted by *Latin America, Regional Reports, Southern Cone* (London:

Latin American Newsletters), 26 June 1981. *Búsqueda* is the press organ of the former minister Vegh Villegas, who directed the Uruguayan reform after 1974.

62. Fidel Castro, *La Historia me absolverá* (Havana, 1967), p. 18.

63. Jerry Weaver, "La élite política de un régimen dominado por los militares: el ejemplo de Guatemala," *Revista latinoamericana de sociología* (Buenos Aires) 1 (1969):24.

64. "Bolivia: The Generation Gap," *Latin America Political Report* (London) 12 January 1979, p. 10.

65. Hugo Abreu, *O Outro lado do Poder* (Porto Alegre, 1978), p. 95.

66. Lowenthal, "The Political Role," pp. 314–316.

67. "Para-quedistas: democracia, volver?" *Movimento* (São Paulo) 16 October 1978.

68. General Abreu backed the candidate of the dissident military, General Euler Bentes, who was supported by the civilian opposition against General Figueiredo in 1978. See "Hugo Abreu, o general dissidente," interview published in the periodical of the extreme left, *Em tempo* (São Paulo), 10 May 1979.

69. Rigoberto Padilla, "El proceso democratizador en Honduras," *Revista internacional* (Prague), no. 12 (1974):69.

70. "Crónica internacional. Considerações sobre a guerra de Coreia," *Revista do Clube militar* (Rio de Janeiro) (July 1950):75–80, quoted by Paul Manor, "Factions et idéologies," pp. 556–586.

71. *Correio da Manha*, 16 December 1950, quoted by Peixoto, "Le Clube militar," p. 88.

72. Document published by Helio Silva in 1964: *Golpe o Contragolpe* (Rio de Janeiro, 1975), pp. 200–201.

73. See especially Leonel Gómez and Bruce Cameron, "El Salvador: the Current Danger. American Myths," in *Foreign Policy*, no. 43 (Summer 1981):75.

74. R. N. Adams, "The Development of the Guatemalan Military", pp. 101–102.

10. REVOLUTION BY THE GENERAL STAFF

1. See the significant headlines of some articles published in France in 1969. For example, C. Morange, "Y a-t-il des gorilles progressistes?" *La Nouvelle Critique* (April 1969), and P. Nourry, "Pérou: des militaires pas comme les autres," *Croissance des jeunes nations* (October 1969).

2. See chapter 4.

3. See Jacques Lambert, *Amérique latine. Structures sociales et institutions politiques* (Paris, 1963), pp. 291–293.

4. On this military progressivism see the case studies published in the collective work, *La Politique de Mars. Les processus politiques au sein des partis militaires*, ed. and intro. A. Rouquié (Paris, 1981), as well as A. Rouquié, "Le camarade et le commandant, réformisme militaire et légitimité institutionnelle," *Revue française de science politique* (June 1979).

5. See the quotations published by Manuel Urriza in his book, *Perú: cuando los militares se van* (Caracas, 1978), pp. 165–166.

6. According to the *Estatuto del gobierno revolucionario*, which became Decree-Law 17.063.

7. "Manifesto del gobierno revolucionario," *El Comercio* (Lima), 4 October 1968.

8. See especially J. Velasco Alvarado in *La Voz de la revolución*, vol. 2 (Lima, 1971), pp. 10–12.

9. See *Plan Inca. Plan del gobierno revolucionario de la fuerza armada* (Lima, n.d.), pp. 46–47.

10. In a "Message to the Nation," published in *La Política del gobierno revolucionario* (Lima) (July 1973), pp. 17–18.

11. Castro mentioned the Peruvian military regime in favorable terms for the first time on 14 July 1969, in a speech to thirty thousand sugar workers at the beginning of the ten-million-ton sugar harvest.

12. See, among others, Bourricaud, "Perú: ¿Los militares porqué y para qué?" *Aportes* (Paris) (April 1970), and Nelson Rimensnyder, "Los militares y la modernización del Perú," *Estudios internacionales* (Santiago de Chile) (April–June 1970), p. 91.

13. Because of the application of an amendment to the *Foreign Military Sales Act* that provided for the suspension of military sales to Peru, the government responded by expelling the North American military mission and refusing a visit by Nelson Rockefeller (May 1969).

14. According to the 1961 census, 83.2 percent of the rural properties were less than 5 hectares in size, and comprised 7 percent of the cultivated land, while .4 percent of the agricultural units were over 500 hectares and comprised 75.6 percent of the land in use. See E. Flores, "La reforma agraria en el Perú," *Trimestre económico* (July–September 1970), and Hernando Aguirre Gamio, "El proceso de la reforma agraria en el Perú," *Mundo nuevo* (Buenos Aires, Paris) (January 1970).

15. "Presidential Message to the Nation," Lima, 24 June 1969, published in *Estudios internacionales* (Santiago de Chile) (October–December, 1969):395.

16. "Decreto-Ley no. 17, 716, article 3 (ley de reforma agraria)" in *Nueva Legislación sobre reforma agraria* (Lima, 1970).

17. A first regulation issued in 1972 aimed at limiting the influence of the APRA-dominated unions excluded from the elections to the administrative bodies of the cooperatives all the former political party and union officers.

18. Ley de reforma agraria, article 39.

19. "Message to the Nation," p. 387.

20. See Jean Piel, "Réforme, problèmes et conflits agraires au Pérou. La situation en 1975," in *Problèmes d'Amérique latine,* no. 36 (May 1975):75, and Ute Schirmer, "Reforma agraria y cooperativismo en el Perú," *Revista mexicana de sociología* (July–September 1977): 799–847.

21. "Message to the Nation," p. 388.

22. Ley de reforma agraria, Article 181. That possibility was not utilized by those who held the agrarian reform bonds, it is true.

23. The marketing of iron ore was transferred to the state in 1971, the export of fishmeal was also taken over in 1970. In 1973, the production of fishmeal was nationalized. It is true that the fishmeal companies were in a very difficult financial situation because of the drop in prices and the reduction in marine life. Fishmeal, in which Peru ranks first in the world in exports, constituted its most important export.

24. See José Martínez, *Una nueva etapa en el proceso revolucionario. La clase obrera ante la ley de industrias (Informe presentado al comité central del partido comunista peruano)* (Lima, 29 and 30 August 1970), p. 24.

25. The Financial Development Corporation, created in 1971 to provide financing to state enterprises and to the social sector (the future enterprises to be created by the workers themselves).

26. The major idea of the regime in its attempt to distinguish itself from capitalism and communism, which was to provide it with its political identity, was the creation of a self-managed area of Social Property. A law was finally issued (Decree-Law 20,558) in April 1974, but its application was soon suspended as a result of the change of government that took place in 1975. It called for a special property sector made up of enterprises created by the workers. The opposition of the military did not permit that form

of property to develop. See Carlos Franco, *Perú Participación popular* (Lima, 1979), pp. 122–126.

27. The Peruvian government initiated campaigns to attract capital through its embassies, governmental missions, and the international press (See *New York Times*, 28 September 1969). The foreign investment was to be carried out on the basis of a contract of limited duration with the state.

28. The second phase of the revolution after the overthrow of General Velasco Alvarado in 1975 led by General Morales Bermudez took steps to cut back or limit the impact of the reforms of the earlier regime before handing back the government to the civilians in 1980.

29. In the opinion of General Velasco Alvarado when he was interviewed by *Le Monde*, 3 February 1973. See the protest of the employers' organization against the "collectivist" orientation of the government, *Expreso* (Lima), 12 August 1970.

30. See Lowenthal, "Peru's Revolutionary Government of the Armed Forces. Background and Context," in Catherine McArdle Kelleher, ed., *Political-Military Systems: Comparative Perspectives* (Beverly Hills, Calif., 1974), p. 148.

31. This is the title of a book by Albert Meister on what he calls "the Peruvian experiment in the management of underdevelopment," (Toulouse, 1981).

32. These words were often used by the minister of mines, General Fernández Maldonado, one of the "initiators" of the process.

33. See Villanueva, ¿*Nueva Mentalidad?* Villanueva is a former commander in the Peruvian army who labored in the ranks of the APRA.

34. This is the theory of Einaudi and Stepan in their study, *Latin American Institutional Development*.

35. Put forward by Henry Pease García in *El Ocaso del poder oligárquico* (Lima, 1977).

36. See, for a sophisticated interpretation along these lines, the study by George E. Philip, *The Rise and Fall of the Peruvian Military Radicals* (London, 1978), p. 40.

37. This is the opinion of Villanueva, ¿*Nueva Mentalidad?* and of Einaudi and Stepan, *Latin American*. See also Luis Valdez, "Antecedentes de la nueva orientación de las fuerzas armadas en el Perú," *Aportes* (Paris) (January 1971):175–178.

38. Such as General Tantaleán or even Velasco Alvarado. On the influence of the writings of the founder of the APRA, Haya de la Torre, see Franco, *Perú, Participación popular*, p. 18.

39. As Urriza correctly notes in his book, *Perú*, pp. 90–92.

40. Interview in *Croissance des jeunes nations*, 1 February 1974, p. 11. See also Edgar Mercado Jarrín, "La seguridad integral en el proceso peruano," *Estrategia* (Buenos Aires) (March 1973):74–84.

41. See "Acción nacionalista revolucionaria. Programa de principios," *El Diario* (La Paz), 31 August 1969, and "Proclamaron a Ovando en Quillacollo," *El Diario*, 13 September 1969.

42. Domitila Barrios de Chungara, *Domitila. Si on me donne la parole. La vie d'une femme de la mine bolivienne*, interview by Moema Viezzer (Paris, 1980), p. 177.

43. René Zavaleta Mercado, "Bolivia, de la Asamblea popular al combate de agosto," in James Petras et al., *América latina. Economía y Política* (Buenos Aires, 1972).

44. Augusto Céspedes, "Bolivia, un Vietnam simbólico y barato," *Marcha* (Montevideo), 1 October 1971.

45. This gave him real popularity after the anti-American demonstrations in 1964. See Larry Piffim, "The Challenge in Panama," *Current History* (January 1966):6.

46. Speech by Torrijos, 9 August 1971, quoted by Gilhodes in his book, *Paysans de Panama*.

47. "Panama: Confrontation," *Latin America Weekly Report* (London), 14 April 1972.

48. See Gilhodes, *Paysans de Panama*, pp. 196–200.

49. According to *Valeurs actuelles*, "Les coffres de Panama," 21 June 1971.

50. "Panama: Another Round," *Latin America Weekly Report*, 30 November 1973. The opposition accused the governor of preparing a celebration of the twentieth anniversary of the attack by Fidel Castro on the Moncada Barracks.

51. The role of the United States in the coup and counter coup of Torrijos remains unclear. Nevertheless, the support by all the pro-American elements of the removal of the leader of the revolution was evident. We should also note that a number of claims have been made that attribute the plane accident that took Torrijos's life to sabotage by the American intelligence services. However, no material proof has yet been produced.

52. According to article 277 of the transitional provisions of 1972, quoted in Gilhodes, *Paysans de Panama*, p. 75.

53. See "Panama After Torrijos," *Newsweek*, 17 August 1981.

54. According to the text entitled, *Filosofía y Plan de acción del gobierno revolucionario nacionalista* (Quito, 1972).

55. See César Verduga, "El proceso económico ecuatoriano contem-

poráneo (análisis del período 1975–1977)," in G. Drekonja et al., eds., *Ecuador hoy* (Bogotá, 1978), pp. 61–64.

56. According to *Lineamientos fundamentales del plan integral de transformación y desarrollo* (Quito, 1972), quoted by Emmanuel Fauroux in his article: "Equateur: les lendemains d'une réforme agraire," *Problèmes d'Amérique latine*, no. 56, p. 106.

57. Jaime Galarza Zavala, "Ecuador, el oro y la pobreza," in *Ecuador hoy*, p. 37.

58. In the words of Stephen Llaidman in the *Washington Post*, 9 December 1973 ("Peru's Junta Tries to Forge a New Society by Decree").

59. "Velasco habla para la revista *Visão*," in *La Autonomía revolucionaria* (Lima) (April–May 1974):6–7.

60. See K. J. Middlebrook and D. Scott Palmer, *Military Government and Political Development: Lessons from Perú* (Beverly Hills, Calif., 1975), p. 16, and Hugo Neira, *Perú: informe urgente (El papel de las fuerzas armadas en el proceso revolucionario)* (Madrid, 1971).

61. This program, published by the radical military in 1974, is supposed to have been developed in 1968 and therefore to have had the support of the entire armed forces.

62. See Franco, *Perú Participación popular*, p. 47.

63. Middlebrook and Palmer, *Military Government*, p. 21.

64. See Richard W. Patch, "Peasantry and National Revolution, Bolivia," in K. H. Silvert, *Expectant Peoples (Nacionalism and Development)* (New York, 1961), pp. 95–126. Carlos Montenegro, who inspired Bolivian nationalism, wrote in a classic book in 1943: "It was in the Chaco that Bolivian national feeling which had disappeared for half a century was reawakened." *Nationalismo y Coloniaje* (Buenos Aires, 1967), p. 221.

65. This was the case with General Juan José Torres who told a French journalist to justify his actions: "In the 1930's we had a conflict with Paraguay which was much more important than the guerrillas, a fratricidal war waged at the instigation of imperialist petroleum interests. My father was killed. He died for the defense of the nation." *Le Monde*, 22 October 1970.

66. Speech of General Ovando, 17 October 1969. Text published in "Bolivia: ¿La segunda revolución nacional?" *Cuadernos de Marcha* (Montevideo) (October 1969):62.

67. See Mario Monteforte Toledo, *Centroamérica. Subdesarrollo y dependencia*, vol. 2 (México, 1972), p. 128. Also, El Salvador, Ministerio de Defensa, *Principios y Objetivos del gobierno revolucionario* (San Salvador, 1955) (see especially no. 2).

68. Charles W. Anderson, "El Salvador, the Army as Reformer," in

Martin C. Needler, *Political Systems of Latin America* (New York, 1970), pp. 70–77.

69. W. W. Rostow, *The Stages of Economic Growth* (New York, 1966).

70. "Changing Role of U.S. Interview with William P. Rogers, Secretary of State," *US News and World Report*, 26 January 1970.

71. *El Espectador* (Bogotá) 27 September 1968.

72. See the book by Louis Mercier-Vega, *La Révolution par l'Etat (Une nouvelle classe dirigeante en Amérique latine)* (Paris, 1978).

11. THE MILITARY STATE AND ITS FUTURE:
ADVENTURES AND MISADVENTURES OF
DEMILITARIZATION

1. We are speaking of General Manuel Odría who gave up power in July 1956 and organized free elections in which his candidate was defeated. On the waves of militarism, see Lieuwen, *Generals versus Presidents, Neo-Militarism in Latin America* (London, 1964).

2. See Adam Przeworski, "Some Problems in the Study of the Transition to Democracy," Working Paper (Washington, D.C., mimeographed, 1979), pp. 5–8.

3. The idea of a "permanent military government" seems as outdated as that of an irresistible rise of democracy. See Mario Esteban Carranza, *Fuerzas armadas y Estado de excepción en América latina* (México, 1978), chapter 5.

4. See Rouquié, *Pouvoir militaire*, passim.

5. See Rouquié, "L'Uruguay, de l'Etat providence à l'Etat garnison," *Etudes* (Paris) (June 1979):750.

6. Speech of General Pinochet on 11 September 1973, quoted by Cristina Hurtado-Beca, "Le processus d'institutionnalisation au Chili," *Problèmes d'Amérique latine* 58 (December 1980):78.

7. See *El Mercurio* (Santiago), 26 and 28 September 1975.

8. Jorge De Esteban and Luis López Guerra, *La Crisis del Estado franquista* (Madrid, 1977), pp. 28–29.

9. See Carlos Semprún Maura, *Franco est mort dans son lit* (Paris, 1978).

10. See Yves Le Bot, "Bolivie. Les militaires, l'Etat, la dépendance: une décennie de pillage," *Amérique latine* (Paris) (July–September 1980):8.

11. According to Rivas, "Vie et mort au Guatemala, réflexions sur la

crise et la violence politique," *Amérique latine* (Paris) (April–June, 1980):5.

12. See "El Salvador: The Process of Political Development and Modernization," in Ronald McDonald, *Party Systems and Election in Latin America* (Chicago, 1971), pp. 260–263.

13. It is not alone. *El Salvador, Election Fact book* (Washington, D.C.: Operations and Policy Research, Inc., Institute for the Comparative Study of Political Systems, 1967), p. 13, states: "Ninety percent of the dozens of political parties which have functioned since 1944 have been in reality military cliques or factions in disguise."

14. See *Latin America Weekly Report* (London), "Mixed Blessings for Government in Panamanian Poll Result," 3 October 1980.

15. See "La visite à Paris du président Royo," *Le Monde*, 8 May 1979.

16. Victor Meza, "Honduras: crisis del reformismo militar y coyuntura política," *Boletín del Instituto de investigaciones económicas y sociales*, no. 98 (Tegucigalpa, September 1980).

17. Ibid., and *Latin America Weekly Report* (London), 22 August 1980.

18. See Salvador Sánchez Estrada, "La répression des Indiens dans la frange transversale nord du Guatemala," *Amérique latine* (April–June 1980):73–77.

19. The anti-Communist right consisted of six parties in 1979, while the legal opposition included the Christian Democratic party, the Social Democratic party, and the United Front of the Revolution. The opposition parties lost a large number of their activists because they were assassinated by paramilitary forces. See Gabriel Aguilera Peralta et al., *Dialéctica del terror en Guatemala* (San José, Costa Rica, 1981), pp. 35, 59.

20. See Jones and Tobias, *Guatemala*, p. 318.

21. In the words of José Alvaro Moises, "Crise política e democracia: a transição difícil," *Revista de cultura e política* (São Paulo), no. 2 (August 1980):13.

22. See L. Martins, "La réorganisation des partis politiques et la crise économique au Brésil," *Problémes d'Amérique latine* 55 (March 1980):23.

23. See Rouquié, "Le modèle brésilien à l'épreuve," *Etudes* (May 1977):628–632.

24. Cardoso, "Les impasses du régime autoritaire: le cas brésilien," *Problèmes d'Amérique latine* 54 (December 1979):104.

25. The electoral reforms aimed at giving advantages and the vote of the conservative parties to the government, combined with sophisticated forms of "gerrymandering," are supposed to guarantee a comfortable majority to the system.

26. See *Le Monde,* 29 November 1980, and *La Prensa* (Buenos Aires), 2 December 1980.

27. See Luis Rico Ortiz, *Uruguay. Un análisis del plebiscito* (Paris, 1981, mimeographed), 37 pp.

28. See Rouquié, "Le retour du général Perón au pouvoir. Les élections générales du 11 mars 1973 et l'élection présidentielle du 23 septembre," *Problèmes d'Amérique latine* 33 (September 1974):20.

29. Ibid., p. 31.

30. *Le Monde,* 14 July 1978.

31. See Rouquié, "Argentine: les fausses sorties de l'armée et l'institutionnalisation du pouvoir militaire," *Problèmes d'Amérique latine* 54 (December 1979):109–129.

32. In 1874 General Pavía at the head of an infantry battalion dissolved the Cortes and put an end to the ephemeral republic before handing over power to Serrano, who ruled as a dictator. See F. G. Bruguera, *Histoire contemporaine d'Espagne, 1789–1950* (1953), p. 286, and Manuel Tuñon de Lara, *La España del siglo XIX, 1808–1914* (Paris, 1961), p. 194.

33. dos Santos, "A ciência política na América latina (Notas preliminares de autocrítica)," *Dados* (Rio de Janeiro) 23, no. 1 (1980):24.

34. See Spoerer, *América latina. Los desafíos del tiempo fecundo* (México, 1980).

35. Thus, henceforth, pensions were to be based on a system of individual "capitalization" and not on the principle of national solidarity; see "Reforma previsional. Compare su futuro," *Ercilla* (Santiago), 26 November 1980.

36. On this theme we refer the reader to Rouquié, "Revolutions militaires et indépendance nationale en Amérique latine, 1968–1971," *Revue française de science politique* 21, nos. 5 and 6 (October and December 1971).

37. See "Declaración del Pacto Andino contra el golpe militar," *El País* (Madrid), 14 November 1979.

38. J. Schumpeter, *Capitalisme, Socialisme, et Democratie* (Paris, 1965), p. 368, (*Capitalism, Socialism, and Democracy,* New York, 1950).

39. Mariano Grondona, *Visión* (México, 1976). See the discussion of this point of view by Daniel Waksman Schinca in *El Día* (Mexico City), 11 May 1976 ("Algo más que simples dictaduras").

40. According to Lucia Pinochet, the daughter of the president, *Hoy,* no. 151 (11 June 1980), quoted by C. Hurtado Beca, "Le processus d'institutionnalisation," p. 89.

41. See Rouquié, "La hipótesis bonapartista y el surgimiento de sistemas políticos semi-competitivos," *Revista mexicana de sociología,* no. E (1978):164–165.

42. On this point see Eliezer Rizzo de Oliveira, "Conflicts militaires et décisions sous la présidence du général Geisel," in Rouquié, ed., *Les Partis militaires au Brésil* (Paris, 1980), pp. 134–139.

43. de Oliveira, ibid., and *As Forças armadas. Política e ideología no Brasil, 1964–1969* (Petropolis, 1976), pp. 10–11.

44. As at various times Goes Monteiro, Dutra, Teixeira Lott, or Albuquerque Lima.

45. This is what Cardoso believes: "Uma constituinte convocada depois de forte derrota do regime nas eleições de 82 significará o fim da dictadura (Entrevista com F.H.C.)," *Movimento* (São Paulo), 23 February 1981.

46. This is how it was explained by General Morales Bermudez in an interview in April 1979: "Un entretien avec le président du Pérou," *Le Monde,* 13 April 1979.

47. According to Hugo Neira, "Au Pérou, le retour de l'oligarchie," *Etudes* (October 1980):304.

48. "Posición oficial ante la Comisión fue expuesta anoche al país por Harguíndeguy," *La Nación* (Buenos Aires), 24 September 1979.

49. *Movimento* (São Paulo), 23 February 1981.

50. This was the term used by Ricardo Balbín, leader of the Argentine Radical party, who was willing to accept the imposition of this law.

51. The relationship with the drug mafia and the protection of the drug traffic by the new masters of the country—from which they benefited (see *Newsweek,* 2 February and 9 March 1981, and *Le Matin-Magazine,* 18 October 1981)—in fact concealed permanent structural phenomena that one can call the "privatization of the state" or "the patrimonialization of the bureaucracy." Laurence Whitehead has described it as "the absence of relations of legitimate authority" and "group domination" in his article, "El Estado y los intereses seccionales: el caso boliviano," *Estudios andinos* (La Paz), no. 10 (1974–1975).

52. See the conclusion of Rouquié, *Pouvoir militaire.*

53. Gérard Fenoy, "L'armée en Colombie," *Cahiers du monde hispanique et luso-brésilien* (Toulouse) 26 (1976):86–87. Only the supporters of the Conservative, Laureano Gómez, were opposed to a military solution of the crisis.

54. See Constantino Urcuyo Fournier, "Les Forces de sécurité publiques et la Politique au Costa Rica, 1960–1978" (thesis, Paris, September 1978), chap. 1.

55. Debray, "Nicaragua, une modération radicale," *Le Monde diplomatique* (September 1979).

56. This is apparent when one reads the military program of the

Sandinista government. See, "Organización de un nuevo ejército nacional," in "Programa de la junta de gobierno de reconstrucción nacional de Nicaragua," published in *Bohemia* (Havana), 3 August 1979.

57. Jorge T. Dominguez, "The Civic Soldier in Cuba," in Kelleher, ed., *Political-Military Systems,* pp. 209–237.

58. See Alfonso Camacho P., "Bolivia: militares en la política," *Aportes* (Paris) (October 1971):73–76.

59. This is the position of the Partido Socialista Obrero Español (PSOE) against its left wing. This position was strengthened by the failed coup of February 24, 1981. See the interview with Felipe González, secretary general of the PSOE in *l'Unité,* 7 March 1981.

60. During the large demonstration in support of democracy after the antiparliamentary coup, former Francoite leaders such as Fraga Iribarne could be seen side by side with Communist, Socialist, and labor leaders of the opposition.

61. Turkey after Kemal Atatürk provides this kind of scenario in the framework of an elective regime granted by the postmilitary state. However with a coup d'état every ten years since 1960 it is hard to cite it as an example of the demilitarization of the political system. See Ergun Ozbudun, "The Nature of the Kemalist Political Origins," in Al Kazancigil and Ergun Ozbudun, eds., *Atatürk, Founder of a Modern State* (London, 1951), pp. 79–102.

62. Self-criticism is rather common in this area on the part of the parties that belonged to Popular Unity in Chile. Moreover the reflection and study on the problem of the military in Chile that have been carried out by the left in exile since 1973 are quite remarkable.

63. See especially the colloquium organized by the University of Vincennes on this subject in 1979, published as Pierre Dommergues, ed., *Le Nouvel Ordre interieur* (Paris, 1980). See also *Le Monde Diplomatique* (March 1979), and Bertram Gross, "Friendly Fascism, A Model for America," *Social Policy* (November–December 1970).

64. Guy Hermet, "Dictatures bourgeoises et modernisation conservatrice, problèmes méthodologiques de l'analyse des situations autoritaires," *Revue Française de Science Politique* (December 1975): 1038–1052.

65. Obviously we are referring to the series of reports that were prepared by the commission on the crisis of democracy. See M. Crozier and S. Huntington, *The Crisis of Democracy* (New York, 1976).

EPILOGUE

1. To be complete we should include Surinam among the continuing military regimes. There has been a partial opening with regard to the former political parties, but the dictatorship of Colonel Deysi Bouterse does not seem to be about to hand over power to an elected civilian government.

2. From 1930 to 1976, 51 percent of the changes of government in Latin America resulted from coups, and 49 percent followed constitutional procedures.

3. See Rouquié, "Argentina, the Departure of the Military: End of a Political Cycle or Just an Episode?" *International Affairs* (London) (Fall 1983).

4. See the official version of the Colorado party in the pamphlet published by the Office of the President in March 1985, entitled, "Uruguay, el Cambio en Paz" (Montevideo). See also Juan Rial, *Partidos Politicos, Democracia, y Autoritarismo,* vol. 2 (Montevideo 1984).

5. See Aníbal Delgado Fiallos, *Honduras, Elecciones 85, Mas Allá de la Fiesta Civica* (Tegucigalpa, 1986).

6. Bolivar Lamounier, "A Trajectoria de un Martir," *Afinal* (São Paulo), 30 April 1985.

7. de Oliveira, "Forças Armadas e Transição Politica, a Politica Militar do Governo Figueiredo," (Campinas, UNICAMP, March 1985, Mimeographed), p. 24.

8. German W. Rama, "La Democratie en Uruguay; un Essai d'Interpretation," *Problèmes d'Amérique Latine,* no. 78 (4th quarter 1985).

9. Juan Rial, "Los Militares en tanto Partido Politico Sustitutivo Frente a la Redemocratizacion" (Santiago, CLASCO, May 1985, mimeographed). See also Cristina Torres, "Las Fuerzas Armadas en la Transición hacia la Democracia," in Charles Gillespie et al., *Uruguay y la Democracia,* vol. 2 (Montevideo, 1985), pp. 161–170.

10. See Rivas, *Crisis del Poder en Centroamérica* (San Jose, Costa Rica, 1981), pp. 145–159. See also Gabriel Aguilera Peralta and Jorge Romeo Imergy, *Dialectica del Terror en Guatemala* (San José, Costa Rica, 1981).

11. Rouquié, "Amérique Latine: Demande Democratique et Désir de Révolution," *Projet* (Paris) (June 1983).

12. See "Nova Republica Sees Resurgence of the Old Right," *Latin American Newsletters* (London), *Brazil Report,* 9 August 1985.

Index

Abreu, Hugo, 304, 305
Acción Democratica party, 194–196, 197, 200
Adams, Richard, 144
Agency for International Development, U.S., 417 n. 30, 433 n. 42
Agriculture: agrarian reform, 314, 325; cooperatives, 329; dominance of, 28; laborers' statute, 24; land grants, 36–37; low efficiency of, 235; military control of, 434 n. 52; rapist, 19; social structure and, 20, 29; tenure system, 20–23; wages, 194. *See also* Landowners
Aguirre Cerda, Pedro, 110
Aleman, Miguel, 201, 205
Alessandri, Arturo, 107, 114
Alessandri, Jorge, 230
Alfonsín, Raul, 392, 394–396, 404
Alfonzo Ravard, R., 200
Alianza Popular Revolucionaria Americana, 415 n. 24
Allende, Salvador, 3, 110, 137, 230, 238
Alliance for Progress, 147, 167, 315, 367
Alvarez, Gustavo, 391
Alvaro Obregon, 201–202
Amado, Jorge, 82, 107
American University: Foreign Area Studies, 423 n. 34; Project Camelot of SORO, 419 n. 51
Amnesty International, 427 n. 58, 430 nn. 3, 4
Anarchy: Chile and, 52; post-civil war, 56; postcolonial, 49; wars of independence and, 47
Andean Pact, 367
Andres Perez, Carlos, 200
Arana Osorio, Carlos, 356
Arbenz, Jacobo, 356, 417
Argentina: agrarian exports, 22; army's state role, 287–292; civil wars in, 66–67; civilian rule in, 374n; coups in, 186; deindustrialization in, 299; demilitarization of, 352; economic culture of, 6, 288–292; generals in, 43; German military model in, 79–84; human rights violations in, 32, 374, 386, 395, 403; Indians of, 21; industrialization in, 298–299; militarism in, 3, 6, 272–277; national security priority, 295; officers of, 89–91; Peronists' return in, 360–361; Radical Civil Union, 105; stratification in, 26; U.S. military aid to, 145–146. *See also* specific leaders
Arias, Arnulfo, 324
Armaments. *See* Weapons
Armed forces: Americanization of, 7, 133–135, 248–249; against state, 49–61; career status of, 45–46; civilians and, 12, 94, 284; civilian control of, 188; compulsory service, 63–64, 71, 94–97; culture of nonparticipation, 330–334; denationalization of, 139; dictator-generals, 153–186; economic function of, 200; establishment of, 39–71; as gatekeepers, 285; ir-

455

Designer:	U.C. Press Staff
Compositor:	Huron Valley Graphics
Text:	11/13 Palatino
Display:	Palatino
Printer:	Edwards Bros., Inc.
Binder:	Edwards Bros., Inc.

469